A STATISTICAL HISTORY
OF THE AMERICAN
PRESIDENTIAL ELECTIONS

Containing 134 statistical compilations, including
a table of votes and percentages for each presidential election,
by states and candidates;

a table of votes and percentages for each state, by elections
and candidates;

a table of votes and percentages, by states and elections, for
each historical party (Democratic, Republican, Whig,
Prohibition, Socialist Labor, Socialist Workers, Populist,
Greenback, Farmer Labor, Communist, and Socialist);

and 28 other tables covering interesting sidelights

A STATISTICAL HISTORY OF THE AMERICAN PRESIDENTIAL ELECTIONS

With Supplementary Tables
Covering 1968-1980

SVEND PETERSEN

Introduction "Our National Elections" by
LOUIS FILLER
Antioch College

GREENWOOD PRESS, PUBLISHERS
WESTPORT, CONNECTICUT

Library of Congress Cataloging in Publication Data

Petersen, Svend, 1911–
    A statistical history of the American presidential
elections.

    Reprint. Originally published: New York : Ungar,
c1968.
    1. Presidents—United States—Election—History.
I. Title.
JK1967.P4 1981   324.973   81-6348
ISBN 0-313-22952-X (lib. bdg.)   AACR2

Reprinted by arrangement with Frederick Ungar
Publishing Co., Inc.

Reprinted in 1981 by Greenwood Press
A division of Congressional Information Service, Inc.
88 Post Road West, Westport, Connecticut 06881

Printed in the United States of America

10 9 8 7 6 5 4 3 2 1

*In memory
of my parents
on the fiftieth anniversary
of our arrival
in this wonderful country*

PREFACE

THIS BOOK is the only publication that gives complete statistics on the American presidential elections. It not only contains tables for each of the forty-four quadrennial elections from 1789 to 1960, but also has tables for each of the fifty states and each of the eleven historical parties, as well as other tables that feature various interesting sidelights.

In compiling this volume, I have tried to reconcile the numerous contradictory figures that appear in various sources. The original records have been consulted whenever that has been possible. Data filed in the National Archives have been available for the period 1888 to 1960; however, I have had to deal with omissions, inconsistencies, and contradictions. The newspaper files at the Library of Congress have been consulted for the period 1824 to 1888 (for which only a few records are to be found at the Archives), as well as, to a more limited extent, for the period 1892 to 1912.

As a general rule, a newspaper figure was not accepted unless it was corroborated by at least two other papers, and not then when one paper merely quoted another. The perpetuation of typographical errata, incomplete returns, and the misleading figures used by extremely partisan publications has thus been avoided as far as possible. Where data were unobtainable from the National Archives records and the Library of Congress newspaper files, I have used the publications listed in subsequent paragraphs.

One of the reasons for the discrepancies in the figures given by the various authorities is that each candidate for elector does not necessarily receive the same number of votes as his fellow candidates. In the 1940 election, for example, New York had forty-seven electors. The Roosevelt nominees received various votes, some getting 3,251,918, some 3,251,917, others 3,251,-916, and the rest 3,251,915. Some of Willkie's candidates received 3,027,478, some 3,027,477, and the rest 3,027,476. The compiler is faced with several alternatives. He can use the high votes, as I have done in all cases where they are determinable; he can use the votes received by each of the higher of the two "at large" candidates for each party, where there were such nominees; he can use the votes received by those whose names appear at the top of the list (these have not necessarily been the "at large" nominees); or he can use the average votes, which would of course produce artificial figures in many instances and would often necessitate the dropping or increasing of ridiculous fractions. Almost all of the states now have the ballots arranged so that the voter ballots for all of the persons listed on the slate of candidates for electors; in other words, there is no "scratching" or possibility of overlooking one or more names.

Some of the differences in the votes cast for nominees for electors have been due to the use of several forms of the same name. In some states, the election judges considered these names as belonging to separate and distinct individuals, while the judges in other states credited them all to one man. In the 1860 election, this factor decided the contest between Breckinridge and Bell in Virginia. For example, four nominees on the Bell slate received 74,524 votes each. Several of the others would each have received the same number, but for the fact that the voters cast their ballots for them under various names. To use only one illustration: A. E. Kennedy had 72,406 votes, Andrew F. Kennedy 995, Andrew S. Kennedy 526, Andrew W. E. Kennedy 462, Andrew E. Keeney 102, and Andrew J. Kennedy 33, for a total of 74,524. At first, Bell was awarded nine electors and Breckinridge six; the Breckinridge nominees, however, refused to accept victory on a technicality and all fifteen votes went to Bell. Final results, which included a few later returns, gave Bell 74,701 and Breckinridge 74,379 (high electors).

While the entire electoral vote of a state usually goes to one candidate, there have been times when the vote was split, due to the closeness of the race and the fact that one or more of the loser's electoral candidates received more votes than did one or more of the winner's. An extraordinary example of this nature occurred in North Dakota's first appearance in the presidential race, in 1892. The Populist slate received 17,700, 17,520, and 17,511, while the Republicans got 17,519, 17,506, and 17,463. The lowest Populist had eight fewer votes than did the highest Republican and therefore failed to become an elector. The Populists were entitled to two electors and the Republicans to one; however, one of the former voted for Cleveland, the Democratic candidate, who was not even on the North Dakota ballot.

Another complicating factor has been the Fusion arrangement which was used in some elections. Two competing parties would agree on a list of candidates for electors in an attempt to prevent a third party from carrying a state. Sometimes one or both of the parties would run one or more nominees on their own slate or slates in order to test their strength. In Michigan in 1884 the Democrats and Greenbackers ran a list of twelve names, while each group also ran one nominee of its own. The Fusion candidates received votes ranging from 189,361 down to 186,927. The Democrats and Greenbackers who ran without support from any but their own parties received 149,835 and 41,390 votes, respectively; these are the figures that I have adopted for 1884. A better name for this arrangement would be Con-Fusion!

Another source of difficulty has been those minor parties which, instead of supporting candidates of their own, have voted for the nominees of other parties. The vote of the American Labor Party, for instance, was necessary for the Democratic candidate to defeat his Republican rivals in New York in 1940 and 1944. It would be absurd not to add its votes to the nominee's regular totals.

One of the features of this book is the inclusion of an analysis for each of the elections where a switch of less than 1% of the major party vote would have changed the outcome. Since the 1824-25 deadlock, there have been only twelve contests that could have been considered overwhelming triumphs for the winners. Five of these occurred successively in the elections of 1920 to 1936, while the others took place in 1832, 1852, 1872, 1904, 1912, 1952, and 1956. In the remaining campaigns, the results could have been reversed by vote shifts ranging from .0002% in 1960 to .95% in 1864. In order to emphasize the importance of a comparative handful of votes, I have included the breakdowns for the states involved in these switches whenever the data have been available.

While these tabulations show the votes in order, with the high figures at the top, the low ones at the bottom, etc., the candidates for electors did not necessarily line up that way. The name at the head of the list may have received fewer votes than the next name; in fact, it may have ranked anywhere down to last. In the 1884 New York breakdown, for example, there are several ways in which the Cleveland and Blaine figures could be shown —the way in which they appeared on the ballots, in alphabetical order, or by descending order from high to low. The latter arrangement is the one which I chose, as I believe it is the fairest. In this, as in other instances where I demonstrated the closeness of results, I used the highest shift figure, 575, although it will be noted that the other shifts range from 574 down to 539.

These shift analyses necessarily overlook factors that play an important part in close elections—the people who stay at home (whether deliberately or through apathy) and the voters who leave the squares for presidential electors blank.

An example of the manner in which I have tried to put the election statistics in a convenient and compact form will be found in the table entitled *Number and Percentage of Votes by Elections and Parties.* If this compilation had not been included in the volume, it would be necessary, for example, to search the tables for thirty-four different elections in order to get a comparative record of the votes and percentages for the Democratic Party for its entire history.

Among the newspapers I consulted are the following:

Albany—*Argus, Journal,* and *Statesman*
Atlanta—*Constitution*
Augusta, Georgia—*Chronicle*
Augusta, Maine—*Kennebec Journal*

Bismarck—*Tribune*
Boise—*Idaho Statesman*
Boston—*Advertiser, Courier, Herald, Journal, Post,* and *Transcript*
Burlington, Vermont—*Free Press & Times*
Cheyenne—*Sun-Leader*
Chicago—*Tribune*
Columbus—*Ohio Statesman*
Concord—*New Hampshire Statesman*
Denver—*Rocky Mountain News*
Guthrie—*Oklahoma State Capital*
Harrisburg—*Patriot* and *Pennsylvania Telegraph*
Hartford—*Courant*
Helena—*Herald*
Indianapolis—*Journal*
Jacksonville—*Florida Times-Union & Citizen*
Little Rock—*Arkansas Gazette*
Louisville—*Commercial* and *Times*
Madison—*Democrat*
Nashville—*American*
New York—*Herald, Journal of Commerce, Post, Times, Tribune,* and
    World
Philadelphia—*Bulletin, Inquirer,* and *National Gazette*
Portland, Maine—*Eastern Argus*
Providence—*Journal*
Raleigh—*North Carolina Standard*
Richmond—*Dispatch* and *Enquirer*
St. Louis—*Republic(an)*
St. Paul—*Globe*
Salem—*Oregon Statesman*
Salt Lake City—*Tribune*
San Francisco—*Alta California* and *Bulletin*
Springfield—*Illinois State Register*
Washington, D. C.—*Globe* and *National Intelligencer*
Wheeling—*Register*
Wilmington—*Republican*

The following reference works were consulted. Each of them was issued in a number of editions, either annually or at various intervals.

A History of the Presidency, by Edward Stanwood
*The National Conventions and Platforms of All Political Parties, 1789
    to 1905,* by Thomas Hudson McKee; sub-title: *Convention, Popular,
    and Electoral Vote.* Earlier editions would have earlier dates in the
    title than 1905

Statistical Abstract of the United States
Statistics of the Congressional and Presidential Elections
The American, World, and *Tribune Almanacs;* the latter was known as
   The Whig Almanac in early years
Encyclopaedia Britannica Book of the Year

SVEND PETERSEN

OUR NATIONAL ELECTIONS

IT IS surprising that so useful a volume as that which Mr. Petersen has prepared has not been made available before. Librarians, analysts in various categories of public service, political scientists, and others in and out of academic life, have long wanted a work which would give them the details of our election experiences. Those who prepare papers and theses on aspects of our history—social and political changes, critical events—especially those involving local and state circumstances, now have a ready reference work calculated to answer many of their questions directly, and generally to strengthen their findings with relevant data.

Mr. Petersen's conscientous labors have independently resulted in such valuable materials that one can examine this work as a matter of general interest. Thus, his study of the states as "barometers" of national preferences not only reduces to rubble that piece of political folklore, "As Maine goes, so goes the Nation," but it raises the question of why it has persisted in public consciousness. Moreover, it results in a table of states (see p. 166) which can be pondered with profit, to determine why some states have so adequately reflected the nation's decision, why others have so persistently voted against victorious candidates.

If there is any one overall conclusion the student of these statistics can derive from his analysis, it is that the nation has on only a few occasions revealed a determination to elect a particular Executive Officer, and that many of the Presidential triumphs and defeats have been products of the merest accident. Clearly, Americans as a nation were unwilling to re-elect Herbert Hoover in 1932, and Franklin D. Roosevelt's 1936 vote was a ringing endorsement of his Administration. But this happens infrequently. Most of the elections show vigorous parties in conflict, and many of the elections have been filled with imponderables.

Although researchers will be grateful for Mr. Petersen's careful compilation of electoral votes for those years, it is unfortunate that we do not have the popular votes for elections prior to 1824. We miss the full excitement and illumination attending the election of 1800, when, for particular reasons, the Democratic-Republicans, then the name for one party, elected to the Presidency *both* of their candidates, Thomas Jefferson and Aaron Burr. As a result, the run-off election was thrown into the House of Representatives, where, ironically, the severely defeated Federalists were in position to decide which of their opponents they preferred to be their Chief Executive. Happily, we have a much better report of the election of 1824, when once again it was given to the House of Representatives to choose the President of the United States. This contest is filled with interesting sidelights. Thus, there were no less than *four* major candidates for the office, John Quincy Adams, Andrew Jackson, Henry Clay, and William Harris Crawford. Crawford, of Georgia, is the least known of these figures; however, there is little question but that he would have been elected to the Presidency, given normal conditions. He was a compromise figure who had filled distinguished government posts, and was very much in demand. So powerful was his following that, even though he had been struck down with paralysis during the campaign, and could not have carried out the duties of a President, an astonishing number of people voted for him, gave him forty-one electoral votes, and prevented the now-major candidates from acquiring the majority of electoral votes they required.

The statistics of this book play havoc with historical rhetoric. The impression that Andrew Jackson was "swept" into the White House, in 1828, after having "buried" the Adams forces loses much of its lustre in consideration of the facts; as the compiler drily notes: "The figures . . . show how a switch of 11,517 votes out of the 1,155,022 cast for Jackson and Adams—.997%—would have made the latter president." Contrarywise, the famous "Log Cabin and Hard Cider" campaign of 1840 was much less of an overwhelming victory for General William Henry Harrison, at the expense of Martin Van Buren, than legend has it: "[A] switch of 8,386 votes out of the 2,405,645 cast for Harrison and Van Buren—.35%— would have kept the latter in office as President." This does not quite end the matter. It needs to be recalled how firmly the Jacksonians had imbedded themselves into the administrative apparatus, by means of the spoils system, appeals to slavery interests, and a variety of democratic slogans. For the Whigs to have overcome this powerful machine was indeed a considerable achievement.

There is no space here to note the numerous fascinating facts which stud election returns from the states: coalitions, reversals, favorite-son endorsements, abstentions, and other political phenomena. They throw light on local circumstances, and continuously remind us of the place which sheer accident has in our most momentous affairs. However, there are a number of electoral high-points which deserve to be noticed, for the light they shed on our experiences in the field, the lessons they suggest to interested citizens.

First, the sensation caused by the small and despised Liberty Party, in 1844. It was not the first "Third Party," and much that is of interest could be said of the Anti-Masonic Party of 1832. But readers studying the table of votes can see for themselves how the Liberty Party's 15,814 votes in New York cost Henry Clay the state (see p. 27) and the entire election, and raised the question of whether the abolitionists had fouled their own

xiii

nest by sinking a moderate slaveholder, thus giving the Presidency to the dedicated pro-slavery advocate and imperialist, James K. Polk. (For good measure, the Liberty Party's 3,632 votes in Michigan deprived Clay of that state, as well.) Thus, for the first time, Americans dramatically learned that a small force could become powerful, when it held the balance of power.

In our time, we learned this fact in 1948, when the farmers, though far descended from their status of the mid-nineteenth century, when they were all-powerful, were able to tip the election to Harry S. Truman, standing as they did between Big Labor and Big Capital.

The significance of Abraham Lincoln's election in 1860 wants no emphasis here. Mr. Petersen provides elaborate tables and commentary explaining aspects of that crucial election, which offered four major candidates to the suffrage.

Readers will also be interested in the details of the election of 1864, carried on in the midst of war, which Lincoln feared he would lose and during which he prepared to turn over the office to his opponent, George B. McClellan.

A word might profitably be said about the election of 1876. Ordinarily, the following statistics help deepen and give meaning to our general understanding of elections. In this case, it is general understanding of the election which is required, if we are to understand the import of the statistics. The Disputed Election of 1876 is one of the critical moments in our history. For there can be no doubt but that the American people in that year elected the Democratic Party candidate, Samuel J. Tilden, to the Presidency. Why he was not permitted to take his high office is a study in conditions of the time, human psychology, and the most unmitigated accident.

The electoral votes of no fewer than four states were in question: those of South Carolina, Florida, Louisiana, and Oregon. If Tilden could carry any *one* of them, the Presidency was his. If Rutherford B. Hayes, for the Republicans, received the electoral votes of *all* four states, he was President —by one electoral vote. The Republicans boldly claimed all four states. South Carolina, in the hands of Federal (that is, Republican) troops, returned a more or less legitimate Republican majority. An incredible amount of both Republican and Democratic skulduggery left the situation in Oregon smoky and uncertain. But in Florida and Louisiana, Republican Party leaders rejected patent Democratic majorities and asserted their own supremacy. Thus, two separate sets of electoral votes from all four states were sent to Washington, and a stalemate resulted. Neither Party would acknowledge the claims of the other; no President stood elected, and a complicated situation in Congress did not permit the relief of a decision by the House of Representatives. No wonder that the incumbent President, Ulysses

S. Grant, fearing violence, fortified the Capital against the possibility of an armed uprising by outraged Democrats.

Many students of this election are convinced that if Tilden had insisted on receiving the office he had won, the Republicans would not have dared gainsay him. They were divided among themselves. The frustrated southerners, feeling they had little to lose, were prepared to endure a crisis in public affairs, even to the point of civil war. But Tilden did not rise to the occasion. He was querulous and legalistic, in a situation for which no legal machinery existed. Hence, it is unlikely that the Republic lost much by losing his services as President. But the entire election is rich with experiences. Incidentally, though it was sordid and uninspiring, it does not show Americans in too bad a light. They organized an *ad hoc* "Electoral Commission" to settle the choice of President, without recourse to arms and barricades. It is doubtful that such a crisis could anywhere else in the world have been settled without bloodshed.

The point to be noticed, so far as the following statistics on the Election of 1876 are concerned, is that the popular and electoral votes recorded are those asserted by the Republican Party. Lost to official history are the distinctly more accurate claims of the beaten Democrats, who, in a famous "deal," exchanged the Presidency for an unofficial agreement which removed the last Federal troops from the South and permitted the reestablishment of white supremacy there.[1]

Reference has already been made to the institution of Third Parties.

[1] The Democratic count gave Tilden 4,300,590 votes, Hayes 4,036,298. The Republicans could do no better for their candidate than a minority vote of 4,033,768, compared with Tilden's 4,285,992. As for the state count, Professor Eugene H. Roseboom's discussion (*A History of Presidential Elections* [1957], 244-45) gives some idea of the complexity of the matter. He is here analyzing the viewpoint of Paul L. Haworth, in his *The Hayes-Tilden Disputed Presidential Election of 1876* (1906):

"[Haworth] states that 'in an absolutely fair and free election' Louisiana would have gone Republican by five to fifteen thousand, basing his figures on the number cf colored and white voters on the registration rolls. He admits that the rolls were padded by the Republicans, but argues that they actually derived little advantage from the excess. He dismisses the census of 1880, which showed more adult white males in the state than colored, as inconclusive because 'many thousands' of the whites were foreigners. If the colored voters outnumbered the whites, in 'an absolutely fair and free election'—which Louisiana had not had since reconstruction began—would some 114,000 colored voters, nine-tenths of them illiterate, have gone to the polls and voted Republican? . . ."

It should be noted that Mr. Petersen's Louisiana figures differ from those quoted by Professor Roseboom, the latter's probably being incomplete.

The high stability of our party system can be remarked from the fact that Presidents have been elected only from Federalist, Democratic-Republican, Democratic, Whig, and Republican ranks. Third Parties have generally made a small impression on this firm tradition, though they have made somewhat more of an impression than is generally realized.[2] Such comments inadequately sum up the effect Third Parties have had on our politics and lives, and the information they impart to us about the tendencies in our national life. The student can profitably follow the American Party through its career in the 1850's, when it represented a desperate effort to break out of an increasingly ominous division between pro-slavery and anti-slavery partisans into an "American" position, alas, at the expense of our newer immigrants. The "Know-Nothings" were a strategic factor in the course of events which resulted in the election of Lincoln. Thereafter, in the elections of 1876, 1880, 1888, and in 1920 and 1924, they are a far less consequential factor, but aspects of their narrow, self-righteous, and essentially romantic viewpoint may be found in other Third Parties.

However, they have been more than tendentious. In the hairbreadth election of 1884, five hundred and seventy-five votes—575—in New York, taken from Grover Cleveland and given to James G. Blaine, would have elected the latter President. The Prohibition Party polled 17,004 votes, mostly taking them from the Republicans. Democrats had more regard for their beer-drinking Irish and other constituents. Needless to say, the Prohibitionists merit constant attention, at least before 1920, as a warning bell that the great experiment of Prohibition is on the way. And in 1916, they once more affect destinies. In that year, it will be recalled, Charles Evans Hughes went to bed under the impression that he had been elected President over the incumbent, Woodrow Wilson. He learned the next morning that the decision had been reversed. The final outcome had been determined in California, where Wilson had defeated him for its thirteen electoral votes by 3,806 votes. The Prohibitionists had polled 27,698. To be sure, the Socialists had polled 43,259 votes in California, but since they repudiated basic principles accepted by both Democrats and Republicans, their votes could not be taken to have deprived either candidate.

But Third Parties have been powerful in their own right. The Populist Party, running the distinguished General James B. Weaver in 1892, received over a million popular votes and twenty-two electoral votes. As notable was its political Platform of that year: the greatest party platform ever drafted,

[2] Mr. Petersen sums up the parties which have carried one or more states since 1828, as follows: Democratic, National Republican, Anti-Masonic, Whig, Republican, Constitutional Union, Populist, Roosevelt Progressive, La Follette Progressive, and States Rights Democratic.

and, in succeeding years, plundered by both the Republican and Democratic Parties. Furthermore, the Populist wing of the Democratic Party was strong enough to capture the Democratic Party for the election year of 1896. It is interesting that not a few persons who are not immediately in contact with the facts imagine that William Jennings Bryan was a Populist. He was a Democrat, of course, but little separated him from his Populist co-workers, in 1896, or, for that matter, later elections.

Theodore Roosevelt, as the candidate of the Progressives in 1912, was peculiar in that he polled more popular and electoral votes than William Howard Taft, the other loser in that significant election. Theoretically, this should have created a promise of permanency for the Progressive Party. That it did not, that it was Progressivism rather than Republicanism which deteriorated, requires a battery of information to explain, but some of it can be drawn from the following statistics. Incidentally, it should be noticed that the name of "Progressive" does not necessarily indicate a direct continuity from one candidate to another. There is, to be sure, some relationship between the Roosevelt campaign of 1912 and the La Follette bid as a Progressive in 1924. There is almost no connection between their Progressivism and that of Henry A. Wallace in 1948.

Enough has been said, perhaps, to indicate the general uses of this statistical history. But it would be unfair not to note that more than the highest matters of state are encompassed by its materials. Their comprehensive nature permits facts which are simply interesting and suggestive in their own right to emerge. Thus, 1880, of all years, was technically the tightest of elections, there being only a 9,457 difference in the popular vote and an amazing equality of suffrage. Thus, too, we have all heard of the career of Populism in the 1890's. We keep it less securely in memory that there were Populist candidates in 1900 and 1904 and 1908. How many persons recall that Theodore Roosevelt, though not an active candidate in 1916, nevertheless polled over 35,000 votes as a Progressive, 20,653 from, of all states, Georgia? Some readers will wish to follow the stories of the Socialist Labor Party candidacy, and of the Socialists and Communists. It still remains a matter of interest that Eugene V. Debs should have polled almost a million Socialist votes in 1920 while incarcerated in a federal penitentiary. William Lemke's 892,390 votes as Union Party candidate in 1936 interested many observers as possible evidence that a national party with fascist tendencies might get a footing on the political scene. Happily, it did not. Strom Thurmond's States' Rights Democratic Party and Henry A. Wallace's Progressive Party, both of 1948, polled between them only some two and a third million votes.

The reader will need no encouragement to examine the figures and conclusions reached respecting the Nixon-Kennedy contest of 1960. Those who have become aware that elections can be excruciatingly tight, and that candidates can be deprived of victory-bearing votes by third party candidates, will learn to watch such manifestations of public sentiment with care and a regard for details.

LOUIS FILLER

Antioch College
Yellow Springs, Ohio

TABLE OF CONTENTS

A STATISTICAL HISTORY
OF THE AMERICAN
PRESIDENTIAL ELECTIONS

TABLES FOR ELECTIONS AND TABLES FOR STATES

While the tables for elections cover the period 1789 to 1960, only the electoral votes are shown for the years prior to 1824. Popular vote records for the early years of the Republic are all but non-existent.

Beginning with 1824 and continuing to the present, the tables contain the electoral and popular votes, as well as the percentage of the latter, for each candidate and party. The highest percentage that each nominee and party received is underlined. When the elections were decided by narrow margins, the small possible vote shifts which would have changed the results are shown. Breakdowns for the states involved are given where such data have been obtainable.

Six state legislatures chose the electors in 1824 and thus indirectly cast the electoral votes of those states, but this number was reduced to two in 1828. The South Carolina legislature continued to choose that state's electors from 1832 to 1860, while the Massachusetts, Florida, and Colorado legislatures selected the electors of their respective states one time each. Massachusetts did so in 1848 because no presidential candidate had received a majority in that state. Florida had just resumed participation in elections after the Civil War when her lawmakers picked the electors in 1868, while Colorado permitted her legislators to name the electors the year she entered the Union—1876. Details of these legislative proceedings are shown where the data have been available.

Following the tables for 1789 to 1960 is a resume which covers the contests from 1824 to 1960, entitled *Number and Percentage of Votes by Elections and Parties*.

The tables for states show how each sovereign state voted from 1824 or from its entrance into the Union to the present. If these tabulations had not been included, it would be necessary to search from thirteen to thirty-five tables in order to get a comparative record of the votes and percentages for an individual state (except for Alaska and Hawaii, which have participated in but one election).

TABLE 1   Electoral Votes to Which Each State Is Entitled

Census / States	C — 1789	1 — 1792	1796 / 1800	2 — 1804 / 1808	3 — 1812	1816	1820	4 — 1824 / 1828	5 — 1832	1836 / 1840
Alabama							3	5	7	7
Alaska										
Arizona										
Arkansas										3
California										
Colorado										
Connecticut	7	9	9	9	9	9	9	8	8	8
Delaware	3	3	3	3	4	4	4	3	3	3
Florida										
Georgia	5	4	4	6	8	8	8	9	11	11
Hawaii										
Idaho										
Illinois							3	3	5	5
Indiana						3	3	5	9	9
Iowa										
Kansas										
Kentucky		4	4	8	12	12	12	14	15	15
Louisiana					3	3	3	5	5	5
Maine							9	9	10	10
Maryland	8	10	10	11	11	11	11	11	10	10
Massachusetts	10	16	16	19	22	22	15	15	14	14
Michigan										3
Minnesota										
Mississippi							3	3	4	4
Missouri							3	3	4	4
Montana										
Nebraska										
Nevada										
New Hampshire	5	6	6	7	8	8	8	8	7	7
New Jersey	6	7	7	8	8	8	8	8	8	8
New Mexico										
New York	8	12	12	19	29	29	29	36	42	42
North Carolina		12	12	14	15	15	15	15	15	15
North Dakota										
Ohio				3	8	8	8	16	21	21
Oklahoma										
Oregon										
Pennsylvania	10	15	15	20	25	25	25	28	30	30
Rhode Island		4	4	4	4	4	4	4	4	4
South Carolina	7	8	8	10	11	11	11	11	11	11
South Dakota										
Tennessee			3	5	8	8	8	11	15	15
Texas										
Utah										
Vermont		4	4	6	8	8	8	7	7	7
Virginia	12	21	21	24	25	25	25	24	23	23
Washington										
West Virginia										
Wisconsin										
Wyoming										
Dist. of Col.										
TOTALS	81	135	138	176	218	221	235	261	288	294

Electoral Votes to Which Each State Is Entitled (continued)

Census	6		7		8		9		10
States	1844	1848	1852 / 1856	1860	1864	1868	1872	1876 / 1880	1884 / 1888
Alabama	9	9	9	9	8	8	10	10	10
Alaska									
Arizona									
Arkansas	3	3	4	4	5	5	6	6	7
California			4	4	5	5	6	6	8
Colorado								3	3
Connecticut	6	6	6	6	6	6	6	6	6
Delaware	3	3	3	3	3	3	3	3	3
Florida		3	3	3	3	3	4	4	4
Georgia	10	10	10	10	9	9	11	11	12
Hawaii									
Idaho									
Illinois	9	9	11	11	16	16	21	21	22
Indiana	12	12	13	13	13	13	15	15	15
Iowa		4	4	4	8	8	11	11	13
Kansas					3	3	5	5	9
Kentucky	12	12	12	12	11	11	12	12	13
Louisiana	6	6	6	6	7	7	8	8	8
Maine	9	9	8	8	7	7	7	7	6
Maryland	8	8	8	8	7	7	8	8	8
Massachusetts	12	12	13	13	12	12	13	13	14
Michigan	5	5	6	6	8	8	11	11	13
Minnesota				4	4	4	5	5	7
Mississippi	6	6	7	7	7	7	8	8	9
Missouri	7	7	9	9	11	11	15	15	16
Montana									
Nebraska						3	3	3	5
Nevada					3	3	3	3	3
New Hampshire	6	6	5	5	5	5	5	5	4
New Jersey	7	7	7	7	7	7	9	9	9
New Mexico									
New York	36	36	35	35	33	33	35	35	36
North Carolina	11	11	10	10	9	9	10	10	11
North Dakota									
Ohio	23	23	23	23	21	21	22	22	23
Oklahoma									
Oregon				3	3	3	3	3	3
Pennsylvania	26	26	27	27	26	26	29	29	30
Rhode Island	4	4	4	4	4	4	4	4	4
South Carolina	9	9	8	8	6	6	7	7	9
South Dakota									
Tennessee	13	13	12	12	10	10	12	12	12
Texas		4	4	4	6	6	8	8	13
Utah									
Vermont	6	6	5	5	5	5	5	5	4
Virginia	17	17	15	15	10	13	11	11	12
Washington									
West Virginia					5	5	5	5	6
Wisconsin		4	5	5	8	8	10	10	11
Wyoming									
Dist. of Col.									
TOTALS	275	290	296	303	314	320	366	369	401

Census	11		12		13	15	16	17		18
States	1892	1896 / 1900	1904	1908	1912 to 1928	1932 1936 1940	1944 1948	1952 1956	1960	1964 1968
Alabama	11	11	11	11	12	11	11	11	11	10
Alaska									3	3
Arizona					3	3	4	4	4	5
Arkansas	8	8	9	9	9	9	9	8	8	6
California	9	9	10	10	13	22	25	32	32	40
Colorado	4	4	5	5	6	6	6	6	6	6
Connecticut	6	6	7	7	7	8	8	8	8	8
Delaware	3	3	3	3	3	3	3	3	3	3
Florida	4	4	5	5	6	7	8	10	10	14
Georgia	13	13	13	13	14	12	12	12	12	12
Hawaii									3	4
Idaho	3	3	3	3	4	4	4	4	4	4
Illinois	24	24	27	27	29	29	28	27	27	26
Indiana	15	15	15	15	15	14	13	13	13	13
Iowa	13	13	13	13	13	11	10	10	10	9
Kansas	10	10	10	10	10	9	8	8	8	7
Kentucky	13	13	13	13	13	11	11	10	10	9
Louisiana	8	8	9	9	10	10	10	10	10	10
Maine	6	6	6	6	6	5	5	5	5	4
Maryland	8	8	8	8	8	8	8	9	9	10
Massachusetts	15	15	16	16	18	17	16	16	16	14
Michigan	14	14	14	14	15	19	19	20	20	21
Minnesota	9	9	11	11	12	11	11	11	11	10
Mississippi	9	9	10	10	10	9	9	8	8	7
Missouri	17	17	18	18	18	15	15	13	13	12
Montana	3	3	3	3	4	4	4	4	4	4
Nebraska	8	8	8	8	8	7	6	6	6	5
Nevada	3	3	3	3	3	3	3	3	3	3
New Hampshire	4	4	4	4	4	4	4	4	4	4
New Jersey	10	10	12	12	14	16	16	16	16	17
New Mexico					3	3	4	4	4	4
New York	36	36	39	39	45	47	47	45	45	43
North Carolina	11	11	12	12	12	13	14	14	14	13
North Dakota	3	3	4	4	5	4	4	4	4	4
Ohio	23	23	23	23	24	26	25	25	25	26
Oklahoma				7	10	11	10	8	8	8
Oregon	4	4	4	4	5	5	6	6	6	6
Pennsylvania	32	32	34	34	38	36	35	32	32	29
Rhode Island	4	4	4	4	5	4	4	4	4	4
South Carolina	9	9	9	9	9	8	8	8	8	8
South Dakota	4	4	4	4	5	4	4	4	4	4
Tennessee	12	12	12	12	12	11	12	11	11	11
Texas	15	15	18	18	20	23	23	24	24	25
Utah		3	3	3	4	4	4	4	4	4
Vermont	4	4	4	4	4	3	3	3	3	3
Virginia	12	12	12	12	12	11	11	12	12	12
Washington	4	4	5	5	7	8	8	9	9	9
West Virginia	6	6	7	7	8	8	8	8	8	7
Wisconsin	12	12	13	13	13	12	12	12	12	12
Wyoming	3	3	3	3	3	3	3	3	3	3
Dist. of Col.										3
TOTALS	444	447	476	483	531	531	531	531	537	538

The original apportionment was based on the *Constitution of the United States,* Article I, Section 2, Paragraph 3. No apportionment was made following the Fourteenth Census.

The following states did not cast their electoral votes, in whole or in part, in the years shown:

1789:   Maryland 2, New York 8, Virginia 2. Total—12.

1792:   Maryland 2, Vermont 1. Total—3.

1808:   Kentucky 1.

1812:   Ohio 1.

1816:   Delaware 1, Maryland 3. Total—4.

1820   Mississippi 1, Pennsylvania 1, Tennessee 1. Total—3.

1832:   Maryland 2.

1864:   Alabama 8, Arkansas 5, Florida 3, Georgia 9, Louisiana 7, Mississippi 7, Nevada 1, North Carolina 9, South Carolina 6, Tennessee 10, Texas 6, Virginia 10. Total —81.

1868:   Mississippi 7, Texas 6, Virginia 13. Total—26.

1872:   Arkansas 6, Georgia 3, Louisiana 8. Total—17.
None of the abstentions affected the results.

TABLE 2

Candidates	Lived	Parties	Elections
Adams, John	1735-1826	Federalist	1789-92-96-1800
Adams, John Quincy	1767-1848	Democratic	1820-24
		National Republican	1828
Adams, Samuel	1722-1803	Federalist	1796
Aiken, John W.	1896-	Socialist Labor	1936-40
Andrews, Thomas Coleman	1899-	Constitution	1956
Armstrong, James	17??-1795		1789
Babson, Roger Ward	1875-	Prohibition	1940
Barker, Wharton	1846-1921	Populist	1900
Bell, John	1797-1869	Constitutional Union	1860
Benson, Allan L.	1871-1940	Socialist	1916
Bentley, Charles Eugene	1841-1905	National Prohibition	1896
Bidwell, John	1819-1900.	Prohibition	1892
Birney, James Gillespie	1792-1857	Liberty	1840-44
Black, James	1823-1893	Prohibition	1872
Blaine, James Gillespie	1830-1893	Republican	1884
Breckinridge, John Cabell	1821-1875	Democratic	1860
Broome	-	American	1852
Browder, Earl Russell	1891-	Communist	1936-40
Brown, Benjamin Gratz	1826-1885	Democratic	1873
Bryan, William Jennings	1860-1925	Democratic	1896-1900-08
Buchanan, James	1791-1868	Democratic	1856
Burr, Aaron	1756-1836	Democratic	1792-96-1800
Butler, Benjamin Franklin	1818-1893	Greenback	1884
Byrd, Harry Flood	1887-	Southern Democratic	1944
		States' Rights	1956
		Unpledged Democratic	1960
Cass, Lewis	1782-1866	Democratic	1848
Chafin, Eugene W.	1852-1920	Prohibition	1908-12
Christensen, Parley Parker	-	Farmer Labor	1920
Clay, Henry	1777-1852	Democratic	1824
		National Republican	1832
		Whig	1844
Cleveland, Stephen Grover	1837-1908	Democratic	1884-88-92
Clinton, DeWitt	1769-1828	Federalist	1812
Clinton, George	1739-1812		1789
		Democratic	1792-96
		Federalist	1808
Coiner, C. Benton	-	Virginia Conservative	1960
Colvin, David Leigh	1880-1959	Prohibition	1936
Coolidge, John Calvin	1872-1933	Republican	1924
Cooper, Peter	1791-1883	Greenback	1876
Corregan, Charles Hunter	1860-1946	Socialist Labor	1904
Cowdrey, Robert H.	-	United Labor	1888
Cox, James Middleton	1870-1957	Democratic	1920
Cox, James R.	-	Jobless	1932
Cox, William W.	1864-1948	Socialist Labor	1920
Coxey, Jacob Sechler	1854-1951	Farmer Labor	1932
Crawford, William Harris	1772-1834	Democratic	1824
Curtis, James Langdon	-	American	1888
Curtis, Merritt B.	-	Constitution	1960

Candidates	Lived	Parties	Elections
Daly, Lar	-	Tax Cut	1960
Davis, David	1815-1886	Democratic	1873
Davis, John William	1873-1955	Democratic	1924
Debs, Eugene Victor	1855-1926	Socialist	1900-04-08-12-20
Decker, Rutherford L.	-	Prohibition	1960
Dewey, Thomas Edmund	1902-	Republican	1944-48
Dobbs, Farrell	1907-	Socialist Workers	1948-52-56-60
Douglas, Stephen Arnold	1813-1861	Democratic	1860
Dow, Neal	1804-1897	Prohibition	1880
Eisenhower, Dwight David	1890-	Republican	1952-56
Ellis, Seth Hockett	1830-1904	Union Reform	1900
Ellsworth, Oliver	1745-1807	Federalist	1796
Faris, Herman Preston	1858-1936	Prohibition	1924
Faubus, Orval Eugene	1910-	National States Rights	1960
Ferguson, James Edward	1871-1944	American	1920
Fillmore, Millard	1800-1874	Whig	1856
Fisk, Clinton Bowen	1828-1890	Prohibition	1888
Floyd, John	1783-1837	Democratic	1832
Foster, William Zebulon	1881-1961	Communist	1924-28-32
Fremont, John Charles	1813-1890	Republican	1856
Garfield, James Abram	1831-1881	Republican	1880
Gillhaus, August	-	Socialist Labor	1908
Grant, Ulysses Simpson	1822-1885	Republican	1868-72
Greeley, Horace	1811-1872	Democratic	1872
Hale, John Parker	1806-1873	Free Soil	1852
Hallinan, Vincent	-	Progressive	1952
Hamblen, Stuart	-	Prohibition	1952
Hancock, John	1737-1793		1789
Hancock, Winfield Scott	1824-1886	Democratic	1880
Hanly, J. Frank	1863-1920	Prohibition	1916
Harding, Warren Gamaliel	1865-1923	Republican	1920
Harrison, Benjamin	1833-1901	Republican	1888-92
Harrison, Robert Hanson	1745-1790		1789
Harrison, William Henry	1773-1841	Whig	1836-40
Harvey, William Hope	1851-1936	Liberty	1932
Hass, Eric	1905-	Socialist Labor	1952-56-60
Hayes, Rutherford Birchard	1822-1893	Republican	1876
Hendricks, Thomas Andrews	1819-1885	Democratic	1873
Henry, John	1750-1798		1796
Hisgen, Thomas L.	1858-1925	Independence	1908
Holcomb, Austin	-	Continental	1904
Holtwick, Enoch A.	-	Prohibition	1956
Hoopes, Darlington	1896-	Socialist	1952-56
Hoover, Herbert Clark	1874-	Republican	1928-32
Hughes, Charles Evans	1862-1948	Republican	1916
Huntington, Samuel	1731-1796		1789
Iredell, James	1751-1799	Federalist	1796

Candidates	Lived	Parties	Elections
Jackson, Andrew	1767-1845	Democratic	1824-28-32
Jay, John	1745-1829	Federalist	1789-96-1800
Jefferson, Thomas	1743-1826	Democratic	1792-96-1800-04
Jenkins, Charles Jones	1805-1883	Democratic	1873
Johns, Frank T.	1889-1928	Socialist Labor	1924
Johnston, Samuel	1733-1816	Federalist	1796
Jones, Walter Burgwyn	1888-	Democratic	1956
Kennedy, John Fitzgerald	1917-	Democratic	1960
King, Clennon	-	Independent Afro-American	1960
King, Rufus	1755-1827	Federalist	1816
Knutson, Alfred	-	Independent	1940
Krajewski, Henry	-	Poor Man's	1952
		American Third Party	1956
LaFollette, Robert Marion	1855-1925	Progressive	1924
Landon, Alfred Mossman	1887-	Republican	1936
Lee, Joseph Bracken	1899-	Conservative	1960
Lemke, William	1878-1950	Union	1936
Leonard, Jonah Fitz Randolph	1832-19??	United Christian	1900
Levering, Joshua	1845-1935	Prohibition	1896
Lincoln, Abraham	1809-1865	Republican	1860-64
Lincoln, Benjamin	1733-1810		1789
MacArthur, Douglas	1880-	Constitution	1952
Macauley, Robert Colvin	-	Single Tax	1920
Madison, James	1751-1836	Democratic	1808-12
Malloney, Joseph F.	-	Socialist Labor	1900
Mangum, Willie Person	1792-1861	Democratic	1836
Matchett, Charles Horatio	1843-1919	Socialist Labor	1896
McClellan, George Brinton	1826-1885	Democratic	1864
McKinley, William	1843-1901	Republican	1896-1900
Milton, John	1740-c.1804		1789
Monroe, James	1758-1831	Democratic	1816-20
Nations, Gilbert Owen	1866-	American	1924
Nixon, Richard Milhous	1913-	Republican	1960
O'Conor, Charles	1804-1884	Labor Reform	1872
Palmer, John McAuley	1817-1900	National Democratic	1896
Parker, Alton Brooks	1852-1926	Democratic	1904
Pelley, William Dudley		Christian	1936
Phelps, John W.	-	American	1880
Pierce, Franklin	1804-1869	Democratic	1852
Pinckney, Charles Cotesworth	1746-1825	Federalist	1796-1800-04-08
Pinckney, Thomas	1750-1828	Federalist	1796
Polk, James Knox	1795-1849	Democratic	1844
Reimer, Arthur E.	1882-19??	Socialist Labor	1912-16
Reynolds, Verne L.	1884-1959	Socialist Labor	1928-32
Roosevelt, Franklin Delano	1882-1945	Democratic	1932-36-40-44
Roosevelt, Theodore	1858-1919	Republican	1904
		Progressive	1912-16
Rutledge, John	1739-1800		1789

9

Candidates	Lived	Parties	Elections
St. John, John Pierce	1833-1916	Prohibition	1884
Scott, Winfield	1786-1866	Whig	1852
Seymour, Horatio	1810-1886	Democratic	1868
Smith, Alfred Emanuel	1873-1944	Democratic	1928
Smith, Gerald Lyman Kenneth	1898?-	America First	1944
Smith, Gerrit	1797-1874	Liberty	1848-52
		Land Reform	1856
			1860
Smith, Green Clay	1832-1895	Prohibition	1876
Stevenson, Adlai Ewing	1900-	Democratic	1952-56
Streeter, Alson J.	-	Union Labor	1888
Sullivan, Charles Loten	1924-	Constitutional	1960
Swallow, Silas C.	1839-1930	Prohibition	1904
Taft, William Howard	1857-1930	Republican	1908-12
Taylor, Zachary	1784-1852	Whig	1848
Teichert, Edward A.	1904-	Socialist Labor	1944-48
Telfair, Edward	1735-1807		1789
Thomas, Norman Mattoon	1884-	Socialist	1928-32-36-40-44-48
Thurmond, James Strom	1902-	States' Rights Democratic	1948
Tilden, Samuel Jones	1814-1886	Democratic	1876
Troup, George Michael	1780-1856	Southern Rights	1852
Truman, Harry S.	1884-	Democratic	1948
Turney, Daniel Braxton	1848-1926	United Christian	1908
Upshaw, William David	1866-1952	Prohibition	1932
Van Buren, Martin	1782-1862	Democratic	1836-40
		Free Soil	1848
Varney, William Frederick	1884-1960	Prohibition	1928
Walker, James B.	-	American	1876
Wallace, Henry Agard	1888-	Progressive	1948
Wallace, William J.	-	Commonwealth Land	1924
Washington, George	1732-1799	Federalist	1789-92-96
Watkins, Aaron Sherman	1863-1941	Prohibition	1920
Watson, Claude A.	1885-	Prohibition	1944-48
Watson, Thomas Edward	1856-1922	Populist	1904-08
Weaver, James Baird	1833-1912	Greenback	1880
		Populist	1892
Webb, Frank Elbridge	1869-1949	Farmer Labor	1928
Webster, Daniel	1782-1852	Whig	1836-52
White, Hugh Lawson	1773-1840	Whig	1836
Willkie, Wendell Lewis	1892-1944	Republican	1940
Wilson, Thomas Woodrow	1856-1924	Democratic	1912-16
Wing, Simon	-	Socialist Labor	1892
Wirt, William	1772-1834	Anti-Masonic	1832
Woolley, John C.	1850-1922	Prohibition	1900
Zahnd, John	1878?-1961	National	1932

TABLE 3   **Election of 1789**

Those who received electoral votes were George Washington, John Adams, John Jay, Robert Hanson Harrison, John Rutledge, John Hancock, George Clinton, Samuel Huntington, John Milton, James Armstrong, Benjamin Lincoln, and Edward Telfair.

The following provision of the *Constitution of the United States* applied to this election:

> The person having the greatest number of votes shall be the President, if such number be a majority of the whole number of electors appointed, and if there be more than one who have such a majority, and have an equal number of votes, then the House of Representatives shall immediately choose by ballot one of them for President. . . . In every case, after the choice of the President, the person having the greatest number of votes of the electors shall be the Vice-President.—Article II, Section 1, Paragraph 3.

Candidates	Conn.	Del.	Ga.	Md.	Mass.	N. H.	N. J.	Penna.	S. C.	Va.	TOTALS
Washington	7	3	5	6	10	5	6	10	7	10	69
Adams	5				10	5	1	8		5	34
Jay		3			.		5			1	9
Harrison				6							6
Rutledge									6		6
Hancock							2		1	1	4
Clinton										3	3
Huntington	2										2
Milton			2								2
Armstrong			1								1
Lincoln			1								1
Telfair			1								1

Washington was chosen unanimously. Eight New York, two Maryland, and two Virginia electors were absent. North Carolina and Rhode Island did not participate, as neither had ratified the *Constitution*. Had they been eligible, the former would have had seven electors and the latter three. The votes of these twenty-two electors could not have prevented the election of either Washington or Adams.

TABLE 4.   **Election of 1793**

Those who received electoral votes were George Washington, John Adams, George Clinton, Thomas Jefferson, and Aaron Burr.

The following provision of the *Constitution of the United States* applied to this election:

> The person having the greatest number of votes shall be the President, if such number be a majority of the whole number of electors appointed, and if there be more than one who have such a majority, and have an equal number of votes, then the House of Representatives shall immediately choose by ballot one of them for President. . . . In every case, after the choice of the President, the person having the greatest number of votes, of the electors shall be the Vice-President.—Article II, Section 1, Paragraph 3.

States	Washington	Adams	Clinton	Jefferson	Burr
Connecticut	9	9			
Delaware	3	3			
Georgia	4		4		
Kentucky	4			4	
Maryland	8	8			
Massachusetts	16	16			
New Hampshire	6	6			
New Jersey	7	7			
New York	12		12		
North Carolina	12		12		
Pennsylvania	15	14	1		
Rhode Island	4	4			
South Carolina	8	7			1
Vermont	3	3			
Virginia	21		21		
TOTALS	132	77	50	4	1

Washington was re-elected unanimously. Two Maryland and one Vermont electors were absent. The votes of these three electors could not have prevented the election of either Washington or Adams.

TABLE 5   Election of 1797

Those who received electoral votes were John Adams, Thomas Jefferson, Thomas Pinckney, Aaron Burr, Samuel Adams, Oliver Ellsworth, George Clinton, John Jay, James Iredell, John Henry, Samuel Johnston, George Washington, and Charles Cotesworth Pinckney. The following provision of the *Constitution of the United States* applied to this election:

> The person having the greatest number of votes shall be the President, if such number be a majority of the whole number of electors appointed, and if there be more than one who have such a majority, and have an equal number of votes, then the House of Representatives shall immediately choose by ballot one of them for President. . . . In every case, after the choice of the President, the person having the greatest number of votes of the electors shall be the Vice-President.—Article II, Section 1, Paragraph 3.

States	J. Adams	Jefferson	T. Pinckney	Burr	S. Adams	Ellsworth	Clinton	Jay	Iredell	Henry	Johnston	Washington	C. Pinckney
Connecticut	9		4					5					
Delaware	3		3										
Georgia		4				4							
Kentucky		4		4									
Maryland	7	4	4	3						2			
Massachusetts	16		13			1					2		
New Hampshire	6					6							
New Jersey	7		7										
New York	12		12										
North Carolina	1	11	1	6					3			1	1
Pennsylvania	1	14	2	13									
Rhode Island	4						4						
South Carolina		8	8										
Tennessee		3		3									
Vermont	4		4										
Virginia	1	20	1	1	15		3					1	
TOTALS	71	68	59	30	15	11	7	5	3	2	2	2	1

TABLE 6 Election of 1801

Those who received electoral votes were Thomas Jefferson, Aaron Burr, John Adams, Charles Cotesworth Pinckney, and John Jay.

The following provision of the *Constitution of the United States* applied to this election:

> The person having the greatest number of votes shall be the President, if such number be a majority of the whole number of electors appointed, and if there be more than one who have such a majority, and have an equal number of votes, then the House of Representatives shall immediately choose by ballot one of them for President. . . . In every case, after the choice of the President, the person having the greatest number of votes of the electors shall be the Vice-President.—Article II, Section 1, Paragraph 3.

States	Jefferson	Burr	Adams	Pinckney	Jay
Connecticut			9	9	
Delaware			3	3	
Georgia	4	4			
Kentucky	4	4			
Maryland	5	5	5	5	
Massachusetts			16	16	
New Hampshire			6	6	
New Jersey			7	7	
New York	12	12			
North Carolina	8	8	4	4	
Pennsylvania	8	8	7	7	
Rhode Island			4	3	1
South Carolina	8	8			
Tennessee	3	3			
Vermont			4	4	
Virginia	21	21			
TOTALS	73	73	65	64	1

Seventy-three electors had intended to elect Jefferson president and Burr vice-president, and sixty-five others had intended to re-elect Adams president and elect Pinckney vice-president. A minority elector in Rhode Island voted for Adams and Jay, which prevented Pinckney from tying Adams. Had one majority elector voted for someone other than Burr, the necessity for a House election would have been avoided.

The figures below show how the House of Representatives voted on the 1st, 35th, and 36th ballots:

States	1st Ballot			35th Ballot			36th Ballot		
	JEFF	BURR	Vote for	JEFF	BURR	Vote for	JEFF	BURR	Vote for
Connecticut		7	BURR		7	BURR		7	BURR
Delaware		1	BURR		1	BURR			Blank
Georgia	1		JEFFERSON	1		JEFFERSON	1		JEFFERSON
Kentucky	2		JEFFERSON	2		JEFFERSON	2		JEFFERSON
Maryland	4	4	Blank	4	4	Blank	4		JEFFERSON
Massachusetts	3	11	BURR	3	11	BURR	3	11	BURR
New Hampshire		4	BURR		4	BURR		4	BURR
New Jersey	3	2	JEFFERSON	3	2	JEFFERSON	3	2	JEFFERSON
New York	6	4	JEFFERSON	6	4	JEFFERSON	6	4	JEFFERSON
North Carolina	9	1	JEFFERSON	7	3	JEFFERSON	7	3	JEFFERSON
Pennsylvania	9	4	JEFFERSON	9	4	JEFFERSON	9	4	JEFFERSON
Rhode Island		2	BURR		2	BURR		2	BURR
South Carolina		5	BURR			Blank			Blank
Tennessee	1		JEFFERSON	1		JEFFERSON	1		JEFFERSON
Vermont	1	1	Blank	1	1	Blank	1		JEFFERSON
Virginia	16	3	JEFFERSON	14	5	JEFFERSON	14	5	JEFFERSON
TOTALS	55	49		51	48		51	42	

	1st	35th	36th
JEFFERSON	8 states	8 states	10 states
BURR	6 states	5 states	4 states
Blank	2 states	3 states	2 states

Each state cast one vote; an evenly divided delegation cast a blank.

A Georgia representative had died before the balloting. On the 1st Ballot, one South Carolina representative was absent, while two were absent on the 35th. The South Carolina vote on the 35th Ballot is uncertain, but was probably one for Jefferson and three for Burr.

This election led to the adoption of the Twelfth Amendment to the *Constitution*, which provides that "The Electors . . . shall name in their ballots the person voted for as President, and in distinct ballots the person voted for as Vice-President."

TABLE 7 **Election of 1805**

Those who received electoral votes were Thomas Jefferson and Charles Cotesworth Pinckney.

States	Jefferson	Pinckney
Connecticut		9
Delaware		3
Georgia	6	
Kentucky	8	
Maryland	9	2
Massachusetts	19	
New Hampshire	7	
New Jersey	8	
New York	19	
North Carolina	14	
Ohio	3	
Pennsylvania	20	
Rhode Island	4	
South Carolina	10	
Tennessee	5	
Vermont	6	
Virginia	24	
	—	—
TOTALS	162	14

TABLE 8 **Election of 1809**

Those who received electoral votes were James Madison, Charles Cotesworth Pinckney, and George Clinton.

States	Madison	Pinckney	Clinton
Connecticut		9	
Delaware		3	
Georgia	6		
Kentucky	7		
Maryland	9	2	
Massachusetts		19	
New Hampshire		7	
New Jersey	8		
New York	13		6
North Carolina	11	3	
Ohio	3		
Pennsylvania	20		
Rhode Island		4	
South Carolina	10		
Tennessee	5		
Vermont	6		
Virginia	24		
	—	—	—
TOTALS	122	47	6

One Kentucky elector was absent.

TABLE 9   **Election of 1813**

Those who received electoral votes were James Madison and DeWitt Clinton.

States	Madison	Clinton
Connecticut		9
Delaware		4
Georgia	8	
Kentucky	12	
Louisiana	3	
Maryland	6	5
Massachusetts		22
New Hampshire		8
New Jersey		8
New York		29
North Carolina	15	
Ohio	7	
Pennsylvania	25	
Rhode Island		4
South Carolina	11	
Tennessee	8	
Vermont	8	
Virginia	25	
TOTALS	128	89

One Ohio elector was absent.

TABLE 10   **Election of 1817**

Those who received electoral votes were James Monroe and Rufus King.

States	Monroe	King
Connecticut		9
Delaware		3
Georgia	8	
Indiana	3	
Kentucky	12	
Louisiana	3	
Maryland	8	
Massachusetts		22
New Hampshire	8	
New Jersey	8	
New York	29	
North Carolina	15	
Ohio	8	
Pennsylvania	25	
Rhode Island	4	
South Carolina	11	
Tennessee	8	
Vermont	8	
Virginia	25	
TOTALS	183	34

Three Maryland and one Delaware electors were absent.

TABLE 11   **Election of 1821**

Those who received electoral votes were James Monroe and John Quincy Adams.

States	Monroe	Adams
Alabama	3	
Connecticut	9	
Delaware	4	
Georgia	8	
Illinois	3	
Indiana	3	
Kentucky	12	
Louisiana	3	
Maine	9	
Maryland	11	
Massachusetts	15	
Mississippi	2	
Missouri	3	
New Hampshire	7	1
New Jersey	8	
New York	29	
North Carolina	15	
Ohio	8	
Pennsylvania	24	
Rhode Island	4	
South Carolina	11	
Tennessee	7	
Vermont	8	
Virginia	25	
TOTALS	231	1

One Mississippi, one Pennsylvania, and one Tennessee electors were absent.

ELECTION OF 1824

Candidates were John Quincy Adams, Andrew Jackson, William Harris Crawford, and Henry Clay, all Democrats. As no candidate received a majority of the electoral vote, the House of Representatives chose the president from the three highest.

Data pertaining to this election are from the following sources:

Connecticut and Massachusetts—High votes. Maryland is also official.

Kentucky, North Carolina, and Ohio—Several newspapers in each case.

Alabama, Illinois, Indiana, Mississippi, Missouri, New Jersey, Rhode Island, Tennessee, and Virginia—Stanwood and *Tribune Almanac*.

Maine and New Hampshire—Stanwood.

Pennsylvania—McKee and *American Almanac*.

The breakdown in Maryland, where the electoral vote was cast by districts, appears below. Jackson received one electoral vote in the 2d district, although he was second to Adams in the popular vote.

District		Jackson	Adams	Crawford	Clay
1	one elector	473	817	380	
2	one elector	628	1,018	397	
3	two electors	4,834	4,398	9	
4	two electors	3,724	2,751	11	695
5	one elector	1,936	976		
6	one elector	1,360	1,259		
7	one elector	817	896	51	
8	one elector	72	1,215	1,407	
9	one elector	679	1,302	1,109	
TOTALS		14,523	14,632	3,364	695

In Connecticut, the nominee for elector who received the highest vote was on both tickets. The breakdown appears below:

Adams	Crawford
9,261	1,978
7,569	1,969
7,556	1,965
7,550	1,961
7,550	1,958
7,504	1,948
7,494	1,911
7,491	

The Delaware legislature of thirty members voted as follows for electors:

Rowland (Adams)	21
Caldwell (Crawford)	15
Tunnel (Crawford)	15
Johns (Adams)	10
Rodney (Adams)	10
Ridgely	8
Gordon (Jackson)	5
Young (Jackson)	3
Tindal	2
Waples (Crawford)	1

Although Caldwell and Tunnel did not receive majorities, they were declared to be elected. The Georgia legislature gave eight Crawford candidates for elector 121 votes each, while the ninth one received 120. Jackson's nine nominees received votes ranging from 42 to 45. In the South Carolina legislature of 159 members, the vote was on a Yea and Nay basis, Jackson succeeding by 132 to 25.

The Vermont legislature voted for Adams, 199 to 0.

Election of 1824

TABLE 12   Electoral and Popular Vote; Percentage of Popular Vote; House Vote

States	J	A	Cr	Cl	Jackson	Adams	Crawford	Clay
Alabama	5				9,443	2,416	1,680	67
Connecticut		8				9,261	1,978	
Delaware		1	2					
Georgia			9					
Illinois	2	1			1,901	1,542	219	1,047
Indiana	5				7,343	3,095		5,315
Kentucky				14	6,455			17,331
Louisiana	3	2						
Maine		9				10,289	2,336	
Maryland	7	3	1		14,523	14,632	3,364	695
Massachusetts		15				30,687	6,616	
Mississippi	3				3,234	1,694	119	
Missouri				3	987	311		1,401
New Hampshire		8				9,389	643	
New Jersey	8				10,985	9,110	1,196	
New York	1	26	5	4				
North Carolina	15				20,415		15,621	
Ohio				16	18,489	12,280		19,255
Pennsylvania	28				36,100	5,440	4,206	1,609
Rhode Island		4				2,145	200	
South Carolina	11							
Tennessee	11				20,197	216	312	
Vermont		7						
Virginia			24		2,861	3,189	8,489	416
TOTALS	99	84	41	37	152,933	115,696	46,979	47,136

States	J	A	Cr	Cl	J	A	Cr
Alabama	69.40	17.76	12.35	.49	**3**		
Connecticut		82.40	17.60			**6**	
Delaware							**1**
Georgia							**7**
Illinois	40.37	32.75	4.65	22.23		**1**	
Indiana	46.61	19.65		33.74	**3**		
Kentucky	27.14			**72.86**	4	**8**	
Louisiana					1	**2**	
Maine		81.50	18.50			**7**	
Maryland	43.73	44.06	10.13	2.09	3	**5**	1
Massachusetts	·	82.26	17.74		1	**12**	
Mississippi	64.08	33.56	2.36		**1**		
Missouri	36.57	11.52		51.91		**1**	
New Hampshire		**93.59**	6.41			**6**	
New Jersey	51.59	42.79	5.62		**5**	1	
New York					2	**18**	14
North Carolina	56.65		43.35		2	1	**10**
Ohio	36.96	24.55		38.49	2	**10**	2
Pennsylvania	76.23	11.49	8.88	3.40	**25**	1	
Rhode Island		91.47	8.53			**2**	
South Carolina					**9**		
Tennessee	**97.45**	1.04	1.51		**9**		
Vermont						**5**	
Virginia	19.13	21.32	**56.76**	2.78	1	1	**19**
TOTALS	42.16	31.89	12.95	12.99	71	87	54

In Delaware, Georgia, Louisiana, New York, South Carolina, and ·Vermont, the legislatures cast the electoral vote. It was cast by districts in Illinois, Kentucky, Maine, Maryland, and Missouri.

Underlined figures in the House vote show who carried the state. Adams carried thirteen states, Jackson seven, and Crawford four.

The highest percentage for each candidate is underlined.

Stanwood designates the Crawford vote in Connecticut, Maine, Massachusetts, and Rhode Island as "Opposition."

ELECTION OF 1828

Candidates were Andrew Jackson, Democrat; and John Quincy Adams, National Republican. Data pertaining to this election are from the following sources:

Connecticut, Georgia, Massachusetts, New Hampshire, and Vermont—High votes.

Alabama, Illinois, Mississippi, and Tennessee—Stanwood.

Louisiana—McKee and *Tribune Almanac.*

All other states—Several newspapers in each case.

In Maine, Maryland, New York, and Tennessee, the electoral vote was cast by districts. The New York breakdown appears below. District 3 had three electoral votes and Districts 20 and 26 each had two. The electors from the thirty districts chose two at-large electors, both of whom were for Jackson.

District	Jackson	Adams	District	Jackson	Adams
1	3,075	2,847	16	3,778	3,982
2	2,936	1,966	17	2,929	3,545
3	15,435	9,638	18	2,658	4,085
4	3,788	3,153	19	4,503	5,042
5	4,680	3,263	20	9,081	9,164
6	3,798	2,586	21	4,329	3,116
7	4,624	2,009	22	4,136	4,974
8	3,446	3,642	23	4,264	3,796
9	4,263	4,650	24	4,159	2,416
10	3,924	4,195	25	5,427	3,755
11	5,331	3,370	26	7,011	9,119
12	3,740	2,584	27	4,631	7,079
13	4,241	3,900	28	5,347	4,395
14	5,136	5,817	29	3,256	6,832
15	3,177	2,510	30	3,660	7,983

| | | | TOTALS | 140,763 | 135,413 |

The figures below show how a switch of 11,517 votes out of the 1,155,022 cast for Jackson and Adams—.997%—would have made the latter president:

States	Adams	Jackson	Shift
	83	178	
Ohio	16	-16	2,101
Kentucky	14	-14	3,968
New York	9	- 9	2,600
Louisiana	5	- 5	255
Indiana	5	- 5	2,593
	132	129	11,517

Details of the New York shift are as follows:

District	Adams	Jackson	Shift
13th	3,900	4,241	171
23d	3,796	4,264	235
4th	3,153	3,788	318
15th	2,510	3,177	334
28th	4,395	5,347	477
2d	1,966	2,936	486
12th	2,584	3,740	579
			2,600

Had Adams received these seven additional electoral votes, he would also have secured the two at large votes.

Jackson carried the Cumberland District in Maine, 4,227 to 4,043, according to the *Boston Patriot.* A shift of 93 votes would have given this electoral vote to Adams. This has not been included in the above tabulation, as the *Patriot's* breakdown for Maine cannot be reconciled with the state's totals.

TABLE 13   Electoral and Popular Vote and Percentage of Popular Vote

States	J	A	Jackson	Adams	Jackson	Adams
Alabama	5		17,138	1,938	89.84	10.16
Connecticut		8	4,448	13,838	24.32	75.68
Delaware		3				
Georgia	9		19,362	642	96.79	3.21
Illinois	3		9,560	4,662	67.22	32.78
Indiana	5		22,237	17,052	56.60	43.40
Kentucky	14		39,394	31,460	55.60	44.40
Louisiana	5		4,605	4,097	52.92	47.08
Maine	1	8	13,927	20,773	40.14	59.86
Maryland	5	6	24,565	25,527	49.04	50.96
Massachusetts		15	6,019	29,837	16.79	83.21
Mississippi	3		6,772	1,581	81.07	18.93
Missouri	3		8,272	3,400	70.87	29.13
New Hampshire		8	20,922	24,124	46.45	53.55
New Jersey		8	21,951	23,764	48.02	51.98
New York	20	16	140,763	135,413	50.97	49.03
North Carolina	15		37,857	13,918	73.12	26.88
Ohio	16		67,597	63,396	51.60	48.40
Pennsylvania	28		101,652	50,848	66.66	33.34
Rhode Island		4	821	2,754	22.97	77.03
South Carolina	11					
Tennessee	11		44,293	2,240	95.19	4.81
Vermont		7	8,385	24,365	25.60	74.40
Virginia	24		26,752	12,101	68.85	31.15
TOTALS	178	83	647,292	507,730	56.04	43.96

The legislatures cast the electoral vote in Delaware and South Carolina.

The highest percentage for each candidate is underlined.

ELECTION OF 1832

Candidates were Andrew Jackson, Democrat; Henry Clay, National Republican; and William Wirt, Anti-Masonic; John Floyd, Democrat, received the electoral vote of South Carolina, where the electors were chosen by the legislature.

Data pertaining to this election are from the following sources: Stanwood, McKee, *American Almanac, Tribune Almanac,* and various newspapers, including *Albany Argus, Kennebec Journal,* and Washington *Globe.*

In Maryland, the electoral vote was cast by districts; the breakdown appears below:

District		Jackson	Clay
1	four electors	5,097	8,458
		5,004	8,451
		5,058	8,447
		5,006	8,445
2	two electors	5,025	4,248
		5,020	4,246
3	one elector	2,905	
4	three electors	6,129	6,446
		6,121	6,454
		6,123	6,380
TOTALS		19,156	19,160

(Totals were obtained by adding the votes of the high man in each district.)

The vote in the South Carolina legislature was 99 for the Anti-Jackson candidates for electors and 57 for the Jackson nominees (32 Union-Jackson and 25 State Rights' Dissenters).

TABLE 14   Electoral and Popular Vote and Percentage of Popular Vote

States	J	C	F	W	Jackson	Clay	Wirt
Alabama	7						
Connecticut		8			11,212	17,617	3,288
Delaware		3			4,194	4,276	
Georgia	11				20,750		
Illinois	5				14,147	5,429	
Indiana	9				31,552	15,472	
Kentucky		15			36,247	43,396	
Louisiana	5				4,049	2,528	
Maine	10				33,984	27,327	841
Maryland	3	5			19,156	19,160	
Massachusetts		14			14,497	33,003	15,233
Mississippi	4				5,919		
Missouri	4				5,192		
New Hampshire	7				25,486	19,010	
New Jersey	8				23,859	23,397	480
New York	42				168,562	154,896	
North Carolina	15				24,862	4,563	
Ohio	21				81,246	76,539	509
Pennsylvania	30				90,983		66,716
Rhode Island		4			2,126	2,810	878
South Carolina			11				
Tennessee	15				28,740	1,436	
Vermont				7	7,870	11,152	13,106
Virginia	23				33,609	11,451	
TOTALS	219	49	11	7	688,242	473,462	101,051

States	Jackson	Clay	Wirt
Alabama			
Connecticut	34.91	54.85	10.24
Delaware	49.52	50.48	
Georgia	100.00		
Illinois	72.27	27.73	
Indiana	67.10	32.90	
Kentucky	45.51	54.49	
Louisiana	61.56	38.44	
Maine	54.68	43.96	1.35
Maryland	49.99	50.01	
Massachusetts	23.11	52.61	24.28
Mississippi	100.00		
Missouri	100.00		
New Hampshire	57.28	42.72	
New Jersey	49.98	49.01	1.01
New York	52.11	47.89	
North Carolina	84.49	15.51	
Ohio	51.33	48.35	.32
Pennsylvania	57.69		42.31
Rhode Island	36.57	48.33	15.10
South Carolina			
Tennessee	95.24	4.76	
Vermont	24.50	34.71	40.79
Virginia	74.59	25.41	
TOTALS	54.50	37.49	8.00

There was no opposition to Jackson in Alabama, Georgia, and Mississippi. According to Stanwood, he had no opposition in Missouri, but according to the *Tribune Almanac* and the *American Almanac,* the figure for Jackson represents his majority in that state.

Two Maryland electors did not vote.

The New York vote for Clay was cast by a coalition for Clay and Wirt.

The highest percentage for each candidate is underlined.

ELECTION OF 1836

Candidates were Martin Van Buren, Democrat; and William Henry Harrison, Daniel Webster, and Hugh Lawson White, Whigs; Willie Person Mangum, Democrat, received South Carolina's electoral vote, which was cast by the legislature.

Data pertaining to this election are from the following sources:

Connecticut, Georgia, Maine, Massachusetts, Michigan, New York, and Rhode Island—High votes.

Tennessee—Stanwood.

Virginia—*Richmond Enquirer.*

All other states—Several newspapers in each case.

The following figures show how a switch of 14,061 votes out of the 1,500,345 cast for Van Buren and the three Whig candidates—.94%—would have prevented Van Buren's election and probably made Harrison president:

	Harrison	Van Buren	White	Webster	Mangum	Shift
New York	73	170	26	14	11	
	42	-42				14,061
	115	128	26	14	11	

With the opportunity for victory, the Whigs would probably have cast all of their electoral votes for Harrison. Even if Van Buren had secured Mangum's eleven votes, the Whigs would still have won, 155 to 139.

A switch of 2,183 votes in Pennsylvania from Van Buren to Harrison would have prevented the former's election without giving Harrison (or White or Webster) the victory. Van Buren would still have led, 140-103-26-14-11, which would have necessitated a decision by the House of Representatives, unless South Carolina cast her eleven votes for Van Buren instead of Mangum.

The vote in the South Carolina legislature for Mangum was unanimous.

TABLE 15   Electoral and Popular Vote

States	V B	H	Wh	We	M	Van Buren	Harrison	White	Webster
Alabama	7					20,506		15,612	
Arkansas	3					2,400		1,238	
Connecticut	8					19,291	18,765		
Delaware		3				4,152	4,734		
Georgia			11			22,333		24,888	
Illinois	5					18,097	14,983		
Indiana		9				32,478	41,281		
Kentucky		15				33,435	36,955		
Louisiana	5					3,653		3,383	
Maine	10					22,900	15,239		
Maryland		10				22,168	25,852		
Massachusetts				14		33,542			41,287
Michigan	3					7,534	4,085		
Mississippi	4					9,979		9,688	
Missouri	4					10,995		7,337	
New Hampshire	7					18,722	6,228		
New Jersey		8				25,847	26,392		
New York	42					166,886	138,765		
North Carolina	15					26,910		23,626	
Ohio		21				96,916	105,417		
Pennsylvania	30					91,475	87,111		
Rhode Island	4					2,966	2,711		
South Carolina					11				
Tennessee			15			26,129		36,168	
Vermont		7				14,039	20,990		
Virginia	23					30,845		23,412	
TOTALS	170	73	26	14	11	764,198	549,508	145,352	41,287

Election of 1836

Percentage of Popular Vote

States	Van B	H	Wh	We
Alabama	56.78		43.22	
Arkansas	65.97		34.03	
Connecticut	50.69	49.31		
Delaware	46.73	53.27		
Georgia	47.29		52.71	
Illinois	54.71	45.29		
Indiana	44.03	55.97		
Kentucky	47.50	52.50		
Louisiana	51.92		48.08	
Maine	60.04	39.96		
Maryland	46.16	53.84		
Massachusetts	44.82			55.18
Michigan	64.84	35.16		
Mississippi	50.74		49.26	
Missouri	59.98		40.02	
New Hampshire	75.04	24.96		
New Jersey	49.48	50.52		
New York	54.60	45.40		
North Carolina	53.25		46.75	
Ohio	47.90	52.10		
Pennsylvania	51.22	48.78		
Rhode Island	52.25	47.75		
South Carolina				
Tennessee	41.94		58.06	
Vermont	40.08	59.92		
Virginia	56.85		43.15	
TOTALS	50.93	36.63	9.69	2.75

The highest percentage for each candidate is underlined.

Candidates were William Henry Harrison, Whig; Martin Van Buren, Democrat; and James Gillespie Birney, Liberty.

Data pertaining to this election are from the following sources: Stanwood, McKee, *American Almanac, Tribune Almanac,* and various newspapers, including *Albany Argus,* Philadelphia *National Gazette,* and Raleigh *North Carolina Standard.*

The figures below show how a switch of 8,386 votes out of the 2,405,645 cast for Harrison and Van Buren—.35%—would have reelected the latter president:

States	Van Buren	Harrison	Shift
	60	234	
New York	42	-42	6,602
Pennsylvania	30	-30	176
Maine	10	-10	226
New Jersey	8	- 8	1,382
	150	144	8,386

In the following tabulation, the nominees for electors are ranked according to the number of votes they received:

States	Van Buren	Harrison	Shift	
Pennsylvania	143,784	144,023	120	
	143,676	144,023	174	
	143,674	144,023	175	
	143,673	144,022	175	
	143,672	144,021	175	(5 electors)
	143,671	144,021	176	
	143,671	144,020	175	(3 electors)
	143,670	144,020	176	
	143,670	144,019	175	(2 electors)
	143,670	144,018	175	(3 electors)
	143,670	144,017	174	(2 electors)
	143,669	144,017	175	(2 electors)
	143,667	144,016	175	
	143,666	144,015	175	
	143,665	144,015	176	
	143,663	144,014	176	
	143,663	144,012	175	
	143,663	144,010	174	
	143,660	143,990	166	
Maine	46,190	46,612	212	(2 electors)
	46,190	46,611	211	(2 electors)
	46,189	46,611	212	
	46,188	46,610	212	(2 electors)
	46,187	46,609	212	
	46,186	46,604	210	
	46,153	46,603	226	
New Jersey	31,034	33,362	1,165	
	31,032	33,352	1,161	
	31,032	33,350	1,160	(2 electors)
	31,031	33,350	1,160	
	31,029	33,349	1,161	
	31,015	33,346	1,166	
	30,578	33,340	1,382	

The vote in the South Carolina legislature for Van Buren was unanimous.

Election of 1840

TABLE 16   Electoral and Popular Vote and Percentage of Popular Vote

States	H	V B	Harrison	Van Buren	Birney	H	Van B	Birney
Alabama		7	28,471	33,991		45.58	54.42.	
Arkansas		3	5,160	6,766		43.27	56.73	
Connecticut	8		31,601	25,296	174	55.37	44.32	.30
Delaware	3		5,967	4,884		54.99	45.01	
Georgia	11		40,349	31,989		55.78	44.22	
Illinois		5	45,574	47,625	159	48.83	51.01	.17
Indiana	9		65,308	51,695	.	55.82	44.18	
Kentucky	15		58,489	32,616		64.20	35.80	
Louisiana	5		11,297	7,617		59.73	40.27	
Maine	10		46,612	46,190	186	50.13	49.67	.20
Maryland	10		33,533	28,759		53.83	46.17	
Massachusetts	14		72,913	52,432	1,621	57.43	41.30	1.28
Michigan	3		22,933	21,131	321	51.67	47.61	.72
Mississippi	4		19,518	16,995		53.45	46.55	
Missouri		4	22,972	29,760		43.56	56.44	
New Hampshire		7	26,434	32,670	126	44.63	55.16	.21
New Jersey	8		33,362	31,034	69	51.75	48.14	.11
New York	42		225,945	212,743	2,790	51.18	48.19	.63
North Carolina	15		46,379	33,782		57.85	42.14	
Ohio	21		148,157	124,782	903	54.10	45.57	.33
Pennsylvania	30		144,023	143,784	343	49.98	49.90	.12
Rhode Island	4		5,278	3,301	42	61.22	38.29	.49
South Carolina		11						
Tennessee	15		60,391	48,289		55.57	44.43	
Vermont	7		32,445	18,009		63.90	35.47	
Virginia		23	42,501	43,893	319	49.19	50.81	.63
TOTALS	234	60	1,275,612	1,130,033	7,053	52.87	46.84	.29

The legislature cast the electoral vote in South Carolina.

The highest percentage for each candidate is underlined.

25

Candidates were James Knox Polk, Democrat; Henry Clay, Whig; and James Gillespie Birney, Liberty.

Data pertaining to this election are from the following sources: Stanwood, McKee; *American Almanac, Tribune Almanac,* and various newspapers, including *New York Journal of Commerce.*

The figures below show how a switch of 2,555 votes out of the 2,640,055 cast for Polk and Clay—.097%—would have made the latter president:

	Clay	Polk	Shift
	105	170	
New York	36	-36	2,555
	—	—	
	141	134	

In the following tabulation, the nominees for electors are ranked according to the number of votes they received:

Polk	Clay	Birney	Shift	Electors
237,588	232,482	15,814	2,554	1
237,574	232,466	15,814	2,555	1
237,573	232,465	15,814	2,555	1
237,572	232,465	15,814	2,554	4
237,572	232,464	15,814	2,555	2
237,571	232,463	15,813	2,555	1
237,570	232,463	15,813	2,554	2
237,569	232,463	15,813	2,554	2
237,568	232,463	15,813	2,553	1
237,567	232,463	15,813	2,553	1
237,567	232,462	15,813	2,553	2
237,567	232,461	15,813	2,554	2
237,566	232,460	15,813	2,554	2
237,565	232,460	15,812	2,553	2
237,565	232,458	15,812	2,554	1
237,564	232,457	15,812	2,554	1
237,564	232,456	15,811	2,555	2
237,562	232,455	15,809	2,554	1
237,561	232,455	15,805	2,554	1
237,559	232,455	15,802	2,553	1
237,548	232,453	15,785	2,548	1
237,537	232,450	15,708	2,544	1
237,486	232,440	15,384	2,524	1
237,447	232,408	15,206	2,520	1
237,343	232,292	14,395	2,526	1

TABLE 17   Electoral and Popular Vote and Percentage of Popular Vote

States	P	C	Polk	Clay	Birney	Polk	Clay	Birney
Alabama	9		37,740	26,084		59.13	40.87	
Arkansas	3		9,546	5,504		63.43	36.57	
Connecticut		6	29,841	32,832	1,943	46.18	50.81	3.01
Delaware		3	5,996	6,278		48.85	51.15	
Georgia	10		44,177	42,106		51.20	48.79	
Illinois	9		58,700	45,790	3,439	54.39	42.43	3.19
Indiana	12		70,181	67,867	2,106	50.07	48.42	1.50
Kentucky		12	51,988	61,255		45.91	54.09	
Louisiana	6		13,782	13,083		51.30	48.70	
Maine	9		45,964	34,619	4,862	53.79	40.52	5.69
Maryland		8	32,676	35,984		47.59	52.41	
Massachusetts		12	52,846	67,418	10,860	40.30	51.42	8.28
Michigan	5		27,759	24,337	3,632	49.81	43.67	6.52
Mississippi	6		25,126	19,206		56.68	43.32	
Missouri	7		41,369	31,251		56.97	43.03	
New Hampshire	6		27,160	17,866	4,161	55.22	36.32	8.46
New Jersey		7	37,495	38,318	131	49.37	50.46	.17
New York	36		237,588	232,482	15,814	48.90	47.85	3.25
North Carolina		11	39,287	43,232		47.61	52.39	
Ohio		23	149,117	155,057	8,050	47.76	49.66	2.58
Pennsylvania	26		167,535	161,203	3,138	50.48	48.57	.95
Rhode Island		4	4,867	7,322	107	39.58	59.55	.87
South Carolina	9							
Tennessee		13	59,904	60,033		49.95	50.05	
Vermont		6	18,041	26,770	3,954	37.00	54.90	8.11
Virginia	17		50,683	44,790		53.09	46.91	
TOTALS	170	105	1,339,368	1,300,687	62,197	49.56	48.13	2.30

The legislature cast the electoral vote in South Carolina.

The highest percentage for each candidate is underlined.

Candidates were Zachary Taylor, Whig; Lewis Cass, Democrat; Martin Van Buren, Free Soil; and Gerrit Smith, Liberty (and Industrial Congress).

Data pertaining to this election are from the following sources: Stanwood, McKee; *American Almanac, Tribune Almanac,* and various newspapers, including *New York Journal of Commerce, Philadelphia Bulletin, Illinois State Register,* and Washington *National Intelligencer.*

The figures below show how a switch of 3,227 votes out of the 2,584,775 cast for Taylor and Cass—.125%—would have made the latter president:

States	Cass	Taylor	Shift
	127	163	
Georgia	10	-10	1,373
Maryland	8	- 8	1,588
Delaware	3	- 3	266
	148	142	3,227

In the following tabulation, the nominees for electors are ranked according to the number of votes they received:

States	Cass	Taylor	Shift
Georgia	44,809	47,538	1,365
	44,795	47,537	1,372 (2 electors)
	44,792	47,536	1,373
	44,791	47,531	1,371
	44,787	47,527	1,371
	44,787	47,525	1,370
	44,787	47,524	1,369
	44,780	47,515	1,368
	44,780	47,508	1,365
Maryland	37,706	34,536	1,586
	37,704	34,532	1,587
	37,704	34,530	1,588
	37,702	34,529	1,587
	37,698	34,528	1,586
	37,696	34,526	1,586
	37,685	34,525	1,581
	37,671	34,517	1,578

The vote in the South Carolina legislature was 129 for the Cass candidates for electors, 27 for the Taylor nominees, and 8 Blank. In the Massachusetts legislature, the vote was: Taylor 196, Cass 65, Van Buren 37, Miscellaneous 1. The lone vote was cast for a complete slate of electors, just as were all the other votes.

Election of 1848

TABLE 18   Electoral and Popular Vote

States	T	C	Taylor	Cass	Van Buren	Smith
Alabama		9	30,482	31,363		
Arkansas		3	7,588	9,300		
Connecticut	6		30,316	27,047	5,005	
Delaware	3		6,441	5,910	80	
Florida	3		4,546	3,243		
Georgia	10		47,538	44,809		
Illinois		9	53,215	56,629	15,804	
Indiana		12	69,907	74,745	8,100	
Iowa		4	11,084	12,093	1,126	
Kentucky	12		67,141	49,720		
Louisiana	6		18,217	15,370		
Maine		9	35,279	40,138	12,124	
Maryland	8		37,706	34,536	130	
Massachusetts	12		61,300	35,398	38,263	
Michigan		5	23,940	30,687	10,389	
Mississippi		6	25,922	26,537		
Missouri		7	32,671	40,077		
New Hampshire		6	14,781	27,763	7,560	
New Jersey	7		40,015	36,901	829	77
New York	36		218,603	114,320	120,510	2,545
North Carolina	11		43,550	34,869	85	
Ohio		23	138,360	154,775	35,354	111
Pennsylvania	26		185,513	171,176	11,263	
Rhode Island	4		6,779	3,646	730	
South Carolina		9				
Tennessee	13		64,705	58,419		
Texas		4	4,509	10,668		
Vermont	6		23,122	10,948	13,837	
Virginia		17	45,124	46,586	9	
Wisconsin		4	13,747	15,001	10,418	
TOTALS	163	127	1,362,101	1,222,674	291,616	2,733

The legislatures cast the electoral vote in Massachusetts and South Carolina. In the former state, it was because no candidate received a majority of the popular vote.

Percentage of Popular Vote

States	T	C	Van B	S
Alabama	49.29	50.71		
Arkansas	44.93	55.07		
Connecticut	48.61	43.37	8.02	
Delaware	51.81	47.54	.64	
Florida	58.36	41.64		
Georgia	51.48	48.52		
Illinois	42.35	45.07	12.58	
Indiana	45.77	48.93	5.30	
Iowa	45.61	49.76	4.63	
Kentucky	57.45	42.55		
Louisiana	54.24	45.76		
Maine	40.30	45.85	13.85	
Maryland	52.10	47.72	.18	
Massachusetts	45.42	26.23	28.35	
Michigan	36.82	47.20	15.98	
Mississippi	49.41	50.59		
Missouri	44.91	55.09		
New Hampshire	29.50	55.41	15.09	
New Jersey	51.42	47.42	1.07	.10
New York	47.94	25.07	26.43	.56
North Carolina	55.47	44.42	.11	
Ohio	42.11	47.10	10.76	.03
Pennsylvania	50.42	46.52	3.06	
Rhode Island	60.77	32.68	6.54	
South Carolina				
Tennessee	52.55	47.45		
Texas	29.71	70.29		
Vermont	48.26	22.85	28.88	
Virginia	49.20	50.79	.01	
Wisconsin	35.10	38.30	26.60	
TOTALS	47.31	42.47	10.13	.09

The highest percentage for each candidate is underlined.

ELECTION OF 1852

Candidates were Franklin Pierce, Democrat; Winfield Scott, Whig; John Parker Hale, Free Soil; Daniel Webster, Whig; George M. Troup, Southern Rights; ———— Broome, Native American; and Gerrit Smith, Liberty. Webster died October 24th, shortly before the election. Data pertaining to this election are from the following sources: Stanwood, McKee, *American Almanac, Tribune Almanac, World Almanac,* and various newspapers, including *Augusta* [Georgia] *Chronicle, Boston Post, Illinois State Register,* and *Pennsylvania Telegraph.* Pierce's slate of electors received 135 votes in the South Carolina legislature; as far as the compiler knows, this was unanimous.

TABLE 19   Electoral and Popular Vote

States	FP	WS	Pierce	Scott	Hale	Webster	Broome	Troup	Smith
Alabama	9		26,881	15,038				2,174	
Arkansas	4		12,173	7,404					
California	4		40,626	35,407	100				
Connecticut	6		33,249	30,359	3,160				
Delaware	3		6,319	6,294	62				
Florida	3		4,318	2,875					
Georgia	10		40,516	16,660		5,324		126	
Illinois	11		80,597	64,934	9,966				
Indiana	13		95,340	80,901	6,929				
Iowa	4		17,763	15,856	1,604				
Kentucky		12	53,806	57,068	265				
Louisiana	6		18,647	17,255					
Maine	8		41,609	32,543	8,030				
Maryland	8		40,028	35,080	54				
Massachusetts		13	45,875	52,683	28,023	1,670	165		
Michigan	6		41,842	33,860	7,237				
Mississippi	7		26,876	17,548					
Missouri	9		38,353	29,984					
New Hampshire	5		29,997	16,147	6,695				
New Jersey	7		44,325	38,553	267		831		
New York	35		262,456	234,906	25,433	413			72
North Carolina	10		39,744	39,058	59				
Ohio	23		169,160	152,626	31,782				
Pennsylvania	27		198,568	179,182	8,524		1,670		
Rhode Island	4		8,735	7,626	644				
South Carolina	8								
Tennessee		12	57,123	58,802					
Texas	4		13,552	4,995					
Vermont		5	13,044	22,173	8,621				
Virginia	15		73,858	58,572					
Wisconsin	5		33,658	22,240	8,842				
TOTALS	254	42	1,609,038	1,386,629	156,297	7,407	2,666	2,300	72

The legislature cast the electoral vote in South Carolina.

Election of 1852

Percentage of Popular Vote

States	Pierce	Scott	Hale	Webster	Broome	Troup	Smith
Alabama	60.96	34.11				<u>4.93</u>	
Arkansas	62.18	37.82					
California	53.36	46.51	.13				
Connecticut	49.80	45.47	4.73				
Delaware	49.85	49.66	.49				
Florida	60.03	39.97					
Georgia	64.70	26.60		<u>8.50</u>		.20	
Illinois	51.83	41.76	6.41				
Indiana	52.05	44.17	3.78				
Iowa	50.43	45.02	4.55				
Kentucky	48.41	<u>51.35</u>	.24				
Louisiana	51.94	48.06					
Maine	50.63	39.60	9.77				
Maryland	53.26	46.67	.07				
Massachusetts	35.72	41.03	<u>21.82</u>	1.30	.12		
Michigan	50.45	40.83	<u>8.73</u>				
Mississippi	60.50	39.50					
Missouri	56.12	43.88					
New Hampshire	56.77	30.56	12.67				
New Jersey	52.78	45.91	.32		<u>.99</u>		
New York	50.16	44.89	4.86	.08			<u>.01</u>
North Carolina	50.40	49.53	.07				
Ohio	47.84	43.17	8.99				
Pennsylvania	51.18	46.19	2.20		.43		
Rhode Island	51.37	44.85	3.79				
South Carolina							
Tennessee	49.28	50.72					
Texas	<u>73.07</u>	26.93					
Vermont	29.76	50.58	19.67				
Virginia	55.77	44.23					
Wisconsin	51.99	34.35	13.66				
TOTALS	50.85	43.82	4.94	.23	.08	.07	.00

The highest percentage for each candidate is underlined.

".00" signifies that the candidate received some votes, but less than .01%.

Candidates were James Buchanan, Democrat; John Charles Fremont, Republican; Millard Fillmore, Whig (and American); and Gerrit Smith, Land Reform.

Data pertaining to this election are from the following sources:

Georgia, Massachusetts, and Wisconsin—High votes.

Arkansas, Maine, and Texas—Stanwood, McKee, and *World Almanac.*

California—*San Francisco Bulletin.*

Kentucky—*Louisville Times.*

Michigan—At least first three candidates high votes; Smith from several newspapers.

New Hampshire—[Concord] *New Hampshire Statesman.*

New York—*Albany Statesman.*

Ohio—First three candidates, several newspapers; Smith from [Columbus] *Ohio Statesman.*

Pennsylvania—High votes were as follows:

Buchanan	230,686 (27 electors)
Straight Fillmore	26,337 (27 electors)
Union ticket (Fremont and Fillmore)	203,534 (26 electors)
Fremont	147,286 (27th "split elector")
Fillmore	55,852 (27th "split elector")
Straight Fremont plus "etc."	64

Smith from several newspapers.

All other states—Several newspapers in each case.

The following figures show how a switch of 17,427 votes out of the 4,030,137 cast for Buchanan, Fremont, and Fillmore—.43%—would have prevented Buchanan's election without giving Fremont the victory. A decision by the House of Representatives would have become necessary.

States	Buchanan	Fremont	Fillmore	Shift
	174	114	8	
Indiana	-13	13		11,929
Illinois	-11	11		4,583
Delaware	- 3		3	915
	147	138	11	17,427

A switch of 13,577 votes in Pennsylvania from Buchanan to the Union ticket of Fremont and Fillmore would likewise have prevented Buchanan's election without giving Fremont the victory, thus necessitating a House decision. Buchanan would still have led, 148 to 140, with Fillmore's 8 representing the balance of power.

The vote in the South Carolina legislature, where 159 members voted, was as follows; the top eight were successful:

Chesnut	156
Nowell	156
Owens	156
T. Pickens	155
Watts	155
Inglis	154
Manning	105
F. Pickens	86
Calhoun	61
Jamison	52
Several (at least six)	1 each

As Manning, F. Pickens, Calhoun, and Jamison were voted on as at-large candidates, it is likely that the opposition to Buchanan was included in the group that received one vote each.

Election of 1856

TABLE 20 Electoral and Popular Vote

States	B	Fr	Fi	Buchanan	Fremont	Fillmore	Smith
Alabama	9			46,817		28,557	
Arkansas	4			21,910		10,787	
California	4			53,365	20,693	36,165	
Connecticut		6		34,995	42,715	2,615	
Delaware	3			8,003	306	6,175	
Florida	3			6,368		4,843	
Georgia	10			56,608		42,477	
Illinois	11			105,344	96,180	37,451	
Indiana	13			118,672	94,816	23,386	
Iowa		4		36,241	44,127	9,444	
Kentucky	12			74,642	373	67,416	
Louisiana	6			22,169		20,709	
Maine		8		39,080	67,379	3,325	
Maryland			8	39,115	281	47,462	
Massachusetts		13		39,240	108,190	19,726	
Michigan		6		52,529	71,969	1,660	150
Mississippi	7			35,665		24,490	
Missouri	9			58,164		48,524	
New Hampshire		5		32,789	38,345	422	
New Jersey	7			46,943	28,351	24,115	
New York		35		195,866	274,707	124,603	160
North Carolina	10			48,246		36,886	
Ohio		23		170,874	187,497	28,125	156
Pennsylvania	27			230,686	147,286	55,852	18
Rhode Island		4		6,680	11,467	1,675	
South Carolina	8						
Tennessee	12			73,638		66,178	
Texas	4			31,169		15,639	
Vermont		5		10,577	39,963	546	
Virginia	15			89,975	291	60,039	
Wisconsin		5		52,867	66,092	580	
TOTALS	174	114	8	1,839,237	1,341,028	849,872	484

The legislature cast the electoral vote in South Carolina.

States	B	Fr	F1	S
Alabama	62.11		37.88	
Arkansas	67.01		32.99	
California	48.42	18.77	32.81	
Connecticut	43.57	53.18	3.26	
Delaware	55.25	2.11	42.63	
Florida	56.81		43.20	
Georgia	57.13		42.87	
Illinois	44.08	40.25	15.67	
Indiana	50.10	40.03	9.87	
Iowa	40.35	49.13	10.52	
Kentucky	52.41	.26	47.33	
Louisiana	51.70		48.30	
Maine	35.60	61.37	3.03	
Maryland	45.03	.32	54.64	
Massachusetts	23.48	64.72	11.80	
Michigan	41.59	56.98	1.31	.12
Mississippi	59.29		40.71	
Missouri	54.52		45.48	
New Hampshire	45.82	53.59	.59	
New Jersey	47.22	28.52	24.26	
New York	32.90	46.14	20.93	.03
North Carolina	56.67		43.33	
Ohio	44.19	48.49	7.27	.04
Pennsylvania	53.17	33.95	12.87	.00
Rhode Island	33.70	57.85	8.45	
South Carolina				
Tennessee	52.67		47.33	
Texas	66.59		33.41	
Vermont	20.70	78.23	1.07	
Virginia	59.86	.19	39.94	
Wisconsin	44.23	55.29	.49	
TOTALS	45.63	33.27	21.08	.01

The highest percentage for each candidate is underlined.

".00" signifies that the candidate received some votes, but less than .01%.

ELECTION OF 1860

Candidates were Abraham Lincoln, Republican; Stephen Arnold Douglas, Democrat; John Cabell Breckinridge, Democrat; and John Bell, Constitutional Union; Gerrit Smith also received votes.

Data pertaining to this election are from the following sources: Stanwood, McKee, *American Almanac, Tribune Almanac, World Almanac,* and various newspapers, including *Ohio Statesman, New York Tribune, Providence Journal,* and *Alta Galifornia.* See notes following *Electoral and Popular Vote* for data pertaining to Illinois and New York.

The following figures explain the split in the New Jersey electoral vote. The opposition to Lincoln appeared on a Fusion ticket.

WINNERS	CANDIDATE	LOSERS	CANDIDATE
62,869	Douglas	58,324	Lincoln
62,388	Douglas	58,322	Lincoln
62,309	Douglas	58,316	Lincoln
58,346	Lincoln	58,022	Breckinridge
58,342	Lincoln	57,770	Bell
58,336	Lincoln	57,552	Bell
58,335	Lincoln	56,237	Breckinridge

The following figures show how a switch of 25,069 votes out of the 3,246,632 cast for Lincoln and Douglas—.77%—would have prevented Lincoln's election and necessitated a decision by the House of Representatives:

	Lincoln	Breckin-ridge	Bell	Douglas	Shift
New York	180 -35	72	39	12 35	25,069
	145	72	39	47	

The political lineup in the House was as follows:

States	Rep.	Dem.	Amn.	Whig
Alabama		7		
Arkansas		2		
California		2		
Connecticut	4			
Delaware		1		
Florida		1		
Georgia		6	2	
Illinois	4	5		
Indiana	7	4		
Iowa	2			
Kansas	1			
Kentucky		5	5	
Louisiana		3	1	
Maine	6			
Maryland		3	3	
Massachusetts	11			
Michigan	4			
Minnesota	2			
Mississippi		5		
Missouri		7		
New Hampshire	3			
New Jersey	1	2	2	
New York	24	7	2	
North Carolina		4	4	
Ohio	15	6		
Oregon		1		
Pennsylvania	20	5		
Rhode Island	2			
South Carolina		6		
Tennessee		3	6	1
Texas		2		
Vermont	3			
Virginia		12	1	
Wisconsin	2	1		
TOTALS	111	100	26	1

The Kansas member was seated January 30, 1861. Kansas did not participate in the presidential election in November.

Had the House failed to elect a president, the vice-president would have assumed the presidency. Only Hannibal Hamlin and Joseph Lane, the running-mates of Lincoln and Breckinridge, would have received votes, as the Senate would have had to choose between the two highest candidates. Both Hamlin and Lane were in the Senate at the time of this "election," as was also Douglas. Breckinridge was vice-president.

The political lineup in the Senate was as follows:

Both Senators Republicans: Connecticut, Iowa, Maine, Massachusetts, Michigan, New Hampshire, New York, Rhode Island, Vermont, and Wisconsin.

Both Senators Democrats: Alabama, Arkansas, California, Delaware, Florida, Georgia, Indiana, Louisiana, Mississippi, Missouri, North Carolina, South Carolina, Tennessee, Texas, and Virginia.

One Senator Republican, one Democrat: Illinois, Minnesota, New Jersey, Ohio, Oregon, and Pennsylvania.

One Senator Democrat, one American: Kentucky and Maryland.

TOTALS: Democrats 38, Republicans 26, Americans 2. (Kansas had no senators.)

The vote in the South Carolina legislature, where 161 members voted, was as follows:

```
McCaa        159
Gist         157
Elliott      156
Williams     156
Calhoun      155
Martin       151
Watson       148
Simons       142
Scattering     4
```

The first eight were chosen electors.

Election of 1860

TABLE 21   Electoral and Popular Vote

States	L	Br	Bl	D	Lincoln	Douglas	Breck.	Bell	Smith
Alabama		9				13,651	48,831	27,875	
Arkansas		4				5,227	28,732	20,094	
California	4				39,173	38,516	34,334	6,817	
Connecticut	6				43,486	17,364	16,558	3,337	
Delaware		3			3,816	1,069	7,344	3,868	
Florida		3				367	8,543	5,437	
Georgia		10				11,613	52,131	43,050	
Illinois	11				172,171	160,205	2,402	4,913	35
Indiana	13				139,033	115,509	12,295	5,306	
Iowa	4				70,409	55,111	1,048	1,763	
Kentucky			12		1,364	25,651	53,143	66,058	
Louisiana		6				7,625	22,681	20,204	
Maine	8				62,811	26,693	6,368	2,046	
Maryland		8			2,895	5,953	42,511	41,875	
Massachusetts	13				106,649	34,492	6,277	22,536	
Michigan	6				88,480	65,057	805	405	
Minnesota	4				22,069	11,920	748	62	
Mississippi		7				3,283	40,797	25,040	
Missouri				9	17,028	58,801	31,317	58,372	
New Hampshire	5				37,519	25,881	2,112	441	
New Jersey	4			3	58,346	62,869			
New York	35				362,646	312,510			
North Carolina		10				2,701	48,539	44,990	
Ohio	23				231,610	187,232	11,405	12,194	136
Oregon	3				5,496	4,127	5,342	976	
Pennsylvania	27				268,030	16,765	178,871	12,776	
Rhode Island	4				12,240	7,753			1
South Carolina		8							
Tennessee			12			11,428	66,440	70,706	
Texas		4					47,548	15,438	
Vermont	5				33,888	8,748	1,859	217	
Virginia			15		1,929	16,292	74,379	74,701	
Wisconsin	5				86,110	65,021	888	161	
TOTALS	180	72	39	12	1,867,198	1,379,434	854,248	591,658	172

The legislature cast the electoral vote in South Carolina.

Connecticut also had 1,852 Fusion votes, mostly for Breckinridge.

In Illinois, the high votes without Monroe and Pulaski Counties were: Lincoln 171,137, Douglas 158,254, Bell, 4,851, and Breckinridge 2,293. The votes for the electoral candidates listed first were the same in the cases of Douglas and Bell, while Lincoln's nominee received 171,106 and Breckinridge's 2,292. The Monroe and Pulaski votes were, respectively: Lincoln 845 and 220, Douglas 1,401 and 550, Bell 17 and 45, and Breckinridge 0 and 110. The grand totals gave the figures used in the above tabulation, except that the official figures gave Breckinridge only 2,332, an obvious error. It is impossible to determine whether the Monroe and Pulaski figures were for the electoral candidates listed first or for the highest vote-getters.

The Massachusetts high votes, as published in the *Boston Advertiser* and *Boston Courier*, differ on Bell's figure. The former has 22,536 and the latter 22,563, most likely a transposition on the part of one or the other. The lower figure was arbitrarily adopted, after the *Herald, Journal, Post,* and *Transcript,* all of Boston, had been checked without result.

In New York, the high votes without Orange and Sullivan Counties were: Lincoln 353,804 and Douglas 305,961. The first at large electoral candidate was the high vote-getter in the case of Lincoln, while Douglas' nominee received 303,329.The Orange and Sullivan votes were, respectively: Lincoln 5,898 and 2,944 and Douglas 6,011 and 3,170. The grand totals give the figures used in the above tabulation. It is impossible to determine whether the Orange and Sullivan figures are for the first at large nominees or for the highest vote-getters. The New York newspapers give Douglas various figures: *Post* 314,176, *Herald* and *World* 313,790, and *Journal of Commerce* and *Tribune* 312,510. The Douglas vote was a Fusion ticket composed of the opposition to Lincoln.

In Pennsylvania, the high votes as published gave Lincoln 267,242 and Bell 12,873. A Fusion ticket, which had fifteen Fusion and twelve Fusion-Douglas candidates, had a high of 194,834, which was cast for two Fusion-Douglas nominees. The high for a Fusion Candidate was 185,6-0 (the next to the last digit being illegible). There were fifteen names on a Straight Douglas ticket, the high vote being 16,634. If the Straight Douglas high is subtracted from the Fusion-Douglas high, Breckinridge will have 178,200. As Stanwood's figures probably include late votes not counted in the published high votes, they have been used in the above tabulation.

1860   Percentage of Popular Vote

States	L	D	Br	Bl	S
Alabama		15.11	54.04	30.85	
Arkansas		9.67	53.16	37.17	
California	32.96	32.41	28.89	5.74	
Connecticut	53.86	21.50	20.51	4.13	
Delaware	23.71	6.64	45.62	24.03	
Florida		2.56	59.55	37.90	
Georgia		10.87	48.81	40.31	
Illinois	50.68	47.16	.71	1.45	.01
Indiana	51.09	42.44	4.52	1.95	
Iowa	54.87	42.94	.82	1.37	
Kentucky	.93	17.54	36.35	45.18	
Louisiana		15.10	44.90	40.00	
Maine	64.15	27.26	6.50	2.09	
Maryland	3.11	6.39	45.60	44.91	
Massachusetts	62.75	20.29	3.69	13.26	
Michigan	57.18	42.04	.52	.26	
Minnesota	63.42	34.25	2.15	.18	
Mississippi		4.75	59.02	36.23	
Missouri	10.29	35.53	18.92	35.27	
New Hampshire	56.89	39.24	3.20	.67	
New Jersey	48.13	51.87			
New York	53.71	46.29			
North Carolina		2.81	50.44	46.75	
Ohio	52.33	42.30	2.58	2.76	.03
Oregon	34.48	25.89	33.51	6.12	
Pennsylvania	56.25	3.52	37.54	2.68	
Rhode Island	61.22	38.78			.01
South Carolina					
Tennessee		7.69	44.72	47.59	
Texas			75.49	24.51	
Vermont	75.79	19.57	4.16	.49	
Virginia	1.15	9.74	44.46	44.65	
Wisconsin	56.58	42.73	.58	.11	
TOTALS	39.79	29.40	18.20	12.61	.00

The highest percentage for each candidate is underlined.

".00" signifies that the candidate received some votes, but less than .01%.

Candidates were Abraham Lincoln, Republican; and George Brinton McClellan, Democrat.
Data pertaining to this election are from the following sources:

Illinois, Kentucky, Maryland, New York, Ohio, and Pennsylvania—High votes.

California—[San Francisco] *Alta California*.

Connecticut, Delaware, Iowa, Massachusetts, Michigan, Minnesota, Nevada, and New Jersey
—Several newspapers in each case.

Indiana—*Indianapolis Journal*.

Kansas, Maine, Missouri, New Hampshire, Rhode Island, Vermont, and West Virginia—
Stanwood and McKee.

Oregon—[Salem] *Oregon Statesman*.

Wisconsin—*World Almanac, Tribune Almanac,* and *American Almanac*.

The figures below show how a switch of 38,111 votes out of the 4,024,425 cast for Lincoln
and McClellan—.95%—would have made the latter president:

States	McClellan	Lincoln	Shift
	21	212	
New York	33	-33	3,378
Pennsylvania	26	-26	10,180
Indiana	13	-13	10,100
Wisconsin	8	- 8	8,788
Maryland	7	- 7	3,745
Connecticut	6	- 6	1,204
Oregon	3	- 3	716
	117	116	38,111

In the following tabulation, the nominees for electors are ranked according to the number of
votes they received:

States	McClellan	Lincoln	Shift
New York	361,986	368,735	3,375
	361,986	368,734	3,375
	361,985	368,733	3,375 (2 electors)
	361,984	368,732	3,375 (2 electors)
	361,984	368,731	3,374
	361,983	368,731	3,375 (2 electors)
	361,982	368,731	3,375
	361,981	368,731	3,376 (3 electors)
	361,981	368,730	3,375
	361,980	368,730	3,376 (2 electors)
	361,979	368,730	3,376
	361,978	368,729	3,376
	361,977	368,729	3,377
	361,975	368,728	3,377
	361,974	368,728	3,378 (3 electors)
	361,973	368,727	3,378 (2 electors)
	361,972	368,726	3,378
	361,971	368,726	3,378
	361,970	368,722	3,377
	361,969	368,720	3,376
	361,968	368,718	3,376
	361,964	368,717	3,377
	361,961	368,700	3,370
	361,953	368,486	3,267

States	McClellan	Lincoln	Shift	
Pennsylvania	276,308	296,389	10,041	
	275,928	296,286	10,180	
	275,928	296,269	10,171	
	275,927	296,224	10,149	
	275,926	296,222	10,149	
	275,926	296,221	10,148	(2 electors)
	275,925	296,220	10,148	(2 electors)
	275,924	296,219	10,148	(3 electors)
	275,924	296,217	10,147	
	275,923	296,216	10,147	
	275,922	296,216	10,148	(3 electors)
	275,921	296,216	10,148	
	275,921	296,215	10,148	
	275,920	296,214	10,148	
	275,919	296,212	10,147	
	275,918	296,211	10,147	
	275,912	296,192	10,141	
	275,909	296,183	10,138	
	275,902	296,177	10,138	
	275,864	293,586	8,862	
Maryland	32,739	40,169	3,716	
	32,730	40,154	3,713	
	32,723	40,153	3,716	
	32,722	40,149	3,714	
	32,718	40,138	3,711	
	32,701	40,128	3,714	
	32,599	40,087	3,745	

Election of 1864

TABLE 22   Electoral and Popular Vote and Percentage of Popular Vote

States	L	McC	Lincoln	McClellan	L	McC
California	5		62,134	43,842	58.63	41.37
Connecticut	6		44,691	42,285	51.38	48.62
Delaware		3	8,157	8,767	48.20	51.80
Illinois	16		189,521	158,829	54.41	45.59
Indiana	13		150,422	130,223	53.60	46.40
Iowa	8		89,075	49,596	64.23	35.77
Kansas	3		14,228	3,871	78.61	21.39
Kentucky		11	27,786	64,301	30.17	69.83
Maine	7		72,278	47,736	60.22	39.78
Maryland	7		40,169	32,739	55.10	44.90
Massachusetts	12		126,742	48,745	72.22	27.78
Michigan	8		85,352	67,370	55.89	44.11
Minnesota	4		25,060	17,375	59.06	40.94
Missouri	11		72,991	31,026	70.17	29.83
Nevada	2		9,826	6,594	59.84	40.16
New Hampshire	5		36,595	33,034	52.56	47.44
New Jersey		7	60,723	68,024	47.16	52.84
New York	33		368,735	361,986	50.46	49.54
Ohio	21		265,154	205,571	56.33	43.67
Oregon	3		9,888	8,457	53.90	46.10
Pennsylvania	26		296,389	276,308	51.75	48.25
Rhode Island	4		14,343	8,718	62.20	37.80
Vermont	5		42,422	13,325	76.10	23.90
West Virginia	5		23,223	10,457	68.95	31.05
Wisconsin	8		83,458	65,884	55.88	44.12
TOTALS	212	21	2,219,362	1,805,063	55.15	44.85

The highest percentage for each candidate is underlined.

Alabama, Arkansas, Florida, Georgia, Louisiana, Mississippi, North Carolina, South Carolina, Tennessee, Texas, and Virginia did not participate, due to the Civil War.

One Nevada elector died before the electoral vote was counted.

In California, the high votes without the soldier vote were: Lincoln 59,534, McClellan 43,843. The soldier vote was: Lincoln 2,600, McClellan 237. The *Alta* uses Lincoln's high, but adopts a lower figure—43,605—for McClellan, to arrive at the totals used in the above table. It is impossible to determine whether the 237 soldier votes were cast for the highest McClellan electoral nominee or for another candidate.

ELECTION OF 1868

Candidates were Ulysses Simpson Grant, Republican; and Horatio Seymour, Democrat.

Data pertaining to this election are from the following sources:

Oregon—National Archives.

California and New York—High votes.

Arkansas, Maryland, Minnesota, Missouri, and Nevada—Stanwood, McKee, *World Almanac*, and *Tribune Almanac*.

Connecticut—*Hartford Courant*.

Maine, South Carolina, and Tennessee—Stanwood, McKee, and *World Almanac*.

Wisconsin—Stanwood and McKee.

All other states—Several newspapers in each case.

The figures below show how a switch of 29,862 votes out of the 5,717,246 cast for Grant and Seymour—.52%—would have made the latter president:

States	Seymour	Grant	Shift
	80	214	
Pennsylvania	26	-26	14,450
Indiana	13	-13	4,787
North Carolina	9	- 9	6,069
Alabama	8	- 8	2,141
Connecticut	6	- 6	1,522
California	5	- 5	261
Nevada	3	- 3	632
	150	144	29,862

In the following tabulation, the nominees for electors are ranked according to the number of votes they received:

	Seymour	Grant	Shift
California	54,078	54,592	258
	54,068	54,588	261
	54,068	54,576	255
	54,068	54,565	249
	54,061	54,551	246

The vote in the Florida legislature was as follows (the top three were successful):

Butler, Republican	39
Meacham, Republican	39
Green, Republican	38
Bloxam, Democrat	9
Call, Democrat	9
Stanley, Democrat	9
Hill, Republican	1

Pearce, Republican, received one vote for each of the three positions.

TABLE 23   Electoral and Popular Vote and Percentage of Popular Vote

States	G	S	Grant	Seymour	G	S
Alabama	8		76,366	72,086	51.44	48.56
Arkansas	5		22,152	19,078	53.73	46.27
California	5		54,592	54,078	50.24	49.76
Connecticut	6		50,995	47,952	51.54	48.46
Delaware		3	7,623	10,980	40.98	59.02
Florida	3					
Georgia		9	57,134	102,822	35.72	64.28
Illinois	16		250,293	199,143	55.69	44.31
Indiana	13		176,552	166,980	51.39	48.61
Iowa	8		120,399	74,040	61.92	38.08
Kansas	3		31,049	14,019	68.89	31.11
Kentucky		11	39,566	115,889	25.45	74.55
Louisiana		7	33,263	80,225	29.31	70.69
Maine	7		70,426	42,396	62.42	37.58
Maryland		7	30,438	62,357	32.80	67.20
Massachusetts	12		136,477	59,408	69.67	30.33
Michigan	8		128,550	97,069	56.98	43.02
Minnesota	4		43,542	28,072	60.80	39.20
Missouri	11		85,671	59,788	58.90	41.10
Nebraska	3		9,729	5,439	64.14	35.86
Nevada	3		6,480	5,218	55.39	44.61
New Hampshire	5		38,191	31,224	55.02	44.98
New Jersey		7	80,121	83,001	49.12	50.88
New York		33	419,915	429,883	49.41	50.59
North Carolina	9		96,226	84,090	53.37	46.63
Ohio	21		280,222	239,032	53.97	46.03
Oregon		3	10,961	11,125	49.63	50.37
Pennsylvania	26		342,280	313,382	52.20	47.80
Rhode Island	4		12,993	6,548	66.49	33.51
South Carolina	6		62,301	45,237	57.93	42.07
Tennessee	10		56,757	26,311	68.33	31.67
Vermont	5		44,167	12,045	78.57	21.43
West Virginia	5		29,025	20,306	58.84	41.16
Wisconsin	8		108,857	84,710	56.24	43.76
TOTALS	214	80	3,013,313	2,703,933	52.71	47.29

The highest percentage for each candidate is underlined.

Mississippi, Texas, and Virginia did not participate, due to Reconstruction.
The legislature cast the electoral vote in Florida.

ELECTION OF 1872

Candidates were Ulysses Simpson Grant, Republican; Horace Greeley, Democrat; Charles O'Conor, Democrat (and Labor Reform); and James Black, Prohibition.

Data pertaining to this election are from the following sources: National Archives (Delaware and Kentucky), Stanwood, McKee, *American Almanac, Tribune Almanac, World Almanac,* and various newspapers, including *Hartford Courant.*

TABLE 24   Electoral and Popular Vote

States	USG	H	B	J	D	Grant	Greeley	O'Conor	Black
Alabama	10					90,272	79,444		
Arkansas						41,373	37,927		
California	6					54,044	40,749	1,068	
Connecticut	6					50,634	45,875	203	186
Delaware	3					11,129	10,208	487	
Florida	4					17,763	15,427		
Georgia			6	2		62,550	76,356	4,000	
Illinois	21					241,944	184,938	3,058	
Indiana	15					186,147	163,632	1,417	
Iowa	11					131,566	71,196	2,221	
Kansas	5					67,048	32,970	596	
Kentucky		8	4			88,970	100,208	2,374	
Louisiana						71,663	57,029		
Maine	7					61,422	29,087		
Maryland		8				66,760	67,687	19	
Massachusetts	13					133,472	59,260		
Michigan	11					138,455	78,355	2,861	1,271
Minnesota	5					55,117	34,423		
Mississippi	8					82,175	47,288		
Missouri			6	8	1	119,196	151,434	2,429	
Nebraska	3					18,329	7,812		
Nevada	3					8,413	6,236		
New Hampshire	5					37,168	31,424	100	200
New Jersey	9					91,661	76,801	606	
New York	35					440,736	387,281	1,454	201
North Carolina	10					94,769	70,094		
Ohio	22					281,852	244,321	1,163	2,100
Oregon	3					11,819	7,730	572	
Pennsylvania	29					349,589	211,041		1,630
Rhode Island	4					13,665	5,329		
South Carolina	7					72,290	22,703	187	
Tennessee		12				85,655	94,391		
Texas		8				47,468	66,546	2,580	
Vermont	5					41,481	10,927	593	
Virginia	11					93,468	91,654	42	
West Virginia	5					32,315	29,451	600	
Wisconsin	10					104,997	86,477	834	
TOTALS	286	42	18	2	1	3,597,375	2,833,711	29,464	5,588

Congress rejected Arkansas' six electoral votes and Louisiana's eight. Greeley died after the popular election and before the counting of the electoral vote. The sixty-six electoral votes which he would ordinarily have received were scattered among Thomas Andrews Hendricks, Benjamin Gratz Brown, Charles Jones Jenkins, and David Davis. Congress rejected the three which Georgia persisted in giving Greeley.

Percentage of Popular Vote

States	USG	H. G.	O'C	B
Alabama	53.19	46.81		
Arkansas	52.17	47.83		
California	56.38	42.51	1.11	
Connecticut	52.25	47.34	.21	.19
Delaware	50.99	46.78	2.23	
Florida	53.52	46.48		
Georgia	43.77	53.43	2.80	
Illinois	56.27	43.01	.71	
Indiana	53.00	46.59	.40	
Iowa	64.18	34.73	1.08	
Kansas	66.64	32.77	.59	
Kentucky	46.45	52.31	1.24	
Louisiana	55.69	44.31		
Maine	67.86	32.14		
Maryland	49.65	50.34	.01	
Massachusetts	69.25	30.75		
Michigan	62.67	35.46	1.29	.58
Minnesota	61.55	38.44		
Mississippi	63.47	36.53		
Missouri	43.65	55.46	.89	
Nebraska	70.12	29.88		
Nevada	57.43	42.57		
New Hampshire	53.95	45.61	.15	.29
New Jersey	54.22	45.43	.36	
New York	53.12	46.68	.18	.02
North Carolina	57.48	42.52		
Ohio	53.24	46.15	.22	.40
Oregon	58.74	38.42	2.84	
Pennsylvania	62.18	37.53		.29
Rhode Island	71.94	28.06		
South Carolina	75.95	23.85	.20	
Tennessee	47.57	52.43		
Texas	40.71	57.07	2.21	
Vermont	78.26	20.62	1.12	
Virginia	50.48	49.50	.02	
West Virginia	51.82	47.22	.96	
Wisconsin	54.60	44.97	.43	
TOTALS	55.63	43.82	.46	.09

The highest percentage for each candidate is underlined.

ELECTION OF 1876

Candidates were Rutherford Birchard Hayes, Republican; Samuel Jones Tilden, Democrat; Peter Cooper, Greenback; Green Clay Smith, Prohibition; and James B. Walker, American.

Data pertaining to this election are from the following sources: National Archives (Oregon), Stanwood, McKee, *American Almanac, Tribune Almanac, World Almanac,* and various newspapers, including *New York Times, Tribune,* and *World, Philadelphia Inquirer, Albany Journal, Harrisburg Patriot,* [Portland, Maine] *Eastern Argus,* and *Burlington Free Press & Times.*

The legislature chose the electors in Colorado. The successful candidates received 50, 50, and 44 votes, while the defeated nominees each received 24. William L. Hadley, the low man on the Republican ticket, would have received the same number of votes as his colleagues, but for the fact that six votes were scattered: William M. Hadley 3, William A. Hadley 2, and William H. Hadley 1.

The figures below show how a switch of 464 votes out of the 8,313,494 cast for Hayes and Tilden—.0056%—would have made the latter president:

	Tilden	Hayes	Shift
	184	185	
Florida	4	- 4	464
	188	181	

As Tilden needed but one electoral vote to win the presidency, an even smaller switch can be figured out. In South Carolina, where the difference between the lowest Republican electoral candidate and the highest Democratic nominee was 230, a shift of 116 votes would have made Tilden president. The breakdown appears below:

Tilden	Hayes	Shift
90,906	91,870	483
90,905	91,852	474
90,896	91,830	468
90,895	91,804	455
90,860	91,786	464
90,798	91,432	318
90,737	91,136	200

The nineteen electoral votes of Florida, Louisiana, and South Carolina were disputed. Other than these, Tilden had 184 votes and Hayes 166; the former thus lacked one of a majority. Congress set up a fifteen-member Electoral Commission, which was to decide whether the electoral votes of the three states should go to Hayes or to Tilden, or partly to each. The former needed all of them to win. In an effort to secure a balance between the two parties, the Commission was to consist of three Republican and two Democratic senators, two Republican and three Democratic representatives, and two from each party from among the Supreme Court justices, another justice to be chosen by the four from among the five others. The justices chose another Republican. By an eight-to-seven margin, the Commission credited Hayes with all of the disputed votes, thus giving him 185 electoral votes.

Election of 1876

TABLE 25

Electoral and Popular Vote

States	H	T	Hayes	Tilden	Cooper	Smith	Walker
Alabama		10	68,708	102,989			
Arkansas		6	38,669	58,083	211		
California	6		79,269	76,465	47		19
Colorado	3						
Connecticut		6	59,034	61,934	774	374	16
Delaware		3	10,752	13,381			
Florida	4		23,849	22,923			
Georgia		11	50,446	130,088			
Illinois	21		278,232	258,601	18,241	249	178
Indiana		15	208,111	213,526	9,533		
Iowa	11		171,327	112,099	9,001	36	
Kansas	5		78,332	37,902	7,776	110	23
Kentucky		12	98,415	160,445	2,003	818	
Louisiana	8		75,135	70,566			
Maine	7		66,300	49,914	662		
Maryland		8	71,981	91,780	33	10	
Massachusetts	13		150,078	108,975	779	84	
Michigan	11		166,534	141,095	9,060	767	71
Minnesota	5		72,962	48,799	2,311	72	
Mississippi		8	52,605	112,173			
Missouri		15	145,029	203,077	3,498	64	97
Nebraska	3		31,916	17,554	2,320	1,599	117
Nevada	3		10,383	9,308			
New Hampshire	5		41,539	38,509	76		
New Jersey		9	103,517	115,962	712	43	
New York		35	489,547	522,612	2,039	2,359	1,828
North Carolina		10	108,417	125,427			
Ohio	22		330,698	323,182	3,057	1,636	76
Oregon	3		15,214	14,157	510	4	
Pennsylvania	29		384,148	366,204	7,204	1,318	83
Rhode Island	4		15,787	10,712	68	60	
South Carolina	7		91,870	90,906			
Tennessee		12	89,566	133,166			
Texas		8	44,800	104,755			
Vermont	5		44,428	20,350			
Virginia		11	95,558	139,670			
West Virginia		5	42,698	56,455	1,373		
Wisconsin	10		130,070	123,926	1,509	27	
TOTALS	185	184	4,035,924	4,287,670	82,797	9,630	2,508

Percentage of Popular Vote

States	H	T	C	S	W
Alabama	40.02	59.98			
Arkansas	39.88	59.90	.22		
California	50.88	49.08	.03		.01
Colorado					
Connecticut	48.34	50.71	.63	.31	.01
Delaware	44.55	55.45			
Florida	50.99	49.01			
Georgia	27.94	72.06			
Illinois	50.09	46.55	3.28	.04	.03
Indiana	48.27	49.52	2.21		
Iowa	58.58	38.33	3.08	.01	
Kansas	63.10	30.53	6.26	.09	.02
Kentucky	37.61	61.31	.77	.31	
Louisiana	51.57	48.43			
Maine	56.73	42.71	.57		
Maryland	43.94	56.03	.02	.01	
Massachusetts	57.74	41.93	.30	.03	
Michigan	52.45	44.44	2.85	.24	.02
Minnesota	58.77	39.31	1.86	.06	
Mississippi	31.92	68.08			
Missouri	41.23	57.73	.99	.02	.03
Nebraska	59.65	32.81	4.34	2.99	.22
Nevada	52.73	47.27			
New Hampshire	51.84	48.06	.09		
New Jersey	47.00	52.65	.32	.02	
New York	48.07	51.32	.20	.23	.18
North Carolina	46.36	53.64			
Ohio	50.21	49.07	.46	.25	.01
Oregon	50.91	47.37	1.71	.01	
Pennsylvania	50.61	48.25	.95	.17	.01
Rhode Island	59.29	40.23	.26	.23	
South Carolina	50.26	49.74			
Tennessee	40.21	59.79			
Texas	29.96	70.04			
Vermont	68.58	31.41			
Virginia	40.62	59.38			
West Virginia	42.47	56.16	1.37		
Wisconsin	50.90	48.50	.59	.01	
TOTALS	47.94	50.93	.98	.11	.03

The highest percentage for each candidate is underlined.

ELECTION OF 1880

Candidates were James Abram Garfield, Republican; Winfield Scott Hancock, Democrat; James Baird Weaver, Greenback; Neal Dow, Prohibition; and John W. Phelps, American. Data pertaining to this election are from the following sources:

California, Colorado, Maine, and Oregon—High votes.

New York—Several newspapers.

All other states, except Phelps vote— Stanwood and *Tribune Almanac*. McKee agrees on all but South Carolina.

Balance of Phelps vote—*New York Tribune*.

The following figures explain the split in the California electoral vote:

WINNERS	PARTY	LOSERS	PARTY
80,443	Democratic	80,282	Republican
80,429	Democratic	80,277	Republican
80,426	Democratic	80,252	Republican
80,420	Democratic	80,242	Republican
80,413	Democratic	80,228	Republican
80,348	Republican	79,885	Democratic

The Maine Democratic and Greenback breakdowns appear below. The highest vote received by a Democratic candidate running on the Fusion slate and the highest received by a Greenback nominee running on his own ticket are used in the table which appears on the next page.

FUSION	PARTY	GREENBACK
69,453	Greenback	
69,435	Greenback	
69,344	Greenback	
68,696	Greenback	
65,171	Democratic	4,480
65,110	Democratic	4,420
64,930	Democratic	4,313

The following figures show how a switch of 10,517 votes out of the 8,899,409 cast for Garfield and Hancock—.12%—would have made the latter president:

States	Hancock	Garfield	Shift
	155	214	
New York	35	-35	10,517
	———	———	
	190	179	

TABLE 26   Electoral and Popular Vote

States	G	H	Garfield	Hancock	Weaver	Dow	Phelps
Alabama		10	56,221	91,185	4,642		
Arkansas		6	42,436	60,775	4,079		
California	1	5	80,348	80,443	3,395	59	
Colorado	3		27,450	24,647	1,435		
Connecticut	6		67,071	64,415	868	409	
Delaware		3	14,133	15,275	120		
Florida		4	23,654	27,964			
Georgia		11	54,086	102,470	969		
Illinois	21		318,037	277,321	26,358	443	153
Indiana	15		232,164	225,522	12,986		
Iowa	11		183,927	105,845	32,701	592	433
Kansas	5		121,549	59,801	19,851	25	
Kentucky		12	106,306	149,068	11,499	258	
Louisiana		8	38,637	65,067	439		
Maine	7		74,056	65,171	4,480	93	142
Maryland		8	78,515	93,706	818		
Massachusetts	13		165,205	111,960	4,548	682	
Michigan	11		185,341	131,597	34,895	942	2
Minnesota	5		93,903	53,315	3,267	286	
Mississippi		8	34,854	75,750	5,797		
Missouri		15	153,567	208,609	35,135		
Nebraska	3		54,979	28,523	3,950		
Nevada		3	8,732	9,613			
New Hampshire	5		44,852	40,794	528	180	
New Jersey		9	120,555	122,565	2,617	191	
New York	35		555,544	534,511	12,373	1,517	75
North Carolina		10	115,874	124,208	1,126		
Ohio	22		375,048	340,821	6,456	2,616	
Oregon	3		20,619	19,955	245		
Pennsylvania	29		444,704	407,428	20,668	1,939	44
Rhode Island	4		18,195	10,779	236	20	
South Carolina		7	58,071	112,312	566		
Tennessee		12	107,677	128,191	5,917	43	
Texas		8	57,893	156,428	27,405		
Vermont	5		45,567	18,316	1,215		105
Virginia		11	84,020	128,586			
West Virginia		5	46,243	57,391	9,079		
Wisconsin	10		144,400	114,649	7,986	69	91
TOTALS	214	155	4,454,433	4,444,976	308,649	10,364	1,045

Percentage of Popular Vote

States	G	H	W	D	P
Alabama	36.98	59.97	3.05		
Arkansas	39.55	56.65	3.80		
California	48.92	48.98	2.07	.04	
Colorado	51.28	46.04	2.68		
Connecticut	50.52	48.52	.65	.31	
Delaware	47.86	51.73	.41		
Florida	45.83	54.17			
Georgia	34.33	65.05	.62		
Illinois	51.11	44.56	4.24	.07	.02
Indiana	49.33	47.91	2.76		
Iowa	56.85	32.72	10.11	.18	.13
Kansas	60.40	29.72	9.87	.01	
Kentucky	39.80	55.80	4.30	.10	
Louisiana	37.10	62.48	.42		
Maine	51.45	45.28	3.11	.06	.10
Maryland	45.37	54.15	.47		
Massachusetts	58.50	39.65	1.61	.24	
Michigan	52.54	37.30	9.89	.27	.00
Minnesota	62.28	35.36	2.17	.19	
Mississippi	29.94	65.08	4.98		
Missouri	38.65	52.51	8.84		
Nebraska	62.87	32.62	4.52		
Nevada	47.60	52.40			
New Hampshire	51.94	47.24	.61	.21	
New Jersey	49.02	49.84	1.06	.08	
New York	50.32	48.41	1.12	.14	.01
North Carolina	48.04	51.49	.47		
Ohio	51.73	47.01	.89	<u>.36</u>	
Oregon	50.51	48.89	.60		
Pennsylvania	50.84	46.57	2.36	.22	.01
Rhode Island	62.25	36.88	.81	.07	
South Carolina	33.97	<u>65.70</u>	.33		
Tennessee	44.53	53.01	2.45	.02	
Texas	23.95	64.71	<u>11.34</u>		
Vermont	<u>69.88</u>	28.09	1.86		<u>.16</u>
Virginia	39.52	60.48			
West Virginia	41.03	50.92	8.05		
Wisconsin	54.04	42.91	2.99	.03	.03
TOTALS	48.32	48.21	3.35	.11	.01

The highest percentage for each candidate is underlined.

".00" signifies that the candidate received some votes, but less than .01%.

ELECTION OF 1884

Candidates were (Stephen) Grover Cleveland, Democrat; James Gillespie Blaine, Republican; Benjamin Franklin Butler, Greenback; and John P. St. John, Prohibition.

Data pertaining to this election are from the following sources: Stanwood, McKee, *American Almanac, Tribune Almanac, World Almanac,* and various newspapers, including *St. Louis Republican* and *Richmond Dispatch.*

The figures below show how a switch of 575 votes out of the 9,728,205 cast for Cleveland and Blaine—.006%—would have made the latter president:

	Blaine	Cleveland	Shift
	182	219	
New York	36	-36	575
	——	——	
	.218	183	

In the following tabulation, the nominees for electors are ranked according to the number of votes they received:

	Blaine	Cleveland	Shift	
New York	562,005	563,154	575	
	562,004	563,151	574	
	562,004	563,150	574	
	562,004	563,148	573	
	562,003	563,148	573	
	562,002	563,147	573	
	562,001	563,146	573	(5 electors)
	562,001	563,145	573	(4 electors)
	562,000	563,144	573	(5 electors)
	561,999	563,143	573	
	561,999	563,142	572	(3 electors)
	561,999	563,141	572	(2 electors)
	561,999	563,140	571	
	561,998	563,139	571	(2 electors)
	561,998	563,138	571	
	561,993	563,137	573	
	561,991	563,137	574	
	561,990	563,137	574	
	561,989	563,135	574	
	561,988	563,133	573	
	561,971	563,048	539	

The Michigan Democratic and Greenback breakdowns appear below. The votes cast for the "split" elector are used in the table which appears on the next page.

DEMOCRATIC	GREENBACK
189,361	
189,294	
189,290	
189,244	
189,152	
188,654	
188,574	
188,554	
188,554	
188,479	
187,924	
186,927	
149,835	41,390

A straight Greenback ticket, which is not included in the table on the next page, received the following votes: 763, 746, 716, 706, 550, and 549.

There was a Democratic-Greenback fusion in Iowa and a Republican-Greenback fusion in Missouri. It is impossible to accurately determine Butler's share of the votes in those states.

Election of 1884

TABLE 27   Electoral and Popular Vote

States	C	Bl	Cleveland	Blaine	Butler	St. John
Alabama	10		93,951	59,591	873	612
Arkansas	7		72,927	50,895	1,847	
California		8	89,288	102,416	2,017	2,920
Colorado		3	27,723	36,290	1,953	761
Connecticut	6		67,182	65,898	1,685	2,494
Delaware	3		17,054	12,778	6	55
Florida	4		31,769	28,031		72
Georgia	12		94,667	48,603	145	195
Illinois		22	312,355	337,474	10,910	12,074
Indiana	15		244,992	238,480	8,716	3,018
Iowa		13	177,286	197,082		1,564
Kansas		9	90,132	154,406	16,341	4,495
Kentucky	13		152,961	118,122	1,691	3,139
Louisiana	8		62,540	46,347	120	338
Maine		6	52,140	72,209	3,953	2,160
Maryland	8		96,932	85,699	531	2,794
Massachusetts		14	122,481	146,724	24,433	10,026
Michigan		13	149,835	192,669	41,390	18,403
Minnesota		7	70,144	111,923	3,587	4,691
Mississippi	9		76,510	43,509		
Missouri	16		235,988	202,929		2,153
Nebraska		5	54,354	76,877		2,858
Nevada		3	5,578	7,193	26	
New Hampshire		4	39,183	43,249	552	1,571
New Jersey	9		127,798	123,440	3,496	6,159
New York	36		563,154	562,005	17,004	25,006
North Carolina	11		142,952	125,068		454
Ohio		23	368,280	400,082	5,179	11,069
Oregon		3	24,604	26,860	726	492
Pennsylvania		30	393,747	474,268	16,992	15,306
Rhode Island		4	12,391	19,030	422	928
South Carolina	9		69,890	21,733		
Tennessee	12		133,270	124,090	957	1,131
Texas	13		225,309	93,141	3,321	3,534
Vermont		4	17,331	39,514	785	1,752
Virginia	12		145,497	139,356		138
West .Virginia	6		67,317	63,096	810	939
Wisconsin		11	146,459	161,157	4,598	7,656
TOTALS	219	182	4,875,971	4,852,234	175,066	150,957

Percentage of Popular Vote

States	C	Bl	Bu	St.J.
Alabama	60.60	38.44	.56	.39
Arkansas	58.03	40.50	1.47	
California	45.41	52.08	1.03	1.48
Colorado	41.55	54.39	2.93	1.14
Connecticut	48.95	48.01	1.23	1.82
Delaware	57.05	42.75	.02	.18
Florida	53.06	46.82		.12
Georgia	65.92	33.84	.10	.14
Illinois	46.43	50.16	1.62	1.79
Indiana	49.47	48.16	1.76	.61
Iowa	47.16	52.42		.42
Kansas	33.96	58.18	6.16	1.69
Kentucky	55.44	42.81	.61	1.14
Louisiana	57.20	42.39	.11	.31
Maine	39.97	55.35	3.03	1.66
Maryland	52.13	46.09	.29	1.50
Massachusetts	40.33	48.32	8.05	3.30
Michigan	37.24	47.89	<u>10.29</u>	<u>4.57</u>
Minnesota	36.85	58.80	1.88	2.46
Mississippi	63.75	36.25		
Missouri	53.50	46.01		.49
Nebraska	40.54	57.33		2.13
Nevada	43.59	56.21	.20	
New Hampshire	46.34	51.15	.65	1.86
New Jersey	48.98	47.31	1.34	2.36
New York	48.25	48.15	1.46	2.14
North Carolina	53.25	46.58		.17
Ohio	46.94	50.99	.66	1.41
Oregon	46.70	50.99	1.38	.93
Pennsylvania	43.73	52.68	1.89	1.70
Rhode Island	37.81	58.07	1.29	2.83
South Carolina	<u>76.28</u>	23.72		
Tennessee	51.37	47.83	.37	.44
Texas	69.26	28.63	1.02	1.09
Vermont	29.19	<u>66.54</u>	1.32	2.95
Virginia	51.05	48.90		.05
West Virginia	50.94	47.74	.61	.71
Wisconsin	45.79	50.38	1.44	2.39
TOTALS	48.50	48.26	1.74	1.50

The highest percentage for each candidate is underlined.

ELECTION OF 1888

Candidates were Benjamin Harrison, Republican; (Stephen) Grover Cleveland, Democrat; Clinton B. Fisk, Prohibition; Alson J. Streeter, Union Labor; Robert H. Cowdrey, United Labor; and James Langdon Curtis, American. The Socialist Labor Party also received votes. Data pertaining to this election are from the official records on file in the National Archives, with these exceptions:

Georgia, Missouri, and Nevada—all from Stanwood.

Maine—all from [Augusta] *Kennebec Journal*.

Mississippi—Streeter from McKee and Stanwood.

Tennessee—Streeter from *Nashville American*.

The figures below show how a switch of 7,189 votes out of the 10,985,634 cast for Harrison and Cleveland—.07%—would have reelected the latter president:

	Cleveland	Harrison	Shift
	168	233	
New York	36	-36	7,189
	204	197	

In the following tabulation, the nominees for electors are ranked according to the number of votes they received:

	Cleveland	Harrison	Shift	
New York	635,965	650,338	7,187	
	635,961	650,337	7,189	
	635,960	650,317	7,179	
	635,959	650,314	7,178	
	635,958	650,313	7,178	
	635,957	650,313	7,179	(2 electors)
	635,956	650,313	7,179	(3 electors)
	635,956	650,312	7,179	
	635,955	650,311	7,179	(2 electors)
	635,954	650,311	7,179	(2 electors)
	635,954	650,310	7,179	
	635,953	650,310	7,179	(3 electors)
	635,953	650,309	7,179	
	635,952	650,309	7,179	(2 electors)
	635,951	650,308	7,179	
	635,950	650,308	7,180	
	635,950	650,307	7,179	
	635,949	650,307	7,180	
	635,948	650,306	7,180	
	635,947	650,305	7,180	
	635,945	650,304	7,180	
	635,939	650,303	7,183	
	635,938	650,300	7,182	
	635,937	650,298	7,181	
	635,929	650,287	7,180	
	635,901	650,243	7,172	
	635,835	648,909	6,538	
	635,757	648,759	6,502	

TABLE 28 Electoral and Popular Vote

States	H	Cl	Harrison	Cleveland	Fisk	Streeter	Cowdrey	S. L.	Curtis
Alabama		10	56,197	117,320	583				
Arkansas		7	60,245	86,717	615	10,671			
California	8		124,816	117,729	5,761				1,591
Colorado	3		50,774	37,567	2,192	1,266			
Connecticut		6	74,586	74,922	4,236	240			
Delaware		3	12,973	16,414	400				
Florida		4	26,654	39,656	418				
Georgia		12	40,496	100,499	1,808	136			
Illinois	22		370,475	348,371	21,703	7,134	150		
Indiana	15		263,361	261,013	9,881	2,694			
Iowa	13		211,598	179,877	3,550	9,105			
Kansas	9		182,904	102,745	6,779	37,788			
Kentucky		13	155,134	183,800	5,225	622			
Louisiana		8	30,701	85,032	127	39			
Maine	6		73,734	50,481	2,691	1,344			
Maryland		8	99,986	106,168	4,767				
Massachusetts	14		183,892	151,905	8,701				
Michigan	13		236,387	213,469	20,945	4,555			
Minnesota	7		142,492	104,385	15,311	1,097			
Mississippi		9	31,120	85,467	258	22			
Missouri		16	236,257	261,974	4,539	18,632			
Nebraska	5		108,425	80,542	9,429	4,226			
Nevada	3		7,229	5,362	41				
New Hampshire	4		45,728	43,456	1,593	42			
New Jersey		9	144,360	151,508	7,933				
New York	36		650,338	635,965	30,231	627	2,668	2,068	
North Carolina		11	134,784	148,336	2,789	37			
Ohio	23		416,054	396,455	24,356	3,496			
Oregon	3		33,291	26,522	1,677	363			
Pennsylvania	30		526,269	447,004	20,966	3,876			
Rhode Island	4		21,969	17,530	1,251	18			
South Carolina		9	13,740	65,825					
Tennessee		12	139,511	158,779	5,975	48			
Texas		13	88,422	234,883	4,749	29,459			
Vermont	4		45,192	16,788	1,460				
Virginia		12	150,449	151,979	1,682				
West Virginia		6	78,171	78,677	1,085	1,508			
Wisconsin	11		176,555	155,243	14,415	8,561			
TOTALS	233	168	5,445,269	5,540,365	250,122	147,606	2,818	2,068	1,591

Percentage of Popular Vote

States	H	Cl	F	S	Co	S.-L.	Cu
Alabama	32.28	67.39	.33				
Arkansas	38.07	54.80	.39	6.74			
California	49.95	47.11	2.31				.64
Colorado	55.31	40.92	2.39	1.38			
Connecticut	48.44	48.66	2.75	.16			
Delaware	43.55	55.10	1.34				
Florida	39.94	59.43	.63				
Georgia	28.33	70.31	1.26	.10			
Illinois	49.54	46.59	2.90	.95	.02		
Indiana	49.05	48.61	1.84	.50			
Iowa	52.36	44.51	.88	2.25			
Kansas	55.39	31.11	2.05	11.44			
Kentucky	44.99	53.31	1.52	.18			
Louisiana	26.48	73.37	.11	.03			
Maine	57.49	39.36	2.10	1.05			
Maryland	47.40	50.34	2.26				
Massachusetts	53.38	44.09	2.53				
Michigan	49.73	44.91	4.41	.96			
Minnesota	54.12	39.65	5.82	.42			
Mississippi	26.63	73.13	.22	.02			
Missouri	45.31	50.24	.87	3.57			
Nebraska	53.51	39.75	4.65	2.09			
Nevada	57.23	42.45	.32				
New Hampshire	50.35	47.84	1.75	.05			
New Jersey	47.52	49.87	2.61				
New York	49.20	48.11	2.29	.05	.20	.16	
North Carolina	47.14	51.88	.98	.01			
Ohio	49.51	47.18	2.90	.42			
Oregon	53.82	42.88	2.71	.59			
Pennsylvania	52.73	44.78	2.10	.39			
Rhode Island	53.89	43.00	3.07	.04			
South Carolina	17.27	82.73					
Tennessee	45.85	52.18	1.96	.02			
Texas	24.73	65.70	1.33	8.24			
Vermont	71.24	26.46	2.30				
Virginia	49.47	49.98	.55				
West Virginia	49.03	49.35	.68	.95			
Wisconsin	49.77	43.76	4.06	2.41			
TOTALS	47.81	48.64	2.20	1.30	.02	.02	.01

The highest percentage for each candidate is underlined.

Extended percentages nationally: Cowdrey .025—%, Socialist Labor .018%.

ELECTION OF 1892

Candidates were (Stephen) Grover Cleveland, Democrat; Benjamin Harrison, Republican; James Baird Weaver, Populist; John Bidwell, Prohibition; and Simon Wing, Socialist-Labor. Data pertaining to this election are from the official records on file in the National Archives, with these exceptions:

Louisiana—Cleveland from Stanwood.

Maine—Weaver from [Portland] *Eastern Argus*.

Montana—all other than Harrison from *Helena Herald*.

North Dakota—all from *Bismarck Tribune*.

Tennessee—all from Stanwood.

In Michigan, the electoral vote was cast by districts; the breakdown appears below:

Districts	Cleveland	Harrison	Weaver	Bidwell
Eastern	108,956	107,418	7,169	8,633
Western	93,340	115,290	12,762	12,224
1st	19,990	18,332	291	340
2d	22,427	20,947	1,072	2,401
3d	15,756	21,233	2,938	2,562
4th		21,402	20,084	2,024
5th	18,173	20,187	1,980	1,967
6th	19,590	21,324	2,070	2,286
7th	15,984	15,723	1,842	777
8th	15,298	16,672	1,218	1,149
9th	12,853	14,036	1,062	1,693
10th	14,972	14,370	1,167	741
11th	12,734	18,379	3,143	1,961
12th	16,888	19,811	1,023	1,851

In Oregon, one of the Populist electoral candidates was successful, due to Democratic indorsement; the breakdown appears below:

WINNERS	PARTY	LOSERS	PARTY
35,811	Populist (Dem. ind.)	34,910	Republican
35,002	Republican	26,965	Populist
34,932	Republican	26,875	Populist
34,928	Republican	26,811	Populist
		14,243	Democratic
		14,217	Democratic
		14,207	Democratic

In North Dakota, two Populists and one Republican elector were successful, but one of the former voted for Cleveland. He had announced his intention before the election. The breakdown appears below:

WINNERS	PARTY	LOSERS	PARTY
17,700	Populist (voted Dem.)	17,511	Populist
17,520	Populist	17,506	Republican
17,519	Republican	17,463	Republican

The following figures explain the splits in the California and Ohio electoral votes:

	WINNERS	PARTY	LOSERS	PARTY
California	118,174	Democratic	117,840	Democratic
	118,151	Democratic	117,747	Republican
	118,112	Democratic	117,743	Republican
	118,109	Democratic	117,717	Republican
	118,096	Democratic	117,711	Republican
	118,029	Democratic	117,670	Republican
	118,027	Republican	117,613	Republican
	118,008	Democratic	117,605	Republican
	117,962	Democratic	117,544	Republican

Ohio	405,187	Republican	402,399	Republican
	404,115	Democratic	401,503	Democratic
	402,706	Republican	401,483	Democratic
	402,551	Republican	401,480	Democratic
	402,544	Republican	401,474	Democratic
	402,541	Republican	401,447	Democratic
	402,540	Republican	401,399	Democratic
	402,527	Republican	401,391	Democratic
	402,526	Republican	401,386	Democratic
	402,518	Republican	401,384	Democratic
	402,518	Republican	401,380	Democratic
	402,497	Republican	401,380	Democratic
	402,495	Republican	401,371	Democratic
	402,493	Republican	401,367	Democratic
	402,476	Republican	401,366	Democratic
	402,465	Republican	401,363	Democratic
	402,456	Republican	401,360	Democratic
	402,454	Republican	401,360	Democratic
	402,451	Republican	401,354	Democratic
	402,450	Republican	401,353	Democratic
	402,449	Republican	401,351	Democratic
	402,425	Republican	401,345	Democratic
	402,423	Republican	401,327	Democratic

The Louisiana Republican and Populist breakdowns appear below. These parties ran two slates of Fusion electors. The highest vote received by any nominee for elector has been assigned to the Republicans, and the highest vote received by any of the lower half of the nominees for electors has been credited to the Populists in the table which appears on the next page.

27,903	2,462
27,712	1,918
27,706	1,890
26,840	1,882
26,134	1,872
26,132	1,863
26,093	1,681
24,968	1,679

The Minnesota Democratic and Populist breakdowns appear below. The highest vote received by a Democratic candidate running on the Fusion slate and the highest received by a Populist nominee running on his own ticket are used in the table which appears on the next page.

FUSION	PARTY	POPULIST
110,465	Populist	
108,337	Populist	
104,759	Populist	
104,568	Populist	
100,920	Democratic	29,313
96,207	Democratic	28,107
95,474	Democratic	26,855
95,193	Democratic	26,648
95,053	Democratic	26,449

The figures below show how a switch of 37,364 votes out of the 11,778,408 cast for Cleveland, Harrison, and Weaver—.32%—would have reelected Harrison president:

States	Harrison	Cleveland	Weaver	Shift
	145	277	22	
New York	36	-36		22,813
Indiana	15	-15		3,563
Wisconsin	12	-12		3,278
New Jersey	10	-10		7,496
California	7	- 7		214
	—	—	—	—
	225	197	22	37,364

In the following tabulation, the nominees for electors are ranked according to the number of votes they received.

States	Harrison	Cleveland	Shift
New York	609,459	654,908	22,725
	609,448	654,906	22,730
	609,445	654,905	22,731 (2 electors)
	609,436	654,902	22,734
	609,416	654,900	22,743
	609,384	654,900	22,759
	609,377	654,898	22,761
	609,371	654,898	22,764
	609,368	654,897	22,765
	609,367	654,897	22,766
	609,364	654,897	22,767
	609,350	654,896	22,774
	609,331	654,895	22,783
	609,285	654,895	22,806
	609,284	654,895	22,806
	609,277	654,895	22,810
	609,276	654,895	22,810
	609,274	654,895	22,811
	609,272	654,895	22,812
	609,272	654,894	22,812
	609,270	654,894	22,813
	609,270	654,893	22,812
	609,268	654,890	22,812
	609,267	654,889	22,812
	609,266	654,889	22,812 (2 electors)
	609,266	654,888	22,812
	609,265	654,887	22,812
	609,264	654,887	22,812
	609,263	654,885	22,812
	609,262	654,884	22,812
	609,260	654,882	22,812
	609,260	654,879	22,810
	609,259	654,868	22,805
	609,252	654,835	22,792
Indiana	255,615	262,740	3,563
	253,878	260,661	3,392
	253,836	260,600	3,383
	253,815	260,600	3,393
	253,808	260,591	3,392
	253,807	260,590	3,392
	253,799	260,586	3,394
	253,793	260,581	3,395
	253,792	260,580	3,395
	253,787	260,575	3,395
	253,777	260,560	3,392
	253,770	260,558	3,395
	253,770	260,547	3,389
	253,767	260,538	3,386
	253,767	260,533	3,384

States	Harrison	Cleveland	Shift
Wisconsin	170,846	177,335	3,245
	170,791	177,314	3,262
	170,786	177,307	3,261
	170,765	177,293	3,265
	170,745	177,291	3,274
	170,741	177,283	3,272
	170,740	177,282	3,272
	170,726	177,281	3,278
	170,717	177,221	3,253
	170,684	177,180	3,249
	170,677	177,171	3,248
	170,525	177,053	3,265
New Jersey	156,101	171,066	7,483
	156,080	171,056	7,489
	156,074	171,054	7,491
	156,072	171,053	7,491
	156,067	171,053	7,494
	156,061	171,052	7,496
	156,060	171,037	7,489
	156,059	171,034	7,488
	156,059	171,027	7,485
	156,050	170,987	7,469
California	117,747	118,174	214
	117,743	118,151	205
	117,717	118,112	198
	117,711	118,109	200
	117,670	118,096	214
	117,613	118,029	209
	117,605	118,008	202
	117,544	117,962	210

TABLE 29 Electoral and Popular Vote

States	C	H	JW	Cleveland	Harrison	Weaver	Bidwell	Wing
Alabama	11			138,138	9,197	85,181	241	
Arkansas	8			87,834	46,974	11,831	130	
California	8	1		118,174	118,027	25,311	8,096	
Colorado			4		38,620	53,584	1,687	
Connecticut	6			82,395	77,032	809	4,026	329
Delaware	3			18,581	18,077	13	564	
Florida	4			30,143		4,843	570	
Georgia	13			129,386	48,305	42,937	988	
Idaho			3	2	8,799	10,520	288	
Illinois	24			426,281	399,288	22,207	25,870	
Indiana	15			262,740	255,615	22,208	13,050	
Iowa		13		196,367	219,795	20,595	6,402	
Kansas			10		157,241	163,111	4,553	
Kentucky	13			175,461	135,441	23,500	6,442	
Louisiana	8			87,922	27,903	2,462		
Maine		6		48,044	62,931	2,045	3,062	336
Maryland	8			113,866	92,736	796	5,877	27
Massachusetts		15		176,858	202,927	3,348	7,539	676
Michigan	5	9		202,296	222,708	20,084	20,857	
Minnesota		9		100,920	122,823	29,313	14,182	
Mississippi	9			40,288	1,395	10,102	995	
Missouri	17			268,188	226,918	41,213	4,331	
Montana		3		17,581	18,851	7,334	549	
Nebraska		8		24,943	87,227	83,134	4,902	
Nevada			3	714	2,811	7,264	89	
New Hampshire		4		42,081	45,658	293	1,297	
New Jersey	10			171,066	156,101	985	8,134	1,337
New York	36			654,908	609,459	16,436	38,193	17,958
North Carolina	11			133,098	100,565	44,732	2,630	
North Dakota	1	1	1		17,519	17,700	899	
Ohio	1	22		404,115	405,187	14,852	26,012	
Oregon		3	1	14,243	35,002	26,965	2,281	
Pennsylvania		32		452,264	516,011	8,714	25,123	898
Rhode Island		4		24,336	26,975	228	1,654	
South Carolina	9			54,698	13,384	2,410		
South Dakota		4		9,081	34,888	26,544		
Tennessee	12			138,874	100,331	23,447	4,851	
Texas	15			239,148	81,444	99,688	2,165	
Vermont		4		16,325	37,992	44	1,424	
Virginia	12			163,977	113,256	12,275	2,798	
Washington		4		29,844	36,460	19,105	2,553	
West Virginia	6			84,467	80,293	4,166	2,145	
Wisconsin	12			177,335	170,846	9,909	13,132	
Wyoming		3			8,454	7,722	530	
TOTALS	277	145	22	5,556,982	5,191,466	1,029,960	271,111	21,561

Percentage of Popular Vote

States	C	H	W'V'R	B	WING
Alabama	59.35	3.95	36.60	.10	
Arkansas	59.84	32.01	8.06	.09	
California	43.84	43.76	9.39	3.00	
Colorado		41.13	57.07	1.80	
Connecticut	50.06	46.80	.49	2.45	.20
Delaware	49.90	48.55	.03	1.51	
Florida	84.78		13.62	1.60	
Georgia	58.38	21.80	19.37	.45	
Idaho	.01	44.87	53.65	1.47	
Illinois	48.79	45.70	2.54	2.96	
Indiana	47.46	46.17	4.01	2.36	
Iowa	44.31	49.60	4.65	1.44	
Kansas		48.40	50.20	1.40	
Kentucky	51.48	39.74	6.89	1.89	
Louisiana	74.33	23.59	2.08		
Maine	41.27	54.06	1.76	2.63	.29
Maryland	53.38	43.48	.37	2.76	.01
Massachusetts	45.19	51.85	.86	1.93	.17
Michigan	43.43	47.81	4.28	4.48	
Minnesota	37.76	45.96	10.97	5.31	
Mississippi	76.33	2.64	19.14	1.89	
Missouri	49.60	41.97	7.62	.80	
Montana	39.67	42.54	16.55	1.24	
Nebraska	12.46	43.57	41.52	2.45	
Nevada	6.56	25.84	66.78	.82	
New Hampshire	47.11	51.11	.33	1.45	
New Jersey	50.67	46.24	.29	2.41	.40
New York	48.99	45.59	1.23	2.86	1.34
North Carolina	47.36	35.79	15.92	.94	
North Dakota		48.50	49.01	2.49	
Ohio	47.53	47.66	1.75	3.06	
Oregon	18.15	44.59	34.35	2.91	
Pennsylvania	45.09	51.45	.87	2.50	.09
Rhode Island	45.75	50.71	.43	3.11	
South Carolina	77.59	18.99	3.42		
South Dakota	12.88	49.48	37.64		
Tennessee	51.91	37.51	8.77	1.81	
Texas	56.61	19.28	23.60	.51	
Vermont	29.26	68.10	.08	2.55	
Virginia	56.10	38.75	4.20	.96	
Washington	33.92	41.45	21.72	2.91	
West Virginia	49.38	46.94	2.44	1.25	
Wisconsin	47.77	46.02	2.67	3.54	
Wyoming		50.60	46.22	3.17	
TOTALS	46.04	43.01	8.53	2.25	.18

The highest percentage for each candidate is underlined.

Candidates were William McKinley, Republican; William Jennings Bryan, Democrat; John McAuley Palmer, National Democrat; Joshua Levering, Prohibition; Charles H. Matchett, Socialist-Labor; and Charles E. Bentley, National Prohibition.

Data pertaining to this election are from the official records on file in the National Archives, with these exceptions:

Delaware—all from *Wilmington Republican*.

Idaho—all from [Boise] *Idaho Statesman*.

Kansas—all from *Chicago Tribune*.

Kentucky—Palmer and Levering from *Louisville Commercial*.

Minnesota—Palmer from *St. Paul Globe*.

Missouri—all from *St. Louis Republic*.

Montana—McKinley and Levering from *Helena Herald*.

North Dakota—Levering from *Bismarck Tribune*.

Ohio—Bryan from Stanwood.

Utah—Palmer from *Salt Lake Tribune*.

Wisconsin—all from *Madison Democrat*.

Wyoming—Levering from *Cheyenne Sun-Leader*.

The following figures explain the splits in the California and Kentucky electoral votes:

	WINNERS	PARTY	LOSERS	PARTY
California	146,688	Republican	144,618	Republican
	146,133	Republican	144,185	Democratic
	145,886	Republican	144,113	Democratic
	145,812	Republican	143,959	Democratic
	145,631	Republican	143,914	Democratic
	145,590	Republican	143,874	Democratic
	145,587	Democratic	143,725	Democratic
	145,474	Republican	143,664	Democratic
	144,766	Democratic	143,024	Democratic
Kentucky	218,171	Republican	215,402	Republican
	217,890	Democratic	215,091	Democratic
	215,459	Republican	215,073	Democratic
	215,431	Republican	215,053	Democratic
	215,426	Republican	215,048	Democratic
	215,423	Republican	215,045	Democratic
	215,415	Republican	215,043	Democratic
	215,409	Republican	215,032	Democratic
	215,408	Republican	215,022	Democratic
	215,408	Republican	215,021	Democratic
	215,407	Republican	215,013	Democratic
	215,404	Republican	214,995	Democratic
	215,402	Republican	214,943	Democratic

As two of the Republican candidates received 215,402 votes each, one of them had to yield his position as a winner.

The figures below show how a switch of 20,396 votes out of the 13,630,456 cast for McKinley and Bryan—.15%—would have made the latter president:

States	Bryan	McKinley	Shift
	176	271	
Indiana	15	-15	9,163
Kentucky	12	-12	1,541
California	8	- 8	1,252
West Virginia	6	- 6	5,447
Oregon	4	- 4	1,074
Delaware	3	- 3	1,919
	___	___	_____
	224	223	20,396

In the following tabulation, the nominees for electors are ranked according to the number of votes they received:

States	Bryan	McKinley	Shift
Indiana	305,573	323,754	9,091
	303,038	321,363	9,163
	303,032	321,315	9,142
	303,027	321,303	9,139
	303,017	321,299	9,142
	303,013	321,289	9,139
	303,010	321,279	9,135
	303,002	321,272	9,136
	302,979	321,271	9,147
	302,972	321,266	9,148
	302,970	321,264	9,148
	302,958	321,263	9,153
	302,949	321,261	9,157
	302,946	321,241	9,148
	302,939	321,236	9,149
Kentucky	215,091	218,171	1,541
	215,073	215,459	194
	215,053	215,431	190
	215,048	215,426	190
	215,045	215,423	190
	215,043	215,415	187
	215,032	215,409	189
	215,022	215,408	193
	215,021	215,408	194
	215,013	215,407	198
	214,995	215,404	205
	214,943	215,402	230
California	144,185	146,688	1,252
	144,113	146,133	1,011
	143,959	145,886	964
	143,914	145,812	950
	143,874	145,631	879
	143,725	145,590	933
	143,664	145,587	962
	143,024	145,474	1,226
West Virginia	94,488	105,379	5,446
	94,487	105,371	5,443
	94,484	105,370	5,444
	94,483	105,369	5,444
	94,475	105,366	5,446
	94,465	105,357	5,447
Oregon	46,739	48,779	1,021
	46,662	48,711	1,025
	46,554	48,700	1,074
	46,518	48,568	1,026

TABLE 30   Electoral and Popular Vote

States	McK	B	McKinley	Bryan	Palmer	Levering	Matchett	Bentley
Alabama		11	54,737	131,226	6,464	2,147		
Arkansas		8	37,512	110,103		889		893
California	8	1	146,688	144,618	2,006	2,573	1,611	1,047
Colorado		4	26,279	161,269	1	1,724	160	386
Connecticut	6		110,297	56,740	4,336	1,806	1,223	
Delaware	3		20,452	16,615	966	602		
Florida		4	11,288	32,736	1,778	654		
Georgia		13	60,107	94,733	2,809	5,613		
Idaho		3	6,324	23,192		181		
Illinois	24		607,130	465,613	6,390	9,818	1,147	793
Indiana	15		323,754	305,573	2,145	3,056	329	2,267
Iowa	13		289,293	223,741	4,586	3,192	453	352
Kansas		10	159,541	173,042	1,209	1,721		630
Kentucky	12	1	218,171	217,890	5,114	4,781		
Louisiana		8	22,037	77,175	1,915			
Maine	6		80,461	34,587	1,867	1,589		
Maryland	8		136,978	104,746	2,507	5,922	588	136
Massachusetts	15		278,976	106,206	11,809	3,060	2,137	
Michigan	14		293,582	237,268	6,968	5,025	297	1,995
Minnesota	9		193,503	139,735	3,216	4,348	954	
Mississippi		9	5,123	63,793	1,071	485		
Missouri		17	304,940	363,652	2,355	2,169	610	292
Montana		3	10,494	42,537		186		
Nebraska		8	103,064	115,999	2,885	1,243	186	797
Nevada		3	1,938	8,376				
New Hampshire	4		57,444	21,650	3,420	776	228	49
New Jersey	10		221,371	133,695	6,378	5,617	3,986	
New York	36		819,838	551,513	19,295	16,086	17,731	
North Carolina		11	155,243	174,488	578	681		253
North Dakota	3		26,335	20,686		358		
Ohio	23		525,991	477,497	1,858	5,084	1,165	2,741
Oregon	4		48,779	46,739	977	919		
Pennsylvania	32		728,300	433,228	11,000	19,274	1,683	873
Rhode Island	4		37,437	14,459	1,166	1,161	558	5
South Carolina		9	9,317	58,801	824			
South Dakota		4	41,042	41,225		683		
Tennessee		12	149,703	168,878	2,106	3,140		
Texas		15	167,520	370,434	5,046	1,786		
Utah		3	13,491	64,607	21			
Vermont	4		51,127	10,640	1,331	733		
Virginia		12	135,388	154,985	2,129	2,344	115	
Washington		4	39,153	51,646	1,668	968		148
West Virginia	6		105,379	94,488	678	1,223		
Wisconsin	12		268,135	165,523	4,584	7,509	1,314	346
Wyoming		3	10,072	10,375		159		
TOTALS	271	176	7,113,734	6,516,722	135,456	131,285	36,475	14,003

Percentage of Popular Vote

States	McK	Br	P	L	Ma	Be
Alabama	28.13	67.44	3.32	1.10		
Arkansas	25.11	73.70		.60		.60
California	49.13	48.44	.67	.86	.54	.35
Colorado	13.84	84.96	.00	.91	.08	.20
Connecticut	63.24	32.53	2.49	1.04	.70	
Delaware	52.94	43.01	2.50	1.56		
Florida	24.30	70.47	3.83	1.41		
Georgia	36.82	58.03	1.72	3.44		
Idaho	21.30	78.10		.61		
Illinois	55.65	42.68	.59	.90	.11	.07
Indiana	50.81	47.96	.34	.48	.05	.36
Iowa	55.46	42.90	.88	.61	.09	.07
Kansas	47.46	51.48	.36	.51		.19
Kentucky	48.92	48.86	1.15	1.07		
Louisiana	21.79	76.31	1.89			
Maine	67.90	29.19	1.58	1.34		
Maryland	54.60	41.75	1.00	2.36	.23	.05
Massachusetts	69.36	26.41	2.94	.76	.53	
Michigan	53.85	43.52	1.28	.92	.05	.37
Minnesota	56.62	40.89	.94	1.27	.28	
Mississippi	7.27	90.52	1.52	.69		
Missouri	45.24	53.95	.35	.32	.09	.04
Montana	19.72	79.93		.35		
Nebraska	45.98	51.75	1.29	.55	.08	.36
Nevada	18.79	81.21				
New Hampshire	68.74	25.91	4.09	.93	.27	.06
New Jersey	59.66	36.03	1.72	1.51	1.07	
New York	57.55	38.72	1.35	1.13	1.24	
North Carolina	46.87	52.68	.17	.21		.08
North Dakota	55.58	43.66		.76		
Ohio	51.86	47.07	.18	.50	.11	.27
Oregon	50.07	47.98	1.00	.94		
Pennsylvania	60.98	36.27	.92	1.61	.14	.07
Rhode Island	68.33	26.39	2.13	2.12	1.02	.01
South Carolina	13.51	85.29	1.20			
South Dakota	49.48	49.70		.82		
Tennessee	46.23	52.15	.65	.97		
Texas	30.75	68.00	.93	.33		
Utah	17.27	82.70	.03			
Vermont	80.10	16.67	2.09	1.15		
Virginia	45.90	52.54	.72	.79	.04	
Washington	41.84	55.19	1.78	1.03		.16
West Virginia	52.23	46.83	.34	.61		
Wisconsin	59.93	37.00	1.02	1.68	.29	.08
Wyoming	48.88	50.35		.77		
TOTALS	51.00	46.72	.97	.94	.26	.10

The highest percentage for each candidate is underlined.

".00" signifies that the candidate received some votes, but less than .01%.

ELECTION OF 1900

Candidates were William McKinley, Republican; William Jennings Bryan, Democrat; John C. Woolley, Prohibition; Eugene Victor Debs, Socialist; Wharton Barker, Populist; Joseph F. Malloney, Socialist-Labor; Seth H. Ellis, Union Reform; and Jonah Fitz Randolph Leonard, United Christian.

Data pertaining to this election are from the official records on file in the National Archives, with these exceptions:

Arkansas—McKinley and Bryan from [Little Rock] *Arkansas Gazette.*

Florida—McKinley from [Jacksonville] *Florida Times-Union & Citizen.*

Tennessee—all from *Abstract.*

West Virginia—all other than McKinley from *Abstract.*

The figures below show how a switch of 74,755 votes out of the 13,577,988 cast for McKinley and Bryan—.55%—would have made the latter president:

States	Bryan	McKinley	Shift
	155	292	
Ohio	23	-23	34,722
Indiana	15	-15	13,859
Kansas	10	-10	11,881
Nebraska	8	- 8	3,962
Maryland	8	- 8	7,074
Utah	3	- 3	1,097
Wyoming	3	- 3	2,160
	225	222	74,755

In the following tabulation, the nominees for electors are ranked according to the number of votes they received:

States	Bryan	McKinley	Shift	States	Bryan	McKinley	Shift
Ohio	474,882	543,918	34,519	Kansas	162,601	185,955	11,678
	473,507	542,921	34,708		161,185	184,946	11,881
	473,476	542,862	34,694		160,931	184,260	11,665
	473,451	542,859	34,705		160,705	183,804	11,550
	473,450	542,840	34,696		160,604	183,700	11,549
	473,410	542,828	34,710		160,487	183,637	11,576
	473,405	542,828	34,712		160,451	183,449	11,500
	473,388	542,819	34,716		160,039	183,214	11,588
	473,378	542,801	34,712		159,948	183,017	11,535
	473,371	542,788	34,709		159,624	182,793	11,585
	473,367	542,786	34,710				
	473,365	542,781	34,709	Nebraska	114,013	121,835	3,912
	473,356	542,774	34,710		113,537	121,415	3,940
	473,341	542,774	34,717		113,512	121,395	3,942
	473,337	542,772	34,718		113,502	121,383	3,941
	473,336	542,765	34,715		113,477	121,383	3,954
	473,336	542,749	34,707		113,426	121,336	3,956
	473,325	542,724	34,700		113,417	121,334	3,959
	473,321	542,723	34,702		113,411	121,333	3,962
	473,321	542,710	34,695				
	473,292	542,706	34,708	Maryland	122,238	136,185	6,974
	473,264	542,706	34,722		122,237	136,175	6,970
	473,256	542,698	34,722		122,228	136,175	6,974
					122,223	136,169	6,974
Indiana	309,584	336,063	13,240		122,210	136,169	6,980
	305,120	332,837	13,859		122,209	136,161	6,977
	305,120	332,694	13,788		122,205	136,154	6,975
	304,995	332,587	13,797		122,004	136,151	7,074
	304,974	332,569	13,798				
	304,970	332,549	13,790	Utah	45,006	47,139	1,067
	304,956	332,548	13,797		44,949	47,089	1,071
	304,938	332,545	13,804		44,878	47,071	1,097
	304,933	332,536	13,802				
	304,923	332,510	13,794	Wyoming	10,164	14,482	2,160
	304,920	332,491	13,786		10,156	14,465	2,155
	304,918	332,488	13,786		10,134	14,409	2,138
	304,917	332,482	13,783				
	304,915	332,475	13,781				
	304,883	332,456	13,787				

Election of 1900

TABLE 31   Electoral and Popular Vote

States	McK	Br	McKinley	Bryan	Woolley	Debs	Barker	Malloney	Ellis	Lnrd
Alabama		11	55,634	96,368	3,796	928	3,751			
Arkansas		8	44,800	81,142	584	27	972		340	
California	9		164,755	124,985	5,087	7,572				
Colorado		4	93,072	122,733	3,790	714	389	684		
Connecticut	6		102,572	74,014	1,617	1,029		908		
Delaware	3		22,535	18,863	546	57				
Florida		4	7,499	28,007	2,234	601	1,070			
Georgia		13	35,056	81,700	1,396		4,584			
Idaho		3	27,198	29,414	857		232			
Illinois	24		597,985	503,061	17,626	9,687	1,141	1,373	672	352
Indiana	15		336,063	309,584	13,718	2,374	1,438	663	254	
Iowa	13		307,808	209,265	9,502	2,790	1,026	259		169
Kansas	10		185,955	162,601	3,605	1,605				
Kentucky		13	226,801	234,899	2,814	770	2,017	299		
Louisiana		8	14,233	53,671						
Maine	6		65,435	. 36,823	2,585	878				
Maryland	8		136,185	122,238	4,574	904		388	145	
Massachusetts	15		239,147	157,016	6,208	9,716		2,610		
Michigan	14		316,269	211,685	11,859	2,826	837	903		
Minnesota	9		190,461	112,901	8,555	3,065		1,329		
Mississippi		9	5,753	51,706			1,644			
Missouri		17	314,092	351,922	5,965	6,139	4,244	1,294		
Montana		3	25,373	37,145	298	708		169		
Nebraska	8		121,835	114,013	3,655	823	1,104			
Nevada		3	3,849	6,347						
New Hampshire	4		54,798	35,489	1,271	790				
New Jersey	10		221,754	164,879	7,190	4,611	691	2,081		
New York	36		822,013	678,462	22,077	12,869		12,622		
North Carolina		11	133,081	157,752	1,009		830			
North Dakota	3		35,898	20,531	735	520	111			
Ohio	23		543,918	474,882	10,203	4,847	251	1,688	4,284	
Oregon	4		46,526	33,385	2,536	1,494	275			
Pennsylvania	32		712,665	424,232	27,908	4,831	642	2,936		
Rhode Island	4		33,784	19,812	1,529			1,423		
South Carolina		9	3,579	47,283						
South Dakota	4		54,530	39,544	1,542	169	339			
Tennessee		12	123,180	145,356	3,882	413	1,322			
Texas		15	130,641	267,432	2,644	1,846	20,981	162		
Utah	3		47,139	45,006	209	720		106		
Vermont	4		42,569	12,849	367		383			
Virginia		12	115,865	146,080	2,150	145	63	167		
Washington	4		57,456	44,833	2,363	2,006		866		
West Virginia	6		119,829	98,807	1,692	219	268			
Wisconsin	12		265,756	159,279	10,022	7,051		505		
Wyoming	3		14,482	10,164						
TOTALS	292	155	7,219,828	6,358,160	210,200	95,744	50,605	33,435	5,695	521

67

Percentage of Popular Vote

States	McK	Br	W	D	Ba	Ma	E	L
Alabama	34.67	60.05	2.37	.58	2.34			
Arkansas	35.04	63.46	.46	.02	.76		.27	
California	54.48	41.33	1.68	2.50				
Colorado	42.04	55.44	1.71	.32	.18	.31		
Connecticut	56.94	41.09	.90	.57		.50		
Delaware	53.65	44.91	1.30	.14				
Florida	19.03	71.06	5.67	1.52	2.71			
Georgia	28.56	66.57	1.14		3.73			
Idaho	47.14	50.98	1.49		.40			
Illinois	52.83	44.44	1.56	.86	.10	.12	.06	.03
Indiana	50.60	46.62	2.07	.36	.22	.10	.04	
Iowa	57.99	39.42	1.79	.53	.19	.05		.03
Kansas	52.56	45.96	1.02	.45				
Kentucky	48.50	50.24	.60	.16	.43	.06		
Louisiana	20.96	79.04						
Maine	61.89	34.83	2.45	.83				
Maryland	51.50	46.23	1.73	.34		.15	.05	
Massachusetts	57.67	37.86	1.50	2.34		.63		
Michigan	58.10	38.89	2.18	.52	.15	.17		
Minnesota	60.21	35.69	2.70	.97		.42		
Mississippi	9.73	87.48			2.78			
Missouri	45.94	51.48	.87	.90	.62	.19		
Montana	39.84	58.32	.47	1.11		.27		
Nebraska	50.46	47.22	1.51	.34	.46			
Nevada	37.75	62.25						
New Hampshire	59.34	38.43	1.38	.86				
New Jersey	55.27	41.10	1.79	1.15	.17	.52		
New York	53.10	43.83	1.43	.83		.82		
North Carolina	45.47	53.90	.34		.28			
North Dakota	62.11	35.52	1.27	.90	.19			
Ohio	52.30	45.66	.98	.47	.02	.16	.41	
Oregon	55.25	39.64	3.01	1.77	.33			
Pennsylvania	60.74	36.16	2.38	.41	.05	.25		
Rhode Island	59.74	35.04	2.70			2.52		
South Carolina	7.04	92.96						
South Dakota	56.73	41.14	1.60	.18	.35			
Tennessee	44.93	53.02	1.42	.15	.48			
Texas	30.83	63.12	.62	.44	4.95	.04		
Utah	50.59	48.30	.22	.77		.11		
Vermont	75.79	22.88	.65		.68			
Virginia	43.81	55.23	.81	.05	.02	.06		
Washington	53.44	41.70	2.20	1.87		.81		
West Virginia	54.27	44.75	.77	.10	.12			
Wisconsin	60.04	35.99	2.26	1.59		.11		
Wyoming	58.76	41.24						
TOTALS	51.67	45.50	1.50	.69	.36	.24	.04	.00

The highest percentage for each candidate is underlined.

".00" signifies that the candidate received some votes, but less than .01%.

Extended percentages for Leonard: Illinois .031%, Iowa .032%.

ELECTION OF 1904

Candidates were Theodore Roosevelt, Republican; Alton Brooks Parker, Democrat; Eugene Victor Debs, Socialist; Silas C. Swallow, Prohibition; Thomas Edward Watson, Populist; Charles H. Corregan, Socialist-Labor; and Austin Holcomb, Continental.

Data pertaining to this election are from the official records on file in the National Archives, with these exceptions:

Alabama—all from *Abstract.*

Colorado—Parker, Debs, Watson, and Corregan from *Abstract;* Swallow from [Denver] *Rocky Mountain News.*

Missouri and Nevada—all other than Roosevelt from *Abstract.*

South Carolina—Debs from *Abstract.*

The following figures explain the split in the Maryland electoral vote:

WINNERS	PARTY	LOSERS	PARTY
109,497	Republican	107,276	Democratic
109,446	Democratic	106,993	Republican
107,477	Democratic	106,896	Republican
107,460	Democratic	106,876	Republican
107,343	Democratic	106,787	Republican
107,333	Democratic	106,721	Republican
107,285	Democratic	106,709	Republican
107,278	Democratic	106,694	Republican

TABLE 32 — Electoral and Popular Vote

States	R	P	Roosevelt	Parker	Debs	Swallow	Watson	Corregan	Holcomb
Alabama		11	22,472	79,857	853	612	5,051		
Arkansas		9	46,860	64,434	1,816	993	2,318		
California	10		205,226	89,404	29,535	7,380			
Colorado	5		134,687	100,105	4,304	3,438	824	335	
Connecticut	7		111,089	72,909	4,543	1,506	495	575	
Delaware	3		23,712	19,359	146	607	51		
Florida		5	8,314	27,046	2,337	5	1,605		
Georgia		13	24,003	83,472	197	685	22,635		
Idaho	3		47,783	18,480	4,949	1,013	353		
Illinois	27		632,645	327,606	69,225	34,770	6,725	4,698	830
Indiana	15		368,289	274,345	12,013	23,496	2,444	1,598	
Iowa	13		307,907	149,141	14,847	11,601	2,406		
Kansas	10		212,955	86,174	15,869	7,306	6,257		
Kentucky		13	205,277	217,170	3,602	6,609	2,511	596	
Louisiana		9	5,205	47,747	995				
Maine	6		64,438	27,648	2,103	1,510	338		
Maryland	1	7	109,497	109,446	2,247	3,034			
Massachusetts	16		257,822	165,772	13,604	4,286	1,299	2,365	
Michigan	14		364,957	135,392	9,042	13,441	1,159	1,108	
Minnesota	11		216,651	55,187	11,692	6,352	2,103	974	
Mississippi		10	3,187	53,374	392		1,424		
Missouri	18		321,446	296,312	13,009	7,191	4,226	1,674	
Montana	3		34,932	21,773	5,676	335	1,520	208	
Nebraska	8		138,558	52,921	7,412	6,323	20,518		
Nevada	3		6,864	3,982	925		344		
New Hampshire	4		54,180	33,995	1,090	749	83		
New Jersey	12		245,164	164,567	9,587	6,845	3,705	2,680	
New York	39		859,533	683,981	36,883	20,787	7,459	9,127	
North Carolina		12	82,625	124,124	125	361	879		
North Dakota	4		52,595	14,273	2,117	1,140	165		
Ohio	23		600,095	344,940	36,260	19,339	1,401	2,633	
Oregon	4		60,455	17,521	7,619	3,806	753		
Pennsylvania	34		840,949	337,998	21,863	33,717	33	2,224	
Rhode Island	4		41,605	24,839	956	768		488	
South Carolina		9	2,554	52,563	22		1		
South Dakota	4		72,083	21,969	3,138	2,965	1,240		
Tennessee		12	105,369	131,653	1,354	1,906	2,506		
Texas		18	51,242	167,200	2,791	4,292	8,062	421	
Utah	3		62,446	33,413	5,767				
Vermont	4		40,459	9,777	859	792			
Virginia		12	47,880	80,648	56	1,383	359	218	
Washington	5		101,540	28,098	10,023	3,229	669	1,592	
West Virginia	7		132,628	100,881	1,574	4,604	339		
Wisconsin	13		280,164	124,107	28,220	9,770	530	223	
Wyoming	3		20,489	8,930	1,077	217			
TOTALS	336	140	7,628,831	5,084,533	402,714	259,163	114,790	33,737	830

Percentage of Popular Vote

States	R	P	D	S	W	C	H
Alabama	20.65	73.37	.78	.56	4.64		
Arkansas	40.25	55.35	1.56	.85	1.99		
California	61.90	26.97	8.91	2.23			
Colorado	55.27	41.08	1.77	1.41	.34	.14	
Connecticut	58.13	38.15	2.38	.79	.26	.30	
Delaware	54.04	44.12	.33	1.38	.12		
Florida	21.15	68.81	5.95	.01	4.08		
Georgia	18.32	63.72	.15	.52	17.28		
Idaho	65.84	25.46	6.82	1.40	.49		
Illinois	58.77	30.43	6.43	3.23	.62	.44	.08
Indiana	53.99	40.22	1.76	3.44	.36	.23	
Iowa	63.37	30.69	3.06	2.39	.50		
Kansas	64.81	26.23	4.83	2.22	1.90		
Kentucky	47.11	49.84	.83	1.52	.58	.14	
Louisiana	9.65	88.51	1.84				
Maine	67.10	28.79	2.19	1.57	.35		
Maryland	48.83	48.81	1.00	1.35			
Massachusetts	57.92	37.24	3.06	.96	.29	.53	
Michigan	69.50	25.78	1.72	2.56	.22	.21	
Minnesota	73.95	18.84	3.99	2.17	.72	.33	
Mississippi	5.46	91.43	.67		2.44		
Missouri	49.92	46.02	2.02	1.12	.66	.26	
Montana	54.21	33.79	8.81	.52	2.36	.32	
Nebraska	61.38	23.44	3.28	2.80	9.09		
Nevada	56.66	32.87	7.64		2.84		
New Hampshire	60.14	37.73	1.21	.83	.09		
New Jersey	56.68	38.05	2.22	1.58	.86	.62	
New York	53.13	42.28	2.28	1.28	.46	.56	
North Carolina	39.70	59.64	.06	.17	.42		
North Dakota	74.83	20.31	3.01	1.62	.23		
Ohio	59.73	34.33	3.61	1.92	.14	.26	
Oregon	67.06	19.43	8.45	4.22	.84		
Pennsylvania	67.99	27.33	1.77	·2.73	.00	.18	
Rhode Island	60.60	36.18	1.39	1.12		.71	
South Carolina	4.63	95.33	.04		.00		
South Dakota	71.09	21.67	3.09	2.92	1.22		
Tennessee	43.40	54.23	.56	.79	1.03		
Texas	21.90	71.45	1.19	1.83	3.45	.18	
Utah	61.45	32.88	5.67				
Vermont	77.98	18.84	1.66	1.53			
Virginia	36.67	61.78	.04	1.06	.28	.17	
Washington	69.95	19.36	6.91	2.22	.46	1.10	
West Virginia	55.26	42.03	.66	1.92	.14		
Wisconsin	63.24	28.01	6.37	2.21	.12	.05	
Wyoming	66.71	29.08	3.51	.71			
TOTALS	56.40	37.59	2.98	1.92	.85	.25	.01

The highest percentage for each candidate is underlined.

".00" signifies that the candidate received some votes, but less than .01%.

ELECTION OF 1908

Candidates were William Howard Taft, Republican; William Jennings Bryan, Democrat; Eugene Victor Debs, Socialist; Eugene W. Chafin, Prohibition; Thomas L. Hisgen, Independence; Thomas Edward Watson, Populist; August Gillhaus, Socialist-Labor; and Daniel B. Turney, United Christian. A group without a party designation also received votes. Data pertaining to this election are from the official records on file in the National Archives, with these exceptions:

Alabama—all other than Bryan from *Abstract.*

Illinois—all from [Springfield] *Illinois State Register.*

Oklahoma—all from [Guthrie] *Oklahoma State Capital.*

Texas—Taft, Debs, and Chafin from *Abstract;* Hisgen, Watson, and Gillhaus from *World Almanac.*

The following figures explain the split in the Maryland electoral vote:

WINNERS	PARTY	LOSERS	PARTY
116,513	Republican	113,635	Democratic
115,908	Democratic	113,575	Democratic
114,161	Democratic	113,570	Republican
113,930	Democratic	113,444	Republican
113,877	Democratic	113,364	Republican
113,823	Democratic	113,315	Republican
113,803	Republican	113,268	Republican
113,750	Democratic	113,252	Republican

In Missouri, the highest Bryan candidate for elector received more votes than the lowest Taft candidate for elector, but Taft was awarded all of the state's electoral vote.

The figures below show how a switch of 75,041 votes out of the 14,089,779 cast for Taft and Bryan—.53%—would have made the latter president:

States	Bryan	Taft	Shift
	162	321	
Ohio	23	-23	34,796
Missouri	18	-18	587
Indiana	15	-15	5,366
Kansas	10	-10	18,004
West Virginia	7	- 7	13,226
Delaware	3	- 3	1,473
Montana	3	- 3	1,504
Maryland	1	- 1	85
	242	241	75,041

In the case of Maryland, the shift of 85 votes is one more than half of 168, the difference between the votes received by the winner with the lowest vote of the electoral nominees and the loser with the highest vote—113,803 and 113,635.

In the following tabulation, the nominees for electors are ranked according to the number of votes they received:

States	Bryan	Taft	Shift	States	Bryan	Taft	Shift
Ohio	502,721	572,312	34,796	Indiana	338,262	348,993	5,366
	501,938	570,726	34,395		334,683	344,198	4,758
	501,935	570,627	34,347		334,281	343,826	4,773
	501,924	570,545	34,311		334,256	343,814	4,780
	501,897	570,487	34,296		334,239	343,787	4,775
	501,865	570,462	34,299		334,214	343,766	4,777
	501,832	570,460	34,315		334,214	343,698	4,743
	501,764	570,425	34,331		334,193	343,649	4,729
	501,757	570,411	34,328		334,174	343,539	4,683
	501,724	570,402	34,340		334,170	343,525	4,678
	501,705	570,328	34,312		334,170	343,501	4,666
	501,686	570,307	34,311		334,148	343,499	4,676
	501,673	570,302	34,315		334,146	343,483	4,669
	501,617	570,299	34,342		334,121	343,384	4,632
	501,612	570,298	34,344		334,082	343,330	4,625
	501,608	570,253	34,323				
	501,592	570,240	34,325	Kansas	161,209	197,216	18,004
	501,577	570,211	34,318		160,697	196,677	17,991
	501,544	570,165	34,311		160,687	196,637	17,976
	501,518	570,137	34,310		160,678	196,625	17,974
	501,507	570,131	34,313		160,643	196,567	17,963
	501,507	570,090	34,292		160,634	196,492	17,930
	501,503	569,774	34,136		160,633	196,460	17,914
					160,621	196,458	17,919
Missouri	346,574	347,203	315		160,575	196,443	17,935
	346,498	347,185	344		160,575	196,402	17,914
	346,494	347,066	287				
	346,466	347,053	587	West	111,418	137,869	13,226
	346,464	347,049	293	Virginia	111,302	137,738	13,219
	346,456	347,038	292		111,297	137,735	13,220
	346,442	347,009	284		111,286	137,732	13,224
	346,410	347,001	296		111,279	137,730	13,226
	346,396	347,000	303		111,276	137,727	13,226
	346,374	346,984	306		111,252	137,659	13,204
	346,357	346,946	295				
	346,346	346,939	297	Delaware	22,071	25,014	1,472
	346,317	346,915	300		22,068	25,008	1,471
	346,285	346,873	295		22,055	24,999	1,473
	346,267	346,824	279				
	346,183	346,798	308	Montana	29,326	32,333	1,504
	345,889	346,764	438		28,605	31,260	1,328
	345,419	346,342	462		28,505	31,010	1,253

Election of 1908

States	Ta	B	Taft	Bryan	Debs	Chafin	Hisgen

TABLE 33   Electoral and Popular Vote

States	Ta	B	Taft	Bryan	Debs	Chafin	Hisgen
Alabama		11	25,308	74,374	1,399	665	495
Arkansas		9	56,760	87,015	5,842	1,194	289
California	10		214,398	127,492	28,659	11,770	4,278
Colorado		5	123,700	126,644	7,974	5,559	
Connecticut	7		112,915	68,255	5,113	2,380	728
Delaware	3		25,014	22,071	239	670	30
Florida		5	10,654	31,104	3,747	553	1,356
Georgia		13	41,692	72,413	584	1,059	77
Idaho	3		52,621	36,162	6,400	1,986	119
Illinois	27		629,932	450,810	34,711	29,364	7,724
Indiana	15		348,993	338,262	13,476	18,045	514
Iowa	13		275,210	200,771	8,287	9,837	404
Kansas	10		197,216	161,209	12,420	5,033	68
Kentucky		13	235,711	244,092	4,060	5,887	200
Louisiana		9	8,958	63,568	2,538		82
Maine	6		66,987	35,403	1,758	1,487	701
Maryland	2	6	116,513	115,908	2,323	3,302	485
Massachusetts	16		265,966	155,543	10,781	4,379	19,239
Michigan	14		335,580	175,771	11,586	16,974	760
Minnesota	11		195,843	109,401	14,527	11,107	426
Mississippi		10	4,392	60,287	978		
Missouri	18		347,203	346,574	15,431	4,231	402
Montana	3		32,333	29,326	5,855	827	481
Nebraska		8	126,997	131,099	3,524	5,179	
Nevada		3	10,775	11,212	2,103		436
New Hampshire	4		53,149	33,655	1,299	905	584
New Jersey	12		265,326	182,567	10,253	4,934	2,922
New York	39		870,070	667,468	38,451	22,667	35,817
North Carolina		12	114,937	136,995	378		
North Dakota	4		57,680	32,885	2,421	1,553	43
Ohio	23		572,312	502,721	33,795	11,402	475
Oklahoma		7	110,550	123,907	21,752		274
Oregon	4		62,530	38,049	7,339	2,682	289
Pennsylvania	34		745,779	448,778	33,913	36,694	1,057
Rhode Island	4		43,942	24,706	1,365	1,016	1,105
South Carolina		9	3,965	62,290	100		43
South Dakota	4		67,536	40,266	2,846	4,039	88
Tennessee		12	118,324	135,608	1,870	300	332
Texas		18	65,666	217,302	7,870	1,634	115
Utah	3		61,028	42,601	4,895		87
Vermont	4		39,552	11,496		802	804
Virginia		12	52,573	82,946	255	1,111	51
Washington	5		106,062	58,691	14,177	4,700	249
West Virginia	7		137,869	111,418	3,679	5,139	46
Wisconsin	13		247,747	166,632	28,170	11,572	
Wyoming	3		20,846	14,918	1,715	66	64
TOTALS	321	162	7,679,114	6,410,665	420,858	252,704	83,739

Electoral and Popular Vote (continued)

States	Watson	Gillhaus	Turney	No Party
Alabama	1,568			
Arkansas	1,026			
California				
Colorado				
Connecticut		608		
Delaware				
Florida	1,946			
Georgia	16,969			
Idaho				
Illinois	633	1,680	400	
Indiana	1,193	643		
Iowa	261			
Kansas				
Kentucky	333	404		
Louisiana				
Maine				
Maryland				
Massachusetts		1,018		
Michigan		1,096		63
Minnesota				
Mississippi	1,276			
Missouri	1,165	868		
Montana				
Nebraska				
Nevada				
New Hampshire				
New Jersey		1,196		
New York		3,877		
North Carolina				
North Dakota				
Ohio	163	720		
Oklahoma	434			
Oregon				
Pennsylvania		1,222		
Rhode Island		183		
South Carolina				
South Dakota				
Tennessee	1,081			
Texas	994	176		
Utah				
Vermont				
Virginia	105	25		
Washington				
West Virginia				
Wisconsin		314		
Wyoming				
TOTALS	29,147	14,030	400	63

Percentage of Popular Vote

States	Ta	B	D	C	H	W	G	Tu	N. P.
Alabama	24.38	71.65	1.35	.64	.48	1.51			
Arkansas	37.31	57.20	3.84	.78	.19	.67			
California	55.46	32.98	7.41	3.04	1.11				
Colorado	46.88	47.99	3.02	2.11					
Connecticut	59.43	35.92	2.69	1.25	.38		.32		
Delaware	52.09	45.96	.50	1.40	.06				
Florida	21.58	63.01	7.59	1.12	2.75	3.94			
Georgia	31.40	54.53	.44	.80	.06	12.78			
Idaho	54.09	37.17	6.58	2.04	.12				
Illinois	54.52	39.02	3.00	2.54	.67	.05	.15	.03	
Indiana	48.40	46.91	1.87	2.50	.07	.17	.09		
Iowa	55.62	40.58	1.67	1.99	.08	.05			
Kansas	52.46	42.88	3.31	1.34	.02				
Kentucky	48.04	49.74	.83	1.20	.04	.07	.08		
Louisiana	11.92	84.59	3.38		.11				
Maine	63.00	33.29	1.65	1.40 ·	.66				
Maryland	48.85	48.59	.97	1.38	.20				
Massachusetts	58.21	34.04	2.36	.96	4.21		.22		
Michigan	61.93	32.44	2.14	3.13	.14		.20		.01
Minnesota	59.11	33.02	4.38	3.35	.13				
Mississippi	6.56	90.07	1.46			1.91			
Missouri	48.50	48.41	2.16	.59	.06	.16	.12		
Montana	46.98	42.61	8.51	1.20	.70				
Nebraska	47.60	49.14	1.32	1.94					
Nevada	43.93	45.71	8.57		1.78				
New Hampshire	59.32	37.56	1.45	1.01	.65				
New Jersey	56.79	39.08	2.19	1.06	.63		.26		
New York	53.11	40.74	2.35	1.38	2.19		.24		
North Carolina	45.55	54.30	.15						
North Dakota	60.87	34.71	2.56	1.64	.05				
Ohio	51.03	44.82	3.01	1.02	.04	.01	.06		
Oklahoma	43.03	48.23	8.47		.11	.17			
Oregon	56.39	34.31	6.62	2.42	.26				
Pennsylvania	58.84	35.41	2.68	2.90	.08		.10		
Rhode Island	60.76	34.16	1.89	1.40	1.53		.25		
South Carolina	5.97	93.81	.15		.06				
South Dakota	58.84	35.08	2.48	3.52	.08				
Tennessee	45.95	52.66	.73	.12	.13	.42			
Texas	22.35	73.97	2.68	.56	.04	.34	.06		
Utah	56.19	39.22	4.51		.08				
Vermont	75.12	21.83		1.52	1.53				
Virginia	38.36	60.52	.19	.81	.04	.08	.02		
Washington	57.47	31.80	7.68	2.55	.13				
West Virginia	53.41	43.16	1.43	1.99	.02				
Wisconsin	54.52	36.67	6.20	2.55			.07		
Wyoming	55.43	39.67	4.56	.18	.17				
TOTALS	51.57	43.05	2.83	1.70	.56	.20	.09	.00	.00

The highest percentage for each candidate is underlined.

".00" signifies that the candidate received some votes, but less than .01%.

ELECTION OF 1912

Candidates were (Thomas) Woodrow Wilson, Democrat; Theodore Roosevelt, Progressive; William Howard Taft, Republican; Eugene Victor Debs, Socialist; Eugene W. Chafin, Prohibition; and Arthur E. Reimer, Socialist-Labor.

Data pertaining to this election are from the official records on file in the National Archives, with these exceptions:

Alabama and Wyoming—all other than Wilson from *Abstract*.

Colorado—all other than Wilson from [Denver] *Rocky Mountain News*.

Georgia—all other than Taft from *Atlanta Constitution*.

Illinois—all from [Springfield] *Illinois State Register*.

Ohio—all from *Abstract*.

Texas—all from Stanwood except Chafin, which is official with three counties unreported.

West Virginia—Wilson, Roosevelt, and Taft from *Wheeling Register*.

The following figures explain the split in the California electoral vote:

WINNERS	PARTY	LOSERS	PARTY
283,610	Progressive	282,594	Progressive
283,436	Democratic	282,594	Democratic
283,193	Progressive	282,579	Democratic
283,057	Progressive	282,578	Democratic
282,910	Progressive	282,530	Democratic
282,888	Progressive	282,516	Democratic
282,868	Progressive	282,432	Democratic
282,790	Progressive	282,383	Progressive
282,781	Progressive	282,325	Democratic
282,676	Progressive	282,309	Democratic
282,671	Progressive	282,215	Democratic
282,653	Progressive	282,213	Democratic
282,651	Democratic	282,198	Democratic

TABLE 34 Electoral and Popular Vote

States	W	TR	T	Wilson	Roosevelt	Taft	Debs	Chafin	Reime
Alabama	12			82,438	22,680	9,732	3,029		
Arizona	3			10,324	6,949	3,021	3,163	265	
Arkansas	9			68,838	21,673	24,467	8,153	898	
California	2	11		283,436	283,610	3,914	79,201	23,366	
Colorado	6			114,232	72,306	58,386	16,418	5,063	47
Connecticut	7			74,561	34,129	68,324	10,056	2,068	1,26
Delaware	3			22,631	8,886	15,997	556	623	
Florida	6			36,417	4,535	4,279	4,806	1,854	
Georgia	14			93,171	22,010	5,191	1,028	148	
Idaho	4			33,921	25,527	32,810	11,960	1,537	
Illinois	29			405,048	386,478	253,613	81,278	15,710	4,06
Indiana	15			281,890	162,007	151,267	36,931	19,249	3,13
Iowa	13			185,325	161,819	119,805	16,967	9,026	
Kansas	10			143,663	120,210	74,845	26,779		
Kentucky	13			219,584	102,766	115,512	11,647	3,233	95
Louisiana	10			61,035	9,323	3,834	5,249		
Maine	6			51,113	48,495	26,545	2,541	946	
Maryland	8			112,674	57,789	54,956	3,996	2,244	32
Massachusetts	18			174,315	142,375	156,139	12,662	2,799	1,27
Michigan		15		150,751	214,584	152,244	23,211	8,934	1,25
Minnesota		12		106,426	125,856	64,334	27,505	7,886	2,21
Mississippi	10			57,227	3,645	1,595	2,061		
Missouri	18			330,746	124,371	207,821	28,466	5,380	1,77
Montana	4			27,941	22,456	18,512	10,885	32	
Nebraska	8			109,008	72,689	54,216	10,185	3,383	
Nevada	3			7,986	5,620	3,196	3,313		
New Hampshire	4			34,724	17,794	32,927	1,980	535	
New Jersey	14			178,559	145,674	89,047	15,928	2,915	1,34
New Mexico	3			20,437	8,347	17,733	2,859		
New York	45			655,475	390,021	455,428	63,381	19,427	4,25
North Carolina	12			144,545	70,144	29,277	128	1,025	
North Dakota	5			29,555	25,726	23,090	6,966	1,243	
Ohio	24			424,834	229,807	278,168	90,144	11,511	2,63
Oklahoma	10			119,156		90,786	42,262	2,185	
Oregon	5			47,064	37,600	34,673	13,343	4,360	
Pennsylvania		38		395,619	447,426	273,305	83,614	19,533	70
Rhode Island	5			30,412	16,878	27,703	2,049	616	23
South Carolina	9			48,357	1,293	536	164		
South Dakota		5		48,962	58,811		4,662	3,910	
Tennessee	12			135,425	54,041	60,674	3,504	834	
Texas	20			221,589	28,853	26,755	25,743	1,738	44
Utah			4	36,579	24,174	42,100	9,023		51
Vermont			4	15,354	22,132	23,332	928	1,095	
Virginia	12			90,332	21,777	23,288	820	709	5
Washington		7		86,840	113,698	70,445	40,134	9,810	1,87
West Virginia	8			113,197	79,112	56,754	15,336	4,534	
Wisconsin	13			164,228	62,460	130,695	33,481	8,586	52
Wyoming	3			15,310	9,232	14,560	2,760	434	
TOTALS	435	88	8	6,301,254	4,127,788	3,485,831	901,255	209,644	29,29

Percentage of Popular Vote

States	W	TR	WHT	D	C	AER
Alabama	69.93	19.24	8.26	2.57		
Arizona	43.52	29.29	12.74	13.33	1.12	
Arkansas	55.50	17.47	19.73	6.57	.72	
California	42.08	42.11	.58	11.76	3.47	
Colorado	42.80	27.09	21.88	6.15	1.90	.18
Connecticut	39.16	17.93	35.88	5.28	1.09	.66
Delaware	46.48	18.25	32.85	1.14	1.28	
Florida	70.18	8.74	8.25	9.26	3.57	
Georgia	76.65	18.11	4.27	.85	.12	
Idaho	32.08	24.14	31.02	11.31	1.45	
Illinois	35.34	33.72	22.13	7.09	1.37	.35
Indiana	43.07	24.75	23.11	5.64	2.94	.48
Iowa	37.60	32.83	24.30	3.44	1.83	
Kansas	39.31	32.89	20.48	7.33		
Kentucky	48.40	22.65	25.46	2.57	.71	.21
Louisiana	76.83	11.74	4.83	6.61		
Maine	39.43	37.41	20.48	1.96	.73	
Maryland	48.57	24.91	23.69	1.72	.97	.14
Massachusetts	35.61	29.08	31.89	2.59	.57	.26
Michigan	27.36	38.95	27.63	4.21	1.62	.23
Minnesota	31.84	37.66	19.25	8.23	2.36	.66
Mississippi	88.69	5.65	2.47	3.19		
Missouri	47.35	17.80	29.75	4.07	.77	.25
Montana	35.00	28.13	23.19	13.64	.04	
Nebraska	43.69	29.14	21.73	4.08	1.36	
Nevada	39.70	27.94	15.89	16.47		
New Hampshire	39.48	20.23	37.43	2.25	.61	
New Jersey	41.19	33.61	20.54	3.67	.67	.31
New Mexico	41.39	16.90	35.91	5.79		
New York	41.28	24.56	28.68	3.99	1.22	.27
North Carolina	58.97	28.62	11.94	.05	.42	
North Dakota	34.14	29.71	26.67	8.05	1.44	
Ohio	40.96	22.16	26.82	8.69	1.11	.25
Oklahoma	46.84		35.69	16.61	.86	
Oregon	34.34	27.44	25.30	9.74	3.18	
Pennsylvania	32.42	36.67	22.40	6.85	1.60	.06
Rhode Island	39.04	21.67	35.57	2.63	.79	.30
South Carolina	96.04	2.57	1.06	.33		
South Dakota	42.08	50.55		4.01	3.36	
Tennessee	53.22	21.24	23.84	1.38	.33	
Texas	72.62	9.46	8.77	8.44	.57	.14
Utah	32.55	21.51	37.46	8.03		.45
Vermont	24.43	35.22	37.13	1.48	1.74	
Virginia	65.95	15.90	17.00	.60	.52	.04
Washington	26.90	35.22	21.82	12.43	3.04	.58
West Virginia	42.09	29.42	21.10	5.70	1.69	
Wisconsin	41.06	15.62	32.68	8.37	2.15	.13
Wyoming	36.20	21.83	34.42	6.53	1.03	
TOTALS	41.85	27.42	23.15	5.99	1.39	.19

The highest percentage for each candidate is underlined.

Extended percentages for Reimer: Connecticut .66177%, Minnesota .66184%.

Candidates were (Thomas) Woodrow Wilson, Democrat; Charles Evans Hughes, Republican; Allan L. Benson, Socialist; J. Frank Hanly, Prohibition; Theodore Roosevelt, Progressive; and Arthur E. Reimer, Socialist-Labor.

Data pertaining to this election are from the official records on file in the National Archives. The following figures explain the split in the West Virginia electoral vote:

WINNERS	PARTY	LOSERS	PARTY
143,124	Republican	140,140	Democratic
142,640	Republican	140,121	Democratic
142,605	Republican	140,031	Democratic
142,603	Republican	139,971	Democratic
142,546	Republican	139,966	Democratic
142,472	Republican	139,926	Democratic
142,422	Republican	139,908	Democratic
140,403	Democratic	137,654	Republican

The figures below show how a switch of 1,983 votes out of the 17,680,446 cast for Wilson and Hughes—.01%—would have made the latter president.

State	Hughes	Wilson	Shift
	254	277	
California	13	-13	1,983
	——	——	
	267	264	

In the following tabulation, nominees are ranked according to the number of votes they received.

	Hughes	Wilson	Shift
California	462,394	466,200	1,904
	461,882	465,847	1,983
	461,706	465,003	1,649
	461,704	464,837	1,567
	461,488	464,735	1,624
	461,466	464,719	1,627
	461,383	464,642	1,630
	461,232	464,591	1,680
	461,179	464,388	1,605
	460,819	464,330	1,756
	460,786	464,144	1,680
	460,704	464,117	1,707
	460,699	463,621	1,462

Election of 1916

TABLE 35   Electoral and Popular Vote

States	W	Hu	Wilson	Hughes	Benson	Hanly	Roosevelt	Reimer
Alabama	12		99,409	28,809	1,925	999		
Arizona	3		33,170	20,524	3,174	1,153		
Arkansas	9		112,186	47,148	6,999	2,015		
California	13		466,200	462,394	43,259	27,698		
Colorado	6		178,816	102,308	10,049	2,793	409	
Connecticut		7	99,786	106,514	5,179	1,789		606
Delaware		3	24,753	26,011	480	566		
Florida	6		55,984	14,611	5,353	4,855		
Georgia	14		125,845	11,225	967		20,653	
Idaho	4		70,054	55,368	8,066	1,127		
Illinois		29	950,229	1,152,549	61,394	26,047		2,488
Indiana		15	334,063	341,005	21,855	16,368	3,915	1,659
Iowa		13	221,699	280,449	11,490	3,371	1,793	
Kansas	10		314,588	277,658	24,685	12,882		
Kentucky	13		269,990	241,854	4,734	3,036		333
Louisiana	10		79,875	6,466	292		6,349	
Maine		6	64,132	69,506	2,177	597		
Maryland	8		138,359	117,347	2,674	2,903		756
Massachusetts		18	247,885	268,812	11,062	2,993		1,125
Michigan		15	286,775	339,097	16,120	8,139		842
Minnesota		12	179,152	179,544	20,117	7,793	290	468
Mississippi	10		80,422	4,253	1,484		520	
Missouri	18		398,032	369,339	14,612	3,884		902
Montana	4		101,063	66,750	9,564		302	
Nebraska	8		158,827	117,771	7,141	2,952		
Nevada	3		17,776	12,127	3,065	348		
New Hampshire	4		43,779	43,723	1,318	303		
New Jersey		14	211,645	269,352	10,462	3,217		890
New Mexico	3		33,693	31,163	1,999	112		
New York		45	759,426	879,287	45,944	19,031		2,666
North Carolina	12		168,383	120,988	490	51		
North Dakota	5		55,206	53,471				
Ohio	24		604,161	514,753	38,092	8,080		
Oklahoma	10		148,113	97,233	45,527	1,646	234	
Oregon		5	120,087	126,813	9,711	4,729	310	
Pennsylvania		38	521,784	703,734	42,637	28,525		417
Rhode Island		5	40,394	44,858	1,914	470		180
South Carolina	9		61,846	1,550	135		259	
South Dakota		5	59,191	64,217	3,760	1,774		
Tennessee	12		153,282	116,223	2,542	147		
Texas	20		286,514	64,999	18,969	1,985		
Utah	4		84,256	54,137	4,460	149		144
Vermont		4	22,708	40,250	798	709		
Virginia	12		102,824	49,356	1,060	683		67
Washington	7		183,388	167,244	\22,800	6,868		730
West Virginia	1	7	140,403	143,124	6,140	179		
Wisconsin		13	193,042	221,323	27,846	7,166		
Wyoming	3		28,316	21,698	1,453	373		
TOTALS	277	254	9,131,511	8,548,935	585,974	220,505	35,034	14,273

States	W	Hu	B	Ha	Ro	Re
Alabama	75.80	21.97	1.47	.76		
Arizona	57.17	35.37	5.47	1.99		
Arkansas	66.64	28.01	4.16	1.20		
California	46.64	46.26	4.33	2.77		
Colorado	60.74	34.75	3.41	.95	.14	
Connecticut	46.66	49.80	2.42	.84		.28
Delaware	47.78	50.20	.93	1.09		
Florida	69.28	18.08	6.62	6.01		
Georgia	79.30	7.07	.61		13.01	
Idaho	52.04	41.13	5.99	.84		
Illinois	43.34	52.56	2.80	1.19		.11
Indiana	46.47	47.44	3.04	2.28	.54	.23
Iowa	42.73	54.06	2.21	.65	.35	
Kansas	49.95	44.09	3.92	2.05		
Kentucky	51.93	46.52	.91	.58		.06
Louisiana	85.90	6.95	.31		6.83	
Maine	47.01	50.95	1.60	.44		
Maryland	52.80	44.78	1.02	1.11		.29
Massachusetts	46.61	50.54	2.08	.56		.21
Michigan	44.05	52.09	2.48	1.25		.13
Minnesota	46.25	46.35	5.19	2.01	.07	.12
Mississippi	92.78	4.91	1.71		.60	
Missouri	50.59	46.94	1.86	.49		.11
Montana	56.88	37.57	5.38		.17	
Nebraska	55.40	41.08	2.49	1.03		
Nevada	53.36	36.40	9.20	1.04		
New Hampshire	49.12	49.06	1.48	.34		
New Jersey	42.71	54.35	2.11	.65		.18
New Mexico	50.31	46.53	2.99	.17		
New York	44.51	51.53	2.69	1.12		.16
North Carolina	58.08	41.73	.17	.02		
North Dakota	50.80	49.20				
Ohio	51.86	44.18	3.27	.69		
Oklahoma	50.59	33.21	15.55	.56	.08	
Oregon	45.90	48.47	3.71	1.81	.12	
Pennsylvania	40.23	54.25	3.29	2.20		.03
Rhode Island	46.00	51.08	2.18	.54		.20
South Carolina	96.95	2.43	.21		.41	
South Dakota	45.91	49.80	2.92	1.38		
Tennessee	56.31	42.70	.93	.05		
Texas	76.92	17.45	5.09	.53		
Utah	58.86	37.82	3.12	.10		.10
Vermont	35.23	62.44	1.24	1.10		
Virginia	66.77	32.05	.69	.44		.04
Washington	48.13	43.89	5.98	1.80		.19
West Virginia	48.44	49.38	2.12	.06		
Wisconsin	42.96	49.25	6.20	1.59		
Wyoming	54.62	41.86	2.80	.72		
TOTALS	49.26	46.12	3.16	1.19	.19	.08

The highest percentage for each candidate is underlined.

ELECTION OF 1920

Candidates were Warren Gamaliel Harding, Republican; James Middleton Cox, Democrat; Eugene Victor Debs, Socialist; Parley Parker Christensen, Farmer-Labor; Aaron Sherman Watkins, Prohibition; James E. Ferguson, American; William W. Cox, Socialist-Labor; and Robert Colvin Macauley, Single Tax. The Black & Tan Republican Party also received votes.

Data pertaining to this election are from the official records on file in the National Archives, with these exceptions:

From *Abstract*: Alabama—all other than J. Cox; Arizona—Debs, Christensen, and Watkins; Michigan—Christensen.

From *Statistics of the Congressional and Presidential Election of November 2, 1920*: Michigan—J. Cox, Watkins, and W. Cox; Nevada—all other than Harding; New Jersey—W. Cox and Macauley; New Mexico—Debs; Ohio—Watkins.

TABLE 36 Electoral and Popular Vote

States	H	JMC	Harding	James Cox	Debs	Christensen	Watkins
Alabama		12	74,690	163,254	2,369		757
Arizona	3		37,016	29,546	222	15	4
Arkansas		9	71,117	107,409	5,111		
California	13		624,992	229,191	64,076		25,204
Colorado	6		173,248	104,936	8,046	3,016	2,807
Connecticut	7		229,238	120,721	10,350	1,947	1,771
Delaware	3		52,858	39,911	988	93	
Florida		6	44,853	90,515	5,189		986
Georgia		14	44,127	109,856	465		5,124
Idaho	4		91,351	46,930	38	6	34
Illinois	29		1,420,480	534,395	74,747	49,630	11,216
Indiana	15		696,370	511,364	24,703	16,499	13,462
Iowa	13		634,674	227,921	16,981	10,321	4,197
Kansas	10		369,268	185,464	15,511		
Kentucky		13	452,480	456,497	6,409		3,325
Louisiana		10	38,538	87,519			
Maine	6		136,355	58,961	2,214		1
Maryland	8		236,117	180,626	8,876		
Massachusetts	18		681,153	276,691	32,269	1,645	
Michigan	15		762,865	233,450	28,947	10,480	9,646
Minnesota	12		519,421	142,994	56,106		11,489
Mississippi		10	11,576	69,277	1,639		
Missouri	18		727,521	574,924	20,242	3,291	5,142
Montana	4		109,430	57,372		12,204	
Nebraska	8		247,498	119,608	9,600		5,947
Nevada	3		15,479	9,851	1,864		
New Hampshire	4		95,196	62,662	1,234		
New Jersey	14		615,333	258,761	27,385	2,264	4,895
New Mexico	3		57,634	46,668	2	1,104	
New York	45		1,871,167	781,238	203,201	18,413	19,653
North Carolina		12	232,848	305,447	446		17
North Dakota	5		160,072	37,422	8,282		
Ohio	24		1,182,022	780,037	57,147		294
Oklahoma	10		243,831	217,053	25,726		
Oregon	5		143,592	80,019	9,801		3,595
Pennsylvania	38		1,218,215	503,202	70,021	15,642	42,612
Rhode Island	5		107,463	55,062	4,351		510
South Carolina		9	2,604	64,170	28		
South Dakota	5		110,692	35,938		34,707	900
Tennessee	12		219,829	206,558	2,268		
Texas		20	114,538	288,767	8,121	4,475	
Utah	4		81,555	56,639	3,159		
Vermont	4		68,212	20,919			774
Virginia		12	87,456	141,670	807	243	857
Washington	7		223,137	84,298	8,913	77,246	3,800
West Virginia	8		282,007	220,789	5,618		1,528
Wisconsin	13		498,576	113,422	85,041		8,647
Wyoming	3		35,091	17,429	1,288	2,180	265
TOTALS	404	127	16,153,785	9,147,353	919,801	265,421	189,467

States	Ferguson	Wm. Cox	B. & T.	Macauley
Alabama				
Arizona				
Arkansas				
California				
Colorado				
Connecticut		1,491		
Delaware				39
Florida				
Georgia				
Idaho				
Illinois		3,471		775
Indiana				566
Iowa		982		
Kansas				
Kentucky				
Louisiana				
Maine				310
Maryland		1,178		
Massachusetts		3,583		
Michigan		2,539		
Minnesota		3,828		
Mississippi				
Missouri		2,164		
Montana				
Nebraska				
Nevada				
New Hampshire				
New Jersey		1,010		603
New Mexico				
New York		4,841		
North Carolina				
North Dakota				
Ohio				2,157
Oklahoma				
Oregon		1,515		
Pennsylvania		755		803
Rhode Island		495		100
South Carolina				
South Dakota				
Tennessee				
Texas	47,968		27,247	
Utah				
Vermont				
Virginia				
Washington		1,321		
West Virginia				
Wisconsin				
Wyoming				
TOTALS	47,968	29,173	27,247	5,353

Percentage of Popular Vote

States	H	J.Cox	D	Ch	W	F	W.Cox	B.&T.	M
Alabama	30.98	67.72	.98		.31				
Arizona	55.41	44.23	.33	.02	.01				
Arkansas	38.73	58.49	2.78						
California	66.24	24.29	6.79		2.67				
Colorado	59.32	35.93	2.75	1.03	.96				
Connecticut	62.72	33.03	2.83	.53	.48		.41		
Delaware	55.71	42.07	1.04	.10	1.04				.04
Florida	30.79	62.13	3.56		3.52				
Georgia	28.57	71.12	.30		.01				
Idaho	66.02	33.92	.03	.00	.02				
Illinois	67.81	25.51	3.57	2.37	.54		.17		.04
Indiana	55.14	40.49	1.96	1.31	1.07				.04
Iowa	70.91	25.46	1.90	1.15	.47		.11		
Kansas	64.76	32.52	2.72						
Kentucky	49.25	49.69	.70		.36				
Louisiana	30.57	69.43							
Maine	68.92	29.80	1.12		.00				.16
Maryland	55.11	42.16	2.07	.38			.27		
Massachusetts	68.55	27.84	3.25				.36		
Michigan	72.80	22.28	2.76	1.00	.92		.24		
Minnesota	70.78	19.49	7.65		1.57		.52		
Mississippi	14.03	83.98	1.99						
Missouri	54.57	43.12	1.52	.25	.39		.16		
Montana	61.13	32.05		6.82					
Nebraska	64.68	31.26	2.51		1.55				
Nevada	56.92	36.22	6.85						
New Hampshire	59.84	39.39	.78						
New Jersey	67.60	28.43	3.01	.25	.54		.11		.07
New Mexico	54.68	44.27	.00	1.05					
New York	64.56	26.95	7.01	.64	.68		.17		
North Carolina	43.22	56.69	.08		.00				
North Dakota	77.79	18.19	4.02						
Ohio	58.47	38.58	2.83		.01				.11
Oklahoma	50.11	44.61	5.29	.					
Oregon	60.20	33.55	4.11		1.51		.64		
Pennsylvania	65.80	27.18	3.78	.84	2.30		.04		.04
Rhode Island	63.97	32.78	2.59		.30		.29		.06
South Carolina	3.90	96.06	.04						
South Dakota	60.74	19.72		19.04	.49				
Tennessee	51.28	48.19	.53						
Texas	23.54	59.34	1.67			9.86		5.60	
Utah	55.93	38.84	2.17	3.07					
Vermont	75.87	23.27			.86				
Virginia	37.85	61.32	.35	.12	.37				
Washington	55.96	21.14	2.24	19.37	.95		.33		
West Virginia	55.30	43.30	1.10		.30				
Wisconsin	70.65	16.07	12.05		1.23				
Wyoming	62.38	30.98	2.29	3.88	.47				
TOTALS	60.31	34.15	3.43	.99	.71	.18	.11	.10	.02

The highest percentage for each candidate is underlined.

".00" signifies that the candidate received some votes, but less than .01%.

Candidates were (John) Calvin Coolidge, Republican; John William Davis, Democrat; Robert Marion LaFollette, Progressive; Herman Preston Faris, Prohibition; Frank T. Johns, Socialist-Labor; William Zebulon Foster, Communist; Gilbert Owen Nations, American; and William J. Wallace, Commonwealth-Land.

Data pertaining to this election are from the official records on file in the National Archives.

Election of 1924

TABLE 37				Electoral and Popular Vote		
States	C	D	LaF	Coolidge	Davis	LaFollette
Alabama		12		45,005	112,966	8,084
Arizona	3			30,516	26,235	17,210
Arkansas		9		40,564	84,795·	13,173
California	13			733,250	105,514	424,649
Colorado	6			195,171	75,238	69,945
Connecticut	7			246,322	110,184	42,416
Delaware	3			52,441	33,445	4,979
Florida		6		30,633	62,083	8,625
Georgia		14		30,300	123,200	12,691
Idaho	4			69,879	24,256	54,160
Illinois	29			1,453,321	576,975	432,027
Indiana	15			703,042	492,245	71,700
Iowa	13			537,635	162,600	272,243
Kansas	10			407,671	156,319	98,461
Kentucky	13			398,966	374,855	38,465
Louisiana		10		24,670	93,218	4,063
Maine	6			138,440	41,964	11,382
Maryland	8			162,414	148,072	47,157
Massachusetts	18			703,489	280,831	141,284
Michigan	15			874,631	152,359	122,014
Minnesota	12			420,759	55,913	339,192
Mississippi		10		8,546	100,475	3,494
Missouri	18			648,486	572,753	84,160
Montana	4			74,138	33,805	65,876
Nebraska	8			218,585	137,289	106,701
Nevada	3			11,243	5,909	9,769
New Hampshire	4			98,575	57,201	8,993
New Jersey	14			676,277	298,043	109,964
New Mexico	3			54,745	48,542	9,543
New York	45			1,820,058	950,796	474,925
North Carolina		12		191,753	284,270	6,697
North Dakota	5			94,931	13,858	89,922
Ohio	24			1,176,130	477,888	357,948
Oklahoma		10		226,242	255,798	41,141
Oregon	5			142,579	67,589	68,403
Pennsylvania	38			1,401,481	409,192	307,567
Rhode Island	5			125,286	76,606	7,628
South Carolina		9		1,123	49,008	620
South Dakota	5			101,299	27,214	75,355
Tennessee		12		130,882	158,537	10,656
Texas		20		130,023	484,605	42,881
Utah	4			77,327	47,001	32,662
Vermont	4			80,498	16,124	5,964
Virginia		12		73,359	139,797	10,379
Washington	7			220,224	42,842	150,727
West Virginia	8			288,635	257,232	36,723
Wisconsin			13	311,614	68,115	453,678
Wyoming	3			41,858	12,868	25,174
TOTALS	382	136	13	15,725,016	8,386,624	4,831,470

States	Faris	Johns	Foster	Nations	Wallace
Alabama	569				
Arizona					
Arkansas					
California	18,365				
Colorado	966	378	562		
Connecticut		1,373			
Delaware					
Florida	5,498			2,315	
Georgia	231			155	
Idaho					
Illinois	2,367	2,334	2,622		421
Indiana	4,416		987		
Iowa			4,037		
Kansas					
Kentucky		1,499		1,299	248
Louisiana					
Maine		406			
Maryland		987			
Massachusetts		1,674	2,637		
Michigan	6,085	5,330			
Minnesota		1,855	4,427		
Mississippi					
Missouri	1,418	909			259
Montana		247	357		
Nebraska	1,594				
Nevada					
New Hampshire					
New Jersey	1,660	368	1,560		
New Mexico					
New York		9,928	8,244		
North Carolina	13				
North Dakota			370		
Ohio	1,246	3,025			
Oklahoma		5,234			
Oregon		917			
Pennsylvania	9,779	636	2,735	13,035	296
Rhode Island		268	289		38
South Carolina					
South Dakota					
Tennessee	100			100	
Texas					
Utah					
Vermont	326				
Virginia		191			
Washington		1,004	761	5,991	
West Virginia				1,072	
Wisconsin	2,918	458	3,773		270
Wyoming					
TOTALS	57,551	39,021	33,361	23,967	1,532

1924			Percentage of Popular Vote					
States	C	D	LaF	Fa	J	Fo	N	W
Alabama	27.01	67.80	4.85	.34				
Arizona	41.26	35.47	23.27					
Arkansas	29.28	61.21	9.51					
California	57.21	8.23	33.13	1.43				
Colorado	57.02	21.98	20.44	.28	.11	.16		
Connecticut	61.54	27.53	10.60		.34			
Delaware	57.71	36.81	5.48					
Florida	28.06	56.88	7.90	5.04			2.12	
Georgia	18.19	73.96	7.62	.14			.09	
Idaho	47.12	16.36	36.52					
Illinois	58.84	23.36	17.49	.10	.09	.11		.02
Indiana	55.25	38.69	5.64	.35		.08		
Iowa	55.06	16.65	27.88			.41		
Kansas	61.54	23.60	14.86					
Kentucky	48.93	45.98	4.72		.18		.16	.03
Louisiana	20.23	76.44	3.33					
Maine	72.03	21.83	5.92		.21			
Maryland	45.29	41.29	13.15		.28			
Massachusetts	62.26	24.85	12.50		.15	.23		
Michigan	75.37	13.13	10.51	.52	.46			
Minnesota	51.18	6.80	41.26		.23	.54		
Mississippi	7.60	89.30	3.11					
Missouri	49.58	43.79	6.43	.11	.07			.02
Montana	42.50	19.38	37.77		.14	.20		
Nebraska	47.09	29.58	22.99	.34				
Nevada	41.76	21.95	36.29					
New Hampshire	59.83	34.72	5.46					
New Jersey	62.16	27.40	10.11	.15	.03	.14		
New Mexico	48.52	43.02	8.46					
New York	55.76	29.13	14.55		.30	.25		
North Carolina	39.72	58.89	1.39	.00				
North Dakota	47.68	6.96	45.17			.19		
Ohio	58.33	23.70	17.75	.06	.15			
Oklahoma	42.82	48.41	7.79		.99			
Oregon	51.01	24.18	24.47		.33			
Pennsylvania	65.35	19.07	14.34	.46	.03	.13	.61	.01
Rhode Island	59.63	36.46	3.63		.13	.14		.02
South Carolina	2.21	96.57	1.22					
South Dakota	49.69	13.35	36.96					
Tennessee	43.59	52.80	3.55	.03			.03	
Texas	19.78	73.70	6.52					
Utah	49.26	29.94	20.81					
Vermont	78.22	15.67	5.80	.32				
Virginia	32.79	62.49	4.64		.09			
Washington	52.24	10.16	35.76		.24	.18	1.42	
West Virginia	49.45	44.07	6.29				.18	
Wisconsin	37.06	8.10	53.96	.35	.05	.45		.03
Wyoming	52.39	16.11	31.51					
TOTALS	54.04	28.82	16.60	.20	.13	.11	.08	.01

The highest percentage for each candidate is underlined.

".00" signifies that the candidate received some votes, but less than .01%.

Extended percentages for Wallace: Kentucky .030%, Wisconsin .032%.

Candidates were Herbert Clark Hoover, Republican; Alfred Emanuel Smith, Democrat; Norman Mattoon Thomas, Socialist; William Zebulon Foster, Communist; Verne L. Reynolds, Socialist-Labor; William Frederick Varney, Prohibition; and Frank E. Webb, Farmer-Labor.

Data pertaining to this election are from the official records on file in the National Archives.

Election of 1928

TABLE 38   Electoral and Popular Vote

States	H	S	Hoover	Smith	Thomas	Foster	Reynolds	Varney	Webb
Alabama		12	120,725	127,797	460				
Arizona	3		52,533	38,537		184			
Arkansas		9	77,751	119,196	429	317			
California	13		1,162,323	614,365	19,595	112			
Colorado	6		253,872	133,131	3,472	675			1,092
Connecticut	7		296,614	252,040	3,019	730	622		
Delaware	3		68,860	36,643	329	59			
Florida	6		144,168	101,764	4,036	3,704			
Georgia		14	99,381	129,602	124	64			
Idaho	4		99,848	53,074	1,308				
Illinois	29		1,769,141	1,313,817	19,138	3,581	1,812		
Indiana	15		848,290	562,691	3,871	321	645	5,496	
Iowa	13		623,818	378,936	2,960	328	230		3,088
Kansas	10		513,672	193,003	6,205	320			
Kentucky	13		558,064	381,070	837	293	340		
Louisiana		10	51,160	164,655					
Maine	6		179,923	81,179	1,068				
Maryland	8		301,479	223,626	1,701	636	906		
Massachusetts		18	775,566	792,758	6,262	2,464	773		
Michigan	15		965,396	396,762	3,516	2,881	799	2,728	
Minnesota	12		560,977	396,451	6,774	4,853	1,921		
Mississippi		10	27,153	124,539					
Missouri	18		834,080	662,562	3,739		340		
Montana	4		113,300	78,578	1,667	563			
Nebraska	8		345,745	197,959	3,434				
Nevada	3		18,327	14,090					
New Hampshire	4		115,404	80,715	455	173			
New Jersey	14		926,050	616,517	4,897	1,257	500	160	
New Mexico	3		69,645	48,211		158			
New York	45		2,193,344	2,089,863	107,332	10,876	4,211		
North Carolina	12		348,992	287,078					
North Dakota	5		131,441	106,648	842	936			
Ohio	24		1,627,546	864,210	8,683	2,836	1,515	3,556	
Oklahoma	10		394,046	219,174	3,924				1,283
Oregon	5		205,341	109,223	2,720	1,094	1,564		
Pennsylvania	38		2,055,382	1,067,586	18,647	4,726	380	3,880	
Rhode Island		5	117,522	118,973		283	416		
South Carolina		9	5,858	62,700	47				
South Dakota	5		157,603	102,660	443	232			927
Tennessee	12		195,388	167,343	631	111			
Texas	20		367,036	341,032	722	209			
Utah	4		94,618	80,985	954	47			
Vermont	4		90,404	44,440				338	
Virginia	12		164,609	140,146	250	174	179		
Washington	7		335,844	156,772	2,615	1,541	4,068		
West Virginia	8		375,551	263,784	1,313	401		1,703	
Wisconsin	13		544,205	450,259	18,213	1,528	381	2,245	
Wyoming	3		52,748	29,299	788				
TOTALS	444	87	21,430,743	15,016,443	267,420	48,667	21,602	20,106	6,390

1928			Percentage of Popular Vote				
States	H	S	T	F	R	V	W
Alabama	48.49	51.33	.18				
Arizona	57.57	42.23		.20			
Arkansas	39.33	60.29	.22	.16			
California	64.70	34.20	1.09	.01			
Colorado	64.72	33.94	.89	.17			.28
Connecticut	53.63	45.57	.55	.13	.11		
Delaware	65.03	34.60	.31	.06			
Florida	56.83	40.12	1.59	1.46			
Georgia	43.37	56.55	.05	.03			
Idaho	64.74	34.41	.85				
Illinois	56.93	42.28	.62	.12	.06		
Indiana	59.68	39.59	.27	.02	.05	.39	
Iowa	61.80	37.54	.29	.03	.02		.31
Kansas	72.02	27.06	.87	.04			
Kentucky	59.33	40.51	.09	.03	.04		
Louisiana	23.71	76.29					
Maine	68.63	30.96	.41				
Maryland	57.06	42.33	.32	.12	.17		
Massachusetts	49.15	50.24	.40	.16	.05		
Michigan	70.36	28.92	.26	.21	.06	.20	
Minnesota	57.77	40.83	.70	.50	.20		
Mississippi	17.90	82.10					
Missouri	55.58	44.15	.25		.02		
Montana	58.37	40.48	.86	.29			
Nebraska	63.19	36.18	.63				
Nevada	56.54	43.46					
New Hampshire	58.66	41.02	.23	.09			
New Jersey	59.77	39.79	.32	.08	.03	.01	
New Mexico	59.01	40.85		.13			
New York	49.79	47.44	2.44	.25	.10		
North Carolina	54.87	45.13					
North Dakota	54.80	44.46	.35	.39			
Ohio	64.89	34.45	.35	.11	.06	.14	
Oklahoma	63.72	35.44	.63				.21
Oregon	64.18	34.14	.85	.34	.49		
Pennsylvania	65.24	33.89	.59	.15	.01	.12	
Rhode Island	49.55	50.16		.12	.18		
South Carolina	8.54	91.39	.07				
South Dakota	60.18	39.20	.17	.09			.35
Tennessee	53.76	46.04	.17	.03			
Texas	51.77	48.10	.10	.03			
Utah	53.58	45.86	.54	.03			
Vermont	66.88	32.87				.25	
Virginia	53.91	45.90	.08	.06	.06		
Washington	67.06	31.30	.52	.31	.81		
West Virginia	58.43	41.04	.20	.06		.26	
Wisconsin	53.52	44.28	1.79	.15	.04	.22	
Wyoming	63.68	35.37	.95				
TOTALS	58.22	40.79	.73	.13	.06	.05	.02

The highest percentage for each candidate is underlined.

ELECTION OF 1932

Candidates were Franklin Delano Roosevelt, Democrat; Herbert Clark Hoover, Republican; Norman Mattoon Thomas, Socialist; William Zebulon Foster, Communist; William D. Upshaw, Prohibition; William Hope Harvey, Liberty; Verne L. Reynolds, Socialist-Labor; Jacob Seligman Coxey, Farmer-Labor; John Zahnd, National; and James R. Cox, Jobless. The Jacksonian Party also received votes.

Data pertaining to this election are from the official records on file in the National Archives.

Election of 1932

TABLE 39   Electoral and Popular Vote

States	Ro	Ho	Roosevelt	Hoover	Thomas	Foster	Upshaw
Alabama	11		207,910	34,675	2,030	406	13
Arizona	3		79,264	36,104	2,618	256	
Arkansas	9		189,602	28,467	1,269	175	
California	22		1,324,157	847,902	63,299	1,023	20,637
Colorado	6		250,877	189,617	13,591	787	1,928
Connecticut		8	281,632	288,420	20,480	1,364	
Delaware		3	54,319	57,073	1,376	133	
Florida	7		206,307	69,170	775		
Georgia	12		234,118	19,863	461	23	1,125
Idaho	4		109,479	71,312	526	491	
Illinois	29		1,882,304	1,432,756	67,258	15,582	6,388
Indiana	14		862,054	677,184	21,388	2,187	10,399
Iowa	11		598,019	414,433	20,467	559	2,111
Kansas	9		424,204	349,498	18,276		
Kentucky	11		580,574	394,716	3,853	272	2,252
Louisiana	10		249,418	18,853			
Maine		5	128,907	166,631	2,489	162	
Maryland	8		314,314	184,184	10,489	1,031	
Massachusetts	17		800,148	736,959	34,305	4,821	1,142
Michigan	19		871,700	739,894	39,205	9,318	2,893
Minnesota	11		600,806	363,959	25,476	6,101	
Mississippi	9		140,168	5,180	686		
Missouri	15		1,025,406	564,713	16,374	568	2,429
Montana	4		127,286	78,078	7,891	1,775	
Nebraska	7		359,082	201,177	9,876		
Nevada	3		28,756	12,674			
New Hampshire		4	100,680	103,629	947	264	
New Jersey	16		806,630	775,684	42,998	2,915	774
New Mexico	3		95,089	54,217	1,776	135	
New York	47		2,534,959	1,937,963	177,397	27,956	
North Carolina	13		497,566	208,344	5,591		
North Dakota	4		178,350	71,772	3,521	830	
Ohio	26		1,301,695	1,227,679	64,094	7,231	7,421
Oklahoma	11		516,468	188,165			
Oregon	5		213,871	136,019	15,450	1,681	
Pennsylvania		36	1,295,948	1,453,540	91,119	5,658	11,319
Rhode Island	4		146,604	115,266	3,138	546	183
South Carolina	8		102,347	1,978	82		
South Dakota	4		183,515	99,212	1,551	364	463
Tennessee	11		259,817	126,806	1,786	234	1,995
Texas	23		760,348	97,959	4,450	207	
Utah	4		116,750	84,795	4,087	947	
Vermont		3	56,266	78,984	1,533	195	
Virginia	11		203,979	89,637	2,382	86	1,843
Washington	8		353,260	208,645	17,080	2,972	1,540
West Virginia	8		405,124	330,731	5,133	444	2,342
Wisconsin	12		707,410	347,741	53,379	3,112	2,672
Wyoming	3		54,370	39,583	2,829	180	
TOTALS	472	59	22,821,857	15,761,841	884,781	102,991	81,869

91

1932	Electoral and Popular Vote (continued)					
States	Harvey	Reynolds	Coxey	Zahnd	Cox	Jackson
Alabama						
Arizona						
Arkansas	1,049					
California	9,827					
Colorado		427	469			
Connecticut		2,287				
Delaware						
Florida						
Georgia						
Idaho	4,712					
Illinois		3,638				
Indiana		2,070		1,645		
Iowa			1,094			
Kansas						
Kentucky		1,396				
Louisiana						
Maine		255				
Maryland		1,036				
Massachusetts		2,668				
Michigan	217	1,401				
Minnesota		770	5,731			
Mississippi						
Missouri		404				
Montana	1,449					
Nebraska						
Nevada						
New Hampshire						
New Jersey		1,062				
New Mexico	398					
New York		10,339				
North Carolina						
North Dakota	1,817					
Ohio		1,968				
Oklahoma						
Oregon		1,730				
Pennsylvania		659			725	
Rhode Island		433				
South Carolina						
South Dakota	3,333					
Tennessee						
Texas	324					104
Utah						
Vermont						
Virginia			15			
Washington	30,308	1,009				
West Virginia						
Wisconsin		494				
Wyoming						
TOTALS	53,434	34,046	7,309	1,645	725	104

Percentage of Popular Vote

States	Ro	Ho	T	F	U	Ha	Re	Coxey	Z	Cox	J
Alabama	84.85	14.15	.83	.17	.01						
Arizona	67.04	30.53	2.21	.22							
Arkansas	85.96	12.91	.58	.08		.48					
California	58.41	37.40	2.79	.05	.91	.43					
Colorado	54.81	41.43	2.97	.17	.42		.09	.10			
Connecticut	47.40	48.54	3.45	.23			.38				
Delaware	48.11	50.55	1.22	.12							
Florida	74.68	25.04	.28								
Georgia	91.60	7.77	.18	.01	.44						
Idaho	58.70	38.23	.28	.26		2.53					
Illinois	55.23	42.04	1.97	.46	.19		.11				
Indiana	54.67	42.94	1.36	.14	.66		.13		.10		
Iowa	57.69	39.98	1.97	.05	.20			.11			
Kansas	53.56	44.13	2.31								
Kentucky	59.06	40.15	.39	.03	.23		.14				
Louisiana	92.97	7.03									
Maine	43.19	55.83	.83	.05			.09				
Maryland	61.50	36.04	2.05	.20			.20				
Massachusetts	50.64	46.64	2.17	.31	.07		.17				
Michigan	52.37	44.45	2.36	.56	.17	.01	.08				
Minnesota	59.91	36.29	2.54	.61			.08		.57		
Mississippi	95.98	3.55	.47								
Missouri	63.69	35.08	1.02	.04	.15		.03				
Montana	58.80	36.07	3.65	.82		.67					
Nebraska	62.98	35.29	1.73								
Nevada	69.41	30.59									
New Hampshire	48.99	50.42	.46	.13							
New Jersey	49.48	47.59	2.64	.18	.05		.07				
New Mexico	62.72	35.76	1.17	.09		.26					
New York	54.07	41.33	3.78	.60			.22				
North Carolina	69.93	29.28	.79								
North Dakota	69.59	28.00	1.37	.32		.71					
Ohio	49.87	47.04	2.46	.28	.28		.08				
Oklahoma	73.30	26.70									
Oregon	58.00	36.89	4.19	.46			.47				
Pennsylvania	45.33	50.84	3.19	.20	.40		.02			.03	
Rhode Island	55.08	43.31	1.18	.21	.07		.16				
South Carolina	98.03	1.89	.08								
South Dakota	63.62	34.40	.54	.13	.16	1.16					
Tennessee	66.51	32.46	.46	.06	.51						
Texas	88.07	11.35	.52	.02		.04					.01
Utah	56.52	41.05	1.98	.46							
Vermont	41.08	57.66	1.12	.14							
Virginia	68.46	30.09	.80	.03	.62			.01			
Washington	57.46	33.94	2.78	.48	.25	4.93	.16				
West Virginia	54.47	44.47	.69	.06	.31						
Wisconsin	63.46	31.19	4.79	.28	.24		.04				
Wyoming	56.07	40.82	2.92	.19							
TOTALS	57.41	39.65	2.23	.26	.21	.13	.09	.02	.00	.00	.00

The highest percentage for each candidate is underlined.

".00" signifies that the candidate received some votes, but less than .01%.

Extended percentages nationally: Zahnd .00004%, Cox .00002%, Jacksonian Party .00000%.

Candidates were Franklin Delano Roosevelt, Democrat; Alfred Mossman Landon, Republican; William Lemke, Union; Norman Mattoon Thomas, Socialist; Earl Russell Browder, Communist; D. Leigh Colvin, Prohibition; John W. Aiken, Socialist-Labor; and William Dudley Pelley, Christian.

Data pertaining to this election are from the official records on file in the National Archives with these exceptions:

From *Statistics of the Congressional Election of November 3, 1936:* Arkansas—Lemke; North Carolina—Thomas and Browder; Ohio—Thomas and Aiken; Oregon—Browder and Colvin.

From *World Almanac:* North Carolina—Lemke.

Election of 1936

TABLE 40 | Electoral and Popular Vote

States	R	La	Roosevelt	Landon	Lemke	Thomas	Browder	Colvin	Aiken	Pelley
Alabama	11		238,196	35,358	551	242	678	719		
Arizona	3		86,722	33,433	3,307	317		384		
Arkansas	9		146,765	32,039	4	446	169			
California	22		1,766,836	836,431		11,331	10,877	12,917		
Colorado	6		295,021	181,267	9,962	1,593	497		344	
Connecticut	8		382,129	278,685	21,805	5,683	1,193		1,228	
Delaware	3		69,702	54,014	442	172	51			
Florida	7		249,117	78,248		775				
Georgia	12		255,364	36,942	141	68		663		
Idaho	4		125,683	66,256	7,684					
Illinois	29		2,282,999	1,570,393	89,439	7,530	801	3,439	1,921	
Indiana	14		934,974	691,570	19,407	3,856	1,090			
Iowa	11		621,756	487,977	29,687	1,373	506	1,182	252	
Kansas	9		464,520	397,727	494	2,766				
Kentucky	11		541,944	369,702	12,501	632	204	929	294	
Louisiana	10		292,894	36,791						
Maine		5	126,333	168,823	7,581	783	257	334	129	
Maryland	8		389,612	231,435		1,629	915		1,305	
Massachusetts	17		942,716	768,613	118,639	5,111	2,930	1,032	1,305	
Michigan	19		1,016,794	699,733	75,795	8,208	3,384	579	600	
Minnesota	11		698,811	350,461	74,296	2,872	2,574		961	
Mississippi	9		157,318	4,443		329				
Missouri	15		1,111,043	697,891	14,630	3,454	417	908	292	
Montana	4		159,690	63,598	5,549	1,066	385	224		
Nebraska	7		347,454	247,731	12,847					
Nevada	3		31,925	11,923						
New Hampshire	4		108,460	104,642	4,819		193			
New Jersey	16		1,083,850	720,322	9,407	3,931	1,639	926	362	
New Mexico	3		106,037	61,727	924	343	43	62		
New York	47		3,293,222	2,180,670		86,897	35,610			
North Carolina	13		616,141	223,283	2	21	11			
North Dakota	4		163,148	72,751	36,708	552	360	197		
Ohio	26		1,747,222	1,127,709	132,212	117	5,251		14	
Oklahoma	11		501,069	245,122		2,221		1,328		
Oregon	5		266,733	122,706	21,831	2,143	104	4	500	
Pennsylvania	36		2,353,788	1,690,300	67,467	14,375	4,060	6,691	1,424	
Rhode Island	4		165,238	125,031	19,569		411		929	
South Carolina	8		113,791	1,646						
South Dakota	4		160,137	125,977	10,338					
Tennessee	11		327,083	146,516	296	687	319	632		
Texas	23		734,485	103,874	3,281	1,075	253	514		
Utah	4		150,246	64,555	1,129	432	280	43		
Vermont		3	62,124	81,023			405			
Virginia	11		234,980	98,336	233	313	98	594	36	
Washington	8		459,579	206,892	17,463	3,496	1,907	1,041	362	1,598
West Virginia	8		502,582	325,358		832		1,173		
Wisconsin	12		802,984	380,828	60,297	10,626	2,197	1,071	557	
Wyoming	3		62,624	38,739	1,653	200	91	75		
TOTALS	523	8	27,751,841	16,679,491	892,390	188,497	80,160	37,661	12,815	1,598

1936 — Percentage of Popular Vote

States	R	La	Le	T	B	C	A	P
Alabama	86.38	12.82	.20	.09	.25	.26		
Arizona	69.85	26.93	2.66	.26		.31		
Arkansas	81.80	17.86	.00	.25	.09			
California	66.97	31.70		.43	.41	.49		
Colorado	60.37	37.09	2.04	.33	.10		.07	
Connecticut	55.32	40.35	3.16	.82	.17		.18	
Delaware	56.04	43.43	.36	.14	.04			
Florida	75.91	23.85		.24				
Georgia	87.10	12.60	.05	.02		.23		
Idaho	62.96	33.19	3.85					
Illinois	57.70	39.69	2.26	.19	.02	.09	.05	
Indiana	56.63	41.89	1.18	.23	.07			
Iowa	54.41	42.70	2.60	.12	.04	.10	.02	
Kansas	53.67	45.95	.06	.32				
Kentucky	58.51	39.92	1.35	.07	.02	.10	.03	
Louisiana	88.84	11.16						
Maine	41.52	55.49	2.49	.26	.08	.11	.04	
Maryland	62.35	37.04		.26	.15		.21	
Massachusetts	51.22	41.76	6.45	.28	.16	.06	.07	
Michigan	56.33	38.76	4.20	.45	.19	.03	.03	
Minnesota	61.84	31.01	6.58	.25	.23		.09	
Mississippi	97.06	2.74		.20				
Missouri	60.76	38.16	.80	.19	.02	.05	.02	
Montana	69.28	27.59	2.41	.46	.17	.09		
Nebraska	57.14	40.74	2.11					
Nevada	72.81	27.19						
New Hampshire	49.73	47.98	2.21		.09			
New Jersey	59.54	39.57	.52	.22	.09	.05	.02	
New Mexico	62.69	36.50	.55	.20	.03	.04		
New York	58.85	38.97		1.55	.64			
North Carolina	73.40	26.60	.00	.00	.00			
North Dakota	59.60	26.58	13.41	.20	.13	.07		
Ohio	58.00	37.43	4.39	.00	.17		.00	
Oklahoma	66.83	32.69		.30		.18		
Oregon	64.42	29.64	5.27	.52	.03	.00	.12	
Pennsylvania	56.88	40.85	1.63	.35	.10	.16	.03	
Rhode Island	53.10	40.18	6.29		.13		.30	
South Carolina	98.57	1.43						
South Dakota	54.02	42.49	3.49					
Tennessee	68.78	30.81	.06	.14	.07	.13		
Texas	87.08	12.31	.39	.13	.03	.06		
Utah	69.34	29.79	.52	.20	.13	.02		
Vermont	43.28	56.44			.28			
Virginia	70.23	29.39	.07	.09	.03	.18	.01	
Washington	66.38	29.88	2.52	.50	.28	.15	.05	.23
West Virginia	60.56	39.20		.10		.14		
Wisconsin	63.80	30.26	4.79	.84	.17	.09	.04	
Wyoming	60.58	37.47	1.60	.19	.09	.07		
TOTALS	60.80	36.54	1.96	.41	.18	.08	.03	.00

The highest percentage for each candidate is underlined.

".00" signifies that the candidate received some votes, but less than .01%.

Candidates were Franklin Delano Roosevelt, Democrat; Wendell Lewis Willkie, Republican; Norman Mattoon Thomas, Socialist; Roger Ward Babson, Prohibition; Earl Russell Browder, Communist; John W. Aiken, Socialist-Labor; and Alfred Knutson, Independent.

Data pertaining to this election are from the official records on file in the National Archives, with these exceptions:

Arkansas—Roosevelt and Willkie from *Abstract,* Thomas from *World Almanac.*

North Carolina and Oregon—all from *Statistics of the Presidential and Congressional Election of November 5, 1940.*

The figures below show how a switch of 433,940 votes out of the 49,576,516 cast for Roosevelt and Willkie—.88%—would have made the latter president:

States	Willkie	Roosevelt	Shift
	82	449	
New York	47	-47	112,221
Illinois	29	-29	51,348
Ohio	26	-26	73,184
New Jersey	16	-16	35,856
Missouri	15	-15	43,733
Wisconsin	12	-12	12,808
Minnesota	11	-11	23,962
Connecticut	8	- 8	27,902
Oregon	5	- 5	19,431
New Hampshire	4	- 4	7,583
Idaho	4	- 4	10,645
Wyoming	3	- 3	3,328
Nevada	3	- 3	5,359
Delaware	3	- 3	6,580
	268	263	433,940

In the following tabulation, the nominees for electors are ranked according to the number of votes they received:

States	Willkie	Roosevelt	Shift	
New York	3,027,478	3,251,918	112,221	(1 elector)
	3,027,478	3,251,917	112,220	(16 electors)
	3,027,478	3,251,916	112,220	(13 electors)
	3,027,477	3,251,916	112,220	(16 electors)
	3,027,476	3,251,915	112,220	(1 elector)
New Jersey	945,475	1,016,808	35,667	
	945,359	1,016,714	35,678	
	945,290	1,016,676	35,694	
	945,285	1,016,541	35,629	
	945,283	1,016,535	35,627	
	945,201	1,016,458	35,629	
	944,810	1,016,400	35,796	
	944,761	1,016,394	35,817	
	944,674	1,016,376	35,852	
	944,629	1,016,339	35,856	
	944,592	1,016,283	35,846	
	944,588	1,016,280	35,847	
	944,588	1,016,270	35,842	
	944,579	1,016,177	35,800	
	944,484	1,016,168	35,843	
	944,472	1,016,103	35,816	
Idaho	106,553	127,842	10,645	
	106,509	127,626	10,559	
	106,397	127,608	10,606	
	106,351	127,418	10,534	
Delaware	61,440	74,599	6,580	
	60,971	73,521	6,276	
	60,938	73,424	6,244	

In the other ten states, each candidate for elector received the same number of votes as his colleagues on the Democratic or Republican ticket.

TABLE 41 Electoral and Popular Vote

States	R	W	Roosevelt	Willkie	Thomas	Babson	Browder	Aiken	Knutson
Alabama	11		250,726	42,184	100	700	509		
Arizona	3		95,267	54,030		742			
Arkansas	9		158,622	42,121	305	793			
California	22		1,877,618	1,351,419	16,506	9,400	13,586		
Colorado		6	265,554	279,576	1,899	1,597	378		
Connecticut	8		417,621	361,819			1,091	971	
Delaware	3		74,599	61,440	115	220			
Florida	7		359,334	126,158					
Georgia	12		265,194	46,376		1,003			
Idaho	4		127,842	106,553	497		276		
Illinois	29		2,149,934	2,047,240	10,914	9,190			
Indiana		14	874,063	899,466	2,075	6,437		706	
Iowa		11	578,800	632,370		2,284	1,524	452	
Kansas		9	364,725	489,169	2,347	4,056			
Kentucky	11		557,222	410,384	1,014	1,443			
Louisiana	10		319,751	52,446					
Maine		5	156,478	163,951			411		
Maryland	8		384,546	269,534	4,093		1,274	657	
Massachusetts	17		1,076,522	939,700	4,091	1,370	3,806	1,492	
Michigan		19	1,032,991	1,039,917	7,593	1,795	2,834	795	
Minnesota	11		644,196	596,274	5,454		2,711	2,553	
Mississippi	9		168,267	7,364	193				
Missouri	15		958,476	871,009	2,226	1,809		209	
Montana	4		145,698	99,579	1,443	664	489		
Nebraska		7	263,677	352,201					
Nevada	3		31,945	21,229					
New Hampshire	4		125,292	110,127					
New Jersey	16		1,016,808	945,475	2,433	873	6,508	455	
New Mexico	3		103,699	79,315	144	100			
New York	47		3,251,918	3,027,478	18,950	3,250			
North Carolina	13		609,015	213,633					
North Dakota		4	124,036	154,590	1,279	325			545
Ohio	26		1,733,139	1,586,773					
Oklahoma	11		474,313	348,872		3,027			
Oregon	5		258,415	219,555	398	154	191	2,487	
Pennsylvania	36		2,171,035	1,889,848	10,967		4,519	1,518	
Rhode Island	4		181,122	138,214		74	239		
South Carolina	8		95,470	4,360					
South Dakota		4	131,362	177,065					
Tennessee	11		351,601	169,186	463	1,606			
Texas	23		840,151	199,152	728	925	212		
Utah	4		154,277	93,151	200		191		
Vermont		3	64,269	78,371			411		
Virginia	11		235,961	109,363	282	882	71	48	
Washington	8		462,145	322,123	4,586	1,686	2,626	667	
West Virginia	8		495,662	372,414					
Wisconsin	12		704,821	679,206	15,071	2,148	2,394	1,882	
Wyoming	3		59,287	52,633	148	172			
TOTALS	449	82	27,243,466	22,334,413	116,514	58,725	46,251	14,892	545

Percentage of Popular Vote

States	R	W	T	Ba	Br	A	K
Alabama	85.22	14.34	.03	.24	.17		
Arizona	63.49	36.01		.49			
Arkansas	78.59	20.87	.15	.39			
California	57.45	41.35	.50	.29	.42		
Colorado	48.37	50.92	.35	.29	.07		
Connecticut	53.44	46.30			.14	.12	
Delaware	54.70	45.05	.08	.16			
Florida	74.01	25.99					
Georgia	84.84	14.84		.32			
Idaho	54.36	45.31	.21		.12		
Illinois	50.98	48.54	.26	.22			
Indiana	49.03	50.45	.12	.36		.04	
Iowa	47.62	52.03		.19	.13	.04	
Kansas	42.40	56.86	.27	.47			
Kentucky	57.44	42.30	.10	.15			
Louisiana	85.91	14.09					
Maine	48.77	51.10			.13		
Maryland	58.26	40.83	.62		.19	.10	
Massachusetts	53.11	46.36	.20	.07	.19	.07	
Michigan	49.52	49.85	.36	.09	.14	.04	
Minnesota	51.49	47.66	.44		.22	.20	
Mississippi	95.70	4.19	.11				
Missouri	52.27	47.50	.12	.10		.01	
Montana	58.78	40.17	.58	.27	.20		
Nebraska	42.81	57.19					
Nevada	60.08	39.92					
New Hampshire	53.22	46.78					
New Jersey	51.55	47.93	.12	.04	.33	.02	
New Mexico	56.59	43.28	.08	.05			
New York	51.60	48.04	.30	.05			
North Carolina	74.03	25.97					
North Dakota	44.18	55.06	.46	.12			.19
Ohio	52.20	47.80					
Oklahoma	57.41	42.23		.37			
Oregon	53.70	45.63	.08	.03	.04	.52	
Pennsylvania	53.24	46.34	.27		.11	.04	
Rhode Island	56.66	43.24		.02	.07		
South Carolina	95.63	4.37					
South Dakota	42.59	57.41					
Tennessee	67.25	32.36	.09	.31			
Texas	80.69	19.13	.07	.09	.02		
Utah	62.25	37.59	.08		.08		
Vermont	44.93	54.79			.29		
Virginia	68.08	31.55	.08	.25	.02	.01	
Washington	58.22	40.58	.58	.21	.33	.08	
West Virginia	57.10	42.90					
Wisconsin	50.15	48.32	1.07	.15	.17	.13	
Wyoming	52.83	46.89	.13	.15			
TOTALS	54.69	44.83	.23	.12	.09	.03	.00

The highest percentage for each candidate is underlined.

".00" signifies that the candidate received some votes, but less than .01%.

ELECTION OF 1944

Candidates were Franklin Delano Roosevelt, Democrat; Thomas Edmund Dewey, Republican; Norman Mattoon Thomas, Socialist; Claude A. Watson, Prohibition; Edward A. Teichert, Socialist-Labor; Harry Flood Byrd, Southern Democrat; and Gerald L. K. Smith, America First. The Texas Regulars also received votes.

Data pertaining to this election are from the official records on file in the National Archives, with these exceptions:

From *Statistics of the Presidential and Congressional Election of November 7, 1944:* Illinois and New Hampshire—Thomas; Kentucky—Thomas, Watson, and Teichert.

The following figures show how a switch of 303,193 votes out of the 47,630,044 cast for Roosevelt and Dewey—.64%—would have made the latter president:

States	Dewey	Roosevelt	Shift
	99	432	
Pennsylvania	35	-35	52,716
Illinois	28	-28	70,083
Michigan	19	-19	11,239
New Jersey	16	-16	13,270
Massachusetts	16	-16	56,974
Missouri	15	-15	23,092
Minnesota	11	-11	31,225
Maryland	8	- 8	11,271
Connecticut	8	- 8	22,310
Idaho	4	- 4	3,632
New Hampshire	4	- 4	4,874
Nevada	3	- 3	2,507
	266	265	303,193

TABLE 42   Electoral and Popular Vote

States	R	D	Roosevelt	Dewey	Regulars	Thomas	Watson	Teichert	Byrd	Smith
Alabama	11		198,918	44,540		190	1,095			
Arizona	4		80,926	56,287			421			
Arkansas	9		148,965	63,551		438				
California	25		1,988,564	1,512,965		2,515	14,770	180		
Colorado		6	234,331	268,731		1,977				
Connecticut	8		435,146	390,527		5,097		1,220		
Delaware	3		68,166	56,747		154	294			
Florida	8		339,377	143,215						
Georgia	12		268,187	59,879			36			
Idaho	4		107,399	100,137		282	503			
Illinois	28		2,079,479	1,939,314		180	7,411	9,677		
Indiana		13	781,403	875,891		2,223	12,574			
Iowa		10	499,876	547,267		1,511	3,752	193		
Kansas		8	287,458	442,096		1,613	2,609			
Kentucky	11		472,589	392,448		535	2,023	326		
Louisiana	10		281,564	67,750						
Maine		5	140,631	155,434				335		
Maryland	8		315,490	292,949						
Massachusetts	16		1,035,296	921,350			973	2,780		1,530
Michigan	19		1,106,899	1,084,423		4,598	6,503	1,264		
Minnesota	11		589,864	527,416		5,073		3,176		
Mississippi	9		168,479	11,601						
Missouri	15		807,357	761,175		1,750	1,175	221		
Montana	4		112,556	93,163		1,296	340			
Nebraska		6	233,246	329,880						
Nevada	3		29,623	24,611						
New Hampshire	4		119,663	109,916		46				
New Jersey	16		987,874	961,335		3,358	4,255	6,939		
New Mexico	4		81,389	70,688			148			
New York	47		3,304,238	2,987,647		10,553		14,352		
North Carolina	14		527,399	263,155						
North Dakota		4	100,144	118,535		943	549			
Ohio		25	1,570,763	1,582,293						
Oklahoma	10		401,549	319,424			1,663			
Oregon	6		248,635	225,365		3,785	2,362			
Pennsylvania	35		1,940,479	1,835,048		11,721	5,750	1,789		
Rhode Island	4		175,356	123,487			433			
South Carolina	8		90,606	4,610			365		7,799	
South Dakota		4	96,711	135,362						
Tennessee	12		308,707	200,311		792	885			
Texas	23		821,605	191,425	135,439	594	1,017			251
Utah	4		150,088	97,891		340				
Vermont		3	53,820	71,527						
Virginia	11		242,276	145,243		417	459	90		
Washington	8		486,774	361,689		3,824	2,396	1,645		
West Virginia	8		392,777	322,819						
Wisconsin		12	650,413	674,532		13,205		1,002		
Wyoming		3	49,419	51,921						
TOTALS	432	99	25,612,474	22,017,570	135,439	79,010	74,761	45,189	7,799	1,781

Percentage of Popular Vote

States	R	D	Regs.	Th	W	Te	B	S
Alabama	81.28	18.20		.08	.45			
Arizona	58.80	40.90			.31			
Arkansas	69.95	29.84		.21				
California	56.51	42.99		.07	.42	.01		
Colorado	46.40	53.21		.39				
Connecticut	52.30	46.94		.61		.15		
Delaware	54.38	45.27		.12	.23			
Florida	70.32	29.68						
Georgia	81.74	18.25			.01			
Idaho	51.55	48.07		.14	.24			
Illinois	51.52	48.05		.00	.18	.24		
Indiana	46.73	52.38		.13	.75			
Iowa	47.49	51.99		.14	.36	.02		
Kansas	39.18	60.25		.22	.36			
Kentucky	54.45	45.22		.06	.23	.04		
Louisiana	80.60	19.40						
Maine	47.45	52.44				.11		
Maryland	51.85	48.15						
Massachusetts	52.81	47.00			.05	.14		
Michigan	50.19	49.18		.21	.29	.06		.07
Minnesota	52.41	46.86		.45		.28		
Mississippi	93.56	6.44						
Missouri	51.37	48.43		.11	.07	.01		
Montana	54.28	44.93		.63	.16			
Nebraska	41.42	58.58						
Nevada	54.62	45.38						
New Hampshire	52.11	47.87		.02				
New Jersey	50.31	48.95		.17	.22	.35		
New Mexico	53.47	46.44			.10			
New York	52.31	47.30		.17		.23		
North Carolina	66.71	33.29						
North Dakota	45.48	53.84		.43	.25			
Ohio	49.82	50.18						
Oklahoma	55.57	44.20			.23			
Oregon	51.78	46.94		.79	.49			
Pennsylvania	51.14	48.36		.31	.15	.05		
Rhode Island	58.59	41.26			.14			
South Carolina	87.64	4.46			.35		7.54	
South Dakota	41.67	58.33						
Tennessee	60.45	39.22		.16	.17			
Texas	71.42	16.64	11.77	.05	.09			.02
Utah	60.44	39.42		.14				
Vermont	42.94	57.06						
Virginia	62.36	37.39		.11	.12	.02		
Washington	56.84	42.24		.45	.28	.19		
West Virginia	54.89	45.11						
Wisconsin	48.57	50.37		.99		.07		
Wyoming	48.77	51.23						
TOTALS	53.39	45.89	.28	.16	.16	.09	.02	.00

The highest percentage for each candidate is underlined.

".00" signifies that the candidate received some votes, but less than .01%.

Extended percentages nationally: Thomas .165%, Watson .156%.

ELECTION OF 1948

Candidates were Harry S. Truman, Democrat; Thomas Edmund Dewey, Republican; James Strom Thurmond, States' Rights Democrat; Henry Agard Wallace, Progressive; Norman Mattoon Thomas, Socialist; Claude A. Watson, Prohibition; Edward A. Teichert, Socialist-Labor; and Farrell Dobbs, Socialist-Workers.

Data pertaining to this election are from the official records on file in the National Archives, with these exceptions:

From *Statistics of the Presidential and Congressional Election of November 2, 1948:* Arkansas and South Carolina—Thomas; Florida—Thurmond.

The following figures show how a switch of 29,294 votes out of the 46,075,034 cast for Truman and Dewey—.06%—would have made the latter president:

States	Dewey	Truman	Shift
	189	303	
Illinois	28	-28	16,807
California	25	-25	8,933
Ohio	25	-25	3,554
	267	225	29,294

A switch of only the California and Ohio votes shown, 12,487, would have prevented Truman's election without giving Dewey the victory, as a decision by the House of Representatives would have become necessary. Truman would still have led, 253 to 239, with Thurmond's 39 representing the balance of power.

TABLE 43   Electoral and Popular Vote

States	Tr	De	Th	Truman	Dewey	Thurmond	Wallace
Alabama			11		40,930	171,443	1,522
Arizona	4			95,251	77,597		3,310
Arkansas	9			149,659	50,959	40,068	751
California	25			1,913,134	1,895,269	1,228	190,381
Colorado	6			267,288	239,714		6,115
Connecticut		8		423,297	437,754		13,713
Delaware		3		67,813	69,588		1,050
Florida	8			281,988	194,280	89,755	11,620
Georgia	12			254,646	76,691	85,055	1,636
Idaho	4			107,370	101,514		4,972
Illinois	28			1,994,715	1,961,103		
Indiana		13		807,833	821,079		9,649
Iowa	10			522,380	494,018		12,125
Kansas		8		351,902	423,039		4,603
Kentucky	11			466,756	341,210	10,411	1,567
Louisiana			10	136,344	72,657	204,290	3,035
Maine		5		111,916	150,234		1,884
Maryland		8		286,521	294,814	2,476	9,983
Massachusetts	16			1,151,788	909,370		38,157
Michigan		19		1,003,448	1,038,595		46,515
Minnesota	11			692,966	483,617		27,866
Mississippi			9	19,384	5,043	167,538	225
Missouri	15			917,315	655,039		3,998
Montana	4			119,071	96,770		7,313
Nebraska		6		224,165	264,774		
Nevada	3			31,291	29,357		1,469
New Hampshire		4		107,995	121,299	7	1,970
New Jersey		16		895,455	981,124		42,683
New Mexico	4			105,464	80,303		1,037
New York		47		2,780,204	2,841,163		509,559
North Carolina	14			459,070	258,572	69,652	3,915
North Dakota		4		95,812	115,139	374	8,391
Ohio	25			1,452,791	1,445,684		37,596
Oklahoma	10			452,782	268,817		
Oregon		6		243,147	260,904		14,978
Pennsylvania		35		1,752,426	1,902,197		55,161
Rhode Island	4			188,736	135,791		2,605
South Carolina			8	34,423	5,386	102,607	154
South Dakota		4		117,653	129,651		2,801
Tennessee	11		1	270,412	202,924	73,826	1,866
Texas	23			750,700	282,240	106,909	3,764
Utah	4			147,359	125,327		2,582
Vermont		3		45,557	75,926		1,279
Virginia	11			200,786	172,070	43,393	2,047
Washington	8			476,165	386,315		31,692
West Virginia	8			429,188	316,251		3,311
Wisconsin	12			647,310	590,959		25,282
Wyoming	3			52,354	47,947		931
TOTALS	303	189	39	24,104,030	21,971,004	1,169,032	1,157,063

States	Thomas	Watson	Teichert	Dobbs
Alabama		1,085		
Arizona		786	121	
Arkansas	1,037·	1		
California	3,459	16,926	195	133
Colorado	1,678		214	228
Connecticut	6,964		1,184	606
Delaware	250	343	29	
Florida				
Georgia		732		
Idaho	332	628		
Illinois	11,522	11,959	3,118	
Indiana	2,179	14,711	763	
Iowa	1,829	3,382	4,274	256
Kansas	2,807	6,468		
Kentucky	1,284	1,245	185	
Louisiana				
Maine	547		206	
Maryland	2,941			
Massachusetts		1,663	5,535	
Michigan	6,063	13,052	1,263	672
Minnesota	4,646		2,525	606
Mississippi				
Missouri	2,222			
Montana	695	429		
Nebraska				
Nevada				
New Hampshire	86		83	
New Jersey	10,521	10,593	3,354	5,825
New Mexico	83	127	49	
New York	40,879		2,729	2,675
North Carolina				
North Dakota	1,000			
Ohio				
Oklahoma				
Oregon	5,051			
Pennsylvania	11,325	10,338	1,461	2,133
Rhode Island	428		130	
South Carolina	1			
South Dakota				
Tennessee	1,291			
Texas	874	2,758		
Utah				71
Vermont	585			
Virginia	726		234	
Washington	3,534	6,117	1,133	103
West Virginia				
Wisconsin	12,547		399	303
Wyoming	137		56	
TOTALS	139,523	103,343	29,240	13,611

1948   Percentage of Popular Vote

States	Tr	De	Thu	Wal	Tho	Wat	Te	Do
Alabama		19.04	79.75	.71		.50		
Arizona	53.79	43.82		1.87		.44	.07	
Arkansas	61.72	21.02	16.52	.31	.43	.00		
California	47.58	47.14	.03	4.73	.09	.42	.00	.00
Colorado	51.88	46.52		1.19	.33		.04	.04
Connecticut	47.91	49.55		1.55	.79		.13	.07
Delaware	48.76	50.04		.75	.18	.25	.02	
Florida	48.82	33.63	15.54	2.01				
Georgia	60.81	18.31	20.31	.39		.17		
Idaho	49.98	47.26		2.31	.15	.29		
Illinois	50.09	49.24			.29	.30	.08	
Indiana	48.78	49.58		.58	.13	.89	.05	
Iowa	50.31	47.58		1.17	.18	.33	.41	.02
Kansas	44.61	53.63		.58	.36	.82		
Kentucky	56.74	41.48	1.27	.19	.16	.15	.02	
Louisiana	32.75	17.45	49.07	.73				
Maine	42.27	56.74		.71	.21		.08	
Maryland	48.01	49.40	.41	1.67	.49			
Massachusetts	54.68	43.17		1.81		.08	.26	
Michigan	47.57	49.23		2.20	.29	.62	.06	.03
Minnesota	57.16	39.89		2.30	.38		.21	.05
Mississippi	10.09	2.62	87.17	.12				
Missouri	58.11	41.50		.25	.14			
Montana	53.09	43.15		3.26	.31	.19		
Nebraska	45.85	54.15						
Nevada	50.37	47.26		2.36				
New Hampshire	46.66	52.41	.00	.85	.04		.04	
New Jersey	45.93	50.33		2.19	.54	.54	.17	.30
New Mexico	56.38	42.93		.55	.04	.07	.03	
New York	45.01	45.99		8.25	.66		.04	.04
North Carolina	58.02	32.68	8.80	.49				
North Dakota	43.41	52.17	.17	3.80	.45			
Ohio	49.48	49.24		1.28				
Oklahoma	62.75	37.25						
Oregon	46.40	49.78		2.86	.96			
Pennsylvania	46.92	50.93		1.48	.30	.28	.04	.06
Rhode Island	57.60	41.44		.79	.13		.04	
South Carolina	24.14	3.78	71.97	.11	.00			
South Dakota	47.04	51.84		1.12				
Tennessee	49.14	36.87	13.42	.34	.23			
Texas	65.44	24.60	9.32	.33	.08	.24		
Utah	53.52	45.52		.94				.03
Vermont	36.93	61.55		1.04	.47		•	
Virginia	47.89	41.04	10.35	.49	.17		.06	
Washington	52.61	42.68		3.50	.39	.68	.13	.01
West Virginia	57.32	42.24		.44				
Wisconsin	50.70	46.28		1.98	.98		.03	.02
Wyoming	51.62	47.27		.92	.14		.06	
TOTALS	49.51	45.13	2.40	2.38	.29	.21	.06	.03

The highest percentage for each candidate is underlined.

".00" signifies that the candidate received some votes, but less than .01%.

ELECTION OF 1952

Candidates were Dwight David Eisenhower, Republican; Adlai Ewing Stevenson, Democrat; Vincent Hallinan, Progressive; Stuart Hamblen, Prohibition; Eric Hass, Socialist-Labor; Darlington Hoopes, Socialist; Douglas MacArthur, Constitution; Farrell Dobbs, Socialist-Workers; and Henry Krajewski, Poor Man's.

Data pertaining to this election are from the official records on file in the National Archives, with these exceptions, which are from *Statistics of the Presidential and Congressional Election of November 4, 1952:*

Arkansas, Nebraska, Ohio, and Vermont—All.

Georgia—Stevenson.

South Carolina—Hamblen.

Election of 1952

TABLE 44 — Electoral and Popular Vote

States	E	S	Eisenhower	Stevenson	Hallinan	Hamblen	Hass
Alabama		11	149,231	275,075		1,814	
Arizona	4		152,042	108,528			
Arkansas		8	177,155	226,300		886	1
California	32		2,897,310	2,197,548	24,106	15,653	273
Colorado	6		379,782	245,504	1,919		352
Connecticut	8		611,012	481,649	1,466		535
Delaware	3		90,059	83,315	155	234	242
Florida	10		544,036	444,950			
Georgia		12	198,979	456,823			
Idaho	4		180,707	95,081	443		
Illinois	27		2,457,327	2,013,920			9,363
Indiana	13		1,136,259	801,530	1,222	15,335	979
Iowa	10		808,906	451,513	5,085	2,882	139
Kansas	8		616,302	273,296		6,038	
Kentucky		10	495,029	495,729	336	1,161	893
Louisiana		10	306,925	345,027			
Maine	5		232,353	118,806	332		156
Maryland	9		499,424	395,337	7,313		
Massachusetts	16		1,292,325	1,083,525	4,636	886	1,957
Michigan	20		1,551,529	1,230,657	3,922	10,331	1,495
Minnesota	11		763,211	608,458	2,666	2,147	2,383
Mississippi		8	112,966	172,566			
Missouri	13		959,429	929,830	987	885	169
Montana	4		157,394	106,213	723	548	
Nebraska	6		421,603	188,057			
Nevada	3		50,502	31,688			
New Hampshire	4		166,287	106,663			
New Jersey	16		1,374,613	1,015,902	5,589	989	5,815
New Mexico	4		132,170	105,661	225	297	35
New York	45		3,952,815	3,104,601	64,211		1,560
North Carolina		14	558,107	652,803			
North Dakota	4		191,712	76,694	344	302	
Ohio	25		2,100,391	1,600,367			
Oklahoma	8		518,045	430,939			
Oregon	6		420,815	270,579	3,665		
Pennsylvania	32		2,415,789	2,146,269	4,200	8,771	1,347
Rhode Island	4		210,935	203,293	187		83
South Carolina		8	168,082	173,004		1	
South Dakota	4		203,857	90,426			
Tennessee	11		446,147	443,710	925	1,441	
Texas	24		1,102,878	969,228	294	1,983	
Utah	4		194,190	135,364			
Vermont	3		109,717	43,355	282		
Virginia	12		349,037	268,677	311		1,160
Washington	9		599,107	492,845	2,460		633
West Virginia		8	419,970	453,578			
Wisconsin	12		979,744	622,175	2,174		770
Wyoming	3		81,047	47,934		194	36
TOTALS	442	89	33,937,252	27,314,992	140,178	72,778	30,376

1952 **Electoral and Popular Vote** (continued)

States	Hoopes	MacArthur	Dobbs	Krajewski
Alabama				
Arizona				
Arkansas		458		
California	206	3,504		
Colorado	365	2,181		
Connecticut	2,244			
Delaware	20			
Florida				
Georgia				
Idaho				
Illinois				
Indiana				
Iowa	219			
Kansas	530			
Kentucky				
Louisiana				
Maine	138			
Maryland				
Massachusetts				
Michigan			655	
Minnesota			618	
Mississippi				
Missouri	227	535		
Montana	159			
Nebraska				
Nevada				
New Hampshire				
New Jersey	8,593		3,850	4,203
New Mexico		220		
New York	2,664		2,212	
North Carolina				
North Dakota		1,075		
Ohio				
Oklahoma				
Oregon				
Pennsylvania	2,684		1,502	
Rhode Island				
South Carolina				
South Dakota				
Tennessee		379		
Texas		1,563		
Utah				
Vermont	185			
Virginia	504			
Washington	254	7,290	119	
West Virginia				
Wisconsin	1,157		1,350	
Wyoming	40			
TOTALS	20,189	17,205	10,306	4,203

1952 — Percentage of Popular Vote

States	E	S	Hal	Ham	Has	Ho	Mac	D	K
Alabama	35.02	64.55		.43					
Arizona	58.35	41.65							
Arkansas	43.76	55.90		.22	.00		.11		
California	56.39	42.77	.47	.30	.01	.00	.07		
Colorado	60.27	38.96	.30		.06	.06	.35		
Connecticut	55.70	43.91	.13		.05	.22			
Delaware	51.75	47.88	.09	.13	.14	.01			
Florida	55.01	44.99							
Georgia	30.34	_69.66_							
Idaho	65.42	34.42	.16						
Illinois	54.84	44.95			.21				
Indiana	58.11	40.99	.06	_.78_	.05				
Iowa	63.76	35.59	.40	.23	.01	.02			
Kansas	68.77	30.50		.67		.06			
Kentucky	49.84	49.91	.03	.12	.09				
Louisiana	47.08	52.92							
Maine	66.05	33.77	.09		.04	.04			
Maryland	55.36	43.83	.81						
Massachusetts	54.22	45.46	.19	.04	.08				
Michigan	55.44	43.97	.14	.37	.05			.02	
Minnesota	55.33	44.11	.19	.16	.17			.04	
Mississippi	39.56	60.44							
Missouri	50.71	49.14	.05	.05	.01	.01	.03		
Montana	59.39	40.07	.27	.21		.06			
Nebraska	69.15	30.85							
Nevada	61.45	38.55							
New Hampshire	60.92	39.08							
New Jersey	56.81	41.99	.23	.04	_.24_	_.36_		_.16_	_.17_
New Mexico	55.39	44.28	.09	.12	.01		.09		
New York	55.45	43.55	_.90_		.02	.04		.03	
North Carolina	46.09	53.91							
North Dakota	70.97	28.39	.13	.11			.40		
Ohio	56.76	43.24							
Oklahoma	54.59	45.41							
Oregon	60.54	38.93	.53						
Pennsylvania	52.74	46.86	.09	.19	.03	.06		.03	
Rhode Island	50.89	49.05	.05		.02				
South Carolina	49.28	50.72		.00					
South Dakota	69.27	30.73							
Tennessee	49.98	49.71	.10	.16			.04		
Texas	53.13	46.69	.01	.10			.08		
Utah	58.93	41.07							
Vermont	_71.46_	28.24	.18			.12			
Virginia	56.32	43.36	.05		.19	.08			
Washington	54.33	44.69	.22		.06	.02	_.66_	.01	
West Virginia	48.08	51.92							
Wisconsin	60.95	38.71	.14		.05	.07		.08	
Wyoming	62.71	37.09		.15	.03	.03			
TOTALS	55.14	44.38	.23	.12	.05	.03	.03	.02	.01

The highest percentage for each candidate is underlined.

".00" signifies that the candidate received some votes, but less than .01%.

Extended percentages nationally: Hoopes .033%, MacArthur .028%.

Candidates were Dwight David Eisenhower, Republican; Adlai Ewing Stevenson, Democrat; T. Coleman Andrews, Constitution; Harry Flood Byrd, States' Rights; Eric Hass, Socialist-Labor; Enoch A. Holtwick, Prohibition; Farrell Dobbs, Socialist-Workers; Darlington Hoopes, Socialist; and Henry Krajewski, American Third Party. Walter B. Jones, Democrat, received one electoral vote.

Data pertaining to this election are from the official records on file in the National Archives, with these exceptions:

From *Statistics of the Presidential and Congressional Election of November 6, 1956:* Arkansas —All; Colorado, New Hampshire, and South Carolina—Andrews; New York—Andrews, Hass, and Hoopes.

From *Encyclopaedia Britannica Book of the Year, 1957:* Georgia—Eisenhower and Stevenson; Rhode Island—All.

From *World Almanac, 1957:* Florida—Andrews.

TABLE 45   Electoral and Popular Vote

States	E	S	J	Eisenhower	Stevenson	Andrews	Byrd
Alabama		10	1	195,694	280,844	20,323	
Arizona	4			176,990	112,880	303	
Arkansas		8		186,287	213,277	7,008	
California	32			3,027,688	2,420,135	5,467	
Colorado	6			394,479	263,997	759	
Connecticut	8			711,837	405,079		
Delaware	3			98,057	79,421		
Florida	10			643,849	480,371	1,348	
Georgia		12		222,874	445,925	2,096	
Idaho	4			166,979	105,868	126	
Illinois	27			2,623,327	1,775,682		
Indiana	13			1,182,811	783,908		
Iowa	10			729,187	501,858	3,202	
Kansas	8			566,878	296,317		
Kentucky	10			572,192	476,453		2,657
Louisiana	10			329,047	243,977	44,520	
Maine	5			249,238	102,468		
Maryland	9			559,738	372,613		
Massachusetts	16			1,393,197	948,190		
Michigan	20			1,713,647	1,359,898		
Minnesota	11			719,302	617,525		
Mississippi		8		60,685	144,498		42,966
Missouri		13		914,486	919,187		
Montana	4			154,933	116,238		
Nebraska	6			378,108	199,029		
Nevada	3			56,049	40,640		
New Hampshire	4			176,519	90,364	111	
New Jersey	16			1,606,942	850,337	5,317	
New Mexico	4			146,788	106,098	364	
New York	45			4,340,340	2,750,769	1,027	
North Carolina		14		575,062	590,530		
North Dakota	4			156,766	96,742	483	
Ohio	25			2,262,610	1,439,655		
Oklahoma	8			473,769	385,581		
Oregon	6			406,393	329,204		
Pennsylvania	32			2,585,252	1,981,769		
Rhode Island	4			229,677	163,521		
South Carolina		8		75,700	136,372	2	88,509
South Dakota	4			171,569	122,288		
Tennessee	11			462,288	456,507	19,886	
Texas	24			1,080,619	859,958	14,591	
Utah	4			215,631	118,364		
Vermont	3			110,390	42,549		
Virginia	12			386,459	267,760	42,964	
Washington	9			620,430	523,002		
West Virginia	8			449,297	381,534		
Wisconsin	12			954,844	586,768	6,918	
Wyoming	3			74,573	49,554	72	
TOTALS	457	73	1	35,589,477	26,035,504	176,887	134,132

Electoral and Popular Vote (continued)

States	Hass	Holtwick	Dobbs	Hoopes	Krajewski
Alabama					
Arizona					
Arkansas					
California	293	11,119	94	118	
Colorado	3,308			531	
Connecticut					
Delaware	110	400			
Florida					
Georgia					
Idaho					
Illinois	8,342				
Indiana	1,334	6,554			
Iowa	125			192	
Kansas		3,048			
Kentucky	358	2,145			
Louisiana					
Maine					
Maryland					
Massachusetts	5,573	1,205			
Michigan		6,923			
Minnesota	2,080		1,098		
Mississippi					
Missouri					
Montana					
Nebraska					
Nevada					
New Hampshire					
New Jersey	6,736	9,147	4,004		1,829
New Mexico	69	607			
New York	150			82	
North Carolina					
North Dakota					
Ohio					
Oklahoma					
Oregon					
Pennsylvania	7,447		2,035		
Rhode Island					
South Carolina					
South Dakota					
Tennessee		789			
Texas					
Utah					
Vermont					
Virginia	351			444	
Washington	7,457				
West Virginia					
Wisconsin	710		564	754	
Wyoming					
TOTALS	44,443	41,937	7,795	2,121	1,829

1956   Percentage of Popular Vote

States	E	S	A	B	Ha	Hol	D	Hoo	K
Alabama	39.39	56.52	4.09						
Arizona	60.99	38.90	.10						
Arkansas	45.82	52.46	1.72						
California	55.40	44.28	.10		.01	.20	.00	.00	
Colorado	59.49	39.81	.11		.50			_.08_	
Connecticut	63.73	36.27							
Delaware	55.09	44.62			.06	.22			
Florida	57.20	42.68	.12						
Georgia	33.22	_66.47_	.31						
Idaho	61.18	38.78	.05						
Illinois	59.52	40.29			.19				
Indiana	59.90	39.70			.07	.33			
Iowa	59.06	40.65	.26		.01			.02	
Kansas	65.44	34.21				.35			
Kentucky	54.30	45.21		.25	.03	.20			
Louisiana	53.28	39.51	_7.21_						
Maine	70.87	29.13							
Maryland	60.04	39.96							
Massachusetts	59.33	40.38			.24	.05			
Michigan	55.63	44.15				.22			
Minnesota	53.68	46.08			.16		.08		
Mississippi	24.46	58.23		17.31					
Missouri	49.87	50.13							
Montana	57.13	42.87							
Nebraska	65.51	34.49							
Nevada	57.97	42.03							
New Hampshire	66.11	33.84	.04						
New Jersey	64.68	34.23	.21		.27	_.37_	_.16_		_.07_
New Mexico	57.81	41.78	.14		.03	_.24_			
New York	61.20	38.78	.01		.00			.00	
North Carolina	49.34	50.66							
North Dakota	61.72	38.09	.19						
Ohio	61.11	38.89							
Oklahoma	55.13	44.87							
Oregon	55.25	44.75							
Pennsylvania	56.49	43.30			.16			.04	
Rhode Island	58.31	41.69							
South Carolina	25.18	45.37	.00	_29.45_					
South Dakota	58.39	41.61							
Tennessee	49.21	48.59	2.12			.08			
Texas	55.27	43.98	.75						
Utah	64.56	35.44							
Vermont	_72.18_	27.82							
Virginia	55.37	38.36	6.16		.05			.06	
Washington	53.91	45.44			_.65_				
West Virginia	54.08	45.92							
Wisconsin	61.58	37.84	.45		.05		.04	.05	
Wyoming	60.04	39.90	.06						
TOTALS	57.37	41.97	.29	.21	.07	.07	.01	.00	.00

The highest percentage for each candidate is underlined.

".00" signifies that the candidate received some votes, but less than .01%.

Extended percentages nationally: Hass .072%, Holtwick .068%; Hoopes .000034%, Krajewski .000029%.

ELECTION OF 1960

Candidates were John Fitzgerald Kennedy, Democrat; Richard Milhous Nixon, Republican; Eric Hass, Socialist Labor; Rutherford L. Decker, Prohibition; Orval Eugene Faubus, National States Rights; Farrell Dobbs, Socialist Workers; Charles Loten Sullivan, Constitutional; Joseph Bracken Lee, Conservative; C. Benton Coiner, Virginia Conservative; Lar Daly, Tax Cut; Clennon King, Independent Afro-American; and Merritt B. Curtis, Constitution. In Alabama and Mississippi, successful Democratic electors who had run unpledged cast their votes for Harry Flood Byrd. The States Rights Party of Louisiana also ran unpledged electors. The Independent American Party likewise had no candidate.

Data pertaining to this election are from the official records on file in the National Archives.

There is no satisfactory way to show the vote of Alabama, where five electors pledged to Kennedy ran on the same slate with six unpledged electors. If only the high elector's figure is included, voters who were able to elect five Kennedy electors are slighted. If both the high unpledged and the high Kennedy electors are shown, over 300,000 voters are counted twice. The latter method, unfortunately, seems to be the more nearly fair of the two alternatives.

The following figures show the split in the Alabama Democratic electoral vote:

Unpledged Electors	Pledged to Kennedy
324,050	318,303
323,018	318,266
322,593	317,226
322,124	317,171
322,084	316,934
320,957	

The unpledged electors voted for Harry Flood Byrd.

The following figures show how a switch of 11,874 votes out of the 68,329,996 cast for Kennedy and Nixon—.0002%—would have made the latter president:

States	Nixon	Kennedy	Shift
	219	303	
Illinois	27	-27	4,430
Missouri	13	-13	4,991
New Mexico	4	- 4	1,148
Hawaii	3	- 3	58
Nevada	3	- 3	1,247
	269	253	11,874

A switch of only the Illinois, Missouri, and Hawaii votes shown, 9,479, would have prevented Kennedy's election without giving Nixon the victory, as a decision by the House of Representatives would have become necessary. Nixon would have led, 262 to 260, with Byrd's 15 representing the balance of power.

TABLE 46   Electoral and Popular Vote

States	Ke	N	B	Kennedy	Nixon	Byrd	St.Rts.	Hass	Decker
Alabama	5		6	318,303	237,981	324,050			2,106
Alaska		3		29,809	30,953				
Arizona		4		176,781	221,241			469	
Arkansas	8			215,049	184,508				
California		32		3,224,099	3,259,722			1,051	21,706
Colorado		6		330,629	402,242			2,803	
Connecticut	8			657,055	565,813				
Delaware	3			99,590	96,373			82	284
Florida		10		748,700	795,476				
Georgia	12			458,638	274,472				
Hawaii	3			92,410	92,295				
Idaho		4		138,853	161,597				
Illinois	27			2,377,846	2,368,988			10,560	
Indiana		13		952,358	1,175,120			1,136	6,746
Iowa		10		550,565	722,381			230	
Kansas		8		363,213	561,474				4,138
Kentucky		10		521,855	602,607				
Louisiana	10			407,339	230,980		169,572		
Maine		5		181,159	240,608				
Maryland	9			565,808	489,538				
Massachusetts	16			1,487,174	976,750			3,892	1,633
Michigan	20			1,687,269	1,620,428			1,718	2,029
Minnesota	11			779,933	757,915			962	
Mississippi			8	108,362	73,561	116,248			
Missouri	13			972,201	962,221				
Montana		4		134,891	141,841				456
Nebraska		6		232,542	380,553				
Nevada	3			54,880	52,387				
New Hampshire		4		137,772	157,989				
New Jersey	16			1,385,415	1,363,324			4,262	
New Mexico	4			156,027	153,733			570	777
New York	45			3,830,085	3,446,420				
North Carolina	14			713,136	655,420				
North Dakota		4		123,963	154,310				
Ohio		25		1,944,248	2,217,611				
Oklahoma		7	1	370,111	533,039				
Oregon		6		367,402	408,060				
Pennsylvania	32			2,556,282	2,439,956			7,185	
Rhode Island	4			258,032	147,502				
South Carolina	8			198,129	188,558				
South Dakota		4		128,070	178,417				
Tennessee		11		481,453	556,577				2,475
Texas	24			1,167,932	1,121,699				3,870
Utah		4		169,248	205,361				
Vermont		3		69,186	98,131				
Virginia		12		362,327	404,521			397	
Washington		9		599,298	629,273			10,895	
West Virginia	8			441,786	395,995				
Wisconsin		12		830,805	895,175			1,310	
Wyoming		3		63,331	77,551				
TOTALS	303	219	15	34,221,349	34,108,647	440,298	169,572	47,522	46,220

States	Faubus	Dobbs	Sullivan	Lee	Coiner	Daly	King	Curtis	I. A.
Alabama	4,357						1,485		
Alaska									
Arizona									
Arkansas	28,952								
California									
Colorado		572							
Connecticut									
Delaware	354								
Florida									
Georgia									
Hawaii									
Idaho									
Illinois									
Indiana									
Iowa		634							
Kansas									
Kentucky									
Louisiana									
Maine									
Maryland									
Massachusetts									
Michigan		4,347				1,767			539
Minnesota		3,077							
Mississippi									
Missouri									
Montana		391							
Nebraska									
Nevada									
New Hampshire									
New Jersey		11,402		8,708					
New Mexico									
New York		14,319							
North Carolina									
North Dakota		158							
Ohio									
Oklahoma									
Oregon									
Pennsylvania		2,678							
Rhode Island									
South Carolina									
South Dakota									
Tennessee	11,304								
Texas			18,169						
Utah		100							
Vermont									
Virginia					4,204				
Washington		705						1,401	
West Virginia									
Wisconsin		1,792							
Wyoming									
TOTALS	44,967	40,175	18,169	8,708	4,204	1,767	1,485	1,401	539

States	Ke	N	B	S.R.	H	De	F	Do	S	L	Co	Da	Ki	Cu	I.A.
Alabama		41.75				.37	.76						.26		
Alaska	49.06	50.94													
Arizona	44.36	55.52			.12										
Arkansas	50.19	43.06					6.76								
California	49.55	50.10			.02	.33									
Colorado	44.91	54.63			.38			.08							
Connecticut	53.73	46.27													
Delaware	50.63	49.00			.04	.14	.18								
Florida	48.49	51.51													
Georgia	62.56	37.44													
Hawaii	50.03	49.97													
Idaho	46.22	53.78													
Illinois	49.98	49.80			.22										
Indiana	44.60	55.03			.05	.32									
Iowa	43.22	56.71			.02			.05							
Kansas	39.10	60.45				.45									
Kentucky	46.41	53.59													
Louisiana	50.42	28.59		20.99											
Maine	42.95	57.05													
Maryland	53.61	46.39													
Massachusetts	60.22	39.55			.16	.07									
Michigan	50.85	48.84			.05	.06		.13				.05			.02
Minnesota	50.58	49.16			.06			.20							
Mississippi	36.34	24.67	38.99												
Missouri	50.26	49.74													
Montana	48.60	51.10					.16	.14							
Nebraska	37.93	62.07													
Nevada	51.16	48.84													
New Hampshire	46.58	53.42													
New Jersey	49.96	49.16			.15				.41	.31					
New Mexico	50.15	49.41			.18	.25									
New York	52.53	47.27						.20							
North Carolina	52.11	47.89													
North Dakota	44.52	55.42						.06							
Ohio	46.72	53.28													
Oklahoma	40.98	59.02													
Oregon	47.38	52.62													
Pennsylvania	51.06	48.74			.14			.05							
Rhode Island	63.63	36.37													
South Carolina	51.24	48.76													
South Dakota	41.79	58.21													
Tennessee	45.77	52.92				.24	1.07								
Texas	50.52	48.52					.17			.79					
Utah	45.17	54.81							.03						
Vermont	41.35	58.65													
Virginia	46.96	52.44			.05							.54			
Washington	48.27	50.68			.88			.06						.11	
West Virginia	52.73	47.27													
Wisconsin	48.05	51.77			.08			.10							
Wyoming	44.95	55.05													
TOTALS	49.71	49.55	.64	.25	.07	.07	.07	.06	.03	.01	.01	.00	.00	.00	.00

The highest percentage for each candidate is underlined.

".00" signifies that the candidate received some votes, but less than .01%.

The Alabama Democratic percentage of 56.85 is based on the 324,050 cast for Byrd; the 318,303 cast for Kennedy has been ignored. The latter figure has also been ignored in determining the nationwide percentages.

Extended percentages nationally: Hass .00071%, Decker .00067%, Faubus .00065%, Lee .00013%, Coiner .00006%, Daly .000026%, King .000022%, Curtis .000020%, Independent American .000008%.

TABLE 47   Number and Percentage of Votes by Elections and Parties

Year	Democratic				Jackson	152,933	42.16	Adams	115,696	31.89
1824	Democratic		Nat'l Republican							
1828	647,292	56.04	507,730	43.96						
1832	688,242	54.50	473,462	37.49	Whig			White		
1836	764,198	50.93	Liberty		549,508	36.63		145,352	9.69	
1840	1,130,033	46.84	7,053	.29	1,275,612	52.87				
1844	1,339,368	49.56	62,197	2.30	1,300,687	48.13	Free Soil		
1848	1,222,674	42.47			1,362,101	47.31	291,616	10.13	
1852	1,609,038	50.85	Republican		1,386,629	43.82	156,297	4.94	
1856	1,839,237	45.63	1,341,028	33.27	849,872	21.08	Breckinridge		
1860	1,379,434	29.40	1,867,198	39.79			854,248	18.20	
1864	1,805,063	44.85	2,219,362	55.15					
1868	2,703,933	47.29	3,013,313	52.71	O'Conor - Demo.				
1872	2,833,711	43.82	3,597,375	55.63	29,464	.46	Greenback		
1876	4,287,670	50.93	4,035,924	47.94			82,797	.98	
1880	4,444,976	48.21	4,454,433	48.32			308,649	3.35	
1884	4,875,971	48.50	4,852,234	48.26	Union Labor		175,066	1.74	
1888	5,540,365	48.64	5,445,269	47.81	147,606	1.30	Populist		
1892	5,556,982	46.04	5,191,466	43.01	Nat'l Democratic		1,029,960	8.53	
1896	6,516,722	46.72	7,113,734	51.00	135,456	.97			
1900	6,358,160	45.50	7,219,828	51.67	Continental		50,605	.36	
1904	5,084,533	37.59	7,628,831	56.40	830	.01	114,790	.85	
1908	6,410,665	43.05	7,679,114	51.57	Theo. Roosevelt		29,147	.20	
1912	6,301,254	41.85	3,485,831	23.15	4,127,788	27.42			
1916	9,131,511	49.26	8,548,935	46.12	35,034	.19	Farmer Labor		
1920	9,147,353	34.15	16,153,785	60.31	LaFollette		265,421	.99	
1924	8,386,624	28.82	15,725,016	54.04	4,831,470	16.60			
1928	15,016,443	40.79	21,430,743	58.22			6,390	.02	
1932	22,821,857	57.41	15,761,841	39.65	Union		7,309	.02	
1936	27,751,841	60.80	16,679,491	36.54	892,390	1.96	Knutson		
1940	27,243,466	54.69	22,334,413	44.83			545	.00	
1944	25,612,474	53.39	22,017,570	45.89	Wallace, etc.		S. R. Democratic		
1948	24,104,030	49.51	21,971,004	45.13	1,157,063	2.38	1,169,032	2.40	
1952	27,314,992	44.38	33,937,252	55.14	140,178	.23	Byrd		
1956	26,035,504	41.97	35,589,477	57.37	States Rights-La		134,132	.21	
1960	34,221,349	49.71	34,108,647	49.55	169,572	.25	440,298	.64	

Year	Single Tax		Commonwealth Land		Jacksonian		
1920	5,353	.02	Commonwealth Land				
1924			1,532	.01			
1928	National		Jobless		Jacksonian		
1932	1,645	.00	725	.00	104	.00	
1936							
1940	America First						
1944	1,781	.00					
1948	Krajewski						
1952	4,203	.01					
1956	1,829	.00	Conservative-Lee		Va. Conservative		Tax Cut
1960			8,708	.01	4,204	.01	1,767	.00

".00" signifies that the party received some votes, but less than .01%.

TABLE 47   Number and Percentage of Votes by Elections and Parties

Year	Clay	Crawford				
1824	47,136 12.99	46,979 12.95				
1828						
1832			**Anti-Masonic** 101,051 8.00			
1836	**Webster** 41,287 2.75					
1840						
1844		**Smith**				
1848		2,733 .09	**American**	**So. Rights**		
1852	7,407 .23	72 .00	2,666 .08	2,300 .07		
1856	**Const. Union**	484 .01				
1860	591,658 12.61	172 .00				
1864						
1868	**Prohibition**					
1872	5,588 .09		**American**			
1876	9,630 .11		2,508 .03			
1880	10,364 .11		1,045 .01			
1884	150,957 1.50	**Soc. Labor**				
1888	250,122 2.20	2,068 .02	1,591 .01	**United Labor** 2,818 .02		
1892	271,111 2.25	21,561 .18		**Nat'l Proh'n**		
1896	131,285 .94	36,475 .26	**Socialist**	14,003 .10	**Union Reform**	**Un'd Chr'n**
1900	210,200 1.50	33,435 .24	95,744 .69		5,695 .04	521 .00
1904	259,163 1.92	33,737 .25	402,714 2.98	**Independence**	**No Party**	
1908	252,704 1.70	14,030 .09	420,858 2.83	83,739 .56	63 .00	400 .00
1912	209,644 1.39	29,290 .19	901,255 5.99			
1916	220,505 1.19	14,273 .08	585,974 3.16		**American**	**B.& T. Rep.**
1920	189,467 .71	29,173 .11	919,801 3.43		47,968 .18	27,247 .10
1924	57,551 .20	39,021 .13		**Communist**	23,967 .08	
1928	20,106 .05	21,602 .06	267,420 .73	33,361 .11	**Liberty**	
1932	81,869 .21	34,046 .09	884,781 2.23	48,667 .13	53,434 .13	
1936	37,661 .08	12,815 .03	188,497 .41	102,991 .26		**Christian**
1940	58,725 .12	14,892 .03	116,514 .23	80,160 .18		1,598 .00
1944	74,761 .16	45,189 .09	79,010 .16	46,251 .09	**Tex. Regulars**	**So. Demo.**
1948	103,343 .21	29,240 .06	139,523 .29	**Soc. Workers** 13,611 .03	135,439 .28	7,799 .02
1952	72,778 .12	30,376 .05	20,189 .03	10,306 .02	**Constitution** 17,205 .03	
1956	41,937 .07	44,443 .07	2,121 .00	7,795 .01	176,887 .29	
1960	46,220 .07	47,522 .07		40,175 .06	18,169 .03	**Natl.St.Rts** 44,967 .07

Year	Afro-American	Const.-Wash.	Indpdt. Am'n
1960	1,485 .00	1,401 .00	539 .00

".00" signifies that the party received some votes, but less than .01%.

Jackson, Adams, Clay, and Crawford divided the 1824 Democratic vote. Harrison got the vote shown in the Whig column for 1836; the vote for White and Webster for that year, as well as the latter's for 1852, was also Whig. Douglas got the vote shown in the Democratic column for 1860. The Liberty Party of 1840 and 1844 was not the same as that of 1932. The American Party of 1852 was not the same as that of 1876 to 1888; neither was the same as that of 1920 and 1924. The votes shown for Theodore Roosevelt in 1912 and 1916, for LaFollette in 1924, and for "Wallace, etc." in 1948 and 1952, were cast for Progressive tickets. These were three separate and distinct parties.

Alabama, which entered the Union in 1819, participated in thirty-five presidential elections during the period 1820 to 1960; it did not take part in 1864, because of the Civil War. It supported seventeen winners and eighteen losers.

TABLE 48 Number and Percentage of Votes by Elections and Parties

Year		Jackson	Adams	Crawford	Clay
1824	Democratic	9,443 69.40	2,416 17.76	1,680 12.35	67 .49
1828	17,138 89.84				
1832		Whig			
1836	20,506 56.78	15,612 43.22			
1840	33,991 54.42	28,471 45.58			
1844	37,740 59.13	26,084 40.87			
1848	31,363 50.71	30,482 49.29	South'n Rights		
1852	26,881 60.96	15,038 34.11	2,174 4.93		
1856	46,817 62.11	28,557 37.88	Const. Union	Douglas	
1860	48,831 54.04		27,875 30.85	13,651 15.11	
1864		Republican			
1868	72,086 48.56	76,366 51.44			
1872	79,444 46.81	90,272 53.19			
1876	102,989 59.98	68,708 40.02	Greenback		
1880	91,185 59.97	56,221 36.98	4,642 3.05		Prohibition
1884	93,951 60.60	59,591 38.44	873 .56		612 .39
1888	117,320 67.39	56,197 32.28	Populist		583 .33
1892	138,138 59.35	9,197 3.95	85,181 36.60	Nat'l Demo.	241 .10
1896	131,226 67.44	54,737 28.13		6,464 3.32	2,147 1.10
1900	96,368 60.05	55,634 34.67	3,751 2.34		3,796 2.37
1904	79,857 73.37	22,472 20.65	5,051 4.64		612 .56
1908	74,374 71.65	25,308 24.38	1,568 1.51	T. Roosevelt	665 .64
1912	82,438 69.93	9,732 8.26		22,680 19.24	
1916	99,409 75.80	28,809 21.97			999 .76
1920	163,254 67.72	74,690 30.98	LaFollette		757 .31
1924	112,966 67.80	45,005 27.01	8,084 4.85		569 .34
1928	127,797 51.33	120,725 48.49	Communist		
1932	207,910 84.85	34,675 14.15	406 .17	Union	13 .01
1936	238,196 86.38	35,358 12.82	678 .25	551 .20	719 .26
1940	250,726 85.22	42,184 14.34	509 .17		700 .24
1944	198,918 81.28	44,540 18.20	S. R. Demo.	Wallace	1,095 .45
1948		40,930 19.04	171,443 79.75	1,522 .71	1,085 .50
1952	275,075 64.55	149,231 35.02		Constitution	1,814 .43
1956	280,844 56.52	195,694 39.39	Unpledged Dem.	20,323 4.09	
1960	318,303	237,981 41.75	324,050		2,106 .37

Year	Nat'l Republ'n
1828	1,938 10.16

Year	Socialist	Independence
1900	928 .58	
1904	853 .78	
1908	1,399 1.35	495 .48
1912	3,029 2.57	
1916	1,925 1.47	
1920	2,369 .98	
1924		
1928	460 .18	
1932	2,030 .83	
1936	242 .09	
1940	100 .03	
1944	190 .08	
1948		
1952		
1956	Nat'l St. Rts.	Afro-American
1960	4,357 .76	1,485 .26

There was no opposition to Jackson in 1832.

The vote in the Whig column for 1836 was cast for White. The vote in the Democratic column for 1860 was cast for Breckinridge.

TABLE 49   Number and Percentage of Votes by Elections and Parties

Year	Democratic		Republican	
1960	29,809	49.06	30,953	50.94

ARIZONA

Arizona, which entered the Union in 1912, participated in thirteen presidential elections during the period 1912 to 1960. It supported twelve winners and one loser.

TABLE 50   Number and Percentage of Votes by Elections and Parties

Year	Democratic		Republican		Socialist		Prohibition		T. Roosevelt	
1912	10,324	43.52	3,021	12.74	3,163	13.33	265	1.12	6,949	29.29
1916	33,170	57.17	20,524	35.37	3,174	5.47	1,153	1.99		
1920	29,546	44.23	37,016	55.41	222	.33	4	.01	LaFollette	
1924	26,235	35.47	30,516	41.26					17,210	23.27
1928	38,537	42.23	52,533	57.57						
1932	79,264	67.04	36,104	30.53	2,618	2.21			Union	
1936	86,722	69.85	33,433	26.93	317	.26	384	.31	3,307	2.66
1940	95,267	63.49	54,030	36.01			742	.49		
1944	80,926	58.80	56,287	40.90	Soc. Labor		421	.31	Wallace	
1948	95,251	53.79	77,597	43.82	121	.07	786	.44	3,310	1.87
1952	108,528	41.65	152,042	58.35			Constitution			
1956	112,880	38.90	176,990	60.99			303	.10		
1960	176,781	44.36	221,241	55.52			469	.12		

Year	Farmer Labor	
1920	15	.02
1924	Communist	
1928	184	.20
1932	256	.22

ARKANSAS

Arkansas, which entered the Union in 1836, participated in thirty-one presidential elections during the period 1836 to 1960; it did not take part in 1864, because of the Civil War. It supported fifteen winners and fifteen losers; its 1872 electoral votes, which were intended for the Republican candidate, were rejected.

TABLE 51   Number and Percentage of Votes by Elections and Parties

Year	Democratic		Whig / Republican		Const. Union / Union Labor / Nat'l Proh'n / T. Roosevelt / LaFollette / Liberty / Wallace / Nat'l S. R.		Douglas / Socialist		Greenback / Populist / Communist / S. R. Demo.	
1836	2,400	65.97	1,238	34.03						
1840	6,766	56.73	5,160	43.27						
1844	9,546	63.43	5,504	36.57						
1848	9,300	55.07	7,588	44.93						
1852	12,173	62.18	7,404	37.82						
1856	21,910	67.01	10,787	32.99	*Const. Union*		*Douglas*			
1860	28,732	53.16			20,094	37.17	5,227	9.67		
1864			*Republican*							
1868	19,078	46.27	22,152	53.73						
1872	37,927	47.83	41,373	52.17					*Greenback*	
1876	58,083	59.90	38,669	39.88					211	.22
1880	60,775	56.65	42,436	39.55					4,079	3.80
1884	72,927	58.03	50,895	40.50	*Union Labor*				1,847	1.47
1888	86,717	54.80	60,245	38.07	10,671	6.74			*Populist*	
1892	87,834	59.84	46,974	32.01	*Nat'l Proh'n*				11,831	8.06
1896	110,103	73.70	37,512	25.11	893	.60	*Socialist*			
1900	81,142	63.46	44,800	35.04			27	.02	972	.76
1904	64,434	55.35	46,860	40.25			1,816	1.56	2,318	1.99
1908	87,015	57.20	56,760	37.31	*T. Roosevelt*		5,842	3.84	1,026	.67
1912	68,838	55.50	24,467	19.73	21,673	17.47	8,153	6.57		
1916	112,186	66.64	47,148	28.01			6,999	4.16		
1920	107,409	58.49	71,117	38.73	*LaFollette*		5,111	2.78		
1924	84,795	61.21	40,564	29.28	13,173	9.51			*Communist*	
1928	119,196	60.29	77,751	39.33	*Liberty*		429	.22	317	.16
1932	189,602	85.96	28,467	12.91	1,049	.48	1,269	.58	175	.08
1936	146,765	81.80	32,039	17.86			446	.25	169	.09
1940	158,622	78.59	42,121	20.87			305	.15		
1944	148,965	69.95	63,551	29.84	*Wallace*		438	.21	*S. R. Demo.*	
1948	149,659	61.72	50,959	21.02	751	.31	1,037	.43	40,068	16.52
1952	226,300	55.90	177,155	43.76						
1956	213,277	52.46	186,287	45.82	*Nat'l S. R.*					
1960	215,049	50.19	184,508	43.06	28,952	6.76				

Year	Prohibition		Union Reform / Independence / Union / Soc. Labor		Constitution	
1888	615	.39				
1892	130	.09				
1896	889	.60	*Union Reform*			
1900	584	.46	340	.27		
1904	993	.85	*Independence*			
1908	1,194	.78	289	.19		
1912	898	.72				
1916	2,015	1.20				
1920						
1924						
1928						
1932			*Union*			
1936			4	.00		
1940	793	.39				
1944						
1948	1	.00	*Soc. Labor*		*Constitution*	
1952	886	.22	1	.00	458	.11
1956					7,008	1.72

The vote in the Whig column for 1836 was cast for White. The vote in the Democratic column for 1860 was cast for Breckinridge.

".00" signifies that the party received some votes, but less than .01%.

CALIFORNIA

California, which entered the Union in 1850, participated in twenty-eight presidential elections during the period 1852 to 1960. It supported twenty-four winners and four losers. In 1880 Hancock led Garfield in California, 48.98% to 48.92%, while losing the election; in 1912 Theodore Roosevelt led Wilson in California, 42.11% to 42.08%, while losing the election; and in 1960 Nixon led Kennedy in California, 50.10% to 49.55%, while losing the election. California was the pivotal state in 1916, when its thirteen electoral votes swung the election from Hughes to Wilson, the latter winning by 277 to 254.

TABLE 52 Number and Percentage of Votes by Elections and Parties

Year	Democratic		Republican		(3rd party)		(4th party)		(5th party)	
1852	40,626	53.36	*Republican*		*Whig* 35,407	46.51	*Free Soil* 100	.13		
1856	53,365	48.42	20,693	18.77	36,165	32.81	*Breckinridge*		*Const. Union*	
1860	38,516	32.41	39,173	32.96			34,334	28.89	6,817	5.74
1864	43,842	41.37	62,134	58.63						
1868	54,078	49.76	54,592	50.24					*O'Conor-Dem.*	
1872	40,749	42.51	54,044	56.38	*Greenback*		*American*		1,068	1.11
1876	76,465	49.08	79,269	50.88	47	.03	19	.01	*Prohibition*	
1880	80,443	48.98	80,348	48.92	3,395	2.07			59	.04
1884	89,288	45.41	102,416	52.08	2,017	1.03			2,920	1.48
1888	117,729	47.11	124,816	49.95	*Populist*		1,591	.64	5,761	2.31
1892	118,174	43.84	118,027	43.76	25,311	9.39	*National Demo.*		8,096	3.00
1896	144,618	48.44	146,688	49.13	*Socialist*		2,006	.67	2,573	.86
1900	124,985	41.33	164,755	54.48	7,572	2.50			5,087	1.68
1904	89,404	26.97	205,226	61.90	29,535	8.91			7,380	2.23
1908	127,492	32.98	214,398	55.46	28,659	7.41	*T. Roosevelt*		11,770	3.04
1912	283,436	42.08	3,914	.58	79,201	11.76	283,610	42.11	23,366	3.47
1916	466,200	46.64	462,394	46.26	43,259	4.33			27,698	2.77
1920	229,191	24.29	624,992	66.24	64,076	6.79	*LaFollette*		25,204	2.67
1924	105,514	8.23	733,250	57.21			424,649	33.13	18,365	1.43
1928	614,365	34.20	1,162,323	64.70	19,595	1.09	*Liberty*			
1932	1,324,157	58.41	847,902	37.40	63,299	2.79	9,827	.43	20,637	.91
1936	1,766,836	66.97	836,431	31.70	11,331	.43			12,917	.49
1940	1,877,618	57.45	1,351,419	41.35	16,506	.50			9,400	.29
1944	1,988,564	56.51	1,512,965	42.99	2,515	.07	*Wallace, etc.*		14,770	.42
1948	1,913,134	47.58	1,895,269	47.14	3,459	.09	190,381	4.73	16,926	.42
1952	2,197,548	42.77	2,897,310	56.39	206	.00	24,106	.47	15,653	.30
1956	2,420,135	44.28	3,027,688	55.40	118	.00			11,119	.20
1960	3,224,099	49.55	3,259,722	50.10					21,706	.33

Year	Socialist Labor		Nat'l Prohibit'n / Independence / Communist / Socialist W'kers		Constitution		S. R. Demo.	
1896	1,611	.54	*Nat'l Prohibit'n* 1,047	.35				
1900								
1904			*Independence*					
1908			4,278	1.11				
1912								
1916								
1920								
1924			*Communist*					
1928			112	.01				
1932			1,023	.05				
1936			10,877	.41				
1940			13,586	.42				
1944	180	.01	*Socialist W'kers*				*S. R. Demo.*	
1948	195	.00	133	.00	*Constitution*		1,228	.03
1952	273	.01			3,504	.07		
1956	293	.01	94	.00	5,467	.10		
1960	1,051	.02						

The vote in the Democratic column for 1860 was cast for Douglas.

".00" signifies that the party received some votes, but less than .01%.

COLORADO

Colorado, which entered the Union in 1876, participated in twenty-two presidential elections during the period 1876 to 1960. It supported fourteen winners and eight losers.

TABLE 53   Number and Percentage of Votes by Elections and Parties

Year	Democratic		Republican		Other			Prohibition		Other	
1880	24,647	46.04	27,450	51.28				761	1.14	Greenback	1,435	2.68
1884	27,723	41.55	36,290	54.39	Union Labor			2,192	2.39		1,953	2.93
1888	37,567	40.92	50,774	55.31		1,266	1.38	1,687	1.80	Populist		
1892			38,620	41.13				1,724	.91		53,584	57.07
1896	161,269	84.96	26,279	13.84	Socialist			3,790	1.71			
1900	122,733	55.44	93,072	42.04		714	.32	3,438	1.41		389	.18
1904	100,105	41.08	134,687	55.27		4,304	1.77	5,559	2.11		824	.34
1908	126,644	47.99	123,700	46.88		7,974	3.02	5,063	1.90	T. Roosevelt		
1912	114,232	42.80	58,386	21.88		16,418	6.15	2,793	.95		72,306	27.09
1916	178,816	60.74	102,308	34.75		10,049	3.41	2,807	.96		409	.14
1920	104,936	35.93	173,248	59.32		8,046	2.75	966	.28	LaFollette		
1924	75,238	21.98	195,171	57.02							69,945	20.44
1928	133,131	33.94	253,872	64.72		3,472	.89					
1932	250,877	54.81	189,617	41.43		13,591	2.97	1,928	.42	Union		
1936	295,021	60.37	181,267	37.09		1,593	.33				9,962	2.04
1940	265,554	48.37	279,576	50.92		1,899	.35	1,597	.29			
1944	234,331	46.40	268,731	53.21		1,977	.39			Wallace, etc.		
1948	267,288	51.88	239,714	46.52		1,678	.33	Constitution			6,115	1.19
1952	245,504	38.96	379,782	60.27		365	.06	2,181	.35		1,919	.30
1956	263,997	39.81	394,479	59.49		531	.08	759	.11			
1960	330,629	44.91	402,242	54.63								

Year	Soc. Labor		Nat'l Prohib'n / Farmer Labor / Soc. Workers		Nat'l Demo. / Communist	
1896	160	.08	Nat'l Prohib'n 386	.20	Nat'l Demo. 1	.00
1900	684	.31				
1904	335	.14				
1908						
1912	475	.18				
1916			Farmer Labor			
1920			3,016	1.03	Communist	
1924	378	.11			562	.16
1928			1,092	.28	675	.17
1932	427	.09	469	.10	787	.17
1936	344	.07			497	.10
1940					378	.07
1944			Soc. Workers			
1948	214	.04	228	.04		
1952	352	.06				
1956	3,308	.50				
1960	2,803	.38	572	.08		

The legislature cast the electoral vote in 1876.

".00" signifies that the party received some votes, but less than .01%.

CONNECTICUT

Connecticut, one of the original states, participated in forty-four presidential elections during the period 1789 to 1960. It supported thirty winners and fourteen losers.

TABLE 54   Number and Percentage of Votes by Elections and Parties

Year	Democratic		Nat'l Republ'n / Liberty / Republican		Adams / Whig / Greenback / Populist / T. Roosevelt / LaFollette / Union / Wallace		Crawford / Anti-Masonic / Free Soil / Breckinridge / O'Conor / Union Labor / Socialist		Const. Union / Prohibition / Communist / Soc. Workers	
1824					Adams 9,261	82.40	Crawford 1,978	17.60		
1828	4,448	24.32	Nat'l Republ'n 13,838	75.68						
1832	11,212	34.91	17,617	54.85			Anti-Masonic 3,288	10.24		
1836	19,291	50.69			Whig 18,765	49.31				
1840	25,296	44.32	Liberty 174	.30	31,601	55.37				
1844	29,841	46.18	1,943	3.01	32,832	50.81				
1848	27,047	43.37			30,316	48.61	Free Soil 5,005	8.02		
1852	33,249	49.80			30,359	45.47	3,160	4.73		
1856	34,995	43.57	Republican 42,715	53.18	2,615	3.26				
1860	17,364	21.50	43,486	53.86			Breckinridge 16,558	20.51	Const. Union 3,337	4.13
1864	42,285	48.62	44,691	51.38						
1868	47,952	48.46	50,995	51.54						
1872	45,875	47.34	50,634	52.25			O'Conor-Demo. 203	.21	Prohibition 186	.19
1876	61,934	50.71	59,034	48.34	Greenback 774	.63			374	.31
1880	64,415	48.52	67,071	50.52	868	.65			409	.31
1884	67,182	48.95	65,898	48.01	1,685	1.23			2,494	1.82
1888	74,922	48.66	74,586	48.44			Union Labor 240	.16	4,236	2.75
1892	82,395	50.06	77,032	46.80	Populist 809	.49			4,026	2.45
1896	56,740	32.53	110,297	63.24					1,806	1.04
1900	74,014	41.09	102,572	56.94			Socialist 1,029	.57	1,617	.90
1904	72,909	38.15	111,089	58.13	495	.26	4,543	2.38	1,506	.79
1908	68,255	35.92	112,915	59.43			5,113	2.69	2,380	1.25
1912	74,561	39.16	68,324	35.88	T. Roosevelt 34,129	17.93	10,056	5.28	2,068	1.09
1916	99,786	46.66	106,514	49.80			5,179	2.42	1,789	.84
1920	120,721	33.03	229,238	62.72			10,350	2.83	1,771	.48
1924	110,184	27.53	246,322	61.54	LaFollette 42,416	10.60	3,019	.55	Communist 730	.13
1928	252,040	45.57	296,614	53.63			20,480	3.45	1,364	.23
1932	281,632	47.40	288,420	48.54			5,683	.82	1,193	.17
1936	382,129	55.32	278,685	40.35	Union 21,805	3.16			1,091	.14
1940	417,621	53.44	361,819	46.30						
1944	435,146	52.30	390,527	46.94			5,097	.61	Soc. Workers 606	.07
1948	423,297	47.91	437,754	49.55	Wallace, etc. 13,713	1.55	6,964	.79		
1952	481,649	43.91	611,012	55.70	1,466	.13	2,244	.22		
1956	405,079	36.27	711,837	63.73						
1960	657,055	53.73	565,813	46.27						

Year	American		Soc. Labor		National Demo. / Independence / Farmer Labor	
1876	16	.01				
1880						
1884						
1888						
1892			329	.20		
1896			1,223	.70	National Demo. 4,336	2.49
1900			908	.50		
1904			575	.30		
1908			608	.32	Independence 728	.38
1912			1,260	.66		
1916			606	.28		
1920			1,491	.41	Farmer Labor 1,947	.53
1924			1,373	.34		
1928			622	.11		
1932			2,287	.38		
1936			1,228	.18		
1940			971	.12		
1944			1,220	.15		
1948			1,184	.13		
1952			535	.05		

The vote in the Whig column for 1836 was cast for Harrison. The vote in the Democratic column for 1860 was cast for Douglas.

Delaware, one of the original states, participated in forty-four presidential elections during the period 1789 to 1960. It supported twenty-five winners and nineteen losers.

TABLE 55   Number and Percentage of Votes by Elections and Parties

Year	Democratic	Nat'l Repub'n / Republican	Whig / other third party	Free Soil / Const. Union / Prohibition	Douglas / Socialist
1832	4,194 49.52	Nat'l Repub'n 4,276 50.48			
1836	4,152 46.73		Whig 4,734 53.27		
1840	4,884 45.01		5,967 54.99		
1844	5,996 48.85		6,278 51.15		
1848	5,910 47.54		6,441 51.81	Free Soil 80 .64	
1852	6,319 49.85	Republican	6,294 49.66	62 .49	
1856	8,003 55.25	306 2.11	6,175 42.63		
1860	7,344 45.62	3,816 23.71		Const. Union 3,868 24.03	Douglas 1,069 6.64
1864	8,767 51.80	8,157 48.20			
1868	10,980 59.02	7,623 40.98	O'Conor-Dem.		
1872	10,208 46.78	11,129 50.99	487 2.23		
1876	13,381 55.45	10,752 44.55	Greenback		
1880	15,275 51.73	14,133 47.86	120 .41	Prohibition	
1884	17,054 57.05	12,778 42.75	6 .02	55 .18	
1888	16,414 55.10	12,973 43.55	Populist	400 1.34	
1892	18,581 49.90	18,077 48.55	13 .03	564 1.51	
1896	16,615 43.01	20,452 52.94		602 1.56	Socialist
1900	18,863 44.91	22,535 53.65		546 1.30	57 .14
1904	19,359 44.12	23,712 54.04	51 .12	607 1.38	146 .33
1908	22,071 45.96	25,014 52.09	T. Roosevelt	670 1.40	239 .50
1912	22,631 46.48	15,997 32.85	8,886 18.25	623 1.28	556 1.14
1916	24,753 47.78	26,011 50.20		566 1.09	480 .93
1920	39,911 42.07	52,858 55.71	LaFollette	986 1.04	988 1.04
1924	33,445 36.81	52,441 57.71	4,979 5.48		329 .31
1928	36,643 34.60	68,860 65.03			1,376 1.22
1932	54,319 48.11	57,073 50.55	Union		172 .14
1936	69,702 56.04	54,014 43.43	442 .36		
1940	74,599 54.70	61,440 45.05		220 .16	115 .08
1944	68,166 54.38	56,747 45.27	Wallace, etc.	294 .23	154 .12
1948	67,813 48.76	69,588 50.04	1,050 .75	343 .25	250 .18
1952	83,315 47.88	90,059 51.75	155 .09	234 .13	20 .01
1956	79,421 44.62	98,057 55.09		400 .22	
1960	99,590 50.63	96,373 49.00		284 .14	

Year	National Dem.	Independence / Farmer Labor / Communist / Soc. Labor	Single Tax / Nat'l S. R.
1896	966 2.50		
1900			
1904		Independence	
1908		30 .06	
1912			
1916		Farmer Labor	Single Tax
1920		93 .10	39 .04
1924		Communist	
1928		59 .06	
1932		133 .12	
1936		51 .04	
1940			
1944		Soc. Labor	
1948		29 .02	
1952		242 .14	
1956		110 .06	Nat'l S. R.
1960		82 .04	354 .18

The legislature cast the electoral vote in 1824 and 1828.

The vote in the Whig column for 1836 was cast for Harrison.

The vote in the Democratic column for 1860 was cast for Breckinridge.

FLORIDA

Florida, which entered the Union in 1845, participated in twenty-eight presidential elections during the period 1848 to 1960; it did not take part in 1864, because of the Civil War. It supported eighteen winners and ten losers. While any of the states that supported Hayes in 1876 could have been said to have swung the election, the Florida margin was the closest in the nation; a shift of 462 votes would have switched the state to Tilden.

TABLE 56   Number and Percentage of Votes by Elections and Parties

Year	Democratic		Whig		Const. Union		Douglas				Prohibition	
1848	3,243	41.64	4,546	58.36								
1852	4,318	60.03	2,875	39.97								
1856	6,368	56.81	4,843	43.20								
1860	8,543	59.55			5,437	37.90	367	2.56				
1864												
1868			Republican									
1872	15,427	46.48	17,763	53.52								
1876	22,923	49.01	23,849	50.99								
1880	27,964	54.17	23,654	45.83							72	.12
1884	31,769	53.06	28,031	46.82							418	.63
1888	39,656	59.43	26,654	39.94	Populist						570	1.60
1892	30,143	84.78			4,843	13.62	Nat'l Demo.				654	1.41
1896	32,736	70.47	11,288	24.30			1,778	3.83			2,234	5.67
1900	28,007	71.06	7,499	19.03	1,070	2.71					5	.01
1904	27,046	68.81	8,314	21.15	1,605	4.08					553	1.12
1908	31,104	63.01	10,654	21.58	1,946	3.94	T. Roosevelt				1,854	3.57
1912	36,417	70.18	4,279	8.25			4,535	8.74			4,855	6.01
1916	55,984	69.28	14,611	18.08							5,124	3.52
1920	90,515	62.13	44,853	30.79	LaFollette						5,498	5.04
1924	62,083	56.88	30,633	28.06	8,625	7.90	Communist					
1928	101,764	40.12	144,168	56.83			3,704	1.46				
1932	206,307	74.68	69,170	25.04								
1936	249,117	76.10	78,248	23.90								
1940	359,334	74.01	126,158	25.99								
1944	339,377	70.32	143,215	29.68	S. R. Demo.		Wallace					
1948	281,988	48.82	194,280	33.63	89,755	15.54	11,620	2.01				
1952	444,950	44.99	544,036	55.01	Constitution							
1956	480,371	42.68	643,849	57.20	1,348	.12						
1960	748,700	48.49	795,476	51.51								

Year	Socialist		Independence		American	
1900	601	1.52				
1904	2,337	5.95				
1908	3,747	7.59	1,356	2.75		
1912	4,806	9.26				
1916	5,353	6.62				
1920	5,189	3.56				
1924					2,315	2.12
1928	4,036	1.59				
1932	775	.28				

The vote in the Democratic column for 1860 was cast for Breckinridge.

The legislature cast the electoral vote in 1868.

Georgia, one of the original states, participated in forty-three presidential elections during the period 1789 to 1960; it did not take part in 1864, because of the Civil War. It supported twenty-five winners and eighteen losers.

TABLE 57   Number and Percentage of Votes by Elections and Parties

Year	Democratic		Nat'l Republ'n / Whig / Republican	
1828	19,362	96.79	642 (Nat'l Republ'n)	3.21
1832	20,750	100.00	(Whig)	
1836	22,333	47.29	24,888	52.71
1840	31,989	44.22	40,349	55.78
1844	44,177	51.20	42,106	48.79
1848	44,809	48.52	47,538	51.48
1852	40,516	64.70	16,660	26.60
1856	56,608	57.13	42,477	42.87
1860	52,131	48.81		
1864			(Republican)	
1868	102,822	64.28	57,134	35.72
1872	76,356	53.43	62,550	43.77
1876	130,088	72.06	50,446	27.94
1880	102,470	65.05	54,086	34.33
1884	94,667	65.92	48,603	33.84
1888	100,499	70.31	40,496	28.33
1892	129,386	58.38	48,305	21.80
1896	94,733	58.03	60,107	36.82
1900	81,700	66.57	35,056	28.56
1904	83,472	63.72	24,003	18.32
1908	72,413	54.53	41,692	31.40
1912	93,171	76.65	5,191	4.27
1916	125,845	79.30	11,225	7.07
1920	109,856	71.12	44,127	28.57
1924	123,200	73.96	30,300	18.19
1928	129,602	56.55	99,381	43.37
1932	234,118	91.60	19,863	7.77
1936	255,364	87.10	36,942	12.60
1940	265,194	84.84	46,376	14.84
1944	268,187	81.74	59,879	18.25
1948	254,646	60.81	76,691	18.31
1952	456,823	69.66	198,979	30.34
1956	445,925	66.47	222,874	33.22
1960	458,638	62.56	274,472	37.44

Minor party votes:

Webster		Southern Rts.	
5,324	8.50	126	.20

Const. Union		Douglas	
43,050	40.31	11,613	10.87

O'Conor-Demo.	
4,000	2.80

Greenback	
969	.62
145	.10

Union Labor	
136	.10

National Dem.	
2,809	1.72

Populist	
42,937	19.37
4,584	3.73
22,635	17.28
16,969	12.78

Prohibition	
195	.14
1,808	1.26
988	.45
5,613	3.44
1,396	1.14
685	.52
1,059	.80
148	.12
8	.01
231	.14
1,125	.44
663	.23
1,003	.32
36	.01
732	.17

T. Roosevelt	
22,010	18.11
20,653	13.01

LaFollette	
12,691	7.62

Communist	
64	.03
23	.01

Union	
141	.05

S. R. Demo.	
85,055	20.31

Wallace	
1,636	.39

Constitution	
2,096	.31

Year	Socialist	
1904	197	.15
1908	584	.44
1912	1,028	.85
1916	967	.61
1920	465	.30
1924		
1928	124	.05
1932	461	.18
1936	68	.02

Independence	
77	.06

American	
155	.09

The legislature cast the electoral vote in 1824.

There was no opposition to Jackson in 1832.

The vote in the Whig column for 1836 was cast for White. The vote in the Democratic column for 1860 was cast for Breckinridge.

HAWAII

TABLE 58   Number and Percentage of Votes by Elections and Parties

Year	Democratic		Republican	
1960	92,410	50.03	92,295	49.97

IDAHO

Idaho, which entered the Union in 1890, participated in eighteen presidential elections during the period 1892 to 1960. It supported fourteen winners and four losers; it supported the winner from 1904 to 1956.

TABLE 59   Number and Percentage of Votes by Elections and Parties

Year	Democratic		Republican		Populist				Prohibition	
1892	2	.01	8,799	44.87	10,520	53.65			288	1.47
1896	23,192	78.10	6,324	21.30					181	.61
1900	29,414	50.98	27,198	47.14	232	.40	*Socialist*		857	1.49
1904	18,480	25.46	47,783	65.84	353	.49	4,949	6.82	1,013	1.40
1908	36,162	37.17	52,621	54.09	*T. Roosevelt*		6,400	6.58	1,986	2.04
1912	33,921	32.08	32,810	31.02	25,527	24.14	11,960	11.31	1,537	1.45
1916	70,054	52.04	55,368	41.13			8,066	5.99	1,127	.84
1920	46,930	33.92	91,351	66.02	*LaFollette*		38	.03	34	.02
1924	24,256	16.36	69,879	47.12	54,160	36.52				
1928	53,074	34.41	99,848	64.74			1,308	.85		
1932	109,479	58.70	71,312	38.23	*Union*		526	.28		
1936	125,683	62.96	66,256	33.19	7,684	3.85				
1940	127,842	54.36	106,553	45.31			497	.21		
1944	107,399	51.55	100,137	48.07	*Wallace, etc.*		282	.14	503	.24
1948	107,370	49.98	101,514	47.26	4,972	2.31	332	.15	628	.29
1952	95,081	34.42	180,707	65.42	443	.16	*Constitution*			
1956	105,868	38.78	166,979	61.18			126	.05		
1960	138,853	46.22	161,597	53.78						

Year	Independence			
1908	119	.12		
1912				
1916	*Farmer Labor*			
1920	6	.00		
1924				
1928	*Communist*		*Liberty*	
1932	491	.26	4,712	2.53
1936				
1940	276	.12		

".00" signifies that the party received some votes, but less than .01%.

Illinois, which entered the Union in 1818, participated in thirty-six presidential elections during the period 1820 to 1960. It supported thirty-two winners and four losers. Only New Mexico, which has been a state only since 1912, has a better record as a barometer.

TABLE 60   Number and Percentage of Votes by Elections and Parties

Year	Democratic		Nat'l Republican		Jackson		Adams		Clay	
1824					1,901	40.37	1,542	32.75	1,047	22.23
1828	9,560	67.22	4,662	32.78						
1832	14,147	72.27	5,429	27.73						
1836	18,097	54.71	*Liberty*		*Whig* 14,983	45.29				
1840	47,625	51.01	159	.17	45,574	48.83				
1844	58,700	54.39	3,439	3.19	45,790	42.43	*Free Soil*			
1848	56,629	45.07			53,215	42.35	15,804	12.58		
1852	80,597	51.83	*Republican*		64,934	41.76	9,966	6.41		
1856	105,344	44.08	96,180	40.25	37,451	15.67	*Const. Union*		*Breckinridge*	
1860	160,205	47.16	172,171	50.68			4,913	1.45	2,402	.71
1864	158,829	45.59	189,521	54.41						
1868	199,143	44.31	250,293	55.69	*O'Conor - Dem.*					
1872	184,938	43.01	241,944	56.27	3,058	.71	*Greenback*		*Prohibition*	
1876	258,601	46.55	278,232	50.09			18,241	3.28	249	.04
1880	277,321	44.56	318,037	51.11			26,358	4.24	443	.07
1884	312,355	46.43	337,474	50.16	*Union Labor*		10,910	1.62	12,074	1.79
1888	348,371	46.59	370,475	49.54	7,134	.95			21,703	2.90
1892	426,281	48.79	399,288	45.70	*National Demo.*		*Soc. Labor*		25,870	2.96
1896	465,613	42.68	607,130	55.65	6,390	.59	1,147	.11	9,818	.90
1900	503,061	44.44	597,985	52.83	*Continental*		1,373	.12	17,626	1.56
1904	327,606	30.43	632,645	58.77	830	.08	4,698	.44	34,770	3.23
1908	450,810	39.02	629,932	54.52	*T. Roosevelt*		1,680	.15	29,364	2.54
1912	405,048	35.34	253,613	22.13	386,478	33.72	4,066	.35	15,710	1.37
1916	950,229	43.34	1,152,549	52.56			2,488	.11	26,047	1.19
1920	534,395	25.51	1,420,480	67.81	*LaFollette*		3,471	.17	11,216	.54
1924	576,975	23.36	1,453,321	58.84	432,027	17.49	2,334	.09	2,367	.10
1928	1,313,817	42.28	1,769,141	56.93			1,812	.06		
1932	1,882,304	55.23	1,432,756	42.04	*Union*		3,638	.11	6,388	.19
1936	2,282,999	57.70	1,570,393	39.69	89,439	2.26	1,921	.05	3,439	.09
1940	2,149,934	50.98	2,047,240	48.54					9,190	.22
1944	2,079,479	51.52	1,939,314	48.05			9,677	.24	7,411	.18
1948	1,994,715	50.09	1,961,103	49.24			3,118	.08	11,959	.30
1952	2,013,920	44.95	2,457,327	54.84			9,363	.21		
1956	1,775,682	40.29	2,623,327	59.52			8,342	.19		
1960	2,377,846	49.98	2,368,988	49.80			10,560	.22		

Year	Crawford	
1824	219	4.65

Year	American		Populist / Communist		United Labor / Socialist		Nat'l Prohib'n / Independence / Farmer Labor		United Chr'n / Single Tax		Union Reform / Commonw. Land	
1876	178	.03										
1880	153	.02										
1884												
1888			*Populist*		*United Labor* 150	.02						
1892			22,207	2.54								
1896					*Socialist*		*Nat'l Prohib'n* 793	.07	*United Chr'n* 352	.03	*Union Reform* 672	.06
1900			1,141	.10	9,687	.86						
1904			6,725	.62	69,225	6.43	*Independence*					
1908			633	.05	34,711	3.00	7,724	.67	400	.03		
1912					81,278	7.09						
1916					61,394	2.80	*Farmer Labor*		*Single Tax* 775	.04		
1920					74,747	3.57	49,630	2.37				
1924			*Communist*								*Commonw. Land* 421	.02
1928			2,622	.11	19,138	.62						
1932			3,581	.12	67,258	1.97						
1936			15,582	.46	7,530	.19						
1940			801	.02	10,914	.26						
1944					180	.00						
1948					11,522	.29						

The vote in the Whig column for 1836 was cast for Harrison.
The vote in the Democratic column for 1860 was cast for Douglas.
".00" signifies that the party received some votes, but less than .01%.

Indiana, which entered the Union in 1816, participated in thirty-seven presidential elections during the period 1816 to 1960. It supported twenty-eight winners and nine losers.

TABLE 61   Number and Percentage of Votes by Elections and Parties

Year	Democratic		Nat'l Republ'n		(col)		(col)		(col)	
1824					*Jackson* 7,343	46.61	*Clay* 5,315	33.74	*Adams* 3,095	19.65
1828	22,237	56.60	17,052	43.40						
1832	31,552	67.10	15,472	32.90	*Whig*					
1836	32,478	44.03			41,281	55.97				
1840	51,695	44.18	*Liberty*		65,308	55.82				
1844	70,181	50.07	2,106	1.50	67,867	48.42	*Free Soil*			
1848	74,745	48.93			69,907	45.77	8,100	5.30		
1852	95,340	52.05	*Republican*		80,901	44.17	6,929	3.78		
1856	118,672	50.10	94,816	40.03	23,386	9.87	*Breckinridge*		*Const. Union*	
1860	115,509	42.44	139,033	51.09			12,295	4.52	5,306	1.95
1864	130,223	46.40	150,422	53.60						
1868	166,980	48.61	176,552	51.39	*O'Conor - Dem.*					
1872	163,632	46.59	186,147	53.00	1,417	.40	*Greenback*			
1876	213,526	49.52	208,111	48.27			9,533	2.21		
1880	225,522	47.91	232,164	49.33			12,986	2.76	*Prohibition*	
1884	244,992	49.47	238,480	48.16	*Union Labor*		8,716	1.76	3,018	.61
1888	261,013	48.61	263,361	49.05	2,694	.50	*Populist*		9,881	1.84
1892	262,740	47.46	255,615	46.17	*National Demo.*		22,208	4.01	13,050	2.36
1896	305,573	47.96	323,754	50.81	2,145	.34			3,056	.48
1900	309,584	46.62	336,063	50.60			1,438	.22	13,718	2.07
1904	274,345	40.22	368,289	53.99			2,444	.36	23,496	3.44
1908	338,262	46.91	348,993	48.40	*T. Roosevelt*		1,193	.17	18,045	2.50
1912	281,890	43.07	151,267	23.11	162,007	24.75			19,249	2.94
1916	334,063	46.47	341,005	47.44	3,915	.54	*Farmer Labor*		16,368	2.28
1920	511,364	40.49	696,370	55.14	*LaFollette*		16,499	1.31	13,462	1.07
1924	492,245	38.69	703,042	55.25	71,700	5.64			4,416	.35
1928	562,691	39.59	848,290	59.68			*National*		5,496	.39
1932	862,054	54.67	677,184	42.94	*Union*		1,645	.10	10,399	.66
1936	934,974	56.63	691,570	41.89	19,407	1.18				
1940	874,063	49.03	899,466	50.45					6,437	.36
1944	781,403	46.73	875,891	52.38	*Wallace, etc.*				12,574	.75
1948	807,833	48.78	821,079	49.58	9,649	.58			14,711	.89
1952	801,530	40.99	1,136,259	58.11	1,222	.06			15,335	.78
1956	783,908	39.70	1,182,811	59.90					6,554	.33
1960	952,358	44.60	1,175,120	55.03					6,746	.32

Year	Soc. Labor		Socialist		Nat'l Prohib'n		(col)	
1896	329	.05			2,267	.36	*Union Reform* 254	.04
1900	663	.10	2,374	.36				
1904	1,598	.23	12,013	1.76	*Independence* 514	.07		
1908	643	.09	13,476	1.87				
1912	3,130	.48	36,931	5.64				
1916	1,659	.23	21,855	3.04	*Single Tax* 566	.04		
1920			24,703	1.96	*Communist*			
1924					987	.08		
1928	645	.05	3,871	.27	321	.02		
1932	2,070	.13	21,388	1.36	2,187	.14		
1936			3,856	.23	1,090	.07		
1940	706	.04	2,075	.12				
1944			2,223	.13				
1948	763	.05	2,179	.13				
1952	979	.05						
1956	1,334	.07						
1960	1,136	.05						

The vote in the Whig column for 1836 was cast for Harrison. The vote in the Democratic column for 1860 was cast for Douglas.

Iowa, which entered the Union in 1846, participated in twenty-nine presidential elections during the period 1848 to 1960. It supported twenty-one winners and eight losers.

TABLE 62   Number and Percentage of Votes by Elections and Parties

Year	Democratic		Republican	
1848	12,093	49.76		
1852	17,763	50.43		
1856	36,241	40.35	44,127	49.13
1860	55,111	42.94	70,409	54.87
1864	49,596	35.77	89,075	64.23
1868	74,040	38.08	120,399	61.92
1872	71,196	34.73	131,566	64.18
1876	112,099	38.33	171,327	58.58
1880	105,845	32.72	183,927	56.85
1884	177,286	47.16	197,082	52.42
1888	179,877	44.51	211,598	52.36
1892	196,367	44.31	219,795	49.60
1896	223,741	42.90	289,293	55.46
1900	209,265	39.42	307,808	57.99
1904	149,141	30.69	307,907	63.37
1908	200,771	40.58	275,210	55.62
1912	185,325	37.60	119,805	24.30
1916	221,699	42.73	280,449	54.06
1920	227,921	25.46	634,674	70.91
1924	162,600	16.65	537,635	55.06
1928	378,936	37.54	623,818	61.80
1932	598,019	57.69	414,433	39.98
1936	621,756	54.41	487,977	42.70
1940	578,800	47.62	632,370	52.03
1944	499,876	47.49	547,267	51.99
1948	522,380	50.31	494,018	47.58
1952	451,513	35.59	808,906	63.76
1956	501,858	40.65	729,187	59.06
1960	550,565	43.22	722,381	56.71

Whig
11,084	45.61
15,856	45.02
9,444	10.52

O'Conor - Dem.
2,221	1.08

American
433	.13

Union Labor
9,105	2.25

National Demo.
4,586	.88

T. Roosevelt
161,819	32.83
1,793	.35

LaFollette
272,243	27.88

Union
29,687	2.60

Wallace, etc.
12,125	1.17
5,085	.40

Free Soil
1,126	4.63
1,604	4.55

Const. Union
1,763	1.37

Greenback
9,001	3.08
32,701	10.11

Populist
20,595	4.65
1,026	.19
2,406	.50
261	.05

Farmer Labor
10,321	1.15
3,088	.31
1,094	.11

Soc. Workers
256	.02
634	.05

Breckinridge
1,048	.82

Prohibition
36	.01
592	.18
1,564	.42
3,550	.88
6,402	1.44
3,192	.61
9,502	1.79
11,601	2.39
9,837	1.99
9,026	1.83
3,371	.65
4,197	.47
2,111	.20
1,182	.10
2,284	.19
3,752	.36
3,382	.33
2,882	.23

Year	Soc. Labor		Socialist		Nat'l Prohib'n		United Chr'n	
1896	453	.09			352	.07	169	.03
1900	259	.05	2,790	.53				
1904			14,847	3.06	Independence 404	.08		
1908			8,287	1.67				
1912			16,967	3.44				
1916			11,490	2.21				
1920	982	.11	16,981	1.90	Communist 4,037	.41		
1924					328	.03		
1928	230	.02	2,960	.29	559	.05		
1932			20,467	1.97	506	.04		
1936	252	.02	1,373	.12	1,524	.13		
1940	452	.04						
1944	193	.02	1,511	.14				
1948	4,274	.41	1,829	.18				
1952	139	.01	219	.02	Constitution 3,202	.26		
1956	125	.01	192	.02				
1960	230	.02						

The vote in the Democratic column for 1860 was cast for Douglas.

KANSAS

Kansas, which entered the Union in 1861, participated in twenty-five presidential elections during the period 1864 to 1960. It supported eighteen winners and seven losers.

TABLE 63 Number and Percentage of Votes by Elections and Parties

Year	Democratic		Republican	
1864	3,871	21.39	14,228	78.61
1868	14,019	31.11	31,049	68.89
1872	32,970	32.77	67,048	66.64
1876	37,902	30.53	78,332	63.10
1880	59,801	29.72	121,549	60.40
1884	90,132	33.96	154,406	58.18
1888	102,745	31.11	182,904	55.39
1892			157,241	48.40
1896	173,042	51.48	159,541	47.46
1900	162,601	45.96	185,955	52.56
1904	86,174	26.23	212,955	64.81
1908	161,209	42.88	197,216	52.46
1912	143,663	39.31	74,845	20.48
1916	314,588	49.95	277,658	44.09
1920	185,464	32.52	369,268	64.76
1924	156,319	23.60	407,671	61.54
1928	193,003	27.06	513,672	72.02
1932	424,204	53.56	349,498	44.13
1936	464,520	53.67	397,727	45.95
1940	364,725	42.40	489,169	56.86
1944	287,458	39.18	442,096	60.25
1948	351,902	44.61	423,039	53.63
1952	273,296	30.50	616,302	68.77
1956	296,317	34.21	566,878	65.44
1960	363,213	39.10	561,474	60.45

Minor parties (center columns):

Year	Greenback / Populist / others		O'Conor – Dem / Union Labor	
1876	Greenback 7,776	6.26	O'Conor – Dem 596	.59
1880	Greenback 19,851	9.87		
1884	Greenback 16,341	6.16		
1888			Union Labor 37,788	11.44
1892	Populist 163,111	50.20		
1904	6,257	1.90		
1912	T. Roosevelt 120,210	32.89		
1924	LaFollette 98,461	14.86		
1936	Union 494	.06		
1948	Wallace 4,603	.58		

Socialist:

Year	Socialist	
1900	1,605	.45
1904	15,869	4.83
1908	12,420	3.31
1912	26,779	7.33
1916	24,685	3.92
1920	15,511	2.72
1928	6,205	.87
1932	18,276	2.31
1936	2,766	.32
1940	2,347	.27
1944	1,613	.22
1948	2,807	.36
1952	530	.06

Prohibition:

Year	Prohibition	
1872	110	.09
1876	25	.01
1884	4,495	1.69
1888	6,779	2.05
1892	4,553	1.40
1896	1,721	.51
1900	3,605	1.02
1904	7,306	2.22
1908	5,033	1.34
1916	12,882	2.05
1940	4,056	.47
1944	2,609	.36
1948	6,468	.82
1952	6,038	.67
1956	3,048	.35
1960	4,138	.45

Year	American / other	
1876	American 23	.02
1880		
1884		
1888		
1892	Nat'l Demo. — Nat'l Prohib'n	
1896	1,209 .36 — 630 .19	
1900		
1904	Independence	
1908	68	.02
1912		
1916		
1920		
1924	Communist	
1928	320	.04

KENTUCKY

Kentucky, which entered the Union in 1792, participated in forty-three presidential elections during the period 1792 to 1960. It supported twenty-five winners and eighteen losers.

TABLE 64 Number and Percentage of Votes by Elections and Parties

Year	Democratic									
			Nat'l Republ'n		Clay		Jackson			
1824					17,331	72.86	6,455	27.14		
1828	39,394	55.60	31,460	44.40						
					Whig					
1832	36,247	45.51	43,396	54.49						
1836	33,435	47.50			36,955	52.50				
1840	32,616	35.80			58,489	64.20				
1844	51,988	45.91			61,255	54.09				
							Free Soil			
1848	49,720	42.55			67,141	57.45				
			Republican							
1852	53,806	48.41			57,068	51.35	265	.24		
							Const. Union		Douglas	
1856	74,642	52.41	373	.26	67,416	47.33				
1860	53,143	36.35	1,364	.93			66,058	45.18	25,651	17.54
1864	64,301	69.83	27,786	30.17						
					O'Conor - Dem.		Greenback		Prohibition	
1868	115,889	74.55	39,566	25.45						
1872	100,208	52.31	88,970	46.45	2,374	1.24				
1876	160,445	61.31	98,415	37.61			2,003	.77	818	.31
1880	149,068	55.80	106,306	39.80			11,499	4.30	258	.10
					Union Labor					
1884	152,961	55.44	118,122	42.81			1,691	.61	3,139	1.14
							Populist			
1888	183,800	53.31	155,134	44.99	622	.18			5,225	1.52
					National Demo.					
1892	175,461	51.48	135,441	39.74			23,500	6.89	6,442	1.89
1896	217,890	48.86	218,171	48.92	5,114	1.15			4,781	1.07
1900	234,899	50.24	226,801	48.50			2,017	.43	2,814	.60
1904	217,170	49.84	205,277	47.11			2,511	.58	6,609	1.52
					T. Roosevelt					
1908	244,092	49.74	235,711	48.04			333	.07	5,887	1.20
1912	219,584	48.40	115,512	25.46	102,766	22.65			3,233	.71
1916	269,990	51.93	241,854	46.52					3,036	.58
					LaFollette					
1920	456,497	49.69	452,480	49.25					3,325	.36
							Communist			
1924	374,855	45.98	398,966	48.93	38,465	4.72				
1928	381,070	40.51	558,064	59.33			293	.03		
					Union					
1932	580,574	59.06	394,716	40.15			272	.03	2,252	.23
1936	541,944	58.51	369,702	39.92	12,501	1.35	204	.02	929	.10
1940	557,222	57.44	410,384	42.30					1,443	.15
					Wallace, etc.		S. R. Demo.			
1944	472,589	54.45	392,448	45.22					2,023	.23
1948	466,756	56.74	341,210	41.48	1,567	.19	10,411	1.27	1,245	.15
							States' Rts.			
1952	495,729	49.91	495,029	49.84	336	.03			1,161	.12
1956	476,453	45.21	572,192	54.30			2,657	.25	2,145	.20
1960	521,855	46.41	602,607	53.59						

Year	Soc. Labor		Socialist					
1900	299	.06	770	.16				
					Independence			
1904	596	.14	3,602	.83				
1908	404	.08	4,060	.83	200	.04		
1912	956	.21	11,647	2.57				
1916	333	.06	4,734	.91				
					American		Commonw. Land	
1920			6,409	.70				
1924	1,499	.18			1,299	.16	248	.03
1928	340	.04	837	.09				
1932	1,396	.14	3,853	.39				
1936	294	.03	632	.07				
1940			1,014	.10				
1944	326	.04	535	.06				
1948	185	.02	1,284	.16				
1952	893	.09						
1956	358	.03						

The vote in the Whig column for 1836 was cast for Harrison. The vote in the Democratic column for 1860 was cast for Breckinridge.

LOUISIANA

Louisiana, which entered the Union in 1812, participated in thirty-seven presidential elections during the period 1812 to 1960; it did not take part in 1864, because of the Civil War. It supported twenty-three winners and thirteen losers; its 1872 electoral votes, which were intended for the Republican candidate, were rejected.

TABLE 65 Number and Percentage of Votes by Elections and Parties

Year	Democratic		Whig / Republican		Other parties
1828	4,605	52.92	Nat'l Republ'n 4,097	47.08	
1832	4,049	61.56	Nat'l Republ'n 2,528	38.44	
1836	3,653	51.92	Whig 3,383	48.08	
1840	7,617	40.27	11,297	59.73	
1844	13,782	51.30	13,083	48.70	
1848	15,370	45.76	18,217	54.24	
1852	18,647	51.94	17,255	48.06	
1856	22,169	51.70	20,709	48.30	
1860	22,681	44.90	Const. Union 20,204	40.00	Douglas 7,625 15.10
1864					
1868	80,225	70.69	Republican 33,263	29.31	
1872	57,029	44.31	71,663	55.69	
1876	70,566	48.43	75,135	51.57	
1880	65,067	62.48	38,637	37.10	Greenback 439 .42
1884	62,540	57.20	46,347	42.39	Greenback 120 .11
1888	85,032	73.37	30,701	26.48	Populist 2,462 2.08; Prohibition 338 .31
1892	87,922	74.33	27,903	23.59	National Demo. 1,915 1.89; Prohibition 127 .11
1896	77,175	76.31	22,037	21.79	
1900	53,671	79.04	14,233	20.96	Socialist 995 1.84
1904	47,747	88.51	5,205	9.65	
1908	63,568	84.59	8,958	11.92	Independence 82 .11; Socialist 2,538 3.38
1912	61,035	76.83	3,834	4.83	T. Roosevelt 9,323 11.74; Socialist 5,249 6.61
1916	79,875	85.90	6,466	6.95	T. Roosevelt 6,349 6.83; Socialist 292 .31
1920	87,519	69.43	38,538	30.57	
1924	93,218	76.44	24,670	20.23	LaFollette 4,063 3.33
1928	164,655	76.29	51,160	23.71	
1932	249,418	92.97	18,853	7.03	
1936	292,894	88.84	36,791	11.16	
1940	319,751	85.91	52,446	14.09	
1944	281,564	80.60	67,750	19.40	
1948	136,344	32.75	72,657	17.45	S. R. Demo. 204,290 49.07; Wallace 3,035 .73
1952	345,027	52.92	306,925	47.08	Constitution 44,520 7.21
1956	243,977	39.51	329,047	53.28	
1960	407,339	50.42	230,980	28.59	States Rights 169,572 20.99

Year	Union Labor	
1888	39	.03

The legislature cast the electoral vote in 1824.

The vote in the Whig column for 1836 was cast for White. The vote in the Democratic column for 1860 was cast for Breckinridge.

MAINE

Maine, which entered the Union in 1820, participated in thirty-six presidential elections during the period 1820 to 1960. It supported twenty-four winners and twelve losers.

TABLE 66   Number and Percentage of Votes by Elections and Parties

Year	Democratic		Party	#	%	Party	#	%	Party	#	%	Party	#	%
1824			Nat'l Republ'n			Adams	10,289	81.50	Crawford	2,336	18.50			
1828	13,927	40.14		20,773	59.86				Anti-Masonic					
1832	33,984	55.03		27,327	43.96	Whig				841	1.35			
1836	22,900	60.04	Liberty				15,239	39.96						
1840	46,190	49.67		186	.20		46,612	50.13						
1844	45,964	53.79		4,862	5.69		34,619	40.52	Free Soil					
1848	40,138	45.85					35,279	40.30		12,124	13.85			
1852	41,609	50.63	Republican				32,543	39.60		8,030	9.77			
1856	39,080	35.60		67,379	61.37		3,325	3.03	Breckinridge			Const. Union		
1860	26,693	27.26		62,811	64.15					6,368	6.50		2,046	2.09
1864	47,736	39.78		72,278	60.22									
1868	42,396	37.58		70,426	62.42									
1872	29,087	32.14		61,422	67.86	Greenback								
1876	49,914	42.71		66,300	56.73		662	.57	Prohibition			American		
1880	65,171	45.28		74,056	51.45		4,480	3.11		93	.06		142	.10
1884	52,140	39.97		72,209	55.35		3,953	3.03		2,160	1.66	Union Labor		
1888	50,481	39.36		73,734	57.49	Populist				2,691	2.10		1,344	1.05
1892	48,044	41.27		62,931	54.06		2,045	1.76		3,062	2.63			
1896	34,587	29.19		80,461	67.90					1,589	1.34	Socialist		
1900	36,823	34.83		65,435	61.89					2,585	2.45		878	.83
1904	27,648	28.79		64,438	67.10		338	.35		1,510	1.57		2,103	2.19
1908	35,403	33.29		66,987	63.00	T. Roosevelt				1,487	1.40		1,758	1.65
1912	51,113	39.43		26,545	20.48		48,495	37.41		946	.73		2,541	1.96
1916	64,132	47.01		69,506	50.95					597	.44		2,177	1.60
1920	58,961	29.80		136,355	68.92	LaFollette				1	.00		2,214	1.12
1924	41,964	21.83		138,440	72.03		11,382	5.92					1,068	.41
1928	81,179	30.96		179,923	68.63								2,489	.83
1932	128,907	43.19		166,631	55.83	Union							783	.26
1936	126,333	41.52		168,823	55.49		7,581	2.49		334	.11			
1940	156,478	48.77		163,951	51.10									
1944	140,631	47.45		155,434	52.44	Wallace, etc.							547	.21
1948	111,916	42.27		150,234	56.74		1,884	.71					138	.04
1952	118,806	33.77		232,353	66.05		332	.09						
1956	102,468	29.13		249,238	70.87									
1960	181,159	42.95		240,608	57.05									

Year	Soc. Labor		Party	#	%
1892	336	.29			
1896			National Demo.	1,867	1.58
1900					
1904			Independence		
1908				701	.66
1912					
1916			Single Tax		
1920				310	.16
1924	406	.21			
1928			Communist		
1932	255	.09		162	.05
1936	129	.04		257	.08
1940				411	.13
1944	335	.11			
1948	206	.08			
1952	156	.04			

The vote in the Whig column for 1836 was cast for Harrison. The vote in the Democratic column for 1860 was cast for Douglas.

".00" signifies that the party received some votes, but less than .01%.

Maryland, one of the original states, participated in forty-four presidential elections during the period 1789 to 1960. It supported twenty-nine winners and fourteen losers; in 1801 it split its electoral vote, giving five each to Jefferson, Burr, John Adams, and Charles C. Pinckney.

TABLE 67 Number and Percentage of Votes by Elections and Parties

Year	Democratic		Nat'l Republ'n / Republican	
1824				
1828	24,565	49.04	25,527	50.96
1832	19,156	49.99	19,160	50.01
1836	22,168	46.16		
1840	28,759	46.17		
1844	32,676	47.59		
1848	34,536	47.72		
1852	40,028	53.26		
1856	39,115	45.03	281	.32
1860	42,511	45.60	2,895	3.11
1864	32,739	44.90	40,169	55.10
1868	62,357	67.20	30,438	32.80
1872	67,687	50.34	66,760	49.65
1876	91,780	56.03	71,981	43.94
1880	93,706	54.15	78,515	45.37
1884	96,932	52.13	85,699	46.09
1888	106,168	50.34	99,986	47.40
1892	113,866	53.38	92,736	43.48
1896	104,746	41.75	136,978	54.60
1900	122,238	46.23	136,185	51.50
1904	109,446	48.81	109,497	48.83
1908	115,908	48.59	116,513	48.85
1912	112,674	48.57	54,956	23.69
1916	138,359	52.80	117,347	44.78
1920	180,626	42.16	236,117	55.11
1924	148,072	41.29	162,414	45.29
1928	223,626	42.33	301,479	57.06
1932	314,314	61.50	184,184	36.04
1936	389,612	62.35	231,435	37.04
1940	384,546	58.26	269,534	40.83
1944	315,490	51.85	292,949	48.15
1948	286,521	48.01	294,814	49.40
1952	395,337	43.83	499,424	55.36
1956	372,613	39.96	559,738	60.04
1960	565,808	53.61	489,538	46.39

1824

Adams		Jackson		Crawford		Clay	
14,632	44.06	14,523	43.73	3,364	10.13	695	2.09

Whig (the vote in the Whig column for 1836 was cast for Harrison)

Year	Whig	
1836	25,852	53.84
1840	33,533	53.83
1844	35,984	52.41
1848	37,706	52.10
1852	35,080	46.67
1856	47,462	54.64

Free Soil

Year	Free Soil	
1848	130	.18
1852	54	.07

1860 (the vote in the Democratic column for 1860 was cast for Breckinridge)

Const. Union		Douglas	
41,875	44.91	5,953	6.39

1872

O'Conor-Dem.		Prohibition	
19	.01	10	.01

Greenback

Year	Greenback	
1876	33	.02
1880	818	.47
1884	531	.29

Populist

Year	Populist	
1892	796	.37

Union Reform

Year	Union Reform	
1900	145	.05

T. Roosevelt

Year	T. Roosevelt	
1912	57,789	24.91

LaFollette

Year	LaFollette	
1924	47,157	13.15

Wallace, etc.

Year	Wallace, etc.	
1948	9,983	1.67
1952	7,313	.81

Socialist

Year	Socialist	
1900	904	.34
1904	2,247	1.00
1908	2,323	.97
1912	3,996	1.72
1916	2,674	1.02
1920	8,876	2.07
1928	1,701	.32
1932	10,489	2.05
1936	1,629	.26
1940	4,093	.62
1948	2,941	.49

Prohibition

Year	Prohibition	
1884	2,794	1.50
1888	4,767	2.26
1892	5,877	2.76
1896	5,922	2.36
1900	4,574	1.73
1904	3,034	1.35
1908	3,302	1.38
1912	2,244	.97
1916	2,903	1.11

Communist

Year	Communist	
1928	636	.12
1932	1,031	.20
1936	915	.15
1940	1,274	.19

S. R. Demo.

Year	S. R. Demo.	
1948	2,476	.41

Soc. Labor

Year	Soc. Labor	
1892	27	.01
1896	588	.23
1900	388	.15
1904		
1908		
1912	322	.14
1916	756	.29
1920	1,178	.27
1924	987	.28
1928	906	.17
1932	1,036	.20
1936	1,305	.21
1940	657	.10

1896

National Demo.		Nat'l Proh'n	
2,507	1.00	136	.05

Independence

485	.20

Farmer Labor

1,645	.38

The vote in the Whig column for 1836 was cast for Harrison. The vote in the Democratic column for 1860 was cast for Breckinridge.

MASSACHUSETTS

Massachusetts, one of the original states, participated in forty-four presidential elections during the period 1789 to 1960. It supported thirty winners and fourteen losers.

TABLE 68 — Number and Percentage of Votes by Elections and Parties

Year	Democratic	Nat'l Republican / Liberty / Republican	Adams / Whig / Free Soil / Greenback / Populist / T. Roosevelt / LaFollette / Union / Wallace, etc.	Crawford / Anti-Masonic / Free Soil / Const. Union / Prohibition	Webster / Breckinridge / Soc. Labor
1824	*Democratic*	*Nat'l Republican*	*Adams* 30,687 82.26	*Crawford* 6,616 17.74	
1828	6,019 16.79	29,837 83.21		*Anti-Masonic*	
1832	14,497 23.11	33,003 52.61	*Whig* .	15,233 24.28	
1836	33,542 44.82	*Liberty*	41,287 55.18		
1840	52,432 41.30	1,621 1.28	72,913 57.43		
1844	52,846 40.30	10,860 8.28	67,418 51.42		
1848	35,398 26.23		61,300 45.42	*Free Soil* 38,263 28.35	*Webster*
1852	45,875 35.72	*Republican*	52,683 41.03	28,023 21.82	1,670 1.30
1856	39,240 23.48	108,190 64.72	19,726 11.80	*Const. Union*	*Breckinridge*
1860	34,492 20.29	106,649 62.75		22,536 · 13.26	6,277 3.69
1864	48,745 27.78	126,742 72.22			
1868	59,408 30.33	136,477 69.67			
1872	59,260 30.75	133,472 69.25	*Greenback*	*Prohibition*	
1876	108,975 41.93	150,078 57.74	779 .30	84 .03	
1880	111,960 39.65	165,205 58.50	4,548 1.61	682 .24	
1884	122,481 40.33	146,724 48.32	24,433 8.05	10,026 3.30	
1888	151,905 44.09	183,892 53.38	*Populist* 3,348 .86	8,701 2.53	*Soc. Labor*
1892	176,858 45.19	202,927 51.85		7,539 1.93	676 .17
1896	106,206 26.41	278,976 69.36		3,060 .76	2,137 .53
1900	157,016 37.86	239,147 57.67		6,208 1.50	2,610 .63
1904	165,772 37.24	257,822 57.92	1,299 .29	4,286 .96	2,365 .53
1908	155,543 34.04	265,966 58.21	*T. Roosevelt*	4,379 .96	1,018 .22
1912	174,315 35.61	156,139 31.89	142,375 29.08	2,799 .57	1,270 .26
1916	247,885 46.61	268,812 50.54	*LaFollette*	2,993 .56	1,125 .21
1920	276,691 27.84	681,153 68.55			3,583 .36
1924	280,831 24.85	703,489 62.26	141,284 12.50		1,674 .15
1928	792,758 50.24	775,566 49.15	*Union*		773 .05
1932	800,148 50.64	736,959 46.64		1,142 .07	2,668 .17
1936	942,716 51.22	768,613 41.76	118,639 6.45	1,032 .06	1,305 .07
1940	1,076,522 53.11	939,700 46.36	*Wallace, etc.*	1,370 .07	1,492 .07
1944	1,035,296 52.81	921,350 47.00		973 .05	2,780 .14
1948	1,151,788 54.68	909,370 43.17	38,157 1.81	1,663 .08	5,535 .26
1952	1,083,525 45.46	1,292,325 54.22	4,636 .19	886 .04	1,957 .08
1956	948,190 40.38	1,393,197 59.33		1,205 .05	5,573 .24
1960	1,487,174 60.22	976,750 39.55		1,633 .07	3,892 .16

Year	American
1852	165 .12

Year	National Demo. / Independence / Communist	Socialist
1896	*National Demo.* 11,809 2.94	
1900		9,716 2.34
1904	*Independence*	13,604 3.06
1908	19,239 4.21	10,781 2.36
1912		12,662 2.59
1916		11,062 2.08
1920		32,269 3.25
1924	*Communist* 2,637 .23	
1928	2,464 .16	6,262 .40
1932	4,821 .31	34,305 2.17
1936	2,930 .16	5,111 .28
1940	3,806 .19	4,091 .20

The vote in the Whig column for 1836 was cast for Webster. The vote in the Democratic column for 1860 was cast for Douglas.

Michigan, which entered the Union in *1837*, participated in thirty-two presidential elections during the period *1836* to 1960. It supported twenty-four winners and eight losers.

TABLE 69   Number and Percentage of Votes by Elections and Parties

Year	Democratic		Liberty / Republican		Whig / other		Free Soil / other		Const. Union / Prohibition	
	Votes	%	Votes	%	Votes	%	Votes	%	Votes	%
1836	7,534	64.84	—	—	Whig 4,085	35.16	—	—	—	—
1840	21,131	47.61	Liberty 321	.72	22,933	51.67	—	—	—	—
1844	27,759	49.81	3,632	6.52	24,337	43.67	—	—	—	—
1848	30,687	47.20	—	—	23,940	36.82	Free Soil 10,389	15.98	—	—
1852	41,842	50.45	—	—	33,860	40.83	7,237	8.73	—	—
1856	52,529	41.59	Republican 71,969	56.98	1,660	1.31	—	—	—	—
1860	65,057	42.04	88,480	57.18	—	—	Breckinridge 805	.52	Const. Union 405	.26
1864	67,370	44.11	85,352	55.89	—	—	—	—	—	—
1868	97,069	43.02	128,550	56.98	—	—	—	—	—	—
1872	78,355	35.46	138,455	62.67	—	—	O'Conor-Demo. 2,861	1.29	Prohibition 1,271	.58
1876	141,095	44.44	166,534	52.45	Greenback 9,060	2.85	—	—	767	.24
1880	131,597	37.30	185,341	52.54	34,895	9.89	—	—	942	.27
1884	149,835	37.24	192,669	47.89	41,390	10.29	—	—	18,403	4.57
1888	213,469	44.91	236,387	49.73	—	—	Union Labor 4,555	.96	20,945	4.41
1892	202,296	43.43	222,708	47.81	Populist 20,084	4.28	—	—	20,857	4.48
1896	237,268	43.52	293,582	53.85	837	.15	—	—	5,025	.92
1900	211,685	38.89	316,269	58.10	1,159	.22	Socialist 2,826	.52	11,859	2.18
1904	135,392	25.78	364,957	69.50	—	—	9,042	1.72	13,441	2.56
1908	175,771	32.44	335,580	61.93	—	—	11,586	2.14	16,974	3.13
1912	150,751	27.36	152,244	27.63	T. Roosevelt 214,584	38.95	23,211	4.21	8,934	1.62
1916	286,775	44.05	339,097	52.00	—	—	16,120	2.48	8,139	1.25
1920	233,450	22.28	762,865	72.80	—	—	28,947	2.76	9,646	.92
1924	152,359	13.13	874,631	75.37	LaFollette 122,014	10.51	—	—	6,085	.52
1928	396,762	28.92	965,396	70.36	—	—	3,516	.26	2,728	.20
1932	871,700	52.37	739,894	44.45	—	—	39,205	2.36	2,893	.17
1936	1,016,794	56.33	699,733	38.76	Union 75,795	4.20	8,208	.45	579	.03
1940	1,032,991	49.52	1,039,917	49.85	—	—	7,593	.36	1,795	.09
1944	1,106,899	50.19	1,084,423	49.18	—	—	4,598	.21	6,503	.29
1948	1,003,448	47.57	1,038,595	49.23	Wallace, etc. 46,515	2.20	6,063	.29	13,052	.62
1952	1,230,657	43.97	1,551,529	55.44	—	—	—	—	10,331	.37
1956	1,359,898	44.15	1,713,647	55.63	—	—	—	—	6,923	.22
1960	1,687,269	50.85	1,620,428	48.84	3,922	.14	—	—	2,029	.06

The vote in the Whig column for 1836 was cast for Harrison. The vote in the Democratic column for 1860 was cast for Douglas.

Year	Smith / American / Socialist Labor		National Demo. / Independence / Farmer Labor / Communist / Socialist W'kers		Nat'l Prohib'n / No Party / Liberty / America First / Tax Cut		Indepdt Am'n	
	Votes	%	Votes	%	Votes	%	Votes	%
1856	Smith 150	.12	—	—	—	—	—	—
1876	American 71	.02	—	—	—	—	—	—
1880	2	.00	—	—	—	—	—	—
1892	—	—	—	—	—	—	—	—
1896	Socialist Labor 297	.05	National Demo. 6,968	1.28	Nat'l Prohib'n 1,995	.37	—	—
1900	903	.17	—	—	—	—	—	—
1904	1,108	.21	—	—	—	—	—	—
1908	1,096	.20	Independence 760	.14	No Party 63	.01	—	—
1912	1,252	.23	—	—	—	—	—	—
1916	842	.13	—	—	—	—	—	—
1920	2,539	.24	Farmer Labor 10,480	1.00	—	—	—	—
1924	5,330	.46	Communist 2,881	.21	—	—	—	—
1928	799	.06	9,318	.56	—	—	—	—
1932	1,401	.08	3,384	.19	Liberty 217	.01	—	—
1936	600	.03	2,834	.14	—	—	—	—
1940	795	.04	—	—	—	—	—	—
1944	1,264	.06	Socialist W'kers 672	.03	America First 1,530	.07	—	—
1948	1,263	.06	655	.02	—	—	—	—
1952	1,495	.05	—	—	—	—	—	—
1956	—	—	—	—	—	—	—	—
1960	1,718	.05	4,347	.13	Tax Cut 1,767	.05	539	.02

MINNESOTA

Minnesota, which entered the Union in 1858, participated in twenty-six presidential elections during the period 1860 to 1960. It supported twenty-two winners and four losers. In 1916 Hughes led Wilson in Minnesota, 46.35% to 46.25%, while losing the election.

TABLE 70   Number and Percentage of Votes by Elections and Parties

Year	Democratic		Republican		Minor party A		Minor party B		Prohibition	
					Breckinridge		*Const. Union*			
1860	11,920	34.25	22,069	63.42	748	2.15	62	.18		
1864	17,375	40.94	25,060	59.06						
1868	28,072	39.20	43,542	60.80						
					Greenback				*Prohibition*	
1872	34,423	38.44	55,117	61.55					72	.06
1876	48,799	39.31	72,962	58.77	2,311	1.86				
1880	53,315	35.36	93,903	62.28	3,267	2.17			286	.19
							Union Labor			
1884	70,144	36.85	111,923	58.80	3,587	1.88			4,691	2.46
					Populist					
1888	104,385	39.65	142,492	54.12			1,097	.42	15,311	5.82
1892	100,920	37.76	122,823	45.96	29,313	10.97			14,182	5.31
							Socialist			
1896	139,735	40.89	193,503	56.62					4,348	1.27
1900	112,901	35.69	190,461	60.21			3,065	.97	8,555	2.70
1904	55,187	18.84	216,651	73.95	2,103	.72	11,692	3.99	6,352	2.17
					T. Roosevelt					
1908	109,401	33.02	195,843	59.11			14,527	4.38	11,107	3.35
1912	106,426	31.84	64,334	19.25	125,856	37.66	27,505	8.23	7,886	2.36
1916	179,152	46.25	179,544	46.35	290	.07	20,117	5.19	7,793	2.01
					LaFollette					
1920	142,994	19.49	519,421	70.78	339,192	41.26	56,106	7.65	11,489	1.57
1924	55,913	6.80	420,759	51.18			6,774	.70		
1928	396,451	40.83	560,977	57.77			25,476	2.54		
					Union					
1932	600,806	59.91	363,959	36.29	74,296	6.58	2,872	.25		
1936	698,811	61.84	350,461	31.01			5,454	.44		
1940	644,196	51.49	596,274	47.66			5,073	.45		
					Wallace, etc.					
1944	589,864	52.41	527,416	46.86	27,866	2.30	4,646	.38		
1948	692,966	57.16	483,617	39.89	2,666	.19				
1952	608,458	44.11	763,211	55.33					2,147	.16
1956	617,525	46.08	719,302	53.68						
1960	779,933	50.58	757,915	49.16						

Year	Soc. Labor		Minor party		Farmer Labor	
			National Demo.			
1896	954	.28	3,216	.94		
1900	1,329	.42				
			Independence			
1904	974	.33				
1908			426	.13		
1912	2,212	.66				
1916	468	.12				
			Communist			
1920	3,828	.52				
1924	1,855	.23	4,427	.54		
1928	1,921	.20	4,853	.50	5,731	.57
1932	770	.08	6,101	.61		
1936	961	.09	2,574	.23		
1940	2,553	.20	2,711	.22		
			Soc. Workers			
1944	3,176	.28				
1948	2,525	.21	606	.05		
1952	2,383	.17	618	.04		
1956	2,080	.16	1,098	.08		
1960	962	.06	3,077	.20		

The vote in the Democratic column for 1860 was cast for Douglas.

MISSISSIPPI

Mississippi, which entered the Union in 1817, participated in thirty-four presidential elections during the period 1820 to 1960; it did not take part in 1864 and 1868, because of the Civil War and Reconstruction. It supported seventeen winners and seventeen losers.

TABLE 71   Number and Percentage of Votes by Elections and Parties

Year	Democratic		Nat'l Repub'n / Whig / Republican							
					Jackson		**Adams**		**Crawford**	
1824					3,234	64.08	1,694	33.56	119	2.36
1828	6,772	81.07	1,581	18.93						
1832	5,919	100.00	*Whig*							
1836	9,979	50.74	9,688	49.26						
1840	16,995	46.55	19,518	53.45						
1844	25,126	56.68	19,206	43.32						
1848	26,537	50.59	25,922	49.41						
1852	26,876	60.50	17,548	39.50						
1856	35,665	59.29	24,490	40.71	**Const. Union**		**Douglas**			
1860	40,797	59.02			25,040	36.23	3,283	4.75		
1864										
1868			*Republican*							
1872	47,288	36.53	82,175	63.47						
1876	112,173	68.08	52,605	31.92	**Greenback**					
1880	75,750	65.08	34,854	29.94	5,797	4.98				
1884	76,510	63.75	43,509	36.25			**Union Labor**		**Prohibition**	
1888	85,467	73.13	31,120	26.63	**Populist**		22	.02	258	.22
1892	40,288	76.33	1,395	2.64	10,102	19.14	**Nat'l Demo.**		995	1.89
1896	63,793	90.52	5,123	7.27			1,071	1.52	485	.69
1900	51,706	87.48	5,753	9.73	1,644	2.78			**Socialist**	
1904	53,374	91.43	3,187	5.46	1,424	2.44			392	.67
1908	60,287	90.07	4,392	6.56	1,276	1.91	**T. Roosevelt**		978	1.46
1912	57,227	88.69	1,595	2.47			3,645	5.65	2,061	3.19
1916	80,422	92.78	4,253	4.91			520	.60	1,484	1.71
1920	69,277	83.98	11,576	14.03	**LaFollette**				1,639	1.99
1924	100,475	89.30	8,546	7.60	3,494	3.11				
1928	124,539	82.10	27,153	17.90						
1932	140,168	95.98	5,180	3.55					686	.47
1936	157,318	97.06	4,443	2.74					329	.20
1940	168,267	95.70	7,364	4.19					193	.11
1944	168,479	93.56	11,601	6.44	**S. R. Demo.**		**Wallace**			
1948	19,384	10.09	5,043	2.62	167,538	87.17	225	.12		
1952	172,566	60.44	112,966	39.56			**States' Rts.**			
1956	144,498	58.23	60,685	24.46	**Unpledged Dem.**		42,966	17.31		
1960	108,362	36.34	73,561	24.67	116,248	38.99				

There was no opposition to Jackson in 1832.

The vote in the Whig column for 1836 was cast for White. The vote in the Democratic column for 1860 was cast for Breckinridge.

Missouri, which entered the Union in 1821, participated in thirty-six presidential elections during the period 1824 to 1960. It supported twenty-six winners and ten losers.

TABLE 72   Number and Percentage of Votes by Elections and Parties

Year	Democratic		Nat'l Republ'n / Republican		Third Party A			Third Party B			Third Party C		
1824					Clay 1,401	51.91		Jackson 987	36.57		Adams 311	11.52	
1828	8,272	70.87	3,400	29.13									
1832	5,192				Whig								
1836	10,995	59.98			7,337	40.02							
1840	29,760	56.44			22,972	43.56							
1844	41,369	56.97			31,251	43.03							
1848	40,077	55.09			32,671	44.91							
1852	38,353	56.12			29,984	43.88							
1856	58,164	54.52	Republican		48,524	45.48		Const. Union			Breckinridge		
1860	58,801	35.53	17,028	10.29				58,372	35.27		31,317	18.92	
1864	31,026	29.83	72,991	70.17									
1868	59,788	41.10	85,671	58.90	O'Conor-Demo.								
1872	151,434	55.46	119,196	43.65	2,429	.89		Greenback			American		
1876	203,077	57.73	145,029	41.23				3,498	.99		97	.03	
1880	208,609	52.51	153,567	38.65				35,135	8.84				
1884	235,988	53.50	202,929	46.01	Union Labor								
1888	261,974	50.24	236,257	45.31	18,632	3.57		Populist					
1892	268,188	49.60	226,918	41.97	National Demo.			41,213	7.62				
1896	363,652	53.95	304,940	45.24	2,355	.35					Socialist		
1900	351,922	51.48	314,092	45.94				4,244	.62		6,139	.90	
1904	296,312	46.02	321,446	49.92				4,226	.66		13,009	2.02	
1908	346,574	48.41	347,203	48.50	T. Roosevelt			1,165	.16		15,431	2.16	
1912	330,746	47.35	207,821	29.75	124,371	17.80					28,466	4.07	
1916	398,032	50.59	369,339	46.94				Farmer Labor			14,612	1.86	
1920	574,924	43.12	727,521	54.57	LaFollette			3,291	.25		20,242	1.52	
1924	572,753	43.79	648,486	49.58	84,160	6.43							
1928	662,562	44.15	834,080	55.58				Communist			3,739	.25	
1932	1,025,406	63.69	564,713	35.08	Union			568	.04		16,374	1.02	
1936	1,111,043	60.76	697,891	38.16	14,630	.80		417	.02		3,454	.19	
1940	958,476	52.27	871,009	47.50							2,226	.12	
1944	807,357	51.37	761,175	48.43	Wallace, etc.						1,750	.11	
1948	917,315	58.11	655,039	41.50	3,998	.25		Constitution			2,222	.14	
1952	929,830	49.14	959,429	50.71	987	.05		535	.03		227	.01	
1956	919,187	50.13	914,486	49.87									
1960	972,201	50.26	962,221	49.74									

According to Stanwood, Jackson had no opposition in 1832, but according to the *Tribune Almanac* and the *American Almanac*, the figure 5,192 represents his majority.

The vote in the Whig column for 1836 was cast for White. The vote in the Democratic column for 1860 was cast for Douglas.

Year	Prohibition		Soc. Labor		Nat'l Prohib'n / etc.	
1876	64	.02				
1880						
1884	2,153	.49				
1888	4,539	.87				
1892	4,331	.80	610	.09	Nat'l Prohib'n 292	.04
1896	2,169	.32	1,294	.19		
1900	5,965	.87	1,674	.26	Independence 402	.06
1904	7,191	1.12	868	.12		
1908	4,231	.59	1,778	.25		
1912	5,380	.77	902	.11		
1916	3,884	.49	2,164	.16	Commonw. Land 259	.02
1920	5,142	.39	909	.07		
1924	1,418	.11	340	.02		
1928			404	.03		
1932	2,429	.15	292	.02		
1936	908	.05	209	.01		
1940	1,809	.10	221	.01		
1944	1,175	.07				
1948						
1952	885	.05	169	.01		

MONTANA

Montana, which entered the Union in 1889, participated in eighteen presidential elections during the period 1892 to 1960. It supported fourteen winners and four losers; it supported the winner from 1904 to 1956.

TABLE 73   Number and Percentage of Votes by Elections and Parties

Year	Democratic		Republican		Populist		Socialist		Prohibition	
1892	17,581	39.67	18,851	42.54	7,334	16.55			549	1.24
1896	42,537	79.93	10,494	19.72			*Socialist*		186	.35
1900	37,145	58.32	25,373	39.84			708	1.11	298	.47
1904	21,773	33.79	34,932	54.21	1,520	2.36	5,676	8.81	335	.52
1908	29,326	42.61	32,333	46.98	*T. Roosevelt*		5,855	8.51	827	1.20
1912	27,941	35.00	18,512	23.19	22,456	28.13	10,885	13.64	32	.04
1916	101,063	56.88	66,750	37.57	302	.17	9,564	5.38		
1920	57,372	32.05	109,430	61.13	*LaFollette*					
1924	33,805	19.38	74,138	42.50	65,876	37.77				
1928	78,578	40.48	113,300	58.37			1,667	.86		
1932	127,286	58.80	78,078	36.07	*Union*		7,891	3.65		
1936	159,690	69.28	63,598	27.59	5,549	2.41	1,066	.46	224	.09
1940	145,698	58.78	99,579	40.17			1,443	.58	664	.27
1944	112,556	54.28	93,163	44.93	*Wallace, etc.*		1,296	.63	340	.16
1948	119,071	53.09	96,770	43.15	7,313	3.26	695	.31	429	.19
1952	106,213	40.07	157,394	59.39	723	.27	159	.06	548	.21
1956	116,238	42.87	154,933	57.13	*Soc. Workers*					
1960	134,891	48.60	141,841	51.10	391	.14			456	.16

Year	Soc. Labor		Independence / Communist		Farmer Labor	
1900	169	.27				
1904	208	.32	*Independence*			
1908			481	.70		
1912						
1916					*Farmer Labor*	
1920			*Communist*		12,204	6.82
1924	247	.14	357	.20		
1928	*Liberty*		563	.29		
1932	1,449	.67	1,775	.82		
1936			385	.17		
1940			489	.20		

NEBRASKA

Nebraska, which entered the Union in 1867, participated in twenty-four presidential elections during the period 1868 to 1960. It supported sixteen winners and eight losers.

TABLE 74   Number and Percentage of Votes by Elections and Parties

Year	Democratic	Republican			
1868	5,439 35.86	9,729 64.14			
1872	7,812 29.88	18,329 70.12	Greenback	American	Prohibition
1876	17,554 32.81	31,916 59.65	2,320 4.34	117 .22	1,599 2.99
1880	28,523 32.62	54,979 62.87	3,950 4.52		
1884	54,354 40.54	76,877 57.33		Union Labor	2,858 2.13
1888	80,542 39.75	108,425 53.51	Populist	4,226 2.09	9,429 4.65
1892	24,943 12.46	87,227 43.57	83,134 41.52		4,902 2.45
1896	115,999 51.75	103,064 45.98		Socialist	1,243 .55
1900	114,013 47.22	121,835 50.46	1,104 .46	823 .34	3,655 1.51
1904	52,921 23.44	138,558 61.38	20,518 9.09	7,412 3.28	6,323 2.80
1908	131,099 49.14	126,997 47.60	T. Roosevelt	3,524 1.32	5,179 1.94
1912	109,008 43.69	54,216 21.73	72,689 29.14	10,185 4.08	3,383 1.36
1916	158,827 55.40	117,771 41.08		7,141 2.49	2,952 1.03
1920	119,608 31.26	247,498 64.68	LaFollette	9,600 2.51	5,947 1.55
1924	137,289 29.58	218,585 47.09	106,701 22.99		1,594 .34
1928	197,959 36.18	345,745 63.19		3,434 .63	
1932	359,082 62.98	201,177 35.29	Union	9,876 1.73	
1936	347,454 57.14	247,731 40.74	12,847 2.11		
1940	263,677 42.81	352,201 57.19			
1944	233,246 41.42	329,880 58.58			
1948	224,165 45.85	264,774 54.15			
1952	188,057 30.85	421,603 69.15			
1956	199,029 34.49	378,108 65.51			
1960	232,542 37.93	380,553 62.07			

Year	Nat'l Demo.	Nat'l Prohib'n	Soc. Labor
1896	2,885 1.29	797 .36	186 .08

NEVADA

Nevada, which entered the Union in 1864, participated in twenty-five presidential elections during the period 1864 to 1960. It supported nineteen winners and six losers.

TABLE 75   Number and Percentage of Votes by Elections and Parties

Year	Democratic	Republican				
1864	6,594 40.16	9,826 59.84				
1868	5,218 44.61	6,480 55.39				
1872	6,236 42.57	8,413 57.43				
1876	9,308 47.27	10,383 52.73				
1880	9,613 52.40	8,732 47.60	Greenback			
1884	5,578 43.59	7,193 56.21	26 .20		Prohibition	
1888	5,362 42.45	7,229 57.23	Populist		41 .32	
1892	714 6.56	2,811 25.84	7,264 66.78		89 .82	
1896	8,376 81.21	1,938 18.79				
1900	6,347 62.25	3,849 37.75		Socialist		
1904	3,982 32.87	6,864 56.66	344 2.84	925 7.64		Independence
1908	11,212 45.71	10,775 43.93	T. Roosevelt	2,103 8.57		436 1.78
1912	7,986 39.70	3,196 15.89	5,620 27.94	3,313 16.47		
1916	17,776 53.36	12,127 36.40		3,065 9.20	348 1.04	
1920	9,851 36.22	15,479 56.92	LaFollette	1,864 6.85		
1924	5,909 21.95	11,243 41.76	9,769 36.29			
1928	14,090 43.46	18,327 56.54				
1932	28,756 69.41	12,674 30.59				
1936	31,925 72.81	11,923 27.19				
1940	31,945 60.08	21,229 39.92				
1944	29,623 54.62	24,611 45.38	Wallace			
1948	31,291 50.37	29,357 47.26	1,469 2.36			
1952	31,688 38.55	50,502 61.45				
1956	40,640 42.03	56,049 57.97				
1960	54,880 51.16	52,387 48.84				

New Hampshire, one of the original states, participated in forty-four presidential elections during the period 1789 to 1960. It supported thirty-two winners and twelve losers.

TABLE 76 Number and Percentage of Votes by Elections and Parties

Year	Democratic		Nat'l Republ'n		Adams		Crawford			
1824					9,389	93.59	643	6.41		
1828	20,922	46.45	24,124	53.55						
1832	25,486	57.28	19,010	42.72						
1836	18,722	75.04	*(Liberty)*		*(Whig)* 6,228	24.96				
1840	32,670	55.16	126	.21	26,434	44.63				
1844	27,160	55.22	4,161	8.46	17,866	36.32	*(Free Soil)*			
1848	27,763	55.41			14,781	29.50	7,560	15.09		
1852	29,997	56.77	*(Republican)*		16,147	30.56	6,695	12.67		
1856	32,789	45.82	38,345	53.59	422	.59	*(Breckinridge)*		*(Const. Union)*	
1860	25,881	39.24	37,519	56.89			2,112	3.20	441	.67
1864	33,034	47.44	36,595	52.56						
1868	31,224	44.98	38,191	55.02			*(O'Conor-Dem.)*		*(Prohibition)*	
1872	31,424	45.61	37,168	53.95	*(Greenback)*		100	.15	200	.29
1876	38,509	48.06	41,539	51.84	76	.09				
1880	40,794	47.24	44,852	51.94	528	.61			180	.21
1884	39,183	46.34	43,249	51.15	552	.65	*(Union Labor)*		1,571	1.86
1888	43,456	47.84	45,728	50.35	*(Populist)*		42	.05	1,593	1.75
1892	42,081	47.11	45,658	51.11	293	.33			1,297	1.45
1896	21,650	25.91	57,444	68.74			*(Socialist)*		776	.93
1900	35,489	38.43	54,798	59.34	83	.09	790	.86	1,271	1.38
1904	33,995	37.73	54,180	60.14	*(T. Roosevelt)*		1,090	1.21	749	.83
1908	33,655	37.56	53,149	59.32			1,299	1.45	905	1.01
1912	34,724	39.48	32,927	37.43	17,794	20.23	1,980	2.25	535	.61
1916	43,779	49.12	43,723	49.06			1,318	1.48	303	.34
1920	62,662	39.39	95,196	59.84	*(LaFollette)*		1,234	.78	*(Communist)*	
1924	57,201	34.72	98,575	59.83	8,993	5.46			173	.09
1928	80,715	41.02	115,404	58.66			455	.23	264	.13
1932	100,680	48.99	103,629	50.42			947	.46	193	.09
1936	108,460	49.73	104,642	47.98	*(Union)* 4,819	2.21			*(S. R. Demo.)*	
1940	125,292	53.22	110,127	46.78			46	.02		
1944	119,663	52.11	109,916	47.87	*(Wallace)*				7	.00
1948	107,995	46.66	121,299	52.41	1,970	.85	86	.04		
1952	106,663	39.08	166,287	60.92	*(Constitution)* 111	.04				
1956	90,364	33.84	176,519	66.11						
1960	137,772	46.58	157,989	53.42						

Year	Soc. Labor		National Demo.		National Pro.	
1896	228	.27	3,420	4.09	49	.06
1900						
1904						
1908			*(Independence)* 584	.65		
1912						
1916						
1920						
1924						
1928						
1932						
1936						
1940						
1944						
1948	83	.04				

The vote in the Whig column for 1836 was cast for Harrison. The vote in the Democratic column for 1860 was cast for Douglas.

".00" signifies that the party received some votes, but less than .01%.

NEW JERSEY

New Jersey, one of the original states, participated in forty-four presidential elections during the period 1789 to 1960. It supported thirty-one winners and thirteen losers.

TABLE 77 Number and Percentage of Votes by Elections and Parties

Year	Democratic	Nat'l Republican / Republican	Jackson / Whig / etc.	Adams / etc.	Crawford / etc.
1824	*Democratic*	*Nat'l Republican*	*Jackson* 10,985 51.59	*Adams* 9,110 42.79	*Crawford* 1,196 5.62
1828	21,951 48.02	23,764 51.98		*Anti-Masonic*	
1832	23,859 49.98	23,397 49.01	*Whig*	480 1.01	
1836	25,847 49.48	*Liberty*	26,392 50.52		
1840	31,034 48.14	69 .11	33,362 51.75		
1844	37,495 49.37	131 .17	38,318 50.46	*Free Soil*	
1848	36,901 47.42		40,015 51.42	829 1.07	*American*
1852	44,325 52.78	*Republican*	38,553 45.91	267 .32	831 .99
1856	46,943 47.22	28,351 28.52	24,115 24.26		
1860	62,869 51.87	58,346 48.13			
1864	68,024 52.84	60,723 47.16			
1868	83,001 50.88	80,121 49.12			*O'Conor-Dem*
1872	76,801 45.43	91,661 54.22	*Greenback*	*Prohibition*	606 .36
1876	115,962 52.65	103,517 47.00	712 .32	43 .02	
1880	122,565 49.84	120,555 49.02	2,617 1.06	191 .08	
1884	127,798 48.98	123,440 47.31	3,496 1.34	6,159 2.36	*Soc. Labor*
1888	151,508 49.87	144,360 47.52	*Populist*	7,933 2.61	1,337 .40
1892	171,066 50.67	156,101 46.24	985 .29	8,134 2.41	3,986 1.07
1896	133,695 36.03	221,371 59.66		5,617 1.51	2,081 .52
1900	164,879 41.10	221,754 55.27	691 .17	7,190 1.79	2,680 .62
1904	164,567 38.05	245,164 56.68	3,705 .86	6,845 1.58	1,196 .26
1908	182,567 39.08	265,326 56.79	*T. Roosevelt*	4,934 1.06	1,347 .31
1912	178,559 41.19	89,047 20.54	145,674 33.61	2,915 .67	890 .18
1916	211,645 42.71	269,352 54.35		3,217 .65	1,010 .11
1920	258,761 28.43	615,333 67.60	*LaFollette*	4,895 .54	368 .03
1924	298,043 27.40	676,277 62.16	109,964 10.11	1,660 .15	500 .03
1928	616,517 39.79	926,050 59.77		160 .01	1,062 .07
1932	806,630 49.48	775,684 47.59	*Union*	774 .05	362 .02
1936	1,083,850 59.54	720,322 39.57	9,407 .52	926 .05	455 .02
1940	1,016,808 51.55	945,475 47.93		873 .04	6,939 .35
1944	987,874 50.31	961,335 48.95	*Wallace, etc.*	4,255 .22	3,354 .17
1948	895,455 45.93	981,124 50.33	42,683 2.19	10,593 .54	5,815 .24
1952	1,015,902 41.99	1,374,613 56.81	5,589 .23	989 .04	6,736 .27
1956	850,337 34.23	1,606,942 64.68		9,147 .37	6,736 .27
1960	1,385,415 49.96	1,363,324 49.16			4,262 .15

Year	Smith
1848	77 .10

Year	National Demo. / Independence / Communist / Socialist W'kers	Socialist / Conservative	Farmer Labor / Krajewski	Single Tax / Constitution
1896	*National Demo.* 6,378 1.72	*Socialist*		
1900		4,611 1.15		
1904	*Independence*	9,587 2.22		
1908	2,922 .63	10,253 2.19		
1912		15,928 3.67		
1916		10,462 2.11	*Farmer Labor*	*Single Tax*
1920	*Communist*	27,385 3.01	2,264 .25	603 .07
1924	1,560 .14			
1928	1,257 .08	4,897 .32		
1932	2,915 .18	42,998 2.64		
1936	1,639 .09	3,931 .22		
1940	6,508 .33	2,433 .12		
1944	*Socialist W'kers*	3,358 .17		
1948	5,825 .30	10,521 .54	*Krajewski*	
1952	3,850 .16	8,593 .36	4,203 .17	*Constitution*
1956	4,004 .16	*Conservative*	1,829 .07	5,317 .21
1960	11,402 .41	8,708 .31		

The vote in the Whig column for 1836 was cast for Harrison. The vote in the Democratic column for 1860 was cast for Douglas.

NEW MEXICO

New Mexico, which entered the Union in 1912, participated in thirteen presidential elections during the period 1912 to 1960. It supported the winner every time.

TABLE 78   Number and Percentage of Votes by Elections and Parties

Year	Democratic		Republican		T. Roosevelt / other		Socialist		Prohibition	
1912	20,437	41.39	17,733	35.91	8,347	16.90	2,859	5.79		
1916	33,693	50.31	31,163	46.53			1,999	2.99	112	.17
1920	46,668	44.27	57,634	54.68	*LaFollette*		2	.00		
1924	48,542	43.02	54,745	48.52	9,543	8.46				
1928	48,211	40.85	69,645	59.01						
1932	95,089	62.72	54,217	35.76	*Union*		1,776	1.17		
1936	106,037	62.69	61,727	36.50	924	.55	343	.20	62	.04
1940	103,699	56.59	79,315	43.28			144	.08	100	.05
1944	81,389	53.47	70,688	46.44	*Wallace, etc.*				148	.10
1948	105,464	56.38	80,303	42.93	1,037	.55	83	.04	127	.07
1952	105,661	44.28	132,170	55.39	225	.09			297	.12
1956	106,098	41.78	146,788	57.81					607	.24
1960	156,027	50.15	153,733	49.41					777	.25

Year	Farmer Labor / Communist / Soc. Labor		Liberty / Constitution	
1920	Farmer Labor 1,104	1.05		
1924	*Communist*			
1928	158	.13	*Liberty*	
1932	135	.09	398	.26
1936	43	.03		
1940				
1944	*Soc. Labor*			
1948	49	.03	*Constitution*	
1952	35	.01	220	.09
1956	69	.03	364	.14
1960	570	.18		

".00" signifies that the party received some votes, but less than .01%.

NEW YORK

New York, one of the original states, participated in forty-three presidential elections during the period 1792 to 1960; it did not take part in 1789. It supported thirty-seven winners and six losers. In 1948 Dewey led Truman in New York, 45.99% to 45.01%, while losing the election. Only Arizona, Illinois, and New Mexico have better records as barometers. Arizona and New Mexico have been states only since 1912, while Illinois has been in seven less campaigns than New York.

New York would have had an all but perfect record, had it not supported its past, present, or future governors in 1812, 1868, 1876, 1916, and 1948, when they were losing presidential candidates.

New York was the pivotal state in 1844, when its thirty-six electoral votes swung the election from Clay to Polk, the latter winning, 170 to 105; in 1880, when its thirty-five votes swung the election from Hancock to Garfield, the latter winning, 214 to 155; in 1884, when its thirty-six votes swung the election from Blaine to Cleveland, the latter winning, 219 to 182; and in 1888, when its thirty-six votes swung the election from Cleveland to Harrison, the latter winning, 233 to 168.

New York could have swung the 1848 election to Cass with its thirty-six votes. He lost to Taylor, 163 to 127, but this was a three-way contest in New York, with Van Buren running second.

New York could have swung the 1797 election from John Adams to Jefferson. Its twelve votes were important in a race which went to the former, 71 to 68.

New York could have swung the 1801 election from a tie between Jefferson and Burr to a victory for Adams or Pinckney. Its twelve votes were important in a race in which the first two tied with 73 each against 65 for Adams and 64 for Pinckney.

New York could have deadlocked the 1836 election by voting for Harrison instead of Van Buren. This switch of forty-two votes would have brought about the following result: Van Buren 128, Harrison 115, White 26, Webster 14, and Mangum 11.

New York could have deadlocked the 1860 election by voting for Douglas instead of Lincoln. This switch of thirty-five votes would have brought about the following result: Lincoln 145, Breckinridge 72, Douglas 47, and Bell 39.

New York could have deadlocked the 1960 election by voting for Nixon instead of Kennedy. This switch of forty-five votes would have brought about the following result: Nixon 264, Kennedy 258, and Byrd 15.

NEW YORK

TABLE 79 Number and Percentage of Votes by Elections and Parties

Main table — Democratic and Republican-lineage columns

Year	Democratic	%	Nat'l Republican / Liberty / Republican	%	Whig	%
1828	140,763	50.97	135,413 (Nat'l Rep.)	49.03		
1832	168,562	52.11	154,896 (Nat'l Rep.)	47.89		
1836	166,886	54.60			138,765	45.40
1840	212,743	48.19	2,790 (Liberty)	.63	225,945	51.18
1844	237,588	48.90	15,814 (Liberty)	3.25	232,482	47.85
1848	114,320	25.07			218,603	47.94
1852	262,456	50.16			234,906	44.89
1856	195,866	32.90	274,707 (Republican)	46.14	124,603	20.93
1860	312,510	46.29	362,646	53.71		
1864	361,986	49.54	368,735	50.46		
1868	429,883	50.59	419,915	49.41		
1872	387,281	46.68	440,736	53.12		
1876	522,612	51.32	489,547	48.07		
1880	534,511	48.41	555,544	50.32		
1884	563,154	48.25	562,005	48.15		
1888	635,965	48.11	650,338	49.20		
1892	654,908	48.99	609,459	45.59		
1896	551,513	38.72	819,838	57.55		
1900	678,462	43.83	822,013	53.10		
1904	683,981	42.28	859,533	53.13		
1908	667,468	40.74	870,070	53.11		
1912	655,475	41.28	455,428	28.68		
1916	759,426	44.51	879,287	51.53		
1920	781,238	26.95	1,871,167	64.56		
1924	950,796	29.13	1,820,058	55.76		
1928	2,089,863	47.44	2,193,344	49.79		
1932	2,534,959	54.07	1,937,963	41.33		
1936	3,293,222	58.85	2,180,670	38.97		
1940	3,251,918	51.60	3,027,478	48.04		
1944	3,304,238	52.31	2,987,647	47.30		
1948	2,780,204	45.01	2,841,163	45.99		
1952	3,104,601	43.55	3,952,815	55.45		
1956	2,750,769	38.78	4,340,340	61.20		
1960	3,830,085	52.53	3,446,420	47.27		

Third-party column (col. 3)

Year	Party	Votes	%
1872	O'Conor – Dem.	1,454	.18
1876	Greenback	2,039	.20
1880	Greenback	12,373	1.12
1884	Greenback	17,004	1.46
1888	United Labor	2,668	.20
1892	Populist	16,436	1.23
1904	(People's)	7,459	.46
1912	T. Roosevelt	390,021	24.56
1924	LaFollette	474,925	14.55
1948	Wallace, etc.	509,559	8.25
1952	Wallace, etc.	64,211	.90

Free Soil / Socialist column (col. 4)

Year	Party	Votes	%
1848	Free Soil	120,510	26.43
1852	Free Soil	25,433	4.86
1900	Socialist	12,869	.83
1904	Socialist	36,883	2.28
1908	Socialist	38,451	2.35
1912	Socialist	63,381	3.99
1916	Socialist	45,944	2.69
1920	Socialist	203,201	7.01
1924	Socialist	107,332	2.44
1928	Socialist	177,397	3.78
1932	Socialist	86,897	1.55
1936	Socialist	18,950	.30
1940	Socialist	10,553	.17
1944	Socialist	40,879	.66
1948	Socialist	2,664	.04
1952	Socialist	82	.00

Smith / Prohibition / Soc. Workers column (col. 5)

Year	Party	Votes	%
1848	Smith	2,545	.56
1852	Smith	72	.01
1856	Smith	160	.03
1872	Prohibition	201	.02
1876	Prohibition	2,359	.23
1880	Prohibition	1,517	.14
1884	Prohibition	25,006	2.14
1888	Prohibition	30,231	2.29
1892	Prohibition	38,193	2.86
1896	Prohibition	16,086	1.13
1900	Prohibition	22,077	1.43
1904	Prohibition	20,787	1.28
1908	Prohibition	22,667	1.38
1912	Prohibition	19,427	1.22
1916	Prohibition	19,031	1.12
1920	Prohibition	19,653	.68
1940		3,250	.05
1944	Soc. Workers	2,675	.04
1948	Soc. Workers	2,212	.03
1960		14,319	.20

Lower-left table

Year	Webster / American / Socialist Labor	Votes	%
1852	Webster	413	.08
1876	American	1,828	.18
1880	American	75	.01
1888	Socialist Labor	2,068	.16
1892	Socialist Labor	17,958	1.34
1896	Socialist Labor	17,731	1.24
1900	Socialist Labor	12,622	.82
1904	Socialist Labor	9,127	.56
1908	Socialist Labor	3,877	.24
1912	Socialist Labor	4,251	.27
1916	Socialist Labor	2,666	.16
1920	Socialist Labor	4,841	.17
1924	Socialist Labor	9,928	.30
1928	Socialist Labor	4,211	.10
1932	Socialist Labor	10,339	.22
1944	Socialist Labor	14,352	.23
1948	Socialist Labor	2,729	.04
1952	Socialist Labor	1,560	.02
1956	Socialist Labor	150	.00

Lower-middle blocks

Year	Party	Votes	%
1888	Union Labor	627	.05
1896	National Demo.	19,295	1.35
1908	Independence	35,817	2.19
1920	Farmer Labor	18,413	.64
1924	Communist	8,244	.25
1928	Communist	10,876	.25
1932	Communist	27,956	.60
1936	Communist	35,610	.64
1956	Constitution	1,027	.01

The legislature cast the electoral vote in 1824.

The vote in the Whig column for 1836 was cast for Harrison. The vote in the Democratic column for 1860 was cast for Douglas.

".00" signifies that the party received some votes, but less than .01%.

NORTH CAROLINA

North Carolina, one of the original states, participated in forty-two presidential elections during the period 1792 to 1960; it did not take part in the first election and abstained in 1864 because of the Civil War. It supported twenty-seven winners and fifteen losers.

TABLE 80   Number and Percentage of Votes by Elections and Parties

Year	Democratic		Nat'l Republ'n / Free Soil / Const. Union / Republican		Other principal opponent		
1824					Jackson	20,415	56.65
1824					Crawford	15,621	43.35
1828	37,857	73.12	Nat'l Republ'n 13,918	26.88			
1832	24,862	84.49	4,563	15.51			
1836	26,910	53.25			Whig 23,626	46.75	
1840	33,782	42.14			46,379	57.85	
1844	39,287	47.61			Whig 43,232	52.39	
1848	34,869	44.42	Free Soil 85	.11	43,550	55.47	
1852	39,744	50.40	59	.07	39,058	49.53	
1856	48,246	56.67	Const. Union		36,886	43.33	
1860	48,539	50.44	44,990	46.75	Douglas 2,701	2.81	
1864			Republican				
1868	84,090	46.63	96,226	53.37			
1872	70,094	42.52	94,769	57.48			
1876	125,427	53.64	108,417	46.36	Greenback		
1880	124,208	51.49	115,874	48.04	1,126	.47	
1884	142,952	53.25	125,068	46.58			
1888	148,336	51.88	134,784	47.14			
1892	133,098	47.36	100,565	35.79	Populist 44,732	15.92	
1896	174,488	52.68	155,243	46.87			
1900	157,752	53.90	133,081	45.47	830	.28	
1904	124,124	59.64	82,625	39.70	879	.42	
1908	136,995	54.30	114,937	45.55	T. Roosevelt		
1912	144,545	58.97	29,277	11.94	70,144	28.62	
1916	168,383	58.08	120,988	41.73			
1920	305,447	56.69	232,848	43.22	LaFollette		
1924	284,270	58.89	191,753	39.72	6,697	1.39	
1928	287,078	45.13	348,992	54.87			
1932	497,566	69.93	208,344	29.28	Communist		
1936	616,141	73.40	223,283	26.60	11	.00	
1940	609,015	74.03	213,633	25.97			
1944	527,399	66.71	263,155	33.29	S. R. Demo.		
1948	459,070	58.02	258,572	32.68	69,652	8.80	
1952	652,803	53.91	558,107	46.09			
1956	590,530	50.66	575,062	49.34			
1960	713,136	52.11	655,420	47.89			

Additional minor-party vote clusters (right-hand columns):

Party	Year	Votes	%
Union Labor	1888	37	.01
Nat'l Demo.	1896	578	.17
Socialist	1900	125	.06
Socialist	1904	378	.15
Socialist	1908	128	.05
Socialist	1912	490	.17
Socialist	1916	446	.08
(Socialist)	1932	5,591	.79
(Communist)	1936	21	.00
Wallace	1948	3,915	.49

Prohibition	Year	Votes	%
Prohibition	1884	454	.17
Prohibition	1888	2,789	.98
Prohibition	1892	2,630	.94
Prohibition	1896	681	.21
Prohibition	1900	1,009	.34
Prohibition	1904	361	.17
Prohibition	1912	1,025	.42
Prohibition	1916	51	.02
Prohibition	1920	17	.00
Prohibition	1924	13	.00
Union	1936	2	.00

Year	Nat'l Prohib'n	
1896	253	.08

The vote in the Whig column for 1836 was cast for White. The vote in the Democratic column for 1860 was cast for Breckinridge.

".00" signifies that the party received some votes, but less than .01%.

NORTH DAKOTA

North Dakota, which entered the Union in 1889, participated in eighteen presidential elections during the period 1892 to 1960. It supported thirteen winners and four losers; in 1892 it gave the Democratic, Republican, and Populist candidates one electoral vote each.

TABLE 81   Number and Percentage of Votes by Elections and Parties

Year	Democratic		Republican		Populist		Socialist		Prohibition	
1892			17,519	48.50	17,700	49.01			899	2.49
1896	20,686	43.66	26,335	55.58			*Socialist*		358	.76
1900	20,531	35.52	35,898	62.11	111	.19	520	.90	735	1.27
1904	14,273	20.31	52,595	74.83	165	.23	2,117	3.01	1,140	1.62
1908	32,885	34.77	57,680	60.98	*T. Roosevelt*		2,421	2.56	1,553	1.64
1912	29,555	34.14	23,090	26.67	25,726	29.71	6,966	8.05	1,243	1.44
1916	55,206	50.80	53,471	49.20						
1920	37,422	18.19	160,072	77.79	*LaFollette*		8,282	4.02		
1924	13,858	6.96	94,931	47.68	89,922	45.17				
1928	106,648	44.46	131,441	54.80			842	.35		
1932	178,350	69.59	71,772	28.00	*Union*		3,521	1.37		
1936	163,148	59.60	72,751	26.58	36,708	13.41	552	.20	197	.07
1940	124,036	44.18	154,590	55.06			1,279	.46	325	.12
1944	100,144	45.48	118,535	53.84	*Wallace, etc.*		943	.43	549	.25
1948	95,812	43.41	115,139	52.17	8,391	3.80	1,000	.45		
1952	76,694	28.39	191,712	70.97	344	.13				
1956	96,742	38.09	156,766	61.72	*Soc. Workers*				302	.11
1960	123,963	44.52	154,310	55.42	158	.06				

Year	Independence		Communist		Liberty / Knutson / Constitution		S.R.Democratic	
1908	43	.05						
1912								
1916								
1920			*Communist*					
1924			370	.19				
1928			936	.39	*Liberty*			
1932			830	.32	1,817	.71		
1936			360	.13	*Knutson*			
1940					545	.19		
1944							*S.R.Democratic*	
1948					*Constitution*		374	.17
1952					1,075	.40		
1956					483	.19		

Ohio, which entered the Union in 1803, participated in forty presidential elections during the period 1804 to 1960. It supported thirty-two winners and eight losers. In 1892 Harrison led Cleveland in Ohio, 47.66% to 47.53%, while losing the election. In 1944 Dewey led Roosevelt in Ohio, 50.18% to 49.82%, while losing the election.

TABLE 82 Number and Percentage of Votes by Elections and Parties

Year	Democratic		Nat'l Republican / Liberty / Republican	
1824				
1828	67,597	51.60	63,396	48.40
1832	81,246	51.33	76,539	48.35
1836	96,916	47.90	*Liberty*	
1840	124,782	45.57	903	.33
1844	149,117	47.76	8,050	2.58
1848	154,775	47.10		
1852	169,160	47.84	*Republican*	
1856	170,874	44.19	187,497	48.49
1860	187,232	42.32	231,610	52.35
1864	205,571	43.67	265,154	56.33
1868	239,032	46.03	280,222	53.97
1872	244,321	46.15	281,852	53.24
1876	323,182	49.07	330,698	50.21
1880	340,821	47.01	375,048	51.73
1884	368,280	46.94	400,082	50.99
1888	396,455	47.18	416,054	49.51
1892	404,115	47.53	405,187	47.66
1896	477,497	47.07	525,991	51.99
1900	474,882	45.66	543,918	52.30
1904	344,940	34.33	600,095	59.73
1908	502,721	44.82	572,312	51.03
1912	424,834	40.96	278,168	26.82
1916	604,161	51.86	.514,753	44.18
1920	780,037	38.58	1,182,022	58.47
1924	477,888	23.70	1,176,130	58.33
1928	864,210	34.45	1,627,546	64.89
1932	1,301,695	49.87	1,227,679	47.04
1936	1,747,222	58.00	1,127,709	37.43
1940	1,733,139	52.20	1,586,773	47.80
1944	1,570,763	49.82	1,582,293	50.18
1948	1,452,791	49.48	1,445,684	49.24
1952	1,600,367	43.24	2,100,391	56.76
1956	1,439,655	38.89	2,262,610	61.11
1960	1,944,248	46.72	2,217,611	53.28

Clay (1824): 19,255 38.49
Jackson (1824): 18,489 36.96
Adams (1824): 12,280 24.55
Anti-Masonic (1832): 509 .32

Year	Whig	
1836	105,417	52.10
1840	148,157	54.10
1844	155,057	49.66
1848	138,360	42.11
1852	152,626	43.17
1856	28,125	7.27

Free Soil	
35,354	10.76
31,782	8.99

Const. Union (1860): 12,194 2.76
Breckinridge (1860): 11,405 2.58
O'Conor-Demo. (1872): 1,163 .22

Greenback	
3,057	.46
6,456	.89
5,179	.66

National Demo. (1896): 1,858 .18
Union Labor (1888): 3,496 .42

Socialist	
4,847	.47
36,260	3.61
33,795	3.01
90,144	8.69
38,092	3.27
57,147	2.83
8,683	.35
64,094	2.46
117	.00

T. Roosevelt (1912): 229,807 22.16
LaFollette (1924): 357,948 17.75
Union (1936): 132,212 4.39
Wallace (1948): 37,596 1.28

Prohibition	
2,100	.40
1,636	.25
2,616	.36
11,069	1.41
24,356	2.90
26,012	3.06
5,084	.50
10,203	.98
19,339	1.92
11,402	1.02
11,511	1.11
8,080	.69
294	.01
1,246	.06
3,556	.14
7,421	.28

Year	Smith		American		Populist		Single Tax / Communist	
1848	111	.03						
1852								
1856	156	.04						
1860								
1864								
1868								
1872			*American*					
1876			76	.01				
1880								
1884								
1888					*Populist*			
1892					14,852	1.75		
1896								
1900					251	.02		
1904					1,401	.14		
1908					163	.01		
1912								
1916								
1920							*Single Tax* 2,157	.11
1924							*Communist*	
1928							2,836	.11
1932							7,231	.28
1936							5,251	.17

The vote in the Whig column for 1836 was cast for Harrison. The vote in the Democratic column for 1860 was cast for Douglas.

".00" signifies that the party received some votes, but less than .01%.

Socialist Labor		National Proh.		Union Reform	
1,165	.12	2,741	.27	4,284	.41
1,688	.16				
2,633	.26	*Independence*			
720	.06	475	.04		
2,630	.25				
3,025	.15				
1,515	.06				
1,968	.08				
14	.00				

OKLAHOMA

Oklahoma, which entered the Union in 1907, participated in fourteen presidential elections during the period 1908 to 1960. It supported eleven winners and three losers.

TABLE 83   Number and Percentage of Votes by Elections and Parties

Year	Democratic		Republican		Socialist		Populist		Prohibition	
1908	123,907	48.23	110,550	43.03	21,752	8.47	434	.17		
1912	119,156	46.84	90,786	35.69	42,262	16.61	T. Roosevelt		2,185	.86
1916	148,113	50.59	97,233	33.21	45,527	15.55	234	.08	1,646	.56
1920	217,053	44.61	243,831	50.11	25,726	5.29	LaFollette			
1924	255,798	48.41	226,242	42.82			41,141	7.79		
1928	219,174	35.44	394,046	63.72	3,924	.63				
1932	516,468	73.30	188,165	26.70						
1936	501,069	66.83	245,122	32.69	2,221	.30			1,328	.18
1940	474,313	57.41	348,872	42.23					3,027	.37
1944	401,549	55.57	319,424	44.20					1,663	.23
1948	452,782	62.75	268,817	37.25						
1952	430,939	45.41	518,045	54.59						
1956	385,581	44.87	473,769	55.13						
1960	370,111	40.98	533,039	59.02						

Year	Independence			
1908	274	.11		
1912				
1916				
1920	Soc. Labor			
1924	5,234	.99	Farmer Labor	
1928			1,283	.21

OREGON

Oregon, which entered the Union in 1859, participated in twenty-six presidential elections during the period 1860 to 1960. It supported twenty winners and six losers.

TABLE 84   Number and Percentage of Votes by Elections and Parties

Year	Democratic #	Dem %	Republican #	Rep %	Other party #	%	Other party #	%	Prohibition #	%
1860	5,342	33.51	5,496	34.48	*Douglas* 4,127	25.89	*Const. Union* 976	6.12		
1864	8,457	46.10	9,888	53.90						
1868	11,125	50.37	10,961	49.63			*O'Conor-Dem.* 572	2.84		
1872	7,730	38.42	11,819	58.74	*Greenback*				*Prohibition*	
1876	14,157	47.37	15,214	50.91	510	1.71			4	.01
1880	19,955	48.89	20,619	50.51	245	.60				
1884	24,604	46.70	26,860	50.99	726	1.38	*Union Labor*		492	.93
1888	26,522	42.88	33,291	53.82	*Populist*		363	.59	1,677	2.71
1892	14,243	18.15	35,002	44.59	26,965	34.35			2,281	2.91
1896	46,739	47.98	48,779	50.07			*Socialist*		919	.94
1900	33,385	39.64	46,526	55.25	275	.33	1,494	1.77	2,536	3.01
1904	17,521	19.43	60,455	67.06	753	.84	7,619	8.45	3,806	4.22
1908	38,049	34.31	62,530	56.39	*T. Roosevelt*		7,339	6.62	2,682	2.42
1912	47,064	34.34	34,673	25.30	37,600	27.44	13,343	9.74	4,360	3.18
1916	120,087	45.90	126,813	48.47	310	.12	9,711	3.71	4,729	1.81
1920	80,019	33.55	143,592	60.20	*LaFollette*		9,801	4.11	3,595	1.51
1924	67,589	24.18	142,579	51.01	68,403	24.47	2,720	.85		
1928	109,223	34.14	205,341	64.18			15,450	4.19		
1932	213,871	58.00	136,019	36.89	*Union*		2,143	.52		
1936	266,733	64.42	122,706	29.64	21,831	5.27	398	.08	4	.00
1940	258,415	53.70	219,555	45.63					154	.03
1944	248,635	51.78	225,365	46.94	*Wallace, etc.*		3,785	.79	2,362	.49
1948	243,147	46.40	260,904	49.78	14,978	2.86	5,051	.96		
1952	270,579	38.93	420,815	60.54	3,665	.53				
1956	329,204	44.75	406,393	55.25						
1960	367,402	47.38	408,060	52.62						

Year	Nat'l Demo. #	%	Independence #	%	Soc. Labor #	%	Communist #	%
1896	977	1.00						
1900								
1904			*Independence*					
1908			289	.26				
1912								
1916					*Soc. Labor*			
1920					1,515	.64		
1924					917	.33	*Communist*	
1928					1,564	.49	1,094	.34
1932					1,730	.47	1,681	.46
1936					500	.12	104	.03
1940					2,487	.52	191	.04

The vote in the Democratic column for 1860 was cast for Breckinridge.

".00" signifies that the party received some votes, but less than .01%.

PENNSYLVANIA

Pennsylvania, one of the original states, participated in forty-four presidential elections during the period 1789 to 1960. It supported thirty-six winners and eight losers. In 1848 Pennsylvania could have swung the election to Cass with its twenty-six votes. As it was, he lost to Taylor, 163 to 127.

TABLE 85 Number and Percentage of Votes by Elections and Parties

Year	Democratic		Nat'l Republican / Liberty / Republican		Jackson / Whig / others		Adams / Anti-Masonic / others		Crawford / others / Prohibition	
1824			*Nat'l Republican*		*Jackson* 36,100	76.23	*Adams* 5,440	11.49	*Crawford* 4,206	8.88
1828	101,652	66.66	50,848	33.34			*Anti-Masonic*			
1832	90,983	57.69			*Whig*		66,716	42.31		
1836	91,475	51.22	*Liberty*		87,111	48.78				
1840	143,784	49.90	343	.12	144,023	49.98				
1844	167,535	50.48	3,138	.95	161,203	48.57				
1848	171,176	46.52			185,513	50.42	*Free Soil* 11,263	3.06		
1852	198,568	51.18			179,182	46.19	8,524	2.20		
1856	230,686	53.17	*Republican* 147,286	33.95	55,852	12.87			*American* 1,670	.43
1860	178,871	37.54	268,030	56.25			*Douglas* 16,765	3.52	*Const. Union* 12,776	2.68
1864	276,308	48.25	296,389	51.75						
1868	313,382	47.80	342,280	52.20					*Prohibition*	
1872	211,041	37.53	349,589	62.18	*Greenback*		*American*		1,630	.29
1876	366,204	48.25	384,148	50.61	7,204	.95	83	.01	1,318	.17
1880	407,428	46.57	444,704	50.84	20,668	2.36	44	.01	1,939	.22
1884	393,747	43.73	474,268	52.68	16,992	1.89	*Union Labor*		15,306	1.70
1888	447,004	44.78	526,269	52.73	*Populist*		3,876	.39	20,966	2.10
1892	452,264	45.09	516,011	51.45	8,714	.87			25,123	2.50
1896	433,228	36.27	728,300	60.98			*Socialist*		19,274	1.61
1900	424,232	36.16	712,665	60.74	642	.05	4,831	.41	27,908	2.38
1904	337,998	27.33	840,949	67.99	33	.00	21,863	1.77	33,717	2.73
1908	448,778	35.41	745,779	58.84	*T. Roosevelt*		33,913	2.68	36,694	2.90
1912	395,619	32.42	273,305	22.40	447,426	36.67	83,614	6.85	19,533	1.60
1916	521,784	40.23	703,734	54.25	*LaFollette*		42,637	3.29	28,525	2.20
1920	503,202	27.18	1,218,215	65.80	307,567	14.34	70,021	3.78	42,612	2.30
1924	409,192	19.07	1,401,481	65.35			18,647	.59	9,779	.46
1928	1,067,586	33.89	2,055,382	65.24	*Union*		91,119	3.19	3,880	.12
1932	1,295,948	45.33	1,453,540	50.84	67,467	1.63	14,375	.35	11,319	.40
1936	2,353,788	56.88	1,690,300	40.85			10,967	.27	6,691	.16
1940	2,171,035	53.24	1,889,848	46.34	*Wallace, etc.*		11,721	.31		
1944	1,940,479	51.14	1,835,048	48.36	55,161	1.48	11,325	.30	5,750	.15
1948	1,752,426	46.92	1,902,197	50.93	4,200	.09	2,684	.06	10,338	.28
1952	2,146,269	46.86	2,415,789	52.74					8,771	.19
1956	1,981,769	43.30	2,585,252	56.49						
1960	2,556,282	51.06	2,439,956	48.74						

The vote in the Whig column for 1836 was cast for Harrison. The vote in the Democratic column for 1860 was cast for Breckinridge.

".00" signifies that the party received some votes, but less than .01%.

Year	Clay	
1824	1,609	3.40

Year	Smith	
1856	18	.00

Year	Socialist Labor	
1892	898	.09
1896	1,683	.14
1900	2,936	.25
1904	2,224	.18
1908	1,222	.10
1912	704	.06
1916	417	.03
1920	755	.04
1924	636	.03
1928	380	.01
1932	659	.02
1936	1,424	.03
1940	1,518	.04
1944	1,789	.05
1948	1,461	.04
1952	1,347	.03
1956	7,447	.16
1960	7,185	.14

National Demo.	
11,000	.92

Independence	
1,057	.08

Farmer Labor	
15,642	.84

Jobless	
725	.03

Socialist W'kers	
2,133	.06
1,502	.03
2,035	.04
2,678	.05

National Proh.	
873	.07

Single Tax	
803	.04

American	
13,035	.61

Communist	
2,735	.13
4,726	.15
5,658	.20
4,060	.10
4,519	.11

Year	Commonw'lth Land	
1924	296	.01

RHODE ISLAND

Rhode Island, one of the original states, participated in forty-three presidential elections during the period 1792 to 1960; it did not take part in the first election. It supported thirty-two winners and eleven losers.

TABLE 86   Number and Percentage of Votes by Elections and Parties

Year	Democratic		Second column		Other parties
1824	*Democratic*		*Nat'l Republ'n*		Adams 2,145 91.47; Crawford 200 8.53
1828	821	22.97	2,754	77.03	Anti-Masonic 878 15.10
1832	2,126	36.57	2,810	48.33	
1836	2,966	52.25	*Liberty*		Whig 2,711 47.75
1840	3,301	38.29	42	.49	Whig 5,278 61.22
1844	4,867	39.58	107	.87	Whig 7,322 59.55
1848	3,646	32.68			Whig 6,779 60.77; Free Soil 730 6.54
1852	8,735	51.37	*Republican*		Whig 7,626 44.85; Free Soil 644 3.79
1856	6,680	33.70	11,467	57.85	Whig 1,675 8.45
1860	7,753	38.78	12,240	61.22	
1864	8,718	37.80	14,343	62.20	
1868	6,548	33.51	12,993	66.49	
1872	5,329	28.06	13,665	71.94	
1876	10,712	40.23	15,787	59.29	Greenback 68 .26; Prohibition 60 .23
1880	10,779	36.88	18,195	62.25	Greenback 236 .81; Prohibition 20 .07
1884	12,391	37.81	19,030	58.07	Greenback 422 1.29; Prohibition 928 2.83; Union Labor 18 .04
1888	17,530	43.00	21,969	53.89	Prohibition 1,251 3.07
1892	24,336	45.75	26,975	50.71	National Dem. 1,166 2.13; Prohibition 1,654 3.11; Soc. Labor 558 1.02
1896	14,459	26.39	37,437	68.33	Prohibition 1,161 2.12; Soc. Labor 1,423 2.52
1900	19,812	35.04	33,784	59.74	Prohibition 1,529 2.70; Soc. Labor 488 .71
1904	24,839	36.18	41,605	60.60	Prohibition 768 1.12; Soc. Labor 183 .25
1908	24,706	34.16	43,942	60.76	T. Roosevelt 16,878 21.67; Prohibition 1,016 1.40; Soc. Labor 236 .30
1912	30,412	39.04	27,703	35.57	Prohibition 616 .79; Soc. Labor 180 .20
1916	40,394	46.00	44,858	51.08	Prohibition 470 .54; Soc. Labor 495 .29
1920	55,062	32.78	107,463	63.97	LaFollette 7,628 3.63; Prohibition 510 .30; Soc. Labor 268 .13
1924	76,606	36.46	125,286	59.63	Soc. Labor 416 .18
1928	118,973	50.16	117,522	49.55	
1932	146,604	55.08	115,266	43.31	Union 19,569 6.29; Prohibition 183 .07; Soc. Labor 433 .16
1936	165,238	53.10	125,031	40.18	Soc. Labor 929 .30
1940	181,122	56.66	138,214	43.24	Prohibition 74 .02
1944	175,356	58.59	123,487	41.26	Prohibition 433 .14
1948	188,736	57.60	135,791	41.44	Wallace, etc. 2,605 .79; Soc. Labor 130 .04
1952	203,293	49.05	210,935	50.89	Wallace, etc. 187 .05; Soc. Labor 83 .02
1956	163,521	41.69	229,677	58.31	
1960	258,032	63.63	147,502	36.37	

Year	Other parties
1892	Populist 228 .43
1896	Nat'l Prohib'n 5 .01
1900	*Socialist*
1904	Socialist 956 1.39
1908	Socialist 1,365 1.89; Independence 1,105 1.53
1912	Socialist 2,049 2.63
1916	Socialist 1,914 2.18; Single Tax 100 .06
1920	Socialist 4,351 2.59
1924	Communist 289 .14; Common. Land 38 .02
1928	Communist 283 .12
1932	Socialist 3,138 1.18; Communist 546 .21
1936	Communist 411 .13
1940	Communist 239 .07
1944	
1948	Socialist 428 .13

The vote in the Whig column for 1836 was cast for Harrison. The vote in the Democratic column for 1860 was cast for Douglas.

153

South Carolina, one of the original states, participated in forty-three presidential elections during the period 1789 to 1960; it did not take part in 1864, because of the Civil War. It supported twenty-four winners and nineteen losers. While any of the states that supported Hayes in 1876 could have been said to have swung the election, the South Carolina percentage was the closest in the nation, 50.26% for Hayes to 49.74% for Tilden.

TABLE 87   Number and Percentage of Votes by Elections and Parties

Year	Democratic		Republican							
1868	45,237	42.07	62,301	57.93	**O'Conor - Dem.**					
1872	22,703	23.85	72,290	75.95	187	.20				
1876	90,906	49.74	91,870	50.26	**Greenback**					
1880	112,312	65.70	58,071	33.97	566	.33				
1884	69,890	76.28	21,733	23.72						
1888	65,825	82.73	13,740	17.27	**Populist**					
1892	54,698	77.59	13,384	18.99	2,410	3.42	**Nat'l Demo.**			
1896	58,801	85.29	9,317	13.51			824	1.20		
1900	47,283	92.96	3,579	7.04			**Socialist**			
1904	52,563	95.33	2,554	4.63	1	.00	22	.04	**Independence**	
1908	62,290	93.81	3,965	5.97	**T. Roosevelt**		100	.15	43	.06
1912	48,357	96.04	536	1.06	1,293	2.57	164	.33		
1916	61,846	96.95	1,550	2.43	259	.41	135	.21		
1920	64,170	96.06	2,604	3.90	**LaFollette**		28	.04		
1924	49,008	96.57	1,123	2.21	620	1.22				
1928	62,700	91.39	5,858	8.54			47	.07		
1932	102,347	98.03	1,978	1.89			82	.08		
1936	113,791	98.57	1,646	1.43						
1940	95,470	95.63	4,360	4.37					**Southern Dem**	
1944	90,606	87.64	4,610	4.46	**S.R.Democratic**				7,799	7.54
1948	34,423	24.14	5,386	3.78	102,607	71.97	1	.00		
1952	173,004	50.72	168,082	49.28	**States' Rights**		**Constitution**			
1956	136,372	45.37	75,700	25.18	88,509	29.45	2	.00		
1960	198,129	51.24	188,558	48.76						

Year	Prohibition		Wallace	
1944	365	.35		
1948			154	.11
1952	1	.00		

The legislature cast the electoral vote from 1824 to 1860.

The vote cast for the Republican candidate in 1952 was 12,088 more than that cast for all of the Republican nominees from 1880 to 1948.

".00" signifies that the party received some votes, but less than .01%.

SOUTH DAKOTA

South Dakota, which entered the Union in 1889, participated in eighteen presidential elections during the period 1892 to 1960. It supported ten winners and eight losers.

TABLE 88   Number and Percentage of Votes by Elections and Parties

Year	Democratic		Republican		Populist		Socialist		Prohibition	
1892	9,081	12.88	34,888	49.48	26,544	37.64				
1896	41,225	49.70	41,042	49.48					683	.82
1900	39,544	41.14	54,530	56.73	339	.35	169	.18	1,542	1.60
1904	21,969	21.67	72,083	71.09	1,240	1.22	3,138	3.09	2,965	2.92
1908	40,266	35.08	67,536	58.84	*T. Roosevelt*		2,846	2.48	4,039	3.52
1912	48,962	42.08			58,811	50.55	4,662	4.01	3,910	3.36
1916	59,191	45.91	64,217	49.80			3,760	2.92	1,774	1.38
1920	35,938	19.72	110,692	60.74	*LaFollette*				900	.49
1924	27,214	13.35	101,299	49.69	75,355	36.96				
1928	102,660	39.20	157,603	60.18	*Liberty*		443	.17		
1932	183,515	63.62	99,212	34.40	3,333	1.16	1,551	.54	463	.16
1936	160,137	54.02	125,977	42.49						
1940	131,362	42.59	177,065	57.41						
1944	96,711	41.67	135,362	58.33	*Wallace*					
1948	117,653	47.04	129,651	51.84	2,801	1.12				
1952	90,426	30.73	203,857	69.27						
1956	122,288	41.61	171,569	58.39						
1960	128,070	41.79	178,417	58.21						

Year	Independence / Farmer Labor / Union		Communist	
1908	*Independence* 88	.08		
1912				
1916	*Farmer Labor*			
1920	34,707	19.04		
1924			*Communist*	
1928	927	.35	232	.09
1932	*Union*		364	.13
1936	10,338	3.49		

155

Tennessee, which entered the Union in 1796, participated in forty-one presidential elections during the period 1796 to 1960; it did not take part in 1864, because of the Civil War. It supported twenty-five winners and sixteen losers.

TABLE 89   Number and Percentage of Votes by Elections and Parties

Year	Democratic	Jackson	Crawford	Adams	Nat'l Rep'n
1824	*Democratic*	20,197 97.45	312 1.51	216 1.04	*Nat'l Rep'n*
1828	44,293 95.19				2,240 4.81
1832	28,740 95.24	*Whig*			1,436 4.76
1836	26,129 41.94	36,168 58.06			
1840	48,289 44.43	60,391 55.57			
1844	59,904 49.95	60,033 50.05			
1848	58,419 47.45	64,705 52.55			
1852	57,123 49.28	58,802 47.59			
1856	73,638 52.67	66,178 47.33	*Const. Union*	*Douglas*	
1860	66,440 44.72		70,706 47.59	11,428 7.69	
1864		*Republican*			
1868	26,311 31.67	56,757 68.33			
1872	94,391 52.43	85,655 47.57			
1876	133,166 59.79	89,566 40.21		*Greenback* 5,917 2.45	*Prohibition* 43 .02
1880	128,191 53.01	107,677 44.53		957 .37	1,131 .44
1884	133,270 51.37	124,090 47.83	*Union Labor*		5,975 1.96
1888	158,779 52.18	139,511 45.85	48 .02	*Populist*	4,851 1.81
1892	138,874 51.91	100,331 37.51	*National Dem.*	23,447 8.77	3,140 .97
1896	168,878 52.15	149,703 46.23	2,106 .65		3,882 1.42
1900	145,356 53.02	123,180 44.93		1,322 .48	1,906 .79
1904	131,653 54.23	105,369 43.40		2,506 1.03	300 .12
1908	135,608 52.66	118,324 45.95	*T. Roosevelt*	1,081 .42	834 .33
1912	135,425 53.22	60,674 23.84	54,041 21.24		147 .05
1916	153,282 56.31	116,223 42.70			
1920	206,558 48.19	219,829 51.28	*LaFollette*		
1924	158,537 52.80	130,882 43.59	10,656 3.55	*Communist*	100 .03
1928	167,343 46.04	195,388 53.76		111 .03	
1932	259,817 66.51	126,806 32.46	*Union*	234 .06	1,995 .51
1936	327,083 68.78	146,516 30.81	296 .06	319 .07	632 .13
1940	351,601 67.25	169,186 32.36			1,606 .31
1944	308,707 60.45	200,311 39.22	*S. R. Demo.*		885 .17
1948	270,412 49.14	202,924 36.87	73,826 13.42	*Constitution*	
1952	443,710 49.71	446,147 49.98		379 .04	1,441 .16
1956	456,507 48.59	462,288 49.21	*N. S. Rights*	19,886 2.12	789 .08
1960	481,453 45.77	556,577 52.92	11,304 1.07		2,475 .24

Year	Socialist	Other
1900	413 .15	
1904	1,354 .56	*Independence*
1908	1,870 .73	332 .13
1912	3,504 1.38	
1916	2,542 .93	
1920	2,268 .53	*American*
1924		100 .03
1928	631 .17	
1932	1,786 .46	
1936	687 .14	
1940	463 .09	
1944	792 .16	*Wallace, etc.*
1948	1,291 .23	1,866 .34
1952		925 .10

The vote in the Whig column for 1836 was cast for White. The vote in the Democratic column for 1860 was cast for Breckinridge.

TEXAS

Texas, which entered the Union in 1845, participated in twenty-seven presidential elections during the period 1848 to 1960; it did not take part in 1864 and 1868, because of the Civil War and Reconstruction. It supported fifteen winners and twelve losers.

TABLE 90   Number and Percentage of Votes by Elections and Parties

Year	Democratic		Whig / Republican		(third parties)		(other)		Prohibition	
1848	10,668	70.29	4,509	29.71						
1852	13,552	73.07	4,995	26.93						
1856	31,169	66.59	15,639	33.41	Const. Union					
1860	47,548	75.49			15,438	24.51				
1864										
1868			Republican		O'Conor-Demo.					
1872	66,546	57.07	47,468	40.71	2,580	2.21				
1876	104,755	70.04	44,800	29.96	Greenback					
1880	156,428	64.71	57,893	23.95	27,405	11.34			Prohibition	
1884	225,309	69.26	93,141	28.63	3,321	1.02	Union Labor		3,534	1.09
1888	234,883	65.70	88,422	24.73	Populist		29,459	8.24	4,749	1.33
1892	239,148	56.61	81,444	19.28	99,688	23.60	National Dem.		2,165	.51
1896	370,434	68.00	167,520	30.75			5,046	.93	1,786	.33
1900	267,432	63.12	130,641	30.83	20,981	4.95			2,644	.62
1904	167,200	71.45	51,242	21.90	8,062	3.45			4,292	1.83
1908	217,302	73.97	65,666	22.35	994	.34	T. Roosevelt		1,634	.56
1912	221,589	72.62	26,755	8.77			28,853	9.46	1,738	.57
1916	286,514	76.92	64,999	17.45	American				1,985	.53
1920	288,767	59.34	114,538	23.54	47,968	9.86	LaFollette			
1924	484,605	73.70	130,023	19.78	Communist		42,881	6.52		
1928	341,032	48.10	367,036	51.77	209	.03	Liberty			
1932	760,348	88.07	97,959	11.35	207	.02	324	.04		
1936	734,485	87.08	103,874	12.31	253	.03			514	.06
1940	840,151	80.69	199,152	19.13	212	.02			925	.09
1944	821,605	71.42	191,425	16.64			S. R. Demo.		1,017	.09
1948	750,700	65.44	282,240	24.60	Constitution		106,909	9.32	2,758	.24
1952	969,228	46.69	1,102,878	53.13	1,563	.08			1,983	.10
1956	859,958	43.98	1,080,619	55.27	14,591	.75				
1960	1,167,932	50.52	1,121,699	48.52	18,169	.79			3,870	.17

Year	Socialist Labor		Socialist		(other)		(other)	
1900	162	.04	1,846	.44				
1904	421	.18	2,791	1.19	Independence			
1908	176	.06	7,870	2.68	115	.04		
1912	442	.14	25,743	8.44				
1916	B. & T. Republ'n		18,969	5.09				
1920	27,247	5.60	8,121	1.67				
1924								
1928			722	.10	Jacksonian			
1932	Union		4,450	.52	104	.01		
1936	3,281	.39	1,075	.13				
1940	Texas Regulars		728	.07	America First			
1944	135,439	11.77	594	.05	251	.02	Wallace, etc.	
1948			874	.08			3,764	.33
1952							294	.01

The vote in the Democratic column for 1860 was cast for Breckinridge.

".00" signifies that the party received some votes, but less than .01%.

UTAH

Utah, which entered the Union in 1896, participated in seventeen presidential elections during the period 1896 to 1960. It supported fourteen winners and three losers.

TABLE 91   Number and Percentage of Votes by Elections and Parties

Year	Democratic		Republican		National Dem.		Socialist		Prohibition		Soc.Workers	
1896	64,607	82.70	13,491	17.27	21	.03			209	.22		
1900	45,006	48.30	47,139	50.59			720	.77				
1904	33,413	32.88	62,446	61.45			5,767	5.67				
1908	42,601	39.22	61,028	56.19	*T. Roosevelt*		4,895	4.51				
1912	36,579	32.55	42,100	37.46	24,174	21.51	9,023	8.03				
1916	84,256	58.86	54,137	37.82			4,460	3.12	149	.10		
1920	56,639	38.84	81,555	55.93	*LaFollette*		3,159	2.17				
1924	47,001	29.94	77,327	49.26	32,662	20.81						
1928	80,985	45.86	94,618	53.58			954	.54				
1932	116,750	56.52	84,795	41.05	*Union*		4,087	1.98				
1936	150,246	69.34	64,555	29.79	1,129	.52	432	.20	43	.02		
1940	154,277	62.25	93,151	37.59			200	.08				
1944	150,088	60.44	97,891	39.42	*Wallace*		340	.14			*Soc.Workers*	
1948	147,359	53.52	125,327	45.52	2,582	.94					71	.03
1952	135,364	41.07	194,190	58.93								
1956	118,364	35.44	215,631	64.56								
1960	169,248	45.17	205,361	54.81							100	.03

Year	Soc. Labor		Other	
1900	106	.11		
1904			*Independence*	
1908			87	.08
1912	510	.45		
1916	144	.10	*Farmer Labor*	
1920			4,475	3.07
1924			*Communist*	
1928			47	.03
1932			947	.46
1936			280	.13
1940			191	.08

Vermont, which entered the Union in 1791, participated in forty-three presidential elections during the period 1792 to 1960. It supported twenty-six winners and seventeen losers.

TABLE 92   Number and Percentage of Votes by Elections and Parties

Year	Democratic		Nat'l Republ'n							
1828	8,385	25.60	24,365	74.40			Anti-Masonic			
1832	7,870	24.50	11,152	34.71	Whig		13,106	40.79		
1836	14,039	40.08	Liberty		20,990	59.92				
1840	18,009	35.47	319	.63	32,445	63.90				
1844	18,041	37.00	3,954	8.11	26,770	54.90	Free Soil			
1848	10,948	22.85			23,122	48.26	13,837	28.88		
1852	13,044	29.76	Republican		22,173	50.58	8,621	19.67		
1856	10,577	20.70	39,963	78.23	546	1.07	Breckinridge		Const. Union	
1860	8,748	19.57	33,888	75.79			1,859	4.16	217	.49
1864	13,325	23.90	42,422	76.10						
1868	12,045	21.43	44,167	78.57	O'Conor-Dem.					
1872	10,927	20.62	41,481	78.26	593	1.12				
1876	20,350	31.41	44,428	68.58	Greenback				American	
1880	18,316	28.09	45,567	69.88	1,215	1.86	Prohibition		105	.16
1884	17,331	29.19	39,514	66.54	785	1.32	1,752	2.95		
1888	16,788	26.46	45,192	71.24			1,460	2.30		
1892	16,325	29.26	37,992	68.10	National Dem.		1,424	2.55		
1896	10,640	16.67	51,127	80.10	1,331	2.09	733	1.15		
1900	12,849	22.88	42,569	75.79			367	.65	Socialist	
1904	9,777	18.84	40,459	77.98			792	1.53	859	1.66
1908	11,496	21.83	39,552	75.12	T. Roosevelt		802	1.52		
1912	15,354	24.43	23,332	37.13	22,132	35.22	1,095	1.74	928	1.48
1916	22,708	35.23	40,250	62.44			709	1.10	798	1.24
1920	20,919	23.27	68,212	75.87	LaFollette		774	.86		
1924	16,124	15.67	80,498	78.22	5,964	5.80	326	.32		
1928	44,440	32.87	90,404	66.88	Communist		338	.25		
1932	56,266	41.08	78,984	57.66	195	.14			1,533	1.12
1936	62,124	43.28	81,023	56.44	405	.28				
1940	64,269	44.93	78,371	54.79	411	.29				
1944	53,820	42.94	71,527	57.06	Wallace, etc.					
1948	45,557	36.93	75,926	61.55	1,279	1.04			585	.47
1952	43,355	28.24	109,717	71.46	282	.18			185	.12
1956	42,549	27.82	110,390	72.18						
1960	69,186	41.35	98,131	58.65						

Year	Populist	
1892	44	.08
1896		
1900	383	.68
1904	Independence	
1908	804	1.53

The legislature cast the electoral vote in 1824.

The vote in the Whig column for 1836 was cast for Harrison. The vote in the Democratic column for 1860 was cast for Douglas.

VIRGINIA

Virginia, one of the original states, participated in forty-two presidential elections during the period 1789 to 1960; it did not take part in 1864 and 1868, because of the Civil War and Reconstruction. It supported twenty-seven winners and fifteen losers.

TABLE 93   Number and Percentage of Votes by Elections and Parties

Year	Democratic		Nat'l Republ'n		Party	Votes	%	Party	Votes	%	Party	Votes	%
1824					Crawford	8,489	56.76	Adams	3,189	21.32	Jackson	2,861	19.13
1828	26,752	68.85	12,101	31.15									
1832	33,609	74.59	11,451	25.41									
1836	30,845	56.85			Whig	23,412	43.15						
1840	43,893	50.81				42,501	49.19						
1844	50,683	53.09				44,790	46.91						
1848	46,586	50.79				45,124	49.20	Free Soil	9	.01			
1852	73,858	55.77	Republican			58,572	44.23						
1856	89,975	59.86	291	.19		60,039	39.94	Const. Union			Douglas		
1860	74,379	44.46	1,929	1.15					74,701	44.65		16,292	9.74
1864													
1868					O'Conor-Demo.								
1872	91,654	49.50	93,468	50.48		42	.02						
1876	139,670	59.38	95,558	40.62									
1880	128,586	60.48	84,020	39.52							Prohibition		
1884	145,497	51.05	139,356	48.90								138	.05
1888	151,979	49.98	150,449	49.47				Populist				1,682	.55
1892	163,977	56.10	113,256	38.75	Nat'l Demo.				12,275	4.20		2,798	.96
1896	154,985	52.54	135,388	45.90		2,129	.72					2,344	.79
1900	146,080	55.23	115,865	43.81					63	.02		2,150	.81
1904	80,648	61.78	47,880	36.67					359	.28		1,383	1.06
1908	82,946	60.52	52,573	38.36	T. Roosevelt				105	.08		1,111	.81
1912	90,332	65.95	23,288	17.00		21,777	15.90					709	.52
1916	102,824	66.77	49,356	32.05								683	.44
1920	141,670	61.32	87,456	37.85	LaFollette							857	.37
1924	139,797	62.49	73,359	32.79		10,379	4.64	Communist					
1928	140,146	45.90	164,609	53.91					174	.06			
1932	203,979	68.46	89,637	30.09	Union				86	.03		1,843	.62
1936	234,980	70.23	98,336	29.39		233	.07		98	.03		594	.18
1940	235,961	68.08	109,363	31.55					71	.02		882	.25
1944	242,276	62.36	145,243	37.39	Wallace, etc.			S. R. Demo.				459	.12
1948	200,786	47.89	172,070	41.04		2,047	.49		43,393	10.35			
1952	268,677	43.36	349,037	56.32		311	.05	Constitution					
1956	267,760	38.36	386,459	55.37	Va. Conserv.				42,964	6.16			
1960	362,327	46.96	404,521	52.44		4,204	.54						

Year	Clay	
1824	416	2.78

Year	Soc. Labor		Socialist		Party	Votes	%
1896	115	.04					
1900	167	.06	145	.05			
1904	218	.17	56	.04	Independence		
1908	25	.02	255	.19		51	.04
1912	50	.04	820	.60			
1916	67	.04	1,060	.69	Farmer Labor		
1920			807	.35		243	.12
1924	191	.09					
1928	179	.06	250	.08			
1932			2,382	.80		15	.01
1936	36	.01	313	.09			
1940	48	.01	282	.08			
1944	90	.02	417	.11			
1948	234	.06	726	.17			
1952	1,160	.19	504	.08			
1956	351	.05	444	.06			
1960	397	.05					

The vote in the Whig column for 1836 was cast for White. The vote in the Democratic column for 1860 was cast for Breckinridge.

WASHINGTON

Washington, which entered the Union in 1889, participated in eighteen presidential elections during the period 1892 to 1960. It supported fourteen winners and four losers.

TABLE 94 Number and Percentage of Votes by Elections and Parties

Year	Democratic		Republican		Populist / Other			Socialist		Prohibition	
1892	29,844	33.92	36,460	41.45	Populist	19,105	21.72			2,553	2.91
1896	51,646	55.19	39,153	41.84						968	1.03
1900	44,833	41.70	57,456	53.44	Socialist			2,006	1.87	2,363	2.20
1904	28,098	19.36	101,540	69.95		669	.46	10,023	6.91	3,229	2.22
1908	58,691	31.92	106,062	57.68	T. Roosevelt			14,177	7.71	4,700	2.56
1912	86,840	26.90	70,445	21.82		113,698	35.22	40,134	12.43	9,810	3.04
1916	183,388	48.13	167,244	43.89				22,800	5.98	6,868	1.80
1920	84,298	21.14	223,137	55.96	LaFollette			8,913	2.24	3,800	.95
1924	42,842	10.16	220,224	52.24		150,727	35.76				
1928	156,772	31.30	335,844	67.06				2,615	.52		
1932	353,260	57.46	208,645	33.94	Union			17,080	2.78	1,540	.25
1936	459,579	66.38	206,892	29.88		17,463	2.52	3,496	.50	1,041	.15
1940	462,145	58.22	322,123	40.58				4,586	.58	1,686	.21
1944	486,774	56.84	361,689	42.24	Wallace, etc.			3,824	.45	2,396	.28
1948	476,165	52.61	386,315	42.68		31,692	3.50	3,534	.39	6,117	.68
1952	492,845	44.69	599,107	54.33		2,460	.22	254	.02		
1956	523,002	45.44	620,430	53.91							
1960	599,298	48.27	629,273	50.68							

Year	Soc. Labor		Nat'l Demo.	Nat'l Prohib'n	Independence	Farmer Labor	Liberty	Communist	Soc. Workers	Constitution	American	Christian
1896			1,668 1.78	148 .16								
1900	866	.81										
1904	1,592	1.10										
1908					249 .14							
1912	1,872	.58										
1916	730	.19										
1920	1,321	.33				77,246 19.37						
1924	1,004	.24						761 .18			5,991 1.42	
1928	4,068	.81						1,541 .31				1,598 .23
1932	1,009	.16					30,308 4.93	2,972 .48				
1936	362	.05						1,907 .28				
1940	667	.08						2,626 .33				
1944	1,645	.19							103 .01			
1948	1,133	.13							119 .01	7,290 .66		
1952	633	.06										
1956	7,457	.65										
1960	10,895	.88							705 .06	1,401 .11		

West Virginia, which entered the Union in 1863, participated in twenty-five presidential elections during the period 1864 to 1960. It supported twenty winners and five losers. In 1916 Hughes led Wilson in West Virginia, 49.38% to 48.44%, while losing the election.

TABLE 95   Number and Percentage of Votes by Elections and Parties

Year	Democratic		Republican	
1864	10,457	31.05	23,223	68.95
1868	20,306	41.16	29,025	58.84
1872	29,451	47.22	32,315	51.82
1876	56,455	56.16	42,698	42.47
1880	57,391	50.92	46,243	41.03
1884	67,317	50.94	63,096	47.74
1888	78,677	49.35	78,171	49.03
1892	84,467	49.38	80,293	46.94
1896	94,488	46.83	105,379	52.23
1900	98,807	44.75	119,829	54.27
1904	100,881	42.03	132,628	55.26
1908	111,418	43.16	137,869	53.41
1912	113,197	42.09	56,754	21.10
1916	140,403	48.44	143,124	49.38
1920	220,789	43.30	282,007	55.30
1924	257,232	44.07	288,635	49.45
1928	263,784	41.04	375,551	58.43
1932	405,124	54.47	330,731	44.47
1936	502,582	60.56	325,358	39.20
1940	495,662	57.10	372,414	42.90
1944	392,777	54.89	322,819	45.11
1948	429,188	57.32	316,251	42.24
1952	453,578	51.92	419,970	48.08
1956	381,534	45.92	449,297	54.08
1960	441,786	52.73	395,995	47.27

O'Conor Dem.
1872	600	.96

Greenback
1876	1,373	1.37
1880	9,079	8.05
1884	810	.61

Union Labor
1888	1,508	.95

Populist
1892	4,166	2.44

1900	268	.12
1904	339	.14

T. Roosevelt
1912	79,112	29.42

LaFollette
1924	36,723	6.29

Wallace
1948	3,311	.44

Socialist
1900	219	.10
1904	1,574	.66
1908	3,679	1.43
1912	15,336	5.70
1916	6,140	2.12
1920	5,618	1.10
1928	1,313	.20
1932	5,133	.69
1936	832	.10

Prohibition
1888	939	.71
1892	1,085	.68
1896	2,145	1.25
1900	1,223	.61
1904	1,692	.77
1908	4,604	1.92
1912	4,534	1.69
1916	179	.06
1920	1,528	.30
1928	1,703	.26
1932	2,342	.31
1936	1,173	.14

Year	Nat'l Demo.	
1896	678	.34

Year	Independence	
1908	46	.02

Year	American	
1924	1,072	.18

Year	Communist	
1928	401	.06
1932	444	.06

WISCONSIN

Wisconsin, which entered the Union in 1848, participated in twenty-nine presidential elections during the period 1848 to 1960. It supported twenty-two winners and seven losers.

TABLE 96   Number and Percentage of Votes by Elections and Parties

Year	Democratic		Republican		Other (A)		Other (B)		Other (C)	
1848	15,001	38.30			13,747	35.10 (Whig)	10,418	26.60 (Free Soil)		
1852	33,658	51.99			22,240	34.35 (Whig)	8,842	13.66 (Free Soil)		
1856	52,867	44.23	66,092	55.29	580	.49 (Whig)				
1860	65,021	42.73	86,110	56.58			888	.58 (Breckinridge)	161	.11 (Const. Union)
1864	65,884	44.12	83,458	55.88						
1868	84,710	43.76	108,857	56.24						
1872	86,477	44.97	104,997	54.60			834	.43 (O'Conor-Demo.)		
1876	123,926	48.50	130,070	50.90	1,509	.59 (Greenback)			27	.01 (Prohibition)
1880	114,649	42.91	144,400	54.04	7,986	2.99 (Greenback)	91	.03 (American)	69	.03
1884	146,459	45.79	161,157	50.38	4,598	1.44 (Greenback)			7,656	2.39
1888	155,243	43.76	176,555	49.77			8,561	2.41 (Union Labor)	14,415	4.06
1892	177,335	47.77	170,846	46.02	9,909	2.67 (Populist)			13,132	3.54
1896	165,523	37.00	268,135	59.93					7,509	1.68
1900	159,279	35.99	265,756	60.04			7,051	1.59 (Socialist)	10,022	2.26
1904	124,107	28.01	280,164	63.24	530	.12	28,220	6.37	9,770	2.21
1908	166,632	36.67	247,747	54.52			28,170	6.20	11,572	2.55
1912	164,228	41.06	130,695	32.68	62,460	15.62 (T. Roosevelt)	33,481	8.37	8,586	2.15
1916	193,042	42.96	221,323	49.25			27,846	6.20	7,166	1.59
1920	113,422	16.07	498,576	70.65			85,041	12.05	8,647	1.23
1924	68,115	8.10	311,614	37.06	453,678	53.96 (LaFollette)			2,918	.35
1928	450,259	44.28	544,205	53.52			18,213	1.79	2,245	.22
1932	707,410	63.46	347,741	31.19			53,379	4.79	2,672	.24
1936	802,984	63.80	380,828	30.26	60,297	4.79 (Union)	10,626	.84	1,071	.09
1940	704,821	50.15	679,206	48.32			15,071	1.07	2,148	.15
1944	650,413	48.57	674,532	50.37			13,205	.99		
1948	647,310	50.70	590,959	46.28	25,282	1.98 (Wallace, etc.)	12,547	.98		
1952	622,175	38.71	979,744	60.95	2,174	.14	1,157	.07		
1956	586,768	37.84	954,844	61.58			754	.05		
1960	830,805	48.05	895,175	51.77					6,918	.45 (Constitution)

Year	Soc. Labor		National Demo.		National Proh.		Communist / Soc. Workers		Commonw. Land	
1896	1,314	.29	4,584	1.02	346	.08				
1900	505	.11								
1904	223	.05								
1908	314	.07								
1912	527	.13								
1916										
1920										
1924	458	.05					3,773	.45 (Communist)	270	.03
1928	381	.04					1,528	.15		
1932	494	.04					3,112	.28		
1936	557	.04					2,197	.17		
1940	1,882	.13					2,394	.17		
1944	1,002	.07					303	.02 (Soc. Workers)		
1948	399	.03					1,350	.08		
1952	770	.05					564	.04		
1956	710	.05								
1960	1,310	.08					1,792	.10		

The vote in the Democratic column for 1860 was cast for Douglas.

WYOMING

Wyoming, which entered the Union in 1890, participated in eighteen presidential elections during the period 1892 to 1960. It supported fourteen winners and four losers.

TABLE 97   Number and Percentage of Votes by Elections and Parties

Year	Democratic		Republican		Populist / Other		Socialist		Prohibition	
1892	Democratic		8,454	50.60	7,722	46.22	Socialist		530	3.17
1896	10,375	50.35	10,072	48.88					159	.77
1900	10,164	41.24	14,482	58.76			1,077	3.51	217	.71
1904	8,930	29.08	20,489	66.71	T. Roosevelt		1,715	4.56	66	.18
1908	14,918	39.67	20,846	55.43			2,760	6.53	434	1.03
1912	15,310	36.20	14,560	34.42	9,232	21.83	1,453	2.80	373	.72
1916	28,316	54.62	21,698	41.86	LaFollette		1,288	2.29	265	.47
1920	17,429	30.98	35,091	62.38	25,174	31.51				
1924	12,868	16.11	41,858	52.39			788	.95		
1928	29,299	35.37	52,748	63.68	Union		2,829	2.92		
1932	54,370	56.07	39,583	40.82	1,653	1.60	200	.19	75	.07
1936	62,624	60.58	38,739	37.47			148	.13	172	.15
1940	59,287	52.83	52,633	46.89	Wallace					
1944	49,419	48.77	51,921	51.23	931	.92	137	.14		
1948	52,354	51.62	47,947	47.27	Constitution		40	.03	194	.15
1952	47,934	37.09	81,047	62.71	72	.06				
1956	49,554	39.90	74,573	60.04						
1960	63,331	44.95	77,551	55.05						

Year	Independence		Farmer Labor		Communist		Soc. Labor	
1908	64	.17						
1912								
1916			Farmer Labor					
1920			2,180	3.88				
1924								
1928					Communist			
1932					180	.19		
1936					91	.09		
1940								
1944							Soc. Labor	
1948							56	.06
1952							36	.03

164

States as Barometers

The absurdity of the statement "As Maine goes, so goes the Nation!" can be proved by a glance at the table *States as Barometers*. Over half of the other forty-nine states have better records as political weather-vanes. Five of Maine's twelve misses were in succession, during the years 1932 to 1948. A state which has given continuous Republican majorities since the first appearance of that party, with the exception of 1912, when the G. O. P. was split, can hardly qualify as a barometer.

The only state, other than Hawaii, with a perfect record is New Mexico, which has voted for the winner every time since its entrance into the Union in 1912. Illinois and New York have missed only four and six times, respectively. Illinois first voted in 1820 while New York began voting in 1792. All but one of the latter's misses have been during campaigns when one of its past, present, or future governors was a candidate.

California, which participated in its first election in 1852, has missed only four times, including two contests in which its electoral vote was divided. Hancock carried it by ninety-five votes in 1880, but Garfield got one of the six electoral votes. In 1912, Roosevelt led Wilson by 174 votes, with the latter getting two of the thirteen electors.

TABLE 98 — States as Barometers

States	1789	1792	1796	1800	1804	1808	1812	1816	1820	1824	1828	1832	1836	1840	1844	1848	1852	1856	1860	1864	1868	1872
New Mexico																						
Hawaii																						
Arizona																						
Illinois													X		X							
New York						X												X		X		
California																						
Minnesota																						
Pennsylvania			X						X													
Utah																						
Ohio												X		X	X		X					
West Virginia																						
Oklahoma																						
Oregon																				X		
North Dakota																						
Nevada																						
Wisconsin														X		X						
Indiana									X			X		X								
Michigan														X		X						
Rhode Island			X		X	X				X	X			X		X						
New Hampshire			X		X	X			X			X		X								
Iowa														X		X						
Missouri												X		X				X				X
Kansas																						
Idaho																						
Montana																						
Washington																						
Wyoming																						
New Jersey			X			X				X	X		X	X							X	X
Connecticut			X	X	X	X	X			X	X			X			X					
Massachusetts			X		X	X	X			X	X	X		X		X	X					
Maryland			T							X	X	X		X				X	X	X	X	X
Maine										X					X	X						
Nebraska																						
Florida																		X	O			
North Carolina	X								X					X				X	O			
Virginia	X								X				X		X			X	O	O		
Louisiana																		X	O	X	O	
Colorado																						
Tennessee	X								X				X		X		X	X	O			X
Vermont		X								X	X	X		X		X	X					
Georgia	X								X					X				X	O		X	X
Kentucky	X										X	X		X		X	X	X	O		X	X
Delaware		X	X	X	X	X			X	X	X	X		X				X	X	X		
South Carolina	X								X			X	X	X		X		X	O			
Texas														X				X	O	O		X
Alabama									X				X		X			X	O			
Mississippi									X					X				X	O	O		
Arkansas													X		X			X	O			O
Alaska																						

The New York electors were absent in 1789.

X indicates that states voted for losers.

T indicates that the candidates received the same number of votes. Maryland cast five votes each for Jefferson, Burr, Adams, and Pinckney in1801, and North Dakota cast one vote each for Cleveland, Harrison, and Weaver in 1892.

O indicates that states did not vote, due to Civil War and Reconstruction.

166

States	1876	1880	1884	1888	1892	1896	1900	1904	1908	1912	1916	1920	1924	1928	1932	1936	1940	1944	1948	1952	1956	1960
New Mexico																						
Hawaii																						
Arizona																						x
Illinois			x				x															
New York	x						x												x			
California		x	x				x															x
Minnesota			x		x		x	x														
Pennsylvania			x		x		x	x					x						x			
Utah						x	x															x
Ohio			x		x													x				x
West Virginia	x	x		x			x									x						
Oklahoma						x				x												x
Oregon			x		x		x												x			x
North Dakota				T													x	x	x			x
Nevada		x	x		x	x	x			x												
Wisconsin			x				x		x									x				x
Indiana	x						x										x	x	x			x
Michigan			x		x		x			x							x	x				
Rhode Island			x		x		x					x										
New Hampshire			x		x								x					x				x
Iowa			x		x		x										x	x				x
Missouri	x	x		x		x	x										x	x			x	
Kansas			x		x		x										x	x	x			x
Idaho					x	x	x															x
Montana					x	x	x															x
Washington					x	x				x												x
Wyoming					x	x												x				x
New Jersey	x	x		x			x												x			
Connecticut	x			x			x						x						x			
Massachusetts		x		x			x					x										
Maryland	x	x		x				x	x										x			
Maine		x		x				x					x	x	x	x	x					x
Nebraska		x		x	x		x										x	x	x			x
Florida		x		x		x	x	x	x				x	x								x
North Carolina	x	x		x		x	x	x	x				x	x						x	x	
Virginia	x	x		x		x	x	x	x				x	x								x
Louisiana		x		x		x	x	x	x	x				x	x							
Colorado		x		x	x					x							x	x				x
Tennessee	x	x		x		x	x	x	x					x								x
Vermont			x	x			x	x					x	x	x	x	x	x				x
Georgia	x	x		x		x	x	x	x				x	x	x					x	x	
Kentucky	x	x		x		x	x	x					x							x	x	x
Delaware	x	x		x					x				x						x			
South Carolina		x		x		x	x	x	x				x	x	x					x	x	x
Texas	x	x		x		x	x	x	x				x	x								x
South Dakota				x	x				x	x					x	x	x					x
Alabama	x	x		x		x	x	x	x				x	x	x				x	x	x	x
Mississippi	x	x		x		x	x	x	x				x	x	x				x	x	x	x
Arkansas	x	x		x		x	x	x	x				x	x	x				x	x		
Alaska																						x

1824: The House of Representatives vote (1825) is used, instead of the Electoral College vote.

1860: New Jersey—Douglas led in popular vote, Lincoln in electoral.

1892: North Dakota—Weaver led in popular vote, but Cleveland, Harrison, and Weaver split electoral evenly.

1904: Maryland—Roosevelt led in popular vote, Parker in electoral.

1908: Maryland—Taft led in popular vote, Bryan in electoral.

States	Voted for Winners	Voted for Losers	Ties	Pct.
New Mexico	13	0		1.000
Hawaii	1	0		1.000
Arizona	12	1		.923
Illinois	32	4		.889
New York	37	6		.860
California	24	4		.857
Minnesota	22	4		.846
Pennsylvania	36	8		.818
Utah	14	3		.824
Ohio	32	8		.800
West Virginia	20	5		.800
Oklahoma	11	3		.786
Oregon	20	6		.769
North Dakota	13	4	1	.765
Nevada	19	6		.760
Wisconsin	22	7		.759
Indiana	28	9		.757
Michigan	24	8		.750
Rhode Island	32	11		.744
New Hampshire	32	12		.727
Iowa	21	8		.724
Missouri	26	10		.722
Kansas	18	7		.720
Idaho	14	4		.714
Montana	14	4		.714
Washington	14	4		.714
Wyoming	14	4		.714
New Jersey	31	13		.705
Connecticut	30	14		.682
Massachusetts	30	14		.682
Maryland	29	14	1	.674
Maine	24	12		.667
Nebraska	16	8		.667
Florida	18	10		.643
North Carolina	27	15		.643
Virginia	27	15		.643
Louisiana	23	13		.639
Colorado	14	8		.636
Tennessee	25	16		.610
Vermont	26	17		.605
Georgia	25	18		.581
Kentucky	25	18		.581
Delaware	25	19		.568
South Carolina	24	19		.558
Texas	15	12		.556
South Dakota	10	8		.556
Alabama	18	17		.514
Mississippi	17	17		.500
Arkansas	15	15		.500
Alaska	0	1		.000
TOTALS	1,059	463	2	.696

The following tabulation shows how many states voted for the winner and how many for the loser:

Year	W	L	Year	W	L	Year	W	L
1789	10	–	1848	15	15	1908	29	17
1792	15	–	1852	27	4	1912	40	8
1796	9	7	1856	19	12	1916	30	18
1800	8	7	1860	18	15	1920	37	11
1804	15	2	1864	22	3	1924	35	13
1808	12	5	1868	26	8	1928	40	8
1812	11	7	1872	29	6	1932	42	6
1816	16	3	1876	21	17	1936	46	2
1820	24	–	1880	19	19	1940	38	10
1824	13	11	1884	20	18	1944	36	12
1828	15	9	1888	20	18	1948	28	20
1832	16	8	1892	23	20	1952	39	9
1836	15	11	1896	23	22	1956	41	7
1840	19	7	1900	28	17	1960	23	27
1844	15	11	1904	32	13			

The House vote (1825) was used instead of the electoral (1824). Non-participating states: 1864—11, 1868—3, 1872—2.

Over fifty different parties received votes in the presidential races during the period 1828 to 1960. Only ten received electoral votes and but three—the Democratic, Whig, and Republican—elected presidents.

There were eight campaigns in which "third" parties offered enough opposition to the dominant parties to obtain electoral votes. The Anti-Masonic Party carried Vermont in 1832. The new Republican Party displaced the Whigs in 1856 and finished second to the Democrats; the only state the Whigs carried was Maryland. Four years later, the Democrats split into Northern and Southern wings, both of which secured electoral votes, as did also the new Constitutional Union Party. The Populists broke into the electoral column in 1892, the Roosevelt Progressives in 1912, the LaFollette Progressives in 1924, the States' Rights Democrats in 1948, and unpledged Democratic slates in 1960. The 1912 Progressives were responsible not only for Taft's defeat by Wilson, but were strong enough to place their own candidate ahead of Taft.

There were other instances besides these eight, but they did not involve minor parties. In 1832 and 1836, South Carolina cast its electoral vote for Democratic candidates other than the ones which the other Democratic states supported. There were three Whig nominees in 1836, all of whom received electoral votes.

The numerous parties which have never broken into the electoral column have on occasion had an influence far out of proportion to their votes. The Liberty Party decided the 1844 election by swinging New York from Clay to Polk. Pivotal New York was swung from Cass to Taylor by the Free Soil Party in 1848. The Prohibition Party received 25,006 votes in pivotal New York in 1884; Cleveland's margin was only 1,149. It got 30,231 in New York in 1888, when the Empire State again decided the contest; Harrison's edge was 14,373. In 1916 the Socialists received 43,259 in California, which was the decisive state; Wilson carried it by 3,806.

The listing below shows the instances in which certain candidates had the balance of power in states in which no candidate received a majority. Sometimes two or more nominees combined held the balance of power. There were also instances, not included in the listing, where a nominee who did not have sufficient votes to constitute the balance of power still had enough to have changed the order among the other candidates, if he had been able to shift his votes.

1828: Only two parties.

1832: Jackson, Democrat—Vermont; Wirt, Anti-Masonic—New Jersey and Rhode Island.

1836: Only two parties.

1840: Birney, Liberty—Pennsylvania.

1844: Birney, Liberty—Michigan, New York, and Ohio.

1848: Cass, Democrat—Massachusetts, New York, and Vermont. Van Buren, Free Soil—Connecticut, Illinois, Indiana, Iowa, Maine, Michigan, Ohio, and Wisconsin.

1852: Hale, Free Soil—Connecticut, Delaware, Massachusetts, and Ohio.

1856: Fremont, Republican—California. Fillmore, Whig—Illinois, Iowa, New Jersey, New York, and Ohio.

1860: Douglas, Democrat—Georgia, Kentucky, Louisiana, Maryland, Oregon, Tennessee, and Virginia. Breckinridge, Democrat—California and Missouri. Lincoln, Republican, and Douglas—Delaware.

1864 and *1868:* Only two parties each time.

1872: Majorities in all states.

1876: Cooper, Greenback—Indiana.

1880: Weaver, Greenback—California, Indiana, and New Jersey.

1884: St. John, Prohibition—New York. Butler, Greenback, and St. John—Connecticut, Indiana, Massachusetts, Michigan, and New Jersey.

1888: Fisk, Prohibition—Connecticut, Indiana, New Jersey, New York, Ohio, and Virginia. Fisk and Streeter, Union Labor—Illinois, Michigan, West Virginia, and Wisconsin. Fisk and Curtis, American—California.

1892: Cleveland, Democrat—Nebraska, Oregon, and South Dakota. Weaver, Populist—California, Indiana, Montana, North Carolina, and Washington. Bidwell, Prohibition—Delaware, North Dakota, and Ohio. Weaver and Bidwell—Illinois, Iowa, Michigan, Minnesota, Missouri, West Virginia, and Wisconsin. Weaver, Bidwell, and Wing, Socialist-Labor—New York.

1896: Palmer, National Democrat—Kentucky. Levering, Prohibition—South Dakota. Palmer, Levering, and Matchett, Socialist-Labor—California.

1900: Majorities in all states.

1904: Swallow, Prohibition—Maryland. Swallow, Debs, Socialist, and Watson, Populist—Kentucky. Swallow, Debs, Watson, and Corregan, Socialist-Labor—Missouri.

1908: Debs, Socialist—Missouri, Montana, Nevada, and Oklahoma. Debs and Chafin, Prohibition—Colorado, Indiana, Kentucky, Maryland, and Nebraska.

1912: Wilson, Democrat—Michigan and Vermont. Roosevelt, Progressive—Connecticut, Delaware, Idaho, Massachusetts, New Hampshire, New Mexico, New York, Rhode Island, Utah, and Wyoming. Taft, Republican—Illinois, Iowa, Kansas, Maine, Minnesota, Montana, Nebraska, New Jersey, North Dakota, Oregon, Pennsylvania, and West Virginia. Debs, Socialist—California and Oklahoma. Roosevelt and Debs—Kentucky, Missouri, Ohio, and Wisconsin. Taft and Debs—Arizona, Colorado, Indiana, Maryland, Nevada, and Washington.

1916: Benson, Socialist—California, Minnesota, New Hampshire, and West Virginia. Benson and Hanly, Prohibition—Indiana, Kansas, Oregon, South Dakota, Washington, and Wisconsin. Benson, Hanly, and Reimer, Socialist-Labor—Connecticut.

1920: Debs, Socialist, and Watkins, Prohibition—Kentucky.

1924: Davis, Democrat—Idaho, Montana, Nevada, North Dakota, and South Dakota. La-Follette, Progressive—Arizona, Kentucky, Maryland, Missouri, Nebraska, New Mexico, Oklahoma, Utah, and West Virginia.

1928: Thomas, Socialist, and Foster, Communist—New York.

1932: Thomas, Socialist—Connecticut and New Jersey. Thomas, Foster, Communist, and Upshaw, Prohibition—Ohio.

1936: Lemke, Union—New Hampshire.

1940: Thomas, Socialist, and Browder, Communist—Michigan.

1944: Majorities in all states.

1948: Dewey, Republican—Louisiana. Thurmond, States' Rights Democrat—Tennessee and Virginia. Wallace, Progressive—California, New York, and Ohio. Thurmond and Wallace—Florida, Wallace and Thomas, Socialist—Connecticut, Maryland, and Oregon. Wallace and Watson, Prohibition—Indiana and Michigan. Wallace, Thomas, and Watson—Idaho.

1952: Hallinan, Progressive, Hamblen, Prohibition, and MacArthur, Constitution—Tennessee. Hamblen and Hass, Socialist-Labor—Kentucky.

1956: Eisenhower, Republican—South Carolina. Andrews, Constitution—Tennessee.

1960: Nixon, Republican—Mississippi. Hass, Socialist-Labor—Illinois. Hass, Dobbs, Socialist Workers, and Lee, Conservative—New Jersey.

On a nation-wide basis, where the popular vote has only an indirect bearing, the following parties have held the balance of power:

1844: Liberty. *1848:* Free Soil. *1856:* Whig. *1860:* Breckinridge Democrat and Constitutional Union. *1880* and *1884:* Greenback. *1888:* Prohibition. *1892:* Populist. *1912:* Republican. *1916:* Socialist and Prohibition. *1948:* States' Rights Democrat, Wallace Progressive, and Socialist.

Tables 99 to 109 give the votes received by the eleven parties which offered candidates in at least three presidential elections during the period 1828 to 1960. These include three parties which have been successful nationally (Democratic, Republican, and Whig), a party which was successful only in certain states (Populist), three others which furnished the balance of power in the national popular vote (Prohibition, Socialist, and Greenback), three minor parties (Socialist Labor, Socialist Workers, and Communist), which furnished the balance of power in part in certain states, and a minor party (Farmer Labor) which had no effect as far as other parties' majorities were concerned.

TABLE 99   Democratic Vote by States and Elections

States	1828	1832	1836	1840	1844	1848
Alabama	17,138		20,506	33,991	37,740	31,363
Alaska						
Arizona						
Arkansas			2,400	6,766	9,546	9,300
California						
Colorado						
Connecticut	4,448	11,212	19,291	25,296	29,841	27,047
Delaware		4,194	4,152	4,884	5,996	5,910
Florida						3,243
Georgia	19,362	20,750	22,333	31,989	44,177	44,809
Hawaii						
Idaho						
Illinois	9,560	14,147	18,097	47,625	58,700	56,629
Indiana	22,237	31,552	32,478	51,695	70,181	74,745
Iowa						12,093
Kansas						
Kentucky	39,394	36,247	33,435	32,616	51,988	49,720
Louisiana	4,605	4,049	3,653	7,617	13,782	15,370
Maine	13,927	33,984	22,900	46,190	45,964	40,138
Maryland	24,565	19,156	22,168	28,759	32,676	34,536
Massachusetts	6,019	14,497	33,542	52,432	52,846	35,398
Michigan			7,534	21,131	27,759	30,687
Minnesota						
Mississippi	6,772	5,919	9,979	16,995	25,126	26,537
Missouri	8,272	5,192	10,995	29,760	41,369	40,077
Montana						
Nebraska						
Nevada						
New Hampshire	20,922	25,486	18,722	32,670	27,160	27,763
New Jersey	21,951	23,859	25,847	31,034	37,495	36,901
New Mexico						
New York	140,763	168,562	166,886	212,743	237,588	114,320
North Carolina	37,857	24,862	26,910	33,782	39,287	34,869
North Dakota						
Ohio	67,597	81,246	96,916	124,782	149,117	154,775
Oklahoma						
Oregon						
Pennsylvania	101,652	90,983	91,475	143,784	167,535	171,176
Rhode Island	821	2,126	2,966	3,301	4,867	3,646
South Carolina						
South Dakota						
Tennessee	44,293	28,740	26,129	48,289	59,904	58,419
Texas						10,668
Utah						
Vermont	8,385	7,870	14,039	18,009	18,041	10,948
Virginia	26,752	33,609	30,845	43,893	50,683	46,586
Washington						
West Virginia						
Wisconsin						15,001
Wyoming						
TOTALS	647,292	688,242	764,198	1,130,033	1,339,368	1,222,674

States	1852	1856	1860	1864	1868	1872
Alabama	26,881	46,817	48,831		72,086	79,444
Alaska						
Arizona						
Arkansas	12,173	21,910	28,732		19,078	37,927
California	40,626	53,365	38,516	43,842	54,078	40,749
Colorado						
Connecticut	33,249	34,995	17,364	42,285	47,952	45,875
Delaware	6,319	8,003	7,344	8,767	10,980	10,208
Florida	4,318	6,368	8,543			15,427
Georgia	40,516	56,608	52,131		102,822	76,356
Hawaii						
Idaho						
Illinois	80,597	105,344	160,205	158,829	199,143	184,938
Indiana	95,340	118,672	115,509	130,223	166,980	163,632
Iowa	17,763	36,241	55,111	49,596	74,040	71,196
Kansas				3,871	14,019	32,970
Kentucky	53,806	74,642	53,143	64,301	115,889	100,208
Louisiana	18,647	22,169	22,681		80,225	57,029
Maine	41,609	39,080	26,693	47,736	42,396	29,087
Maryland	40,028	39,115	42,511	32,739	62,357	67,687
Massachusetts	45,875	39,240	34,492	48,745	59,408	59,260
Michigan	41,842	52,529	65,057	67,370	97,069	78,355
Minnesota			11,920	17,375	28,072	34,423
Mississippi	26,876	35,665	40,797			47,288
Missouri	38,353	58,164	58,801	31,026	59,788	151,434
Montana						
Nebraska					5,439	7,812
Nevada				6,594	5,218	6,236
New Hampshire	29,997	32,789	25,881	33,034	31,224	31,424
New Jersey	44,325	46,943	62,869	68,024	83,001	76,801
New Mexico						
New York	262,456	195,866	312,510	361,986	429,883	387,281
North Carolina	39,744	48,246	48,539		84,090	70,094
North Dakota						
Ohio	169,160	170,874	187,232	205,571	239,032	244,321
Oklahoma						
Oregon			5,342	8,457	11,125	7,730
Pennsylvania	198,568	230,686	178,871	276,308	313,382	211,041
Rhode Island	8,735	6,680	7,753	8,718	6,548	5,329
South Carolina					45,237	22,703
South Dakota						
Tennessee	57,123	73,638	66,440		26,311	94,391
Texas	13,552	31,169	47,548			66,546
Utah						
Vermont	13,044	10,577	8,748	13,325	12,045	10,927
Virginia	73,858	89,975	74,379			91,654
Washington						
West Virginia				10,457	20,306	29,451
Wisconsin	33,658	52,867	65,021	65,884	84,710	86,477
Wyoming						
TOTALS	1,609,038	1,839,237	1,379,434	1,805,063	2,703,933	2,833,711

For 1860, the Douglas vote is used for California, Connecticut, Illinois, Indiana, Iowa, Maine, Massachusetts, Michigan, Minnesota, Missouri, New Hampshire, New Jersey, New York, Ohio, Rhode Island, Vermont, and Wisconsin. The Breckinridge vote is used for the remaining states. The 1860 total is Douglas'; Breckinridges's was 854,248. Most states cast votes for both.

States	1876	1880	1884	1888	1892	1896
Alabama	102,989	91,185	93,951	117,320	138,138	131,226
Alaska						
Arizona						
Arkansas	58,083	60,775	72,927	86,717	87,834	110,103
California	76,465	80,443	89,288	117,729	118,174	144,618
Colorado		24,647	27,723	37,567		161,269
Connecticut	61,934	64,415	67,182	74,922	82,395	56,740
Delaware	13,381	15,275	17,054	16,414	18,581	16,615
Florida	22,923	27,964	31,769	39,656	30,143	32,736
Georgia	130,088	102,470	94,667	100,499	129,386	94,733
Hawaii						
Idaho					2	23,192
Illinois	258,601	277,321	312,355	348,371	426,281	465,613
Indiana	213,526	225,522	244,992	261,013	262,740	305,573
Iowa	112,099	105,845	177,286	179,877	196,367	223,741
Kansas	37,902	59,801	90,132	102,745		173,042
Kentucky	160,445	149,068	152,961	183,800	175,461	217,890
Louisiana	70,566	65,067	62,540	85,032	87,922	77,175
Maine	49,914	65,171	52,140	50,481	48,044	34,587
Maryland	91,780	93,706	96,932	106,168	113,866	104,746
Massachusetts	108,975	111,960	122,481	151,905	176,858	106,206
Michigan	141,095	131,597	149,835	213,469	202,296	237,268
Minnesota	48,799	53,315	70,144	104,385	100,920	139,735
Mississippi	112,173	75,750	76,510	85,467	40,288	63,793
Missouri	203,077	208,609	235,988	261,974	268,188	363,652
Montana					17,581	42,537
Nebraska	17,554	28,523	54,354	80,542	24,943	115,999
Nevada	9,308	9,613	5,578	5,362	714	8,376
New Hampshire	38,509	40,794	39,183	43,456	42,081	21,650
New Jersey	115,962	122,565	127,798	151,508	171,066	133,695
New Mexico						
New York	522,612	534,511	563,154	635,965	654,908	551,513
North Carolina	125,427	124,208	142,952	148,336	133,098	174,488
North Dakota						20,686
Ohio	323,182	340,821	368,280	396,455	404,115	477,497
Oklahoma						
Oregon	14,157	19,955	24,604	26,522	14,243	46,739
Pennsylvania	366,204	407,428	393,747	447,004	452,264	433,228
Rhode Island	10,712	10,779	12,391	17,530	24,336	14,459
South Carolina	90,906	112,312	69,890	65,825	54,698	58,801
South Dakota					9,081	41,225
Tennessee	133,166	128,191	133,270	158,779	138,874	168,878
Texas	104,755	156,428	225,309	234,883	239,148	370,434
Utah						64,607
Vermont	20,350	18,316	17,331	16,788	16,325	10,640
Virginia	139,670	128,586	145,497	151,979	163,977	154,985
Washington					29,844	51,646
West Virginia	56,455	57,391	67,317	78,677	84,467	94,488
Wisconsin	123,926	114,649	146,459	155,243	177,335	165,523
Wyoming						10,375
TOTALS	4,287,670	4,444,976	4,875,971	5,540,365	5,556,982	6,516,722

States	1900	1904	1908	1912	1916	1920
Alabama	96,368	79,857	74,374	82,438	99,409	163,254
Alaska						
Arizona				10,324	33,170	29,546
Arkansas	81,142	64,434	87,015	68,838	112,186	107,409
California	124,985	89,404	127,492	283,436	466,200	229,191
Colorado	122,733	100,105	126,644	114,232	178,816	104,936
Connecticut	74,014	72,909	68,255	74,561	99,786	120,721
Delaware	18,863	19,359	22,071	22,631	24,753	39,911
Florida	28,007	27,046	31,104	36,417	55,984	90,515
Georgia	81,700	83,472	72,413	93,171	125,845	109,856
Hawaii						
Idaho	29,414	18,480	36,162	33,921	70,054	46,930
Illinois	503,061	327,606	450,810	405,048	950,229	534,395
Indiana	309,584	274,345	338,262	281,890	334,063	511,364
Iowa	209,265	149,141	200,771	185,325	221,699	227,921
Kansas	162,601	86,174	161,209	143,663	314,588	185,464
Kentucky	234,899	217,170	244,092	219,584	269,990	456,497
Louisiana	53,671	47,747	63,568	61,035	79,875	87,519
Maine	36,823	27,648	35,403	51,113	64,132	58,961
Maryland	122,238	109,446	115,908	112,674	138,359	180,626
Massachusetts	157,016	165,772	155,543	174,315	247,885	276,691
Michigan	211,685	135,392	175,771	150,751	286,775	233,450
Minnesota	112,901	55,187	109,401	106,426	179,152	142,994
Mississippi	51,706	53,374	60,287	57,227	80,422	69,277
Missouri	351,922	296,312	346,574	330,746	398,032	574,924
Montana	37,145	21,773	29,326	27,941	101,063	57,372
Nebraska	114,013	52,921	131,099	109,008	158,827	119,608
Nevada	6,347	3,982	11,212	7,986	17,776	9,851
New Hampshire	35,489	33,995	33,655	34,724	43,779	62,662
New Jersey	164,879	164,567	182,567	178,559	211,645	258,761
New Mexico				20,437	33,693	46,668
New York	678,462	683,981	667,468	655,475	759,426	781,238
North Carolina	157,752	124,124	136,995	144,545	168,383	305,447
North Dakota	20,531	14,273	32,885	29,555	55,206	37,422
Ohio	474,882	344,940	502,721	424,834	604,161	780,037
Oklahoma			123,907	119,156	148,113	217,053
Oregon	33,385	17,521	38,049	47,064	120,087	80,019
Pennsylvania	424,232	337,998	448,778	395,619	521,784	503,202
Rhode Island	19,812	24,839	24,706	30,412	40,394	55,062
South Carolina	47,283	52,563	62,290	48,357	61,846	64,170
South Dakota	39,544	21,969	40,266	48,962	59,191	35,938
Tennessee	145,356	131,653	135,608	135,425	153,282	206,558
Texas	267,432	167,200	217,302	221,589	286,514	288,767
Utah	45,006	33,413	42,601	36,579	84,256	56,639
Vermont	12,849	9,777	11,496	15,354	22,708	20,919
Virginia	146,080	80,648	82,946	90,332	102,824	141,670
Washington	44,833	28,098	58,691	86,840	183,388	84,298
West Virginia	98,807	100,881	111,418	113,197	140,403	220,789
Wisconsin	159,279	124,107	166,632	164,228	193,042	113,422
Wyoming	10,164	8,930	14,918	15,310	28,316	17,429
TOTALS	6,358,160	5,084,533	6,410,665	6,301,254	9,131,511	9,147,353

Democratic Vote by States and Elections (continued)

States	1924	1928	1932	1936	1940
Alabama	112,966	127,797	207,910	238,196	250,726
Alaska					
Arizona	26,235	38,537	79,264	86,722	95,267
Arkansas	84,795	119,196	189,602	146,765	158,622
California	105,514	614,365	1,324,157	1,766,836	1,877,618
Colorado	75,238	133,131	250,877	295,021	265,554
Connecticut	110,184	252,040	281,632	382,129	417,621
Delaware	33,445	36,643	54,319	69,702	74,599
Florida	62,083	101,764	206,307	249,117	359,334
Georgia	123,200	129,602	234,118	255,364	265,194
Hawaii					
Idaho	24,256	53,074	109,479	125,683	127,842
Illinois	576,975	1,313,817	1,882,304	2,282,999	2,149,934
Indiana	492,245	562,691	862,054	934,974	874,063
Iowa	162,600	378,936	598,019	621,756	578,800
Kansas	156,319	193,003	424,204	464,520	364,725
Kentucky	374,855	381,070	580,574	541,944	557,222
Louisiana	93,218	164,655	249,418	292,894	319,751
Maine	41,964	81,179	128,907	126,333	156,478
Maryland	148,072	223,626	314,314	389,612	384,546
Massachusetts	280,831	792,758	800,148	942,716	1,076,522
Michigan	152,359	396,762	871,700	1,016,794	1,032,991
Minnesota	55,913	396,451	600,806	698,811	644,196
Mississippi	100,475	124,539	140,168	157,318	168,267
Missouri	572,753	662,562	1,025,406	1,111,043	958,476
Montana	33,805	78,578	127,286	159,690	145,698
Nebraska	137,289	197,959	359,082	347,454	263,677
Nevada	5,909	14,090	28,756	31,925	31,945
New Hampshire	57,201	80,715	100,680	108,460	125,292
New Jersey	298,043	616,517	806,630	1,083,850	1,016,808
New Mexico	48,542	48,211	95,089	106,037	103,699
New York	950,796	2,089,863	2,534,959	3,293,222	3,251,918
North Carolina	284,270	287,078	497,566	616,141	609,015
North Dakota	13,858	106,648	178,350	163,148	124,036
Ohio	477,888	864,210	1,301,695	1,747,222	1,733,139
Oklahoma	255,798	219,174	516,468	501,069	474,313
Oregon	67,589	109,223	213,871	266,733	258,415
Pennsylvania	409,192	1,067,586	1,295,948	2,353,788	2,171,035
Rhode Island	76,606	118,973	146,604	165,238	181,122
South Carolina	49,008	62,700	102,347	113,791	95,470
South Dakota	27,214	102,660	183,515	160,137	131,362
Tennessee	158,537	167,343	259,817	327,083	351,601
Texas	484,605	341,032	760,348	734,485	840,151
Utah	47,001	80,985	116,750	150,246	154,277
Vermont	16,124	44,440	56,266	62,124	64,269
Virginia	139,797	140,146	203,979	234,980	235,961
Washington	42,842	156,772	353,260	459,579	462,145
West Virginia	257,232	263,784	405,124	502,582	495,662
Wisconsin	68,115	450,259	707,410	802,984	704,821
Wyoming	12,868	29,299	54,370	62,624	59,287
TOTALS	8,386,624	15,016,443	22,821,857	27,751,841	27,243,466

States	1944	1948	1952	1956	1960
Alabama	198,918		275,075	280,844	324,050
Alaska					29,809
Arizona	80,926	95,251	108,528	112,880	176,781
Arkansas	148,965	149,659	226,300	213,277	215,049
California	1,988,564	1,913,134	2,197,548	2,420,135	3,224,099
Colorado	234,331	267,288	245,504	263,997	330,629
Connecticut	435,146	423,297	481,649	405,079	657,055
Delaware	68,166	67,813	83,315	79,421	99,590
Florida	339,377	281,988	444,950	480,371	748,700
Georgia	268,187	254,646	456,823	445,925	458,638
Hawaii					.92,410
Idaho	107,399	107,370	95,081	105,868	138,853
Illinois	2,079,479	1,994,715	2,013,920	1,775,682	2,377,846
Indiana	781,403	807,833	801,530	783,908	952,358
Iowa	499,876	522,380	451,513	501,858	550,565
Kansas	287,458	351,902	273,296	296,317	363,213
Kentucky	472,589	466,756	495,729	476,453	521,855
Louisiana	281,564	136,344	345,027	243,977	407,339
Maine	140,631	111,916	118,806	102,468	181,159
Maryland	315,490	286,521	395,337	372,613	565,808
Massachusetts	1,035,296	1,151,788	1,083,525	948,190	1,487,174
Michigan	1,106,899	1,003,448	1,230,657	1,359,898	1,687,269
Minnesota	589,864	692,966	608,458	617,525	779,933
Mississippi	168,479	19,384	172,566	144,498	108,362
Missouri	807,357	917,315	929,830	919,187	972,201
Montana	112,556	119,071	106,213	116,238	134,891
Nebraska	233,246	224,165	188,057	199,029	232,542
Nevada	29,623	31,291	31,688	40,640	54,880
New Hampshire	119,663	107,995	106,663	90,364	137,772
New Jersey	987,874	895,455	1,015,902	850,337	1,385,415
New Mexico	81,389	105,464	105,661	106,098	156,027
New York	3,304,238	2,780,204	3,104,601	2,750,769	3,830,085
North Carolina	527,399	459,070	652,803	590,530	713,136
North Dakota	100,144	95,812	76,694	96,742	123,963
Ohio	1,570,763	1,452,791	1,600,367	1,439,655	1,944,248
Oklahoma	401,549	452,782	430,939	385,581	370,111
Oregon	248,635	243,147	270,579	329,204	367,402
Pennsylvania	1,940,479	1,752,426	2,146,269	1,981,769	2,556,282
Rhode Island	175,356	188,736	203,293	163,521	258,032
South Carolina	90,606	34,423	173,004	136,372	198,129
South Dakota	96,711	117,653	90,426	122,288	128,070
Tennessee	308,707	270,412	443,710	456,507	481,453
Texas	821,605	750,700	969,228	859,958	1,167,932
Utah	150,088	147,359	135,364	118,364	169,248
Vermont	53,820	45,557	43,355	42,549	69,186
Virginia	242,276	200,786	268,677	267,760	362,327
Washington	486,774	476,165	492,845	523,002	599,298
West Virginia	392,777	429,188	453,578	381,534	441,786
Wisconsin	650,413	647,310	622,175	586,768	830,805
Wyoming	49,419	52,354	47,934	49,554	63,331
TOTALS	25,612,474	24,104,030	27,314,992	26,035,504	34,227,096

States	1828	1832	1836	1840	1844	1848	1852
Alabama	89.84		56.78	54.42	59.13	50.71	60.96
Alaska							
Arizona							
Arkansas			65.97	56.73	63.43	55.07	62.18
California							53.36
Colorado							
Connecticut	24.32	34.91	50.69	44.32	46.18	43.37	49.80
Delaware		49.52	46.73	45.01	48.85	47.54	49.85
Florida						41.64	60.03
Georgia	96.79	100.00	47.29	44.22	51.20	48.52	64.70
Hawaii							
Idaho							
Illinois	67.22	72.27	54.71	51.01	54.39	45.07	51.83
Indiana	56.60	67.10	44.03	44.18	50.07	48.93	52.05
Iowa						49.76	50.43
Kansas							
Kentucky	55.60	45.51	47.50	35.80	45.91	42.55	48.41
Louisiana	52.92	61.56	51.92	40.27	51.30	45.76	51.94
Maine	40.14	54.68	60.04	49.67	53.79	45.85	50.63
Maryland	49.04	49.99	46.16	46.17	47.59	47.72	53.26
Massachusetts	16.79	23.11	44.82	41.30	40.30	26.23	35.72
Michigan			64.84	47.61	49.81	47.20	50.45
Minnesota							
Mississippi	81.07	100.00	50.74	46.55	56.68	50.59	60.50
Missouri	70.87	100.00	59.98	56.44	56.97	55.09	56.12
Montana							
Nebraska							
Nevada							
New Hampshire	46.45	57.28	75.04	55.16	55.22	55.41	56.77
New Jersey	48.02	49.98	49.48	48.14	49.37	47.42	52.78
New Mexico							
New York	50.97	52.11	54.60	48.19	48.90	25.07	50.16
North Carolina	73.12	84.49	53.25	42.14	47.61	44.42	50.40
North Dakota							
Ohio	51.60	51.33	47.90	45.57	47.76	47.10	47.84
Oklahoma							
Oregon							
Pennsylvania	66.66	57.69	51.22	49.90	50.48	46.52	51.18
Rhode Island	22.97	36.57	52.25	38.29	39.58	32.68	51.37
South Carolina							
South Dakota.							
Tennessee	95.19	95.24	41.94	44.43	49.95	47.45	49.28
Texas						70.29	73.07
Utah							
Vermont	25.60	24.50	40.08	35.47	37.00	22.85	29.76
Virginia	68.85	74.59	56.85	50.81	53.09	50.79	55.77
Washington							
West Virginia							
Wisconsin						38.30	51.99
Wyoming							
TOTALS	56.04	54.50	50.93	46.84	49.56	42.47	50.85

The highest percentage for each election is underlined.

States	1856	1860	1864	1868	1872	1876	1880
Alabama	62.11	54.04		48.56	46.81	59.98	59.97
Alaska							
Arizona							
Arkansas	67.01	53.16		46.27	47.83	59.90	56.65
California	48.42	32.41	41.37	49.76	42.51	49.08	48.98
Colorado							46.04
Connecticut	43.57	21.50	48.62	48.46	47.34	50.71	48.52
Delaware	55.25	45.62	51.80	59.02	46.78	55.45	51.73
Florida	56.81	59.55			46.48	49.01	54.17
Georgia	57.13	48.81		64.28	53.43	72.06	65.05
Hawaii							
Idaho							
Illinois	44.08	47.16	45.59	44.31	43.01	46.55	44.56
Indiana	50.10	42.44	46.40	48.61	46.59	49.52	47.91
Iowa	40.35	42.94	35.77	38.08	34.73	38.33	32.72
Kansas			21.39	31.11	32.77	30.53	29.72
Kentucky	52.41	36.35	69.83	74.55	52.31	61.31	55.80
Louisiana	51.70	44.90		70.69	44.31	48.43	62.48
Maine	35.60	27.26	39.78	37.58	32.14	42.71	45.28
Maryland	45.03	45.60	44.90	67.20	50.34	56.03	54.15
Massachusetts	23.48	20.29	27.78	30.33	30.75	41.93	39.65
Michigan	41.59	42.04	44.11	43.02	35.46	44.44	37.30
Minnesota		34.25	40.94	39.20	38.44	39.31	35.36
Mississippi	59.29	59.02			36.53	68.08	65.08
Missouri	54.52	35.53	29.83	41.10	55.46	57.73	52.51
Montana							
Nebraska				35.86	29.88	32.81	32.62
Nevada			40.16	44.61	42.57	47.27	52.40
New Hampshire	45.82	39.24	47.44	44.98	45.61	48.06	47.24
New Jersey	47.22	51.87	52.84	50.88	45.43	52.65	49.84
New Mexico							
New York	32.90	46.29	49.54	50.59	46.68	51.32	48.41
North Carolina	56.67	50.44		46.63	42.52	53.64	51.49
North Dakota							
Ohio	44.19	42.30	43.67	46.03	46.15	49.07	47.01
Oklahoma							
Oregon		33.51	46.10	50.37	38.42	47.37	48.89
Pennsylvania	53.17	37.54	48.25	47.80	37.53	48.25	46.57
Rhode Island	33.70	38.78	37.80	33.51	28.06	40.23	36.88
South Carolina				42.07	23.85	49.74	65.70
South Dakota							
Tennessee	52.67	44.72		31.67	52.43	59.79	53.01
Texas	66.59	75.49			57.07	70.04	64.71
Utah							
Vermont	20.70	19.57	23.90	21.43	20.62	31.41	28.09
Virginia	59.86	44.46			49.50	59.38	60.48
Washington							
West Virginia			31.05	41.16	47.22	56.16	50.92
Wisconsin	44.23	42.73	44.12	43.76	44.97	48.50	42.91
Wyoming							
TOTALS	45.63	29.40	44.85	47.29	43.82	50.93	48.21

For 1860, the Douglas vote is used for California, Connecticut, Illinois, Indiana, Iowa, Maine, Massachusetts, Michigan, Minnesota, Missouri, New Hampshire, New Jersey, New York, Ohio, Rhode Island, Vermont, and Wisconsin. The Breckinridge vote is used for the remaining states. The 1860 total is Douglas'; Breckinridge's was 18.20. Most states cast votes for both. The highest percentage for Douglas was cast in New Jersey and the highest for Breckinridge in Texas.

Percentage of Democratic Vote by States and Elections (continued)

States	1884	1888	1892	1896	1900	1904	1908
Alabama	60.60	67.39	59.35	67.44	60.05	73.37	71.65
Alaska							
Arizona							
Arkansas	58.03	54.80	59.84	73.70	63.46	55.35	57.20
California	45.41	47.11	43.84	48.44	41.33	26.97	32.98
Colorado	41.55	40.92		84.96	55.44	41.08	47.99
Connecticut	48.95	48.66	50.06	32.53	41.09	38.15	35.92
Delaware	57.05	55.10	49.90	43.01	44.91	44.12	45.96
Florida	53.06	59.43	84.78	70.47	71.06	68.81	63.01
Georgia	65.92	70.31	58.38	58.03	66.57	63.72	54.53
Hawaii							
Idaho			.01	78.10	50.98	25.46	37.17
Illinois	46.43	46.59	48.79	42.68	44.44	30.43	39.02
Indiana	49.47	48.61	47.46	47.96	46.62	40.22	46.91
Iowa	47.16	44.51	44.31	42.90	39.42	30.69	40.58
Kansas	33.96	31.11		51.48	45.96	26.23	42.88
Kentucky	55.44	53.31	51.48	48.86	50.24	49.84	49.74
Louisiana	57.20	73.37	74.33	76.31	79.04	88.51	84.59
Maine	39.97	39.36	41.27	29.19	34.83	28.79	33.29
Maryland	52.13	50.34	53.38	41.75	46.23	48.81	48.59
Massachusetts	40.33	44.09	45.19	26.41	37.86	37.24	34.04
Michigan	37.24	44.91	43.43	43.52	38.89	25.78	32.44
Minnesota	36.85	39.65	37.76	40.89	35.69	18.84	33.02
Mississippi	63.75	73.13	76.33	90.52	87.48	91.43	90.07
Missouri	53.50	50.24	49.60	53.95	51.48	46.02	48.41
Montana			39.67	79.93	58.32	33.79	42.61
Nebraska	40.54	39.75	12.46	51.75	47.22	23.44	49.14
Nevada	43.59	42.45	6.56	81.21	62.25	32.87	45.71
New Hampshire	46.34	47.84	47.11	25.91	38.43	37.73	37.56
New Jersey	48.98	49.87	50.67	36.03	41.10	38.05	39.08
New Mexico							
New York	48.25	48.11	48.99	38.72	43.83	42.28	40.74
North Carolina	53.25	51.88	47.36	52.68	53.90	59.64	54.30
North Dakota				43.66	35.52	20.31	34.71
Ohio	46.94	47.18	47.53	47.07	45.66	34.33	44.82
Oklahoma							48.23
Oregon	46.70	42.88	18.15	47.98	39.64	19.43	34.31
Pennsylvania	43.73	44.78	45.09	36.27	36.16	27.33	35.41
Rhode Island	37.81	43.00	45.75	26.39	35.04	36.18	34.16
South Carolina	76.28	82.73	77.59	85.29	92.96	95.33	93.81
South Dakota			12.88	49.70	41.14	21.67	35.08
Tennessee	51.37	52.18	51.91	52.15	53.02	54.23	52.66
Texas	69.26	65.70	56.61	68.00	63.12	71.45	73.97
Utah				82.70	48.30	32.88	39.22
Vermont	29.19	26.46	29.26	16.67	22.88	18.84	21.83
Virginia	51.05	49.98	56.10	52.54	55.23	61.78	60.52
Washington			33.92	55.19	41.70	19.36	31.80
West Virginia	50.94	49.35	49.38	46.83	44.75	42.03	43.16
Wisconsin	45.79	43.76	47.77	37.00	35.99	28.01	36.67
Wyoming				50.35	41.24	29.08	39.67
TOTALS	48.50	48.64	46.04	46.72	45.50	37.59	43.05

States	1912	1916	1920	1924	1928	1932	1936
Alabama	69.93	75.80	67.72	67.80	51.33	84.85	86.38
Alaska							
Arizona	43.52	57.17	44.23	35.47	42.23	67.04	69.85
Arkansas	55.50	66.64	58.49	61.21	60.29	85.96	81.80
California	42.08	46.64	24.29	8.23	34.20	58.41	66.97
Colorado	42.80	60.74	35.93	21.98	33.94	54.81	60.37
Connecticut	39.16	46.66	33.03	27.53	45.57	47.40	55.32
Delaware	46.48	47.78	42.07	36.81	34.60	48.11	56.04
Florida	70.18	69.28	62.13	56.88	40.12	74.68	75.91
Georgia	76.65	79.30	71.12	73.96	56.55	91.60	87.10
Hawaii							
Idaho	32.08	52.04	33.92	16.36	34.41	58.70	62.96
Illinois	35.34	43.34	25.51	23.36	42.28	55.23	57.70
Indiana	43.07	46.47	40.49	38.69	39.59	54.67	56.63
Iowa	37.60	42.73	25.46	16.65	37.54	57.69	54.41
Kansas	39.31	49.95	32.52	23.60	27.06	53.56	53.67
Kentucky	48.40	51.93	49.69	45.98	40.51	59.06	58.51
Louisiana	76.83	85.90	69.43	76.44	76.29	92.97	88.84
Maine	39.43	47.01	29.80	21.83	30.96	43.19	41.52
Maryland	48.57	52.80	42.16	41.29	42.33	61.50	62.35
Massachusetts	35.61	46.61	27.84	24.85	50.24	50.64	51.22
Michigan	27.36	44.05	22.28	13.13	28.92	52.37	56.33
Minnesota	31.84	46.25	19.49	6.80	40.83	59.91	61.84
Mississippi	88.69	92.78	83.98	89.30	82.10	95.98	97.06
Missouri	47.35	50.59	43.12	43.79	44.15	63.69	60.76
Montana	35.00	56.88	32.05	19.38	40.48	58.80	69.28
Nebraska	43.69	55.40	31.26	29.58	36.18	62.98	57.14
Nevada	39.70	53.36	36.22	21.95	43.46	69.41	72.81
New Hampshire	39.48	49.12	39.39	34.72	41.02	48.99	49.73
New Jersey	41.19	42.71	28.43	27.40	39.79	49.48	59.54
New Mexico	41.39	50.31	44.27	43.02	40.85	62.72	62:69
New York	41.28	44.51	26.95	29.13	47.44	54.07	58.85
North Carolina	58.97	58.08	56.69	58.89	45.13	69.93	73.40
North Dakota	34.14	50.80	18.19	6.96	44.46	69.59	59.60
Ohio	40.96	51.86	38.58	23.70	34.45	49.87	58.00
Oklahoma	46.84	50.59	44.61	48.41	35.44	73.30	66.83
Oregon	34.34	45.90	33.55	24.18	34.14	58.00	64.42
Pennsylvania	32.42	40.23	27.18	19.07	33.89	45.33	56.88
Rhode Island	39.04	46.00	32.78	36.46	50.16	55.08	53.10
South Carolina	96.04	96.95	96.06	96.57	91.39	98.03	98.57
South Dakota	42.08	45.91	19.72	13.35	39.20	63.62	54.02
Tennessee	53.22	56.31	48.19	52.80	46.04	66.51	68.78
Texas	72.62	76.92	59.34	73.70	48.10	88.07	87.08
Utah	32.55	58.86	38.84	29.94	45.86	56.52	69.34
Vermont	24.43	35.23	23.27	15.67	32.87	41.08	43.28
Virginia	65.95	66.77	61.32	62.49	45.90	68.46	70.23
Washington	26.90	48.13	21.14	10.16	31.30	57.46	66.38
West Virginia	42.09	48.44	43.30	44.07	41.04	54.47	60.56
Wisconsin	41.06	42.96	16.07	8.10	44.28	63.46	63.80
Wyoming	36.20	54.62	30.98	16.11	35.37	56.07	60.58
TOTALS	41.85	49.26	34.15	28.82	40.79	57.41	60.80

States	1940	1944	1948	1952	1956	1960
Alabama	85.22	81.28		64.55	56.52	56.85
Alaska						49.06
Arizona	63.49	58.80	53.79	41.65	38.90	44.36
Arkansas	78.59	69.95	61.72	55.90	52.46	50.19
California	57.45	56.51	47.58	42.77	44.28	49.55
Colorado	48.37	46.40	51.88	38.96	39.81	44.91
Connecticut	53.44	52.30	47.91	43.91	36.27	53.73
Delaware	54.70	54.38	48.76	47.88	44.62	50.63
Florida	74.01	70.32	48.82	44.99	42.68	48.49
Georgia	84.84	81.74	60.81	69.66	66.47	62.56
Hawaii						50.03
Idaho	54.36	51.55	49.98	34.42	38.78	46.22
Illinois	50.98	51.52	50.09	44.95	40.29	49.98
Indiana	49.03	46.73	48.78	40.99	39.70	44.60
Iowa	47.62	47.49	50.31	35.59	40.65	43.22
Kansas	42.40	39.18	44.61	30.50	34.21	39.10
Kentucky	57.44	54.45	56.74	49.91	45.21	46.41
Louisiana	85.91	80.60	32.75	52.92	39.51	50.42
Maine	48.77	47.45	42.27	33.77	29.13	42.95
Maryland	58.26	51.85	48.01	43.83	39.96	53.61
Massachusetts	53.11	52.81	54.68	45.46	40.38	60.22
Michigan	49.52	50.19	47.57	43.97	44.15	50.85
Minnesota	51.49	52.41	57.16	44.11	46.08	50.58
Mississippi	95.70	93.56	10.09	60.44	58.23	36.34
Missouri	52.27	51.37	58.11	49.14	50.13	50.26
Montana	58.78	54.28	53.09	40.07	42.87	48.60
Nebraska	42.81	41.42	45.85	30.85	34.49	37.93
Nevada	60.08	54.62	50.37	38.55	42.03	51.16
New Hampshire	53.22	52.11	46.66	39.08	33.84	46.58
New Jersey	51.55	50.31	45.93	41.99	34.23	49.96
New Mexico	56.59	53.47	56.38	44.28	41.78	50.15
New York	51.60	52.31	45.01	43.55	38.78	52.53
North Carolina	74.03	66.71	58.02	53.91	50.66	52.11
North Dakota	44.18	45.48	43.41	28.39	38.09	44.52
Ohio	52.20	49.82	49.48	43.24	38.89	46.72
Oklahoma	57.41	55.57	62.75	45.41	44.87	40.98
Oregon	53.70	51.78	46.40	38.93	44.75	47.38
Pennsylvania	53.24	51.14	46.92	46.86	43.30	51.06
Rhode Island	56.66	58.59	57.60	49.05	41.69	63.63
South Carolina	95.63	87.64	24.14	50.72	45.37	51.24
South Dakota	42.59	41.67	47.04	30.73	41.61	41.79
Tennessee	67.25	60.45	49.14	49.71	48.59	45.77
Texas	80.69	71.42	65.44	46.69	43.98	50.52
Utah	62.25	60.44	53.52	41.07	35.44	45.17
Vermont	44.93	42.94	36.93	28.24	27.82	41.35
Virginia	68.08	62.36	47.89	43.36	38.36	46.96
Washington	58.22	56.84	52.61	44.69	45.44	48.27
West Virginia	57.10	54.89	57.32	51.92	45.92	52.73
Wisconsin	50.15	48.57	50.70	38.71	37.84	48.05
Wyoming	52.83	48.77	51.62	37.09	39.90	44.95
TOTALS	54.69	53.39	49.51	44.38	41.97	49.71

TABLE 100 Republican Vote by States and Elections

States	1856	1860	1864	1868	1872	1876
Alabama				76,366	90,272	68,708
Alaska						
Arizona						
Arkansas				22,152	41,373	38,669
California	20,693	39,173	62,134	54,592	54,044	79,269
Colorado						
Connecticut	42,715	43,486	44,691	50,995	50,634	59,034
Delaware	306	3,816	8,157	7,623	11,129	10,752
Florida					17,763	23,849
Georgia				57,134	62,550	50,446
Hawaii						
Idaho						
Illinois	96,180	172,171	189,521	250,293	241,944	278,232
Indiana	94,816	139,033	150,422	176,552	186,147	208,111
Iowa	44,127	70,409	89,075	120,399	131,566	171,327
Kansas			14,228	31,049	67,048	78,332
Kentucky	373	1,364	27,786	39,566	88,970	98,415
Louisiana				33,263	71,663	75,135
Maine	67,379	62,811	72,278	70,426	61,422	66,300
Maryland	281	2,895	40,169	30,438	66,760	71,981
Massachusetts	108,190	106,649	126,742	136,477	133,472	150,078
Michigan	71,969	88,480	85,352	128,550	138,455	166,534
Minnesota		22,069	25,060	43,542	55,117	72,962
Mississippi					82,175	52,605
Missouri		17,028	72,991	85,671	119,196	145,029
Montana						
Nebraska				9,729	18,329	31,916
Nevada			9,826	6,480	8,413	10,383
New Hampshire	38,345	37,519	36,595	38,191	37,168	41,539
New Jersey	28,351	58,346	60,723	80,121	91,661	103,517
New Mexico						
New York	274,707	362,646	368,735	419,915	440,736	489,547
North Carolina				96,226	94,769	108,417
North Dakota						
Ohio	187,497	231,610	265,154	280,222	281,852	330,698
Oklahoma						
Oregon		5,496	9,888	10,961	11,819	15,214
Pennsylvania	147,286	268,030	296,389	342,280	349,589	384,148
Rhode Island	11,467	12,240	14,343	12,993	13,665	15,787
South Carolina				62,301	72,290	91,870
South Dakota						
Tennessee				56,757	85,655	89,566
Texas					47,468	44,800
Utah						
Vermont	39,963	33,888	42,422	44,167	41,481	44,428
Virginia	291	1,929			93,468	95,558
Washington						
West Virginia			23,223	29,025	32,315	42,698
Wisconsin	66,092	86,110	83,458	108,857	104,997	130,070
Wyoming						
TOTALS	1,341,028	1,867,198	2,219,362	3,013,313	3,597,375	4,035,924

States	1880	1884	1888	1892	1896	1900
Alabama	56,221	59,591	56,197	9,197	54,737	55,634
Alaska						
Arizona						
Arkansas	42,436	50,895	60,245	46,974	37,512	44,800
California	80,348	102,416	124,816	118,027	146,688	164,755
Colorado	27,450	36,290	50,774	38,620	26,279	93,072
Connecticut	67,071	65,898	74,586	77,032	110,297	102,572
Delaware	14,133	12,778	12,973	18,077	20,452	22,535
Florida	23,654	28,031	26,654		11,288	7,499
Georgia	54,086	48,603	40,496	48,305	60,107	35,056
Hawaii						
Idaho				8,799	6,324	27,198
Illinois	318,037	337,474	370,475	399,288	607,130	597,985
Indiana	232,164	238,480	263,361	255,615	323,754	336,063
Iowa	183,927	197,082	211,598	219,795	289,293	307,808
Kansas	121,549	154,406	182,904	157,241	159,541	185,955
Kentucky	106,306	118,122	155,134	135,441	218,171	226,801
Louisiana	38,637	46,347	30,701	27,903	22,037	14,233
Maine	74,056	72,209	73,734	62,931	80,461	65,435
Maryland	78,515	85,699	99,986	92,736	136,978	136,185
Massachusetts	165,205	146,724	183,892	202,927	278,976	239,147
Michigan	185,341	192,669	236,387	222,708	293,582	316,269
Minnesota	93,903	111,923	142,492	122,823	193,503	190,461
Mississippi	34,854	43,509	31,120	1,395	5,123	5,753
Missouri	153,567	202,929	236,257	226,918	304,940	314,092
Montana				18,851	10,494	25,373
Nebraska	54,979	76,877	108,425	87,227	103,064	121,835
Nevada	8,732	7,193	7,229	2,811	1,938	3,849
New Hampshire	44,852	43,249	45,728	45,658	57,444	54,798
New Jersey	120,555	123,440	144,360	156,101	221,371	221,754
New Mexico						
New York	555,544	562,005	650,338	609,459	819,838	822,013
North Carolina	115,874	125,068	134,784	100,565	155,243	133,081
North Dakota				17,519	26,335	35,898
Ohio	375,048	400,082	416,054	405,187	525,991	543,918
Oklahoma						
Oregon	20,619	26,860	33,291	35,002	48,779	46,526
Pennsylvania	444,704	474,268	526,269	516,011	728,300	712,665
Rhode Island	18,195	19,030	21,969	26,975	37,437	33,784
South Carolina	58,071	21,733	13,740	13,384	9,317	3,579
South Dakota				34,888	41,042	54,530
Tennessee	107,677	124,090	139,511	100,331	149,703	123,180
Texas	57,893	93,141	88,422	81,444	167,520	130,641
Utah					13,491	47,139
Vermont	45,567	39,514	45,192	37,992	51,127	42,569
Virginia	84,020	139,356	150,449	113,256	135,388	115,865
Washington				36,460	39,153	57,456
West Virginia	46,243	63,096	78,171	80,293	105,379	119,829
Wisconsin	144,400	161,157	176,555	170,846	268,135	265,756
Wyoming				8,454	10,072	14,482
TOTALS	4,454,433	4,852,234	5,445,269	5,191,466	7,113,734	7,219,828

States	1904	1908	1912	1916	1920
Alabama	22,472	25,308	9,732	28,809	74,690
Alaska					
Arizona			3,021	20,524	37,016
Arkansas	46,860	56,760	24,467	47,148	71,117
California	205,226	214,398	3,914	462,394	624,992
Colorado	134,687	123,700	58,386	102,308	173,248
Connecticut	111,089	112,915	68,324	106,514	229,238
Delaware	23,712	25,014	15,997	26,011	52,858
Florida	8,314	10,654	4,279	14,611	44,853
Georgia	24,003	41,692	5,191	11,225	44,127
Hawaii					
Idaho	47,783	52,621	32,810	55,368	91,351
Illinois	632,645	629,932	253,613	1,152,549	1,420,480
Indiana	368,289	348,993	151,267	341,005	696,370
Iowa	307,907	275,210	119,805	280,449	634,674
Kansas	212,955	197,216	74,845	277,658	369,268
Kentucky	205,277	235,711	115,512	241,854	452,480
Louisiana	5,205	8,958	3,834	6,466	38,538
Maine	64,438	66,987	26,545	69,506	136,355
Maryland	109,497	116,513	54,956	117,347	236,117
Massachusetts	257,822	265,966	156,139	268,812	681,153
Michigan	364,957	335,580	152,244	339,097	762,865
Minnesota	216,651	195,843	64,334	179,544	519,421
Mississippi	3,187	4,392	1,595	4,253	11,576
Missouri	321,446	347,203	207,821	369,339	727,521
Montana	34,932	32,333	18,512	66,750	109,430
Nebraska	138,558	126,997	54,216	117,771	247,498
Nevada	6,864	10,775	3,196	12,127	15,479
New Hampshire	54,180	53,149	32,927	43,723	95,196
New Jersey	245,164	265,326	89,047	269,352	615,333
New Mexico			17,733	31,163	57,634
New York	859,533	870,070	455,428	879,287	1,871,167
North Carolina	82,625	114,937	29,277	120,988	232,848
North Dakota	52,595	57,680	23,090	53,471	160,072
Ohio	600,095	572,312	278,168	514,753	1,182,022
Oklahoma		110,550	90,786	97,233	243,831
Oregon	60,455	62,530	34,673	126,813	143,592
Pennsylvania	840,949	745,779	273,305	703,734	1,218,215
Rhode Island	41,605	43,942	27,703	44,858	107,463
South Carolina	2,554	3,965	536	1,550	2,604
South Dakota	72,083	67,536		64,217	110,692
Tennessee	105,369	118,324	60,674	116,223	219,829
Texas	51,242	65,666	26,755	64,999	114,538
Utah	62,446	61,028	42,100	54,137	81,555
Vermont	40,459	39,552	23,332	40,250	68,212
Virginia	47,880	52,573	23,288	49,356	87,456
Washington	101,540	106,062	70,445	167,244	223,137
West Virginia	132,628	137,869	56,754	143,124	282,007
Wisconsin	280,164	247,747	130,695	221,323	498,576
Wyoming	20,489	20,846	14,560	21,698	35,091
TOTALS	7,628,831	7,679,114	3,485,831	8,548,935	16,153,785

States	1924	1928	1932	1936	1940
Alabama	45,005	120,725	34,675	35,358	42,184
Alaska					
Arizona	30,516	52,533	36,104	33,433	54,030
Arkansas	40,564	77,751	28,467	32,039	42,121
California	733,250	1,162,323	847,902	836,431	1,351,419
Colorado	195,171	253,872	189,617	181,267	279,576
Connecticut	246,322	296,614	288,420	278,685	361,819
Delaware	52,441	68,860	57,073	54,014	61,440
Florida	30,633	144,168	69,170	78,248	126,158
Georgia	30,300	99,381	19,863	36,942	46,376
Hawaii					
Idaho	69,879	99,848	71,312	66,256	106,553
Illinois	1,453,321	1,769,141	1,432,756	1,570,393	2,047,240
Indiana	703,042	848,290	677,184	691,570	899,466
Iowa	537,635	623,818	414,433	487,977	632,370
Kansas	407,671	513,672	349,498	397,727	489,169
Kentucky	398,966	558,064	394,716	369,702	410,384
Louisiana	24,670	51,160	18,853	36,791	52,446
Maine	138,440	179,923	166,631	168,823	163,951
Maryland	162,414	301,479	184,184	231,435	269,534
Massachusetts	703,489	775,566	736,959	768,613	939,700
Michigan	874,631	965,396	739,894	699,733	1,039,917
Minnesota	420,759	560,977	363,959	350,461	596,274
Mississippi	8,546	27,153	5,180	4,443	7,364
Missouri	648,486	834,080	564,713	697,891	871,009
Montana	74,138	113,300	78,078	63,598	99,579
Nebraska	218,585	345,745	201,177	247,731	352,201
Nevada	11,243	18,327	12,674	11,923	21,229
New Hampshire	98,575	115,404	103,629	104,642	110,127
New Jersey	676,277	926,050	775,684	720,322	945,475
New Mexico	54,745	69,645	54,217	61,727	79,315
New York	1,820,058	2,193,344	1,937,963	2,180,670	3,027,478
North Carolina	191,753	348,992	208,344	223,283	213,633
North Dakota	94,931	131,441	71,772	72,751	154,590
Ohio	1,176,130	1,627,546	1,227,679	1,127,709	1,586,773
Oklahoma	226,242	394,046	188,165	245,122	348,872
Oregon	142,579	205,341	136,019	122,706	219,555
Pennsylvania	1,401,481	2,055,382	1,453,540	1,690,300	1,889,848
Rhode Island	125,286	117,522	115,266	125,031	138,214
South Carolina	1,123	5,858	1,978	1,646	4,360
South Dakota	101,299	157,603	99,212	125,977	177,065
Tennessee	130,882	195,388	126,806	146,516	169,186
Texas	130,023	367,036	97,959	103,874	199,152
Utah	77,327	94,618	84,795	64,555	93,151
Vermont	80,498	90,404	78,984	81,023	78,371
Virginia	73,359	164,609	89,637	98,336	109,363
Washington	220,224	335,844	208,645	206,892	322,123
West Virginia	288,635	375,551	330,731	325,358	372,414
Wisconsin	311,614	544,205	347,741	380,828	679,206
Wyoming	41,858	52,748	39,583	38,739	52,633
TOTALS	15,725,016	21,430,743	15,761,841	16,679,491	22,334,413

States	1944	1948	1952	1956	1960
Alabama	44,540	40,930	149,231	195,694	237,981
Alaska					30,953
Arizona	56,287	77,597	152,042	176,990	221,241
Arkansas	63,551	50,959	177,155	186,287	184,508
California	1,512,965	1,895,269	2,897,310	3,027,688	3,259,722
Colorado	268,731	239,714	379,782	394,479	402,242
Connecticut	390,527	437,754	611,012	711,837	565,813
Delaware	56,747	69,588	90,059	98,057	96,373
Florida	143,215	194,280	544,036	643,849	795,476
Georgia	59,879	76,691	198,979	222,874	274,472
Hawaii					92,295
Idaho	100,137	101,514	180,707	166,979	161,597
Illinois	1,939,314	1,961,103	2,457,327	2,623,327	2,368,988
Indiana	875,891	821,079	1,136,259	1,182,811	1,175,120
Iowa	547,267	494,018	808,906	729,187	722,381
Kansas	442,096	423,039	616,302	566,878	561,474
Kentucky	392,448	341,210	495,029	572,192	602,607
Louisiana	67,750	72,657	306,925	329,047	230,980
Maine	155,434	150,234	232,353	249,238	240,608
Maryland	292,949	294,814	499,424	559,738	489,538
Massachusetts	921,350	909,370	1,292,325	1,393,197	976,750
Michigan	1,084,423	1,038,595	1,551,529	1,713,647	1,620,428
Minnesota	527,416	483,617	763,211	719,302	757,915
Mississippi	11,601	5,043	112,966	60,685	73,561
Missouri	761,175	655,039	959,429	914,486	962,221
Montana	93,163	96,770	157,394	154,933	141,841
Nebraska	329,880	264,774	421,603	378,108	380,553
Nevada	24,611	29,357	50,502	56,049	52,387
New Hampshire	109,916	121,299	166,287	176,519	157,989
New Jersey	961,335	981,124	1,374,613	1,606,942	1,363,324
New Mexico	70,688	80,303	132,170	146,788	153,733
New York	2,987,647	2,841,163	3,952,815	4,340,340	3,446,420
North Carolina	263,155	258,572	558,107	575,062	655,420
North Dakota	118,535	115,139	191,712	156,766	154,310
Ohio	1,582,293	1,445,684	2,100,391	2,262,610	2,217,611
Oklahoma	319,424	268,817	518,045	473,769	533,039
Oregon	225,365	260,904	420,815	406,393	408,060
Pennsylvania	1,835,048	1,902,197	2,415,789	2,585,252	2,439,956
Rhode Island	123,487	135,791	210,935	229,677	147,502
South Carolina	4,610	5,386	168,082	75,700	188,558
South Dakota	135,362	129,651	203,857	171,569	178,417
Tennessee	200,311	202,924	446,147	462,288	556,577
Texas	191,425	282,240	1,102,878	1,080,619	1,121,699
Utah	97,891	125,327	194,190	215,631	205,361
Vermont	71,527	75,926	109,717	110,390	98,131
Virginia	145,243	172,070	349,037	386,459	404,521
Washington	361,689	386,315	599,107	620,430	629,273
West Virginia	322,819	316,251	419,970	449,297	395,995
Wisconsin	674,532	590,959	979,744	954,844	895,175
Wyoming	51,921	47,947	81,047	74,573	77,551
TOTALS	22,017,570	21,971,004	33,937,252	35,589,477	34,108,647

States	1856	1860	1864	1868	1872	1876	1880
Alabama				51.44	53.19	40.02	36.98
Alaska							
Arizona							
Arkansas				53.73	52.17	39.88	39.55
California	18.77	32.96	58.63	50.24	56.38	50.88	48.92
Colorado							51.28
Connecticut	53.18	53.86	51.38	51.54	52.25	48.34	50.52
Delaware	2.11	23.71	48.20	40.98	50.99	44.55	47.86
Florida					53.52	50.99	45.83
Georgia				35.72	43.77	27.94	34.33
Hawaii							
Idaho							
Illinois	40.25	50.68	54.41	55.69	56.27	50.09	51.11
Indiana	40.03	51.09	53.60	51.39	53.00	48.27	49.33
Iowa	49.13	54.87	64.23	61.92	64.18	58.58	56.85
Kansas				78.61	66.64	63.10	60.40
Kentucky	.26	.93	30.17	25.45	46.45	37.61	39.80
Louisiana				29.31	55.69	51.57	37.10
Maine	61.37	64.15	60.22	62.42	67.86	56.73	51.45
Maryland	.32	3.11	55.10	32.80	49.65	43.94	45.37
Massachusetts	64.72	62.75	72.22	69.67	69.25	57.74	58.50
Michigan	56.98	57.18	55.89	56.98	62.67	52.45	52.54
Minnesota		63.42	59.06	60.80	61.55	58.77	62.28
Mississippi					63.47	31.92	29.94
Missouri		10.29	70.17	58.90	43.65	41.23	38.65
Montana							
Nebraska				64.14	70.12	59.65	62.87
Nevada			59.84	55.39	57.43	52.73	47.60
New Hampshire	53.59	56.89	52.56	55.02	53.95	51.84	51.94
New Jersey	28.52	48.13	47.16	49.12	54.22	47.00	49.02
New Mexico							
New York	46.14	53.71	50.46	49.41	53.12	48.07	50.32
North Carolina				53.37	57.48	46.36	48.04
North Dakota							
Ohio	48.49	52.33	56.33	53.97	53.24	50.21	51.73
Oklahoma							
Oregon		34.48	53.90	49.63	58.74	50.91	50.51
Pennsylvania	33.95	56.25	51.75	52.20	62.18	50.61	50.84
Rhode Island	57.85	61.22	62.20	66.49	71.94	59.29	62.25
South Carolina				57.93	75.95	50.26	33.97
South Dakota							
Tennessee				68.33	47.57	40.21	44.53
Texas					40.71	29.96	23.95
Utah							
Vermont	78.23	75.79	76.10	78.57	78.26	68.58	69.88
Virginia	.19	1.15			50.48	40.62	39.52
Washington							
West Virginia			68.95	58.84	51.82	42.47	41.03
Wisconsin	55.29	56.58	55.88	56.24	54.60	50.90	54.04
Wyoming							
TOTALS	33.27	39.79	55.15	52.71	55.63	47.94	48.32

The highest percentage for each election is underlined.

States	1884	1888	1892	1896	1900	1904	1908
Alabama	38.44	32.28	3.95	28.13	34.67	20.65	24.38
Alaska							
Arizona							
Arkansas	40.50	38.07	32.01	25.11	35.04	40.25	37.31
California	52.08	49.95	43.76	49.13	54.48	61.90	55.46
Colorado	54.39	55.31	41.13	13.84	42.04	55.27	46.88
Connecticut	48.01	48.44	46.80	63.24	56.94	58.13	59.43
Delaware	42.75	43.55	48.55	52.94	53.65	54.04	52.09
Florida	46.82	39.94		24.30	19.03	21.15	21.58
Georgia	33.84	28.33	21.80	36.82	28.56	18.32	31.40
Hawaii							
Idaho			44.87	21.30	47.14	65.84	54.09
Illinois	50.16	49.54	45.70	55.65	52.83	58.77	54.52
Indiana	48.16	49.05	46.17	50.81	50.60	53.99	48.40
Iowa	52.42	52.36	49.60	55.46	57.99	63.37	55.62
Kansas	58.18	55.39	48.40	47.46	52.56	64.81	52.46
Kentucky	42.81	44.99	39.74	48.92	48.50	47.11	48.04
Louisiana	42.39	26.48	23.59	21.79	20.96	9.65	11.92
Maine	55.35	57.49	54.06	67.90	61.89	67.10	63.00
Maryland	46.09	47.40	43.48	54.60	51.50	48.83	48.85
Massachusetts	48.32	53.38	51.85	69.36	57.67	57.92	58.21
Michigan	47.89	49.73	47.81	53.85	58.10	69.50	61.93
Minnesota	58.80	54.12	45.96	56.62	60.21	73.95	59.11
Mississippi	36.25	26.63	2.64	7.27	9.73	5.46	6.56
Missouri	46.01	45.31	41.97	45.24	45.94	49.92	48.50
Montana			42.54	19.72	39.84	54.21	46.98
Nebraska	57.33	53.51	43.57	45.98	50.46	61.38	47.60
Nevada	56.21	57.23	25.84	18.79	37.75	56.66	43.93
New Hampshire	51.15	50.35	51.11	68.74	59.34	60.14	59.32
New Jersey	47.31	47.52	46.24	59.66	55.27	56.68	56.79
New Mexico							
New York	48.15	49.20	45.59	57.55	53.10	53.13	53.11
North Carolina	46.58	47.14	35.79	46.87	45.47	39.70	45.55
North Dakota			48.50	55.58	62.11	74.83	60.87
Ohio	50.99	49.51	47.66	51.86	52.30	59.73	51.03
Oklahoma							43.03
Oregon	50.99	53.82	44.59	50.07	55.25	67.06	56.39
Pennsylvania	52.68	52.73	51.45	60.98	60.74	67.99	58.84
Rhode Island	58.07	53.89	50.71	68.33	59.74	60.60	60.76
South Carolina	23.72	17.27	18.99	13.51	7.04	4.63	5.97
South Dakota			49.48	49.48	56.73	71.09	58.84
Tennessee	47.83	45.85	37.51	46.23	44.93	43.40	45.95
Texas	28.63	24.73	19.28	30.75	30.83	21.90	22.35
Utah				17.27	50.59	61.45	56.19
Vermont	66.54	71.24	68.10	80.10	75.79	77.98	75.12
Virginia	48.90	49.47	38.75	45.90	43.81	36.67	38.36
Washington			41.45	41.84	53.44	69.95	57.47
West Virginia	47.74	49.03	46.94	52.23	54.27	55.26	53.41
Wisconsin	50.38	49.77	46.02	59.93	60.04	63.24	54.52
Wyoming			50.60	48.88	58.76	66.71	55.43
TOTALS	48.26	47.81	43.01	51.00	51.67	56.40	51.57

States	1912	1916	1920	1924	1928	1932	1936
Alabama	8.26	21.97	30.98	27.01	48.49	14.15	12.82
Alaska							
Arizona	12.74	35.37	55.41	41.26	57.57	30.53	26.93
Arkansas	19.73	28.01	38.73	29.28	39.33	12.91	17.86
California	.58	46.26	66.24	57.21	64.70	37.40	31.70
Colorado	21.88	34.75	59.32	57.02	64.72	41.43	37.09
Connecticut	35.88	49.80	62.72	61.54	53.63	48.54	40.35
Delaware	32.85	50.20	55.71	57.71	65.03	50.55	43.43
Florida	8.25	18.08	30.79	28.06	56.83	25.04	23.85
Georgia	4.27	7.07	28.57	18.19	43.37	7.77	12.60
Hawaii							
Idaho	31.02	41.13	66.02	47.12	64.74	38.23	33.19
Illinois	22.13	52.56	67.81	58.84	56.93	42.04	39.69
Indiana	23.11	47.44	55.14	55.25	59.68	42.94	41.89
Iowa	24.30	54.06	70.91	55.06	61.80	39.98	42.70
Kansas	20.48	44.09	64.76	61.54	72.02	44.13	45.95
Kentucky	25.46	46.52	49.25	48.93	59.33	40.15	39.92
Louisiana	4.83	6.95	30.57	20.23	23.71	7.03	11.16
Maine	20.48	50.95	68.92	72.03	68.63	55.83	55.49
Maryland	23.69	44.78	55.11	45.29	57.06	36.04	37.04
Massachusetts	31.89	50.54	68.55	62.26	49.15	46.64	41.76
Michigan	27.63	52.09	72.80	75.37	70.36	44.45	38.76
Minnesota	19.25	46.35	70.78	51.18	57.77	36.29	31.01
Mississippi	2.47	4.91	14.03	7.60	17.90	3.55	2.74
Missouri	29.75	46.94	54.57	49.58	55.58	35.08	38.16
Montana	23.19	37.57	61.13	42.50	58.37	36.07	27.59
Nebraska	21.73	41.08	64.68	47.09	63.19	35.29	40.74
Nevada	15.89	36.40	56.92	41.76	56.54	30.59	27.19
New Hampshire	37.43	49.06	59.84	59.83	58.66	50.42	47.98
New Jersey	20.54	54.35	67.60	62.16	59.77	47.59	39.57
New Mexico	35.91	46.53	54.68	48.52	59.01	35.76	36.50
New York	28.68	51.53	64.56	55.76	49.79	41.33	38.97
North Carolina	11.94	41.73	43.22	39.72	54.87	29.28	26.60
North Dakota	26.67	49.20	77.79	47.68	54.80	28.00	26.58
Ohio	26.82	44.18	58.47	58.33	64.89	47.04	37.43
Oklahoma	35.69	33.21	50.11	42.82	63.72	26.70	32.69
Oregon	25.30	48.47	60.20	51.01	64.18	36.89	29.64
Pennsylvania	22.40	54.25	65.80	65.35	65.24	50.84	40.85
Rhode Island	35.57	51.08	63.97	59.63	49.55	43.31	40.18
South Carolina	1.06	2.43	3.90	2.21	8.54	1.89	1.43
South Dakota		49.80	60.74	49.69	60.18	34.40	42.49
Tennessee	23.84	42.70	51.28	43.59	53.76	32.46	30.81
Texas	8.77	17.45	23.54	19.78	51.77	11.35	12.31
Utah	37.46	37.82	55.93	49.26	53.58	41.05	29.79
Vermont	37.13	62.44	75.87	78.22	66.88	57.66	56.44
Virginia	17.00	32.05	37.85	32.79	53.91	30.09	29.39
Washington	21.82	43.89	55.96	52.24	67.06	33.94	29.88
West Virginia	21.10	49.38	55.30	49.45	58.43	44.47	39.20
Wisconsin	32.68	49.25	70.65	37.06	53.52	31.19	30.26
Wyoming	34.42	41.86	62.38	52.39	63.68	40.82	37.47
TOTALS	23.15	46.12	60.31	54.04	58.22	39.65	36.54

States	1940	1944	1948	1952	1956	1960
Alabama	14.34	18.20	19.04	35.02	39.39	41.75
Alaska						50.94
Arizona	36.01	40.90	43.82	58.35	60.99	55.52
Arkansas	20.87	29.84	21.02	43.76	45.82	43.06
California	41.35	42.99	47.14	56.39	55.40	50.10
Colorado	50.92	53.21	46.52	60.27	59.49	54.63
Connecticut	46.30	46.94	49.55	55.70	63.73	46.27
Delaware	45.05	45.27	50.04	51.75	55.09	49.00
Florida	25.99	29.68	33.63	55.01	57.20	51.51
Georgia	14.84	18.25	18.31	30.34	33.22	37.44
Hawaii						49.97
Idaho	45.31	48.07	47.26	65.42	61.18	53.78
Illinois	48.54	48.05	49.24	54.84	59.52	49.80
Indiana	50.45	52.38	49.58	58.11	59.90	55.03
Iowa	52.03	51.99	47.58	63.76	59.06	56.71
Kansas	56.86	60.25	53.63	68.77	65.44	60.45
Kentucky	42.30	45.22	41.48	49.84	54.30	53.59
Louisiana	14.09	19.40	17.45	47.08	53.28	28.59
Maine	51.10	52.44	56.74	66.05	70.87	57.05
Maryland	40.83	48.15	49.40	55.36	60.04	46.39
Massachusetts	46.36	47.00	43.17	54.22	59.33	39.55
Michigan	49.85	49.18	49.23	55.44	55.63	48.84
Minnesota	47.66	46.86	39.89	55.33	53.68	49.16
Mississippi	4.19	6.44	2.62	39.56	24.46	24.67
Missouri	47.50	48.43	41.50	50.71	49.87	49.74
Montana	40.17	44.93	43.15	59.39	57.13	51.10
Nebraska	57.19	58.58	54.15	69.15	65.51	62.07
Nevada	39.92	45.38	47.26	61.45	57.97	48.84
New Hampshire	46.78	47.87	52.41	60.92	66.11	53.42
New Jersey	47.93	48.95	50.33	56.81	64.68	49.16
New Mexico	43.28	46.44	42.93	55.39	57.81	49.41
New York	48.04	47.30	45.99	55.45	61.20	47.27
North Carolina	25.97	33.29	32.68	46.09	49.34	47.89
North Dakota	55.06	53.84	52.17	70.97	61.72	55.42
Ohio	47.80	50.18	49.24	56.76	61.11	53.28
Oklahoma	42.23	44.20	37.25	54.59	55.13	59.02
Oregon	45.63	46.94	49.78	60.54	55.25	52.62
Pennsylvania	46.34	48.36	50.93	52.74	56.49	48.74
Rhode Island	43.24	41.26	41.44	50.89	58.31	36.37
South Carolina	4.37	4.46	3.78	49.28	25.18	48.76
South Dakota	57.41	58.33	51.84	69.27	58.39	58.21
Tennessee	32.36	39.22	36.87	49.98	49.21	52.92
Texas	19.13	16.64	24.60	53.13	55.27	48.52
Utah	37.59	39.42	45.52	58.93	64.56	54.81
Vermont	54.79	57.06	61.55	71.46	72.18	58.65
Virginia	31.55	37.39	41.04	56.32	55.37	52.44
Washington	40.58	42.24	42.68	54.33	53.91	50.68
West Virginia	42.90	45.11	42.24	48.08	54.08	47.27
Wisconsin	48.32	50.37	46.28	60.95	61.58	51.77
Wyoming	46.89	51.23	47.27	62.71	60.04	55.05
TOTALS	44.83	45.89	45.13	55.14	57.37	49.55

TABLE 101   Whig Vote by States and Elections

States	1836	1840	1844	1848	1852	1856
Alabama	15,612	28,471	26,084	30,482	15,038	28,557
Arkansas	1,238	5,160	5,504	7,588	7,404	10,787
California					35,407	36,165
Connecticut	18,765	31,601	32,832	30,316	30,359	2,615
Delaware	4,734	5,967	6,278	6,441	6,294	6,175
Florida				4,546	2,875	4,843
Georgia	24,888	40,349	42,106	47,538	16,660	42,477
Illinois	14,983	45,574	45,790	53,215	64,934	37,451
Indiana	41,281	65,308	67,867	69,907	80,901	23,386
Iowa				11,084	15,856	9,444
Kentucky	36,955	58,489	61,255	67,141	57,068	67,416
Louisiana	3,383	11,297	13,083	18,217	17,255	20,709
Maine	15,239	46,612	34,619	35,279	32,543	3,325
Maryland	25,852	33,533	35,984	37,706	35,080	47,462
Massachusetts	41,287	72,913	67,418	61,300	52,683	19,726
Michigan	4,085	22,933	24,337	23,940	33,860	1,660
Mississippi	9,688	19,518	19,206	25,922	17,548	24,490
Missouri	7,337	22,972	31,251	32,671	29,984	48,524
New Hampshire	6,228	26,434	17,866	14,781	16,147	422
New Jersey	26,392	33,362	38,318	40,015	38,553	24,115
New York	138,765	225,945	232,482	218,603	234,906	124,603
North Carolina	23,626	46,379	43,232	43,550	39,058	36,886
Ohio	105,417	148,157	155,057	138,360	152,626	28,125
Pennsylvania	87,111	144,023	161,203	185,513	179,182	55,852
Rhode Island	2,711	5,278	7,322	6,779	7,626	1,675
South Carolina						
Tennessee	36,168	60,391	60,033	64,705	58,802	66,178
Texas				4,509	4,995	15,639
Vermont	20,990	32,445	26,770	23,122	22,173	546
Virginia	23,412	42,501	44,790	45,124	58,572	60,039
Wisconsin				13,747	22,240	580
TOTALS	736,147	1,275,612	1,300,687	1,362,101	1,386,629	849,872

The electoral vote was cast by the legislature in South Carolina in all six campaigns.

In 1836, Harrison received the votes of Connecticut, Delaware, Illinois, Indiana, Kentucky, Maine, Maryland, Michigan, New Hampshire, New Jersey, New York, Ohio, Pennsylvania, Rhode Island, and Vermont. White received those of Alabama, Arkansas, Georgia, Louisiana, Mississippi, Missouri, North Carolina, Tennessee, and Virginia. Webster received those of Massachusetts. In 1852, Webster got 5,324 votes (8.50%) in Georgia, 1,670 (1.30%) in Massachusetts, and 413 (.08%) in New York; these were in addition to those shown above. His national total was 7,407 and his national percentage was .23.

Percentage of Whig Vote by States and Elections

States	1836	1840	1844	1848	1852	1856
Alabama	43.22	45.58	40.87	49.29	34.11	37.88
Arkansas	34.03	43.27	36.57	44.93	37.82	32.99
California					46.51	32.81
Connecticut	49.31	55.37	50.81	48.61	45.47	3.26
Delaware	53.27	54.99	51.15	51.81	49.66	42.63
Florida				58.36	39.97	43.20
Georgia	52.71	55.78	48.79	51.48	26.60	42.87
Illinois	45.29	48.83	42.43	42.35	41.76	15.67
Indiana	55.97	55.82	48.42	45.77	44.17	9.87
Iowa				45.61	45.02	10.52
Kentucky	52.50	64.20	54.09	57.45	51.35	47.33
Louisiana	48.08	59.73	48.70	54.24	48.06	48.30
Maine	39.96	50.13	40.52	40.30	39.60	3.03
Maryland	53.84	53.83	52.41	52.10	46.67	54.64
Massachusetts	55.18	57.43	51.42	45.42	41.03	11.80
Michigan	35.16	51.67	43.67	36.82	40.83	1.31
Mississippi	49.26	53.45	43.32	49.41	39.50	40.71
Missouri	40.02	43.56	43.03	44.91	43.88	45.48
New Hampshire	24.96	44.63	36.32	29.50	30.56	.59
New Jersey	50.52	51.75	50.46	51.42	45.91	24.26
New York	45.40	51.18	47.85	47.94	44.89	20.93
North Carolina	46.75	57.85	52.39	55.47	49.53	43.33
Ohio	52.10	54.10	49.66	42.11	43.17	7.27
Pennsylvania	48.78	49.98	48.57	50.42	46.19	12.87
Rhode Island	47.75	61.22	59.55	60.77	44.85	8.45
South Carolina						
Tennessee	58.06	55.57	50.05	52.55	50.72	47.33
Texas				29.71	26.93	33.41
Vermont	59.92	63.90	54.90	48.26	50.58	1.07
Virginia	43.15	49.19	46.91	49.20	44.23	39.94
Wisconsin				35.10	34.35	.49
TOTALS	49.07	52.87	48.13	47.31	43.82	21.08

The highest percentage for each election is underlined.

TABLE 102   Prohibition Vote by States and Elections

States	1872	1876	1880	1884	1888	1892
Alabama				612	583	241
Arizona						
Arkansas					615	130
California			59	2,920	5,761	8,096
Colorado				761	2,192	1,687
Connecticut	186	374	409	2,494	4,236	4,026
Delaware				55	400	564
Florida				72	418	570
Georgia				195	1,808	988
Idaho						288
Illinois		249	443	12,074	21,703	25,870
Indiana				3,018	9,881	13,050
Iowa		36	592	1,564	3,550	6,402
Kansas		110	25	4,495	6,779	4,553
Kentucky		818	258	3,139	5,225	6,442
Louisiana				338	127	
Maine			93	2,160	2,691	3,062
Maryland		10		2,794	4,767	5,877
Massachusetts		84	682	10,026	8,701	7,539
Michigan	1,271	767	942	18,403	20,945	20,857
Minnesota		72	286	4,691	15,311	14,182
Mississippi					258	995
Missouri		64		2,153	4,539	4,331
Montana						549
Nebraska		1,599		2,858	9,429	4,902
Nevada					41	89
New Hampshire	200		180	1,571	1,593	1,297
New Jersey		43	191	6,159	7,933	8,134
New Mexico						
New York	201	2,359	1,517	25,006	30,231	38,193
North Carolina				454	2,789	2,630
North Dakota						899
Ohio	2,100	1,636	2,616	11,069	24,356	26,012
Oklahoma						
Oregon		4		492	1,677	2,281
Pennsylvania	1,630	1,318	1,939	15,306	20,966	25,123
Rhode Island		60	20	928	1,251	1,654
South Carolina						
South Dakota						
Tennessee			43	1,131	5,975	4,851
Texas				3,534	4,749	2,165
Utah						
Vermont				1,752	1,460	1,424
Virginia				138	1,682	2,798
Washington						2,553
West Virginia				939	1,085	2,145
Wisconsin		27	69	7,656	14,415	13,132
Wyoming						530
TOTALS	5,588	9,630	10,364	150,957	250,122	271,111

States	1896	1900	1904	1908	1912	1916
Alabama	2,147	3,796	612	665		999
Arizona					265	1,153
Arkansas	889	584	993	1,194	898	2,015
California	2,573	5,087	7,380	11,770	23,366	27,698
Colorado	1,724	3,790	3,438	5,559	5,063	2,793
Connecticut	1,806	1,617	1,506	2,380	2,068	1,789
Delaware	602	546	607	670	623	566
Florida	·654	2,234	5	553	1,854	4,855
Georgia	5,613	1,396	685	1,059	148	
Idaho	181	857	1,013	1,986	1,537	1,127
Illinois	9,818	17,626	34,770	29,364	15,710	26,047
Indiana	3,056	13,718	23,496	18,045	19,249	16,368
Iowa	3,192	9,502	11,601	9,837	9,026	3,371
Kansas	1,721	3,605	7,306	5,033		12,882
Kentucky	4,781	2,814	6,609	5,887	3,233	3,036
Louisiana						
Maine	1,589	2,585	1,510	1,487	946	597
Maryland	5,922	4,574	3,034	3,302	2,244	2,903
Massachusetts	3,060	6,208	4,286	4,379	2,799	2,993
Michigan	5,025	11,859	13,441	16,974	8,934	8,139
Minnesota	4,348	8,555	6,352	11,107	7,886	7,793
Mississippi	485					
Missouri	2,169	5,965	7,191	4,231	5,380	3,884
Montana	186	298	335	827	32	
Nebraska	1,243	3,655	6,323	5,179	3,383	2,952
Nevada						348
New Hampshire	776	1,271	749	905	535	303
New Jersey	5,617	7,190	6,845	4,934	2,915	3,217
New Mexico						112
New York	16,086	22,077	20,787	22,667	19,427	19,031
North Carolina	681	1,009	361		1,025	51
North Dakota	358	735	1,140	1,553	1,243	
Ohio	5,084	10,203	19,339	11,402	11,511	8,080
Oklahoma					2,185	1,646
Oregon	919	2,536	3,806	2,682	4,360	4,729
Pennsylvania	19,274	27,908	33,717	36,694	19,533	28,525
Rhode Island	1,161	1,529	768	1,016	616	470
South Carolina						
South Dakota	683	1,542	2,965	4,039	3,910	1,774
Tennessee	3,140	3,882	1,906	300	834	147
Texas	1,786	2,644	4,292	1,634	1,738	1,985
Utah		209				149
Vermont	733	367	792	802	1,095	709
Virginia	2,344	2,150	1,383	1,111	709	683
Washington	968	2,363	3,229	4,700	9,810	6,868
West Virginia	1,223	1,692	4,604	5,139	4,534	179
Wisconsin	7,509	10,022	9,770	11,572	8,586	7,166
Wyoming	159		217	66	434	373
TOTALS	131,285	210,200	259,163	252,704	209,644	220,505

Prohibition Vote by States and Elections (continued)

States	1920	1924	1928	1932	1936	1940
Alabama	757	569		13	719	700
Arizona	4				384	742
Arkansas						793
California	25,204	18,365		20,637	12,917	9,400
Colorado	2,807	966		1,928		1,597
Connecticut	1,771					
Delaware	986					220
Florida	5,124	5,498				
Georgia	8	231		1,125	663	1,003
Idaho	34					
Illinois	11,216	2,367		6,388	3,439	9,190
Indiana	13,462	4,416	5,496	10,399		6,437
Iowa	4,197			2,111	1,182	2,284
Kansas						4,056
Kentucky	3,325			2,252	929	1,443
Louisiana						
Maine	1				334	
Maryland						
Massachusetts				1,142	1,032	1,370
Michigan	9,646	6,085	2,728	2,893	579	1,795
Minnesota	11,489					
Mississippi						
Missouri	5,142	1,418		2,429	908	1,809
Montana					224	664
Nebraska	5,947	1,594				
Nevada						
New Hampshire						
New Jersey	4,895	1,660	160	774	926	873
New Mexico					62	100
New York	19,653					3,250
North Carolina	17	13				
North Dakota					197	325
Ohio	294	1,246	3,556	7,421		
Oklahoma					1,328	3,027
Oregon	3,595				4	154
Pennsylvania	42,612	9,779	3,880	11,319	6,691	
Rhode Island	510			183		74
South Carolina						
South Dakota	900			463		
Tennessee		100		1,995	632	1,606
Texas					514	925
Utah					43	
Vermont	774	326	338			
Virginia	857			1,843	594	882
Washington	3,800			1,540	1,041	1,686
West Virginia	1,528		1,703	2,342	1,173	
Wisconsin	8,647	2,918	2,245	2,672	1,071	2,148
Wyoming	265				75	172
TOTALS	189,467	57,551	20,106	81,869	37,661	58,725

States	1944	1948	1952	1956	1960
Alabama	1,095	1,085	1,814		2,106
Arizona	421	786			
Arkansas		1	886		
California	14,770	16,926	15,653	11,119	21,706
Colorado					
Connecticut					
Delaware	294	343	234	400	284
Florida					
Georgia	36	732			
Idaho	503	628			
Illinois	7,411	11,959			
Indiana	12,574	14,711	15,335	6,554	6,746
Iowa	3,752	3,382	2,882		
Kansas	2,609	6,468	6,038	3,048	4,138
Kentucky	2,023	1,245	1,161	2,145	
Louisiana					
Maine					
Maryland					
Massachusetts	973	1,663	886	1,205	1,633
Michigan	6,503	13,052	10,331	6,923	2,029
Minnesota			2,147		
Mississippi					
Missouri	1,175		885		
Montana	340	429	548		456
Nebraska					
Nevada					
New Hampshire					
New Jersey	4,255	10,593	989	9,147	
New Mexico	148	127	297	607	777
New York					
North Carolina					
North Dakota	549		302		
Ohio					
Oklahoma	1,663				
Oregon	2,362				
Pennsylvania	5,750	10,338	8,771		
Rhode Island	433				
South Carolina	365		1		
South Dakota					
Tennessee	885		1,441	789	2,475
Texas	1,017	2,758	1,983		3,870
Utah					
Vermont					
Virginia	459				
Washington	2,396	6,117			
West Virginia					
Wisconsin					
Wyoming			194		
TOTALS	74,761	103,343	72,778	41,937	46,220

197

States	1872	1876	1880	1884	1888	1892	1896	1900
Alabama				.39	.33	.10	1.10	2.37
Arizona								
Arkansas					.39	.09	.60	.46
California			.04	1.48	2.31	3.00	.86	1.68
Colorado				1.14	2.39	1.80	.91	1.71
Connecticut	.19	.31	.31	1.82	2.75	2.45	1.04	.90
Delaware				.18	1.34	1.51	1.56	1.30
Florida				.12	.63	1.60	1.41	5.67
Georgia				.14	1.26	.45	3.44	1.14
Idaho						1.47	.61	1.49
Illinois		.04	.07	1.79	2.90	2.96	.90	1.56
Indiana				.61	1.84	2.36	.48	2.07
Iowa		.01	.18	.42	.88	1.44	.61	1.79
Kansas		.09	.01	1.69	2.05	1.40	.51	1.02
Kentucky		.31	.10	1.14	1.52	1.89	1.07	.60
Louisiana				.31	.11			
Maine			.06	1.66	2.10	2.63	1.34	2.45
Maryland		.01		1.50	2.26	2.76	2.36	1.73
Massachusetts		.03	.24	3.30	2.53	1.93	.76	1.50
Michigan	.58	.24	.27	4.57	4.41	4.48	.92	2.18
Minnesota		.06	.19	2.46	5.82	5.31	1.27	2.70
Mississippi					.22	1.89	.69	
Missouri		.02		.49	.87	.80	.32	.87
Montana						1.24	.35	.47
Nebraska		2.99		2.13	4.65	2.45	.55	1.51
Nevada					.32	.82		
New Hampshire	.29		.21	1.86	1.75	1.45	.93	1.38
New Jersey		.02	.08	2.36	2.61	2.41	1.51	1.79
New Mexico								
New York	.02	.23	.14	2.14	2.29	2.86	1.13	1.43
North Carolina				.17	.98	.94	.21	.34
North Dakota						2.49	.76	1.27
Ohio	.40	.25	.36	1.41	2.90	3.06	.50	.98
Oklahoma								
Oregon		.01		.93	2.71	2.91	.94	3.01
Pennsylvania	.29	.17	.22	1.70	2.10	2.50	1.61	2.38
Rhode Island		.23	.07	2.83	3.07	3.11	2.12	2.70
South Carolina							.82	1.60
South Dakota				.44	1.96	1.81	.97	1.42
Tennessee			.02	.44	1.96	1.81	.97	1.42
Texas				1.09	1.33	.51	.33	.62
Utah								.22
Vermont				2.95	2.30	2.55	1.15	.65
Virginia				.05	.55	.96	.79	.81
Washington						2.91	1.03	2.20
West Virginia				.71	.68	1.25	.61	.77
Wisconsin		.01	.03	2.39	4.06	3.54	1.68	2.26
Wyoming						3.17	.77	
TOTALS	.09	.11	.11	1.50	2.20	2.25	.94	1.50

The highest percentage for each election is underlined.

".00" signifies that the party received some votes, but less than .01%

198

States	1904	1908	1912	1916	1920	1924	1928	1932
Alabama	.56	.64		.76	.31	.34		.01
Arizona			1.12	1.99	.01			
Arkansas	.85	.78	.72	1.20				
California	2.23	3.04	3.47	2.77	2.67	1.43		.91
Colorado	1.41	2.11	1.90	.95	.96	.28		.42
Connecticut	.79	1.25	1.09	.84	.48			
Delaware	1.38	1.40	1.28	1.09	1.04			
Florida	.01	1.12	3.57	6.01	3.52	5.04		
Georgia	.52	.80	.12		.01	.14		.44
Idaho	1.40	2.04	1.45	.84	.02			
Illinois	3.23	2.54	1.37	1.19	.54	.10		.19
Indiana	3.44	2.50	2.94	2.28	1.07	.35	.39	.66
Iowa	2.39	1.99	1.83	.65	.47			.20
Kansas	2.22	1.34		2.05				
Kentucky	1.52	1.20	.71	.58	.36			.23
Louisiana								
Maine	1.57	1.40	.73	.44	.00			
Maryland	1.35	1.38	.97	1.11				
Massachusetts	.96	.96	.57	.56				.07
Michigan	2.56	3.13	1.62	1.25	.92	.52	.20	.17
Minnesota	2.17	3.35	2.36	2.01	1.57			
Mississippi								
Missouri	1.12	.59	.77	.49	.39	.11		.15
Montana	.52	1.20	.04					
Nebraska	2.80	1.94	1.36	1.03	1.55	.34		
Nevada				1.04				
New Hampshire	.83	1.01	.61	.34				
New Jersey	1.58	1.06	.67	.65	.54	.15	.01	.05
New Mexico				.17				
New York	1.28	1.38	1.22	1.12	.68			
North Carolina	.17		.42	.02	.00	.00		
North Dakota	1.62	1.64	1.44					
Ohio	1.92	1.02	1.11	.69	.01	.06	.14	.28
Oklahoma			.86	.56				
Oregon	4.22	2.42	3.18	1.81	1.51			
Pennsylvania	2.73	2.90	1.60	2.20	2.30	.46	.12	.40
Rhode Island	1.12	1.40	.79	.54	.30			.07
South Carolina								
South Dakota	2.92	3.52	3.36	1.38	.49			.16
Tennessee	.79	.12	.33	.05		.03		.51
Texas	1.83	.56	.57	.53				
Utah				.10				
Vermont	1.53	1.52	1.74	1.10	.86	.32	.25	
Virginia	1.06	.81	.52	.44	.37			.62
Washington	2.22	2.55	3.04	1.80	.95			.25
West Virginia	1.92	1.99	1.69	.06	.30		.26	.31
Wisconsin	2.21	2.55	2.15	1.59	1.23	.35	.22	.24
Wyoming	.71	.18	1.03	.72	.47			
TOTALS	1.92	1.70	1.39	1.19	.71	.20	.05	.21

States	1936	1940	1944	1948	1952	1956	1960
Alabama	.26	.24	.45	.50	.43		.37
Arizona	.31	.49	.31	.44			
Arkansas		.39		.00	.22		
California	.49	.29	.42	.42	.30	.20	.33
Colorado		.29					
Connecticut							
Delaware		.16	.23	.25	.13	.22	.14
Florida							
Georgia	.23	.32	.01	.17			
Idaho			.24	.29			
Illinois	.09	.22	.18	.30			
Indiana		.36	.75	.89	.78	.33	.32
Iowa	.10	.19	.36	.33	.23		
Kansas		.47	.36	.82	.67	.35	.45
Kentucky	.10	.15	.23	.15	.12	.20	
Louisiana							
Maine	.11						
Maryland							
Massachusetts	.06	.07	.05	.08	.04	.05	.07
Michigan	.03	.09	.29	.62	.37	.22	.06
Minnesota					.16		
Mississippi							
Missouri	.05	.10	.07		.05		
Montana	.09	.27	.16	.19	.21		.16
Nebraska							
Nevada							
New Hampshire							
New Jersey	.05	.04	.22	.54	.04	.37	
New Mexico	.04	.05	.10	.07	.12	.24	.25
New York		.05					
North Carolina							
North Dakota	.07	.12	.25		.11		
Ohio							
Oklahoma	.18	.37	.23				
Oregon	.00	.03	.49				
Pennsylvania	.16		.15	.28	.19		
Rhode Island		.02	.14				
South Carolina			.35		.00		
South Dakota							
Tennessee	.13	.31	.17		.16	.08	.24
Texas	.06	.09	.09	.24	.10		.17
Utah	.02						
Vermont							
Virginia	.18	.25	.12				
Washington	.15	.21	.28	.68			
West Virginia	.14						
Wisconsin	.09	.15					
Wyoming	.07	.15			.15		
TOTALS	.08	.12	.16	.21	.12	.07	.07

TABLE 103 Socialist Labor Vote by States and Elections

States	1888	1892	1896	1900	1904	1908	1912
Arizona							
Arkansas							
California			1,611				
Colorado			160	684	335		475
Connecticut		329	1,223	908	575	608	1,260
Delaware							
Illinois			1,147	1,373	4,698	1,680	4,066
Indiana			329	663	1,598	643	3,130
Iowa			453	259			
Kentucky				299	596	404	956
Maine		336					
Maryland		27	588	388			322
Massachusetts		676	2,137	2,610	2,365	1,018	1,270
Michigan			297	903	1,108	1,096	1,252
Minnesota			954	1,329	974		2,212
Missouri			610	1,294	1,674	868	1,778
Montana				169	208		
Nebraska			186				
New Hampshire			228				
New Jersey		1,337	3,986	2,081	2,680	1,196	1,347
New Mexico							
New York	2,068	17,958	17,731	12,622	9,127	3,877	4,251
Ohio			1,165	1,688	2,633	720	2,630
Oklahoma							
Oregon							
Pennsylvania		898	1,683	2,936	2,224	1,222	704
Rhode Island			558	1,423	488	183	236
Texas				162	421	176	442
Utah				106			510
Virginia			115	167	218	25	50
Washington				866	1,592		1,872
Wisconsin			1,314	505	223	314	527
Wyoming							
TOTALS	2,068	21,561	36,475	33,435	33,737	14,030	29,290

States	1916	1920	1924	1928	1932	1936
Arizona						
Arkansas						
California						
Colorado			378		427	344
Connecticut	606	1,491	1,373	622	2,287	1,228
Delaware						
Illinois	2,488	3,471	2,334	1,812	3,638	1,921
Indiana	1,659			645	2,070	
Iowa		982		230		252
Kentucky	333		1,499	340	1,396	294
Maine			406		255	129
Maryland	756	1,178	987	906	1,036	1,305
Massachusetts	1,125	3,583	1,674	773	2,668	1,305
Michigan	842	2,539	5,330	799	1,401	600
Minnesota	468	3,828	1,855	1,921	770	961
Missouri	902	2,164	909	340	404	292
Montana			247			
Nebraska						
New Hampshire						
New Jersey	890	1,010	368	500	1,062	362
New Mexico						
New York	2,666	4,841	9,928	4,211	10,339	
Ohio			3,025	1,515	1,968	14
Oklahoma			5,234			
Oregon		1,515	917	1,564	1,730	500
Pennsylvania	417	755	636	380	659	1,424
Rhode Island	180	495	268	416	433	929
Texas						
Utah	144					
Virginia	67		191	179		36
Washington	730	1,321	1,004	4,068	1,009	362
Wisconsin			458	381	494	557
Wyoming						
TOTALS	14,273	29,173	39,021	21,602	34,046	12,815

Socialist Labor Vote by States and Elections (continued)

States	1940	1944	1948	1952	1956	1960
Arizona			121			469
Arkansas				1		
California		180	195	273	293	1,051
Colorado			214	352	3,308	2,803
Connecticut	971	1,220	1,184	535		
Delaware			29	242	110	82
Illinois		9,677	3,118	9,363	8,342	10,560
Indiana	706		763	979	1,334	1,136
Iowa	452	193	4,274	139	125	230
Kentucky		326	185	893	358	
Maine		335	206	156		
Maryland	657					
Massachusetts	1,492	2,780	5,535	1,957	5,573	3,892
Michigan	795	1,264	1,263	1,495		1,718
Minnesota	2,553	3,176	2,525	2,383	2,080	962
Missouri	209	221		169		
Montana						
Nebraska						
New Hampshire			83			
New Jersey	455	6,939	3,354	5,815	6,736	4,262
New Mexico			49	35	69	570
New York		14,352	2,729	1,560	150	
Ohio						
Oklahoma						
Oregon	2,487					
Pennsylvania	1,518	1,789	1,461	1,347	7,447	7,185
Rhode Island			130	83		
Texas						
Utah						
Virginia	48	90	234	1,160	351	397
Washington	667	1,645	1,133	633	7,457	10,895
Wisconsin	1,882	1,002	399	770	710	1,310
Wyoming			56	36		
TOTALS	14,892	45,189	29,240	30,376	44,443	47,522

TABLE 103 (continued) **Percentage of Socialist Labor Vote by States and Elections**

States	1888	1892	1896	1900	1904	1908	1912	1916	1920	1924
Arizona										
Arkansas										
California			.54							
Colorado			.08	.31	.14		.18			.11
Connecticut		.20	.70	.50	.30	<u>.32</u>	.66	.28	.41	.34
Delaware										
Illinois			.11	.12	.44	.15	.35	.11	.17	.09
Indiana			.05	.10	.23	.09	.48	.23		
Iowa			.09	.05						
Kentucky				.06	.14	.08	.21	.06		.18
Maine		.29								.21
Maryland		.01	.23	.15			.14	<u>.29</u>	.27	.28
Massachusetts		.17	.53	.63	.53	.22	.26	.21	.36	.15
Michigan			.05	.17	.21	.20	.23	.13	.24	.46
Minnesota			.28	.42	.33		<u>.66</u>	.12	.52	.23
Missouri			.09	.19	.26	.12	.25	.11	.16	.07
Montana				.27	.32					.14
Nebraska			.08							
New Hampshire			.27							
New Jersey		.40	1.07	.52	.62	.26	.31	.18	.11	.03
New Mexico										
New York	<u>.16</u>	<u>1.34</u>	1.24	.82	.56	.24	.27	.16	.17	.30
Ohio				.11	.16	.26	.06	.25		.15
Oklahoma										<u>.99</u>
Oregon									<u>.64</u>	.33
Pennsylvania		.09	.14	.25	.18	.10	.06	.03	.04	.03
Rhode Island			1.02	<u>2.52</u>	.71	.25	.30	.20	.29	.13
Texas				.04	.18	.06	.14			
Utah				.11			.45	.10		
Virginia			.04	.06	.17	.02	.04	.04		.09
Washington				.81	<u>1.10</u>		.58	.19	.33	.24
Wisconsin			.29	.11	.05	.07	.13			.05
Wyoming										
TOTALS	.02	.18	.26	.24	.25	.09	.19	.08	.11	.13

The highest percentage for each election is underlined.

".00" signifies that the party received some votes, but less than .01%.

Extended percentages, 1912: Connecticut .6618, Minnesota .6619.

Percentage of Socialist Labor Vote by States and Elections (continued)

States	1928	1932	1936	1940	1944	1948	1952	1956	1960
Arizona						.07			.12
Arkansas							.00		
California					.01	.00	.01	.01	.02
Colorado		.09	.07			.04	.06	.50	.38
Connecticut	.11	.38	.18	.12	.15	.13	.05		
Delaware						.02	.14	.06	.04
Illinois	.06	.11	.05		.24	.08	.21	.19	.22
Indiana	.05	.13		.04		.05	.05	.07	.05
Iowa	.02		.02	.04	.02	.41	.01	.01	.02
Kentucky	.04	.14	.03		.04	.02	.09	.03	
Maine		.09	.04		.11	.08	.04		
Maryland	.17	.20	.21	.10					
Massachusetts	.05	.17	.07	.07	.14	.26	.08	.24	.16
Michigan	.06	.08	.03	.04	.06	.06	.05		.05
Minnesota	.20	.08	.09	.20	.28	.21	.17	.16	.06
Missouri	.02	.03	.02	.01	.01		.01		
Montana									
Nebraska									
New Hampshire						.04			
New Jersey	.03	.07	.02	.02	.35	.17	.24	.27	.15
New Mexico						.03	.01	.03	.18
New York	.10	.22			.23	.04	.02	.00	
Ohio	.06	.08	.00						
Oklahoma									
Oregon	.49	.47	.12	.52					
Pennsylvania	.01	.02	.03	.04	.05	.04	.03	.16	.14
Rhode Island	.18	.16	.30			.04	.02		
Texas									
Utah									
Virginia	.06		.01	.01	.02	.06	.19	.05	.05
Washington	.81	.16	.05	.08	.19	.13	.06	.65	.88
Wisconsin	.04	.04	.04	.13	.07	.03	.05	.05	.08
Wyoming						.06	.03		
TOTALS	.06	.09	.03	.03	.09	.06	.05	.07	.07

TABLE 104   Socialist Workers Vote by States and Elections

Number and Percentage of Votes

States	1948	1952	1956	1960	1948	1952	1956	1960
California	133		94		.00		.00	
Colorado	228			572	.04			.08
Connecticut	606				.07			
Iowa	256			634	.02			.05
Michigan	672	655		4,347	.03	.02		.13
Minnesota	606	618	1,098	3,077	.05	.04	.08	.20
Montana				391				.14
New Jersey	5,825	3,850	4,004	11,402	.30	.16	.16	.41
New York	2,675	2,212		14,319	.04	.03		.20
North Dakota				158				.06
Pennsylvania	2,133	1,502	2,035	2,678	.06	.03	.04	.05
Utah	71			100	.03			.03
Washington	103	119		705	.01	.01		.06
Wisconsin	303	1,350	564	1,792	.02	.08	.04	.10
TOTALS	13,611	10,306	7,795	40,175	.03	.02	.01	.06

The highest percentage for each election is underlined.

".00" signifies that the party received some votes, but less than .01%.

TABLE 105   Populist Vote by States and Elections

Number and Percentage of Votes

States	1892	1900	1904	1908	1892	1900	1904	1908
Alabama	85,181	3,751	5,051	1,568	36.60	2.34	4.64	1.51
Arkansas	11,831	972	2,318	1,026	8.06	.76	1.99	.67
California	25,311				9.39			
Colorado	53,584	389	824		57.07	.18	.34	
Connecticut	809		495		.49		.26	
Delaware	13		51		.03		.12	
Florida	4,843	1,070	1,605	1,946	13.62	2.71	4.08	3.94
Georgia	42,937	4,584	22,635	16,969	19.37	3.73	17.28	12.78
Idaho	10,520	232	353		53.65	.40	.49	
Illinois	22,207	1,141	6,725	633	2.54	.10	.62	.05
Indiana	22,208	1,438	2,444	1,193	4.01	.22	.36	.17
Iowa	20,595	1,026	2,406	261	4.65	.19	.50	.05
Kansas	163,111		6,257		50.20		1.90	
Kentucky	23,500	2,017	2,511	333	6.89	.43	.58	.07
Louisiana	2,462				2.08			
Maine	2,045		338		1.76		.35	
Maryland	796				.37			
Massachusetts	3,348		1,299		.86		.29	
Michigan	20,084	837	1,159		4.28	.15	.22	
Minnesota	29,313		2,103		10.97		.72	
Mississippi	10,102	1,644	1,424	1,276	19.14	2.78	2.44	1.91
Missouri	41,213	4,244	4,226	1,165	7.62	.62	.66	.16
Montana	7,334		1,520		16.55		2.36	
Nebraska	83,134	1,104	20,518		41.52	.46	9.09	
Nevada	7,264		344		66.78		2.84	
New Hampshire	293		83		.33		.09	
New Jersey	985	691	3,705		.29	.17	.86	
New York	16,436		7,459		1.23		.46	
North Carolina	44,732	830	879		15.92	.28	.42	
North Dakota	17,700	111	165		49.01	.19	.23	
Ohio	14,852	251	1,401	163	1.75	.02	.14	.01
Oklahoma				434				.17
Oregon	26,965	275	753		34.35	.33	.84	
Pennsylvania	8,714	642	33		.87	.05	.00	
Rhode Island	228				.43			
South Carolina	2,410		1		3.42		.00	
South Dakota	26,544	339	1,240		37.64	.35	1.22	
Tennessee	23,447	1,322	2,506	1,081	8.77	.48	1.03	.42
Texas	99,688	20,981	8,062	994	23.60	4.95	3.45	.34
Vermont	44	383			.08	.68		
Virginia	12,275	63	359	105	4.20	.02	.28	.08
Washington	19,105		669		21.72		.46	
West Virginia	4,166	268	339		2.44	.12	.14	
Wisconsin	9,909		530		2.67		.12	
Wyoming	7,722				46.22			
TOTALS	1,029,960	50,605	114,790	29,147	8.53	.36	.85	.20

The Populist Party supported the Democratic Party nominee in 1896.

The highest percentage for each election is underlined.

".00" signifies that the party received some votes, but less than .01%.

TABLE 106 Greenback Vote by States and Elections

Number and Percentage of Votes

States	1876	1880	1884	1876	1880	1884
Alabama		4,642	873		3.05	.56
Arkansas	211	4,079	1,847	.22	3.80	1.47
California	47	3,395	2,017	.03	2.07	1.03
Colorado		1,435	1,953		2.68	2.93
Connecticut	774	868	1,685	.63	.65	1.23
Delaware		120	6		.41	.02
Georgia		969	145		.62	.10
Illinois	18,241	26,358	10,910	3.28	4.24	1.62
Indiana	9,533	12,986	8,716	2.21	2.76	1.76
Iowa	9,001	32,701		3.08	10.11	
Kansas	7,776	19,851	16,341	<u>6.26</u>	9.87	6.16
Kentucky	2,003	11,499	1,691	<u>.77</u>	4.30	.61
Louisiana		439	120		.42	.11
Maine	662	4,480	3,953	.57	3.11	3.03
Maryland	33	818	531	.02	.47	.29
Massachusetts	779	4,548	24,433	.30	1.61	8.05
Michigan	9,060	34,895	41,390	2.85	9.89	<u>10.29</u>
Minnesota	2,311	3,267	3,587	1.86	2.17	1.88
Mississippi		5,797			4.98	
Missouri	3,498	35,135		.99	8.84	
Nebraska	2,320	3,950		4.34	4.52	
Nevada			26			.20
New Hampshire	76	528	552	.09	.61	.65
New Jersey	712	2,617	3,496	.32	1.06	1.34
New York	2,039	12,373	17,004	.20	1.12	1.46
North Carolina		1,126			.47	
Ohio	3,057	6,456	5,179	.46	.89	.66
Oregon	510	245	726	1.71	.60	1.38
Pennsylvania	7,204	20,668	16,992	.95	2.36	1.89
Rhode Island	68	236	422	.26	.81	1.29
South Carolina		566			.33	
Tennessee		5,917	957		2.45	.37
Texas		27,405	3,321		<u>11.34</u>	1.02
Vermont		1,215	785		1.86	1.32
West Virginia	1,373	9,079	810	1.37	8.05	.61
Wisconsin	1,509	7,986	4,598	.59	2.99	1.44
TOTALS	82,797	308,649	175,066	.98	3.35	1.74

The highest percentage for each election is underlined.

TABLE 107   Farmer-Labor Vote by States and Elections

Number and Percentage of Votes

States	1920	1928	1932	1920	1928	1932
Arizona	15			.02		
Colorado	3,016	1,092	469	1.03	.28	.10
Connecticut	1,947			.53		
Delaware	93			.10		
Idaho	6			.00		
Illinois	49,630			2.37		
Indiana	16,499			1.31		
Iowa	10,321	3,088	1,094	1.15	.31	.11
Maryland	1,645			.38		
Michigan	10,480			1.00		
Minnesota			5,731			.57
Missouri	3,291			.25		
Montana	12,204			6.82		
New Jersey	2,264			.25		
New Mexico	1,104			1.05		
New York	18,413			.64		
Oklahoma		1,283			.21	
Pennsylvania	15,642			.84		
South Dakota	34,707	927		19.04	.35	
Utah	4,475			3.07		
Virginia	243		15	.12		.01
Washington	77,246			19.37		
Wyoming	2,180			3.88		
TOTALS	265,421	6,390	7,309	.99	.02	.02

The Farmer Labor Party supported the Progressive Party nominee in 1924.

The highest percentage for each election is underlined.
".00" signifies that the party received some votes, but less than .01%.

TABLE 108 Communist Vote by States and Elections

Number and Percentage of Votes

States	1924	1928	1932	1936	1940	1924	1928	1932	1936	1940
Alabama			406	678	509			.17	.25	.17
Arizona		184	256				.20	.22		
Arkansas		317	175	169			.16	.08	.09	
California		112	1,023	10,877	13,586		.01	.05	.41	.42
Colorado	562	675	787	497	378	.16	.17	.17	.10	.07
Connecticut		730	1,364	1,193	1,091		.13	.23	.17	.14
Delaware		59	133	51			.06	.12	.04	
Florida		3,704					1.46			
Georgia		64	23				.03	.01		
Idaho			491		276			.26		.12
Illinois	2,622	3,581	15,582	801		.11	.12	.46	.02	
Indiana	987	321	2,187	1,090		.08	.02	.14	.07	
Iowa	4,037	328	559	506	1,524	.41	.03	.05	.04	.13
Kansas		320					.04			
Kentucky		293	272	204			.03	.03	.02	
Maine			162	257	411			.05	.08	.13
Maryland		636	1,031	915	1,274		.12	.20	.15	.19
Massachusetts	2,637	2,464	4,821	2,930	3,806	.23	.16	.31	.16	.19
Michigan		2,881	9,318	3,384	2,834		.21	.56	.19	.14
Minnesota	4,427	4,853	6,101	2,574	2,711	.54	.50	.61	.23	.22
Missouri			568	417				.04	.02	
Montana	357	563	1,775	385	489	.20	.29	.82	.17	.20
New Hampshire		173	264	193			.09	.13	.09	
New Jersey	1,560	1,257	2,915	1,639	6,508	.14	.08	.18	.09	.33
New Mexico		158	135	43			.13	.09	.03	
New York	8,244	10,876	27,956	35,610		.25	.25	.60	.64	
North Carolina				11					.00	
North Dakota	370	936	830	360		.19	.39	.32	.13	
Ohio		2,836	7,231	5,251			.11	.28	.17	
Oregon		1,094	1,681	104	191		.34	.46	.03	.04
Pennsylvania	2,735	4,726	5,658	4,060	4,519	.13	.15	.20	.10	.11
Rhode Island	289	283	546	411	239	.14	.12	.21	.13	.07
South Dakota		232	364				.09	.13		
Tennessee		111	234	319			.03	.06	.07	
Texas		209	207	253	212		.03	.02	.03	.02
Utah		47	947	280	191		.03	.46	.13	.08
Vermont			195	405	411			.14	.28	.29
Virginia		174	86	98	71		.06	.03	.03	.02
Washington	761	1,541	2,972	1,907	2,626	.18	.31	.48	.28	.33
West Virginia		401	444				.06	.06		
Wisconsin	3,773	1,528	3,112	2,197	2,394	.45	.15	.28	.17	.17
Wyoming			180	91				.19	.09	
TOTALS	33,361	48,667	102,991	80,160	46,251	.11	.13	.26	.18	.09

The highest percentage for each election is underlined.

".00" signifies that the party received some votes, but less than .01%

States	1900	1904	1908	1912	1916	1920
Alabama	928	853	1,399	3,029	1,925	2,369
Arizona				3,163	3,174	222
Arkansas	27	1,816	5,842	8,153	6,999	5,111
California	7,572	29,535	28,659	79,201	43,259	64,076
Colorado	714	4,304	7,974	16,418	10,049	8,046
Connecticut	1,029	4,543	5,113	10,056	5,179	10,350
Delaware	57	146	239	556	480	988
Florida	601	2,337	3,747	4,806	5,353	5,189
Georgia		197	584	1,028	967	465
Idaho		4,949	6,400	11,960	8,066	38
Illinois	9,687	69,225	34,711	81,278	61,394	74,747
Indiana	2,374	12,013	13,476	36,931	21,855	24,703
Iowa	2,790	14,847	8,287	16,967	11,490	16,981
Kansas	1,605	15,869	12,420	26,779	24,685	15,511
Kentucky	770	3,602	4,060	11,647	4,734	6,409
Louisiana		995	2,538	5,249	292	
Maine	878	2,103	1,758	2,541	2,177	2,214
Maryland	904	2,247	2,323	3,996	2,674	8,876
Massachusetts	9,716	13,604	10,781	12,662	11,062	32,269
Michigan	2,826	9,042	11,586	23,211	16,120	28,947
Minnesota	3,065	11,692	14,527	27,505	20,117	56,106
Mississippi		392	978	2,061	1,484	1,639
Missouri	6,139	13,009	15,431	28,466	14,612	20,242
Montana	708	5,676	5,855	10,885	9,564	
Nebraska	823	7,412	3,524	10,185	7,141	9,600
Nevada		925	2,103	3,313	3,065	1,864
New Hampshire	790	1,090	1,299	1,980	1,318	1,234
New Jersey	4,611	9,587	10,253	15,928	10,462	27,385
New Mexico				2,859	1,999	2
New York	12,869	36,883	38,451	63,381	45,944	203,201
North Carolina		125	378	128	490	446
North Dakota	520	2,117	2,421	6,966		8,282
Ohio	4,847	36,260	33,795	90,144	38,092	57,147
Oklahoma			21,752	42,262	45,527	25,726
Oregon	1,494	7,619	7,339	13,343	9,711	9,801
Pennsylvania	4,831	21,863	33,913	83,614	42,637	70,021
Rhode Island		956	1,365	2,049	1,914	4,351
South Carolina		22	100	164	135	28
South Dakota	169	3,138	2,846	4,662	3,760	
Tennessee	413	1,354	1,870	3,504	2,542	2,268
Texas	1,846	2,791	7,870	25,743	18,969	8,121
Utah	720	5,767	4,895	9,023	4,460	3,159
Vermont		859		928	798	
Virginia	145	56	255	820	1,060	807
Washington	2,006	10,023	14,177	40,134	22,800	8,913
West Virginia	219	1,574	3,679	15,336	6,140	5,618
Wisconsin	7,051	28,220	28,170	33,481	27,846	85,041
Wyoming		1,077	1,715	2,760	1,453	1,288
TOTALS	95,744	402,714	420,858	901,255	585,974	919,801

TABLE 109   Socialist Vote by States and Elections

States	1928	1932	1936	1940	1944	1948	1952	1956
Alabama	460	2,030	242	100	190			
Arizona		2,618	317					
Arkansas	429	1,269	446	305	438	1,037		
California	19,595	63,299	11,331	16,506	2,515	3,459	206	118
Colorado	3,472	13,591	1,593	1,899	1,977	1,678	365	531
Connecticut	3,019	20,480	5,683		5,097	6,964	2,244	
Delaware	329	1,376	172	115	154	250	20	
Florida	4,036	775	775					
Georgia	124	461	68					
Idaho	1,308	526		497	282	332		
Illinois	19,138	67,258	7,530	10,914	180	11,522		
Indiana	3,871	21,388	3,856	2,075	2,223	2,179		
Iowa	2,960	20,467	1,373		1,511	1,829	219	192
Kansas	6,205	18,276	2,766	2,347	1,613	2,807	530	
Kentucky	837	3,853	632	1,014	535	1,284		
Louisiana								
Maine	1,068	2,489	783			547	138	
Maryland	1,701	10,489	1,629	4,093		2,941		
Massachusetts	6,262	34,305	5,111	4,091				
Michigan	3,516	39,205	8,208	7,593	4,598	6,063		
Minnesota	6,774	25,476	2,872	5,454	5,073	4,646		
Mississippi		686	329	193				
Missouri	3,739	16,374	3,454	2,226	1,750	2,222	227	
Montana	1,667	7,891	1,066	1,443	1,296	695	159	
Nebraska	3,434	9,876						
Nevada								
New Hampshire	455	947			46	86		
New Jersey	4,897	42,998	3,931	2,433	3,358	10,521	8,593	
New Mexico		1,776	343	144		83		
New York	107,332	177,397	86,897	18,950	10,553	40,879	2,664	82
North Carolina		5,591	21					
North Dakota	842	3,521	552	1,279	943	1,000		
Ohio	8,683	64,094	117					
Oklahoma	3,924		2,221					
Oregon	2,720	15,450	2,143	398	3,785	5,051		
Pennsylvania	18,647	91,119	14,375	10,967	11,721	11,325	2,684	
Rhode Island		3,138				428		
South Carolina	47	82				1		
South Dakota	443	1,551						
Tennessee	631	1,786	687	463	792	1,291		
Texas	722	4,450	1,075	728	594	874		
Utah	954	4,087	432	200	340			
Vermont		1,533				585	185	
Virginia	250	2,382	313	282	417	726	504	444
Washington	2,615	17,080	3,496	4,586	3,824	3,534	254	
West Virginia	1,313	5,133	832					
Wisconsin	18,213	53,379	10,626	15,071	13,205	12,547	1,157	754
Wyoming	788	2,829	200	148		137	40	
TOTALS	267,420	884,781	188,497	116,514	79,010	139,523	20,189	2,121

The Socialist Party supported the Progressive Party nominee in 1924.

States	1900	1904	1908	1912	1916	1920	1928
Alabama	.58	.78	1.35	2.57	1.47	.98	.18
Arizona				13.33	5.47	.33	
Arkansas	.02	1.56	3.84	6.57	4.16	2.78	.22
California	2.50	8.91	7.41	11.76	4.33	6.79	1.09
Colorado	.32	1.77	3.02	6.15	3.41	2.75	.89
Connecticut	.57	2.38	2.69	5.28	2.42	2.83	.55
Delaware	.14	.33	.50	1.14	.93	1.04	.31
Florida	1.52	5.95	7.59	9.26	6.62	3.56	1.59
Georgia		.15	.44	.85	.61	.30	.05
Idaho		6.82	6.58	11.31	5.99	.03	.85
Illinois	.86	6.43	3.00	7.09	2.80	3.57	.62
Indiana	.36	1.76	1.87	5.64	3.04	1.96	.27
Iowa	.53	3.06	1.67	3.44	2.21	1.90	.29
Kansas	.45	4.83	3.31	7.33	3.92	2.72	.87
Kentucky	.16	.83	.83	2.57	.91	.70	.09
Louisiana		1.84	3.38	6.61	.31		
Maine	.83	2.19	1.65	1.96	1.60	1.12	.41
Maryland	.34	1.00	.97	1.72	1.02	2.07	.32
Massachusetts	2.34	3.06	2.36	2.59	2.08	3.25	.40
Michigan	.52	1.72	2.14	4.21	2.48	2.76	.26
Minnesota	.97	3.99	4.38	8.23	5.19	7.65	.70
Mississippi		.67	1.46	3.19	1.71	1.99	
Missouri	.90	2.02	2.16	4.07	1.86	1.52	.25
Montana	1.11	8.81	8.51	13.64	5.38		.86
Nebraska	.34	3.28	1.32	4.08	2.49	2.51	.63
Nevada		7.64	8.57	16.47	9.20	6.85	
New Hampshire	.86	1.21	1.45	2.25	1.48	.78	.23
New Jersey	1.15	2.22	2.19	3.67	2.11	3.01	.32
New Mexico				5.79	2.99	.00	
New York	.83	2.28	2.35	3.99	2.69	7.01	2.44
North Carolina		.06	.15	.05	.17	.08	
North Dakota	.90	3.01	2.56	8.05		4.02	.35
Ohio	.47	3.61	3.01	8.69	3.27	2.83	.35
Oklahoma			8.47	16.61	15.55	5.29	.63
Oregon	1.77	8.45	6.62	9.74	3.71	4.11	.85
Pennsylvania	.41	1.77	2.68	6.85	3.29	3.78	.59
Rhode Island		1.39	1.89	2.63	2.18	2.59	
South Carolina		.04	.15	.33	.21	.04	.07
South Dakota	.18	3.09	2.48	4.01	2.92		.17
Tennessee	.15	.56	.73	1.38	.93	.53	.17
Texas	.44	1.19	2.68	8.44	5.09	1.67	.10
Utah	.77	5.67	4.51	8.03	3.12	2.17	.54
Vermont		1.66		1.48	1.24		
Virginia	.05	.04	.19	.60	.69	.35	.08
Washington	1.87	6.91	7.68	12.43	5.98	2.24	.52
West Virginia	.10	.66	1.43	5.70	2.12	1.10	.20
Wisconsin	1.59	6.37	6.20	8.37	6.20	12.05	1.79
Wyoming		3.51	4.56	6.53	2.80	2.29	.95
TOTALS	.69	2.98	2.83	5.99	3.16	3.43	.73

States	1932	1936	1940	1944	1948	1952	1956
Alabama	.83	.09	.03	.08			
Arizona	2.21	.26					
Arkansas	.58	.25	.15	.21	.43		
California	2.79	.43	.50	.07	.09	.00	.00
Colorado	2.97	.33	.35	.39	.33	.06	<u>.08</u>
Connecticut	3.45	.82		.61	.79	.22	
Delaware	1.22	.14	.08	.12	.18	.01	
Florida	.28						
Georgia	.18	.02					
Idaho	.28		.21	.14	.15		
Illinois	1.97	.19	.26	.00	.29		
Indiana	1.36	.23	.12	.13	.13		
Iowa	1.97	.12		.14	.18	.02	.02
Kansas	2.31	.32	.27	.22	.36	.06	
Kentucky	.39	.07	.10	.06	.16		
Louisiana							
Maine	.83	.26			.21	.04	
Maryland	2.05	.26	.62		.49		
Massachusetts	2.17	.28	.20				
Michigan	2.36	.45	.36	.21	.29		
Minnesota	2.54	.25	.44	.45	.38		
Mississippi	.47	.20	.11				
Missouri	1.02	.19	.12	.11	.14	.01	
Montana	3.65	.46	.58	.63	.31	.06	
Nebraska	1.73						
Nevada							
New Hampshire	.46			.02	.04		
New Jersey	2.64	.22	.12	.17	.54	<u>.36</u>	
New Mexico	1.17	.20	.08		.04		
New York	3.78	<u>1.55</u>	.30	.17	.66	.04	.00
North Carolina	.79	.00					
North Dakota	1.37	.20	.46	.43	.45		
Ohio	2.46	.00					
Oklahoma		.30					
Oregon	4.19	.52	.08	.79	.96		
Pennsylvania	3.19	.35	.27	.31	.30	.06	
Rhode Island	1.18				.13		
South Carolina	.08				.00		
South Dakota	.54						
Tennessee	.46	.14	.09	.16	.23		
Texas	.52	.13	.07	.05	.08		
Utah	1.98	.20	.08	.14			
Vermont	1.12				.47	.12	
Virginia	.80	.09	.08	.11	.17	.08	.06
Washington	2.78	.50	.58	.45	.39	.02	
West Virginia	.69	.10					
Wisconsin	<u>4.79</u>	.84	<u>1.07</u>	<u>.99</u>	<u>.98</u>	.07	.05
Wyoming	2.92	.19	.13		.14	.03	
TOTALS	2.23	.41	.23	.16	.29	.03	.00

The highest percentage for each election is underlined.

".00" signifies that the party received some votes, but less than .01%.

TABLE 110   Times Parties Carried States

1828 to 1960 (Popular Vote, except when cast by legislatures.)

The following parties have carried states: Democratic, National Republican, Anti-Masonic, Whig, Republican, Constitutional Union, Populist, Roosevelt Progressive, LaFollette Progressive, States' Rights Democratic, and unpledged Democratic.

States	Dem.	Rep.	Whig	N.R.	T.R.	Pop.	S.R.	C.U.	Total
Alabama	30	2					1		33
Alaska		1							1
Arizona	7	6							13
Arkansas	29	2							31
California	10	17			1				28
Colorado	8	13				1			22
Connecticut	11	18	3	2					34
Delaware	15	13	4	2					34
Florida	20	6	1						27
Georgia	30		3						33
Hawaii	1								1
Idaho	9	8				1			18
Illinois	16	18							34
Indiana	12	20	2						34
Iowa	6	23							29
Kansas	5	19				1			25
Kentucky	22	5	5	1				1	34
Louisiana	27	3	2				1		33
Maine	6	26	1	1					34
Maryland	16	11	5	2					34
Massachusetts	8	19	5	2					34
Michigan	8	22	1		1				32
Minnesota	6	19			1				26
Mississippi	28	1	1				1		32
Missouri	26	8							34
Montana	9	9							18
Nebraska	6	18							24
Nevada	12	12				1			25
New Hampshire	11	22		1					34
New Jersey	17	12	4	1					34
New Mexico	8	5							13
New York	15	17	2						34
North Carolina	27	3	3						33
North Dakota	4	13				1			18
Ohio	10	21	3						34
Oklahoma	9	5							14
Oregon	6	20							26
Pennsylvania	10	21	2		1				34
Rhode Island	10	19	3	2					34
South Carolina	29	3					1		33
South Dakota	3	14			1				18
Tennessee	21	6	5					1	33
Texas	24	3							27
Utah	7	10							17
Vermont		27	5	1					34
Virginia	26	5						1	32
Washington	7	10			1				18
West Virginia	13	12							25
Wisconsin	8	20							29
Wyoming	7	11							18
TOTALS	16	16	2						34

The Anti-Masonic Party carried Vermont once and the LaFollette Progressives carried Wisconsin once. Unpledged Democratic slates carried Alabama and Mississippi once each, however, the Alabama vote has been included in the Democratic column above, inasmuch as the Unpledged and Democratic electors ran in a fusion arrangement.

South Carolina voted for Floyd in 1832 and Mangum in 1836; both were Democrats.

In 1860, Breckinridge carried Alabama, Arkansas, Delaware, Florida, Georgia, Louisiana,

Maryland, Mississippi, North Carolina, South Carolina, and Texas, while Douglas carried Missouri and New Jersey; both were Democrats.

Alabama voted for both Kennedy and Unpledged Democratic electors in 1960, each winning some electoral votes. The latter cast their electoral votes for Byrd.

TABLE 111   States in Which Successful Parties Received Pluralities and Majorities

(Successful parties are those which elected presidents.)

Year	DEMOCRATIC Carried	DEMOCRATIC Majority	REPUBLICAN Carried	REPUBLICAN Majority	WHIG Carried	WHIG Majority
1828	15- 9	14- 8				
1832	16- 8	14- 8				
1836	15-11	15-10			10-16	10-15
1840	7-19	6-19			19- 7	18- 7
1844	15-11	12-13			11-15	10-15
1848	15-15	7-22			15-15	11-18
1852	27- 4	23- 7			4-27	3-27
1856	19-12	15-15	11-20	8-12	1-30	1-29
1860	13-20	7-25	17-16	15- 8		
1864	3-22	3-22	22- 3	22- 3		
1868	9-25	8-25	26- 8	25- 8		
1872	6-29	6-31	29- 6	31- 6		
1876	17-21	16-21	21-17	20-17		
1880	19-19	17-21	19-19	18-20		
1884	20-18	16-22	18-20	16-22		
1888	18-20	14-24	20-18	13-25		
1892	23-21	14-26	16-28	7-36		
1896	22-23	21-24	23-22	21-24		
1900	17-28	17-28	28-17	28-17		
1904	12-33	11-34	33-12	31-14		
1908	16-30	11-35	30-16	26-20		
1912	40- 8	11-37	2-46	0-47		
1916	30-18	26-22	18-30	11-37		
1920	11-37	10-38	37-11	37-11		
1924	12-36	11-37	35-13	22-26		
1928	8-40	8-40	40- 8	39- 9		
1932	42- 6	40- 8	6-42	5-43		
1936	46- 2	45- 3	2-46	2-46		
1940	38-10	38-10	10-38	9-39		
1944	36-12	36-12	12-36	12-36		
1948	28-20	22-25	16-32	10-38		
1952	9-39	8-40	39- 9	38-10		
1956	7-41	6-42	41- 7	40- 8		
1960	23-27	21-29	26-24	26-24		

The totals of the "Carried" columns disagree with the totals of the "Majority" columns in some instances, for the following reasons:

The electoral vote was cast by the legislature in the following states in the years given: Delaware, 1828; South Carolina, 1828 to 1860 (Floyd in 1832 and Mangum in 1836, instead of regular Democratic candidates); Florida, 1868; and Colorado, 1876.

The Democrats had no opposition in Alabama in 1832.They received no votes in Colorado, Kansas, North Dakota, and Wyoming in 1892 and none in Alabama in 1948. The Republicans got none in Alabama, Arkansas, Florida, Georgia, Louisiana, Mississippi, North Carolina, Tennessee, and Texas in 1860; none in Florida in 1892; and none in South Dakota in 1912. In 1872 the Arkansas and Louisiana electoral votes, intended for the Republicans, were rejected by Congress.

For 1860, the Douglas vote is used in the Democratic columns for Missouri and New Jersey, and the Breckinridge vote for Alabama, Arkansas, Delaware, Florida, Georgia, Louisiana, Maryland, Mississippi, North Carolina, South Carolina, and Texas. The latter received majorities in Alabama, Arkansas, Florida, Mississippi, North Carolina, and Texas; Douglas got a majority in New Jersey.

Discrepancies between the electoral and popular votes occurred in the following states in the years given: The Republicans received four electoral votes and the Douglas Democrats three in New Jersey in 1860, although the latter had a popular majority. The Democrats, Republicans, and Populists received one electoral vote each in North Dakota in 1892, although the Populists had a popular plurality. The Democrats received seven electoral votes and the Republicans one in Maryland in 1904, although the latter had a popular plurality. The Democrats received six electoral votes and the Republicans two in Maryland in 1908, although the latter had a popular plurality.

TABLE 112 High Votes for Parties in Each State

States	DEMOCRATIC		REPUBLICAN		WHIG		POPULIST	
	Vote	Year	Vote	Year	Vote	Year	Vote	Year
Alabama	324,050	1960	237,981	1960	30,482	1848	85,181	1892
Alaska	29,809	1960	30,953	1960				
Arizona	176,781	1960	221,241	1960				
Arkansas	226,300	1952	186,287	1956	10,787	1856	11,831	1892
California	3,224,099	1960	3,259,722	1960	36,165	1856	25,311	1892
Colorado	330,629	1960	402,242	1960			53,584	1892
Connecticut	657,055	1960	711,837	1956	32,832	1844	809	1892
Delaware	99,590	1960	98,057	1956	6,441	1848	51	1904
Florida	748,700	1960	795,476	1960	4,843	1856	4,843	1892
Georgia	458,638	1960	274,472	1960	47,538	1848	42,937	1892
Hawaii	92,410	1960	92,295	1960				
Idaho	138,853	1960	180,707	1952			10,520	1892
Illinois	2,377,846	1960	2,623,327	1956	64,934	1852	22,207	1892
Indiana	952,358	1960	1,182,811	1956	80,901	1852	22,208	1892
Iowa	621,756	1936	808,906	1952	15,856	1852	20,595	1892
Kansas	464,520	1936	616,302	1952			163,111	1892
Kentucky	580,574	1932	602,607	1960	67,416	1856	23,500	1892
Louisiana	407,339	1960	329,047	1956	20,709	1856	2,462	1892
Maine	181,159	1960	249,238	1956	46,612	1840	2,045	1892
Maryland	565,808	1960	559,738	1956	47,462	1856	796	1892
Massachusetts	1,487,174	1960	1,393,197	1956	72,913	1840	3,348	1892
Michigan	1,687,269	1960	1,713,647	1956	33,860	1852	20,084	1892
Minnesota	779,933	1960	763,211	1952			29,313	1892
Mississippi	172,566	1952	112,966	1952	25,922	1848	10,102	1892
Missouri	1,111,043	1936	962,221	1960	48,524	1856	41,213	1892
Montana	159,690	1936	157,394	1952			7,334	1892
Nebraska	359,082	1932	421,603	1952			83,134	1892
Nevada	54,830	1960	56,049	1956			7,264	1892
New Hampshire	137,772	1960	176,519	1956	26,434	1840	293	1892
New Jersey	1,385,415	1960	1,606,942	1956	40,015	1848	3,705	1904
New Mexico	156,027	1960	153,733	1960				
New York	3,830,085	1960	4,340,340	1956	234,906	1852	16,436	1892
North Carolina	713,136	1960	655,420	1960	46,379	1840	44,732	1892
North Dakota	178,350	1932	191,712	1952			17,700	1892
Ohio	1,944,248	1960	2,262,610	1956	155,057	1844	14,852	1892
Oklahoma	516,468	1932	533,039	1960			434	1908
Oregon	367,402	1960	420,815	1952			26,965	1892
Pennsylvania	2,556,282	1960	2,585,252	1956	185,513	1848	8,714	1892
Rhode Island	258,032	1960	229,677	1956	7,626	1852	228	1892
South Carolina	198,129	1960	188,558	1960			2,410	1892
South Dakota	183,515	1932	203,857	1952			26,544	1892
Tennessee	481,453	1960	556,577	1960	66,178	1856	23,447	1892
Texas	1,167,932	1960	1,121,699	1960	15,639	1856	99,688	1892
Utah	169,248	1960	215,631	1956				
Vermont	69,186	1960	110,390	1956	32,445	1840	383	1900
Virginia	362,327	1960	404,521	1960	60,039	1856	12,275	1892
Washington	599,298	1960	629,273	1960			19,105	1892
West Virginia	502,582	1936	449,297	1956			4,166	1892
Wisconsin	802,984	1936	979,744	1952	22,240	1852	9,909	1892
Wyoming	63,331	1960	81,047	1952			7,722	1892
United States	34,227,096	1960	35,589,477	1956	1,386,629	1852	1,029,960	1892

States	SOCIALIST		GREENBACK		PROHIBITION		FARMER LABOR		COMMUNIST	
	Vote	Year	Vote	Year	Vote	Year	Vote	Year	Vote	Year
Alabama	3,029	1912	4,642	1880	3,796	1900			678	1936
Alaska										
Arizona	3,174	1916			1,153	1916	15	1920	256	1932
Arkansas	8,153	1912	4,079	1880	2,015	1916			317	1928
California	79,201	1912	3,395	1880	27,698	1916			13,586	1940
Colorado	16,418	1912	1,953	1884	5,559	1908	3,016	1920	787	1932
Connecticut	20,480	1932	1,685	1884	4,236	1888	1,947	1920	1,364	1932
Delaware	1,376	1932	120	1880	986	1920	93	1920	133	1932
Florida	5,353	1916			5,498	1924			3,704	1928
Georgia	1,028	1912	969	1880	5,613	1896			64	1928
Hawaii										
Idaho	11,960	1912			1,986	1908	6	1920	491	1932
Illinois	81,278	1912	26,358	1880	34,770	1904	49,630	1920	15,582	1932
Indiana	36,931	1912	12,986	1880	23,496	1904	16,499	1920	2,187	1932
Iowa	20,467	1932	32,701	1880	11,601	1904	10,321	1920	4,037	1924
Kansas	26,779	1912	19,851	1880	12,882	1916			320	1928
Kentucky	11,647	1912	11,499	1880	6,609	1904			293	1928
Louisiana	5,249	1912	439	1880	338	1884				
Maine	2,541	1912	4,480	1880	3,062	1892			411	1940
Maryland	10,489	1932	818	1880	5,922	1896	1,645	1920	1,274	1940
Massachusetts	34,305	1932	24,433	1884	10,026	1884			4,821	1932
Michigan	39,205	1932	41,390	1884	20,945	1888	10,480	1920	9,318	1932
Minnesota	56,106	1920	3,587	1884	15,311	1888	5,731	1932	6,101	1932
Mississippi	2,061	1912	5,797	1880	995	1892				
Missouri	28,466	1912	35,135	1880	7,191	1904	3,291	1920	568	1932
Montana	10,885	1912			827	1908	12,204	1920	1,775	1932
Nebraska	10,185	1912	3,950	1880	9,429	1888				
Nevada	3,313	1912	26	1884	348	1916				
New Hampshire	1,980	1912	552	1884	1,593	1888			264	1932
New Jersey	42,998	1932	3,496	1884	10,593	1948	2,264	1920	6,508	1940
New Mexico	2,859	1912			777	1960	1,104	1920	158	1928
New York	203,201	1920	17,004	1884	38,193	1892	18,413	1920	35,610	1936
North Carolina	5,591	1932	1,126	1880	2,789	1888			11	1936
North Dakota	8,282	1920			1,553	1908			936	1928
Ohio	90,144	1912	6,456	1880	26,012	1892			7,231	1932
Oklahoma	45,527	1916			3,027	1940	1,283	1928		
Oregon	15,450	1932	726	1884	4,729	1916			1,681	1932
Pennsylvania	91,119	1932	20,668	1880	42,612	1920	15,642	1920	5,658	1932
Rhode Island	4,351	1920	422	1884	1,654	1892			546	1932
South Carolina	164	1912	566	1880	365	1944				
South Dakota	4,662	1912			4,039	1908	34,707	1920	364	1932
Tennessee	3,504	1912	5,917	1880	5,975	1888			319	1936
Texas	25,743	1912	27,405	1880	4,749	1888			253	1936
Utah	9,023	1912			209	1900	4,475	1920	947	1932
Vermont	1,533	1932	1,215	1880	1,752	1884			411	1940
Virginia	2,382	1932			2,798	1892	243	1920	174	1928
Washington	40,134	1912			9,810	1912	77,246	1920	2,972	1932
West Virginia	15,336	1912	9,079	1880	5,139	1908			444	1932
Wisconsin	85,041	1920	7,986	1880	14,415	1888			3,773	1924
Wyoming	2,829	1932			530	1892	2,180	1920	180	1932
United States	919,801	1920	308,649	1880	271,111	1892	265,421	1920	102,991	1932

TABLE 112 High Votes for Parties in Each State (continued)

States	SOCIALIST LABOR Vote	Year	SOCIALIST WORKERS Vote	Year	MISCELLANEOUS PARTIES Vote		Year
Alabama					171,443	States' Rights Demo.	1948
Alaska							
Arizona	469	1960			17,210	LaFollette	1924
Arkansas					40,068	States' Rights Demo.	1948
California	1,611	1896	133	1948	424,649	LaFollette	1924
Colorado	3,308	1956	572	1960	72,306	T. Roosevelt	1912
Connecticut	2,287	1932	606	1948	42,416	LaFollette	1924
Delaware	242	1952			8,886	T. Roosevelt	1912
Florida					89,755	States' Rights Demo.	1948
Georgia					85,055	States' Rights Demo.	1948
Hawaii							
Idaho					54,160	LaFollette	1924
Illinois	10,560	1960			432,027	LaFollette	1924
Indiana	3,130	1912			162,007	T. Roosevelt	1912
Iowa	4,274	1948	634	1960	272,243	LaFollette	1924
Kansas					120,210	T. Roosevelt	1912
Kentucky	1,499	1924			102,766	T. Roosevelt	1912
Louisiana					204,290	States' Rights Demo.	1948
Maine	406	1924			48,495	T. Roosevelt	1912
Maryland	1,305	1936			57,789	T. Roosevelt	1912
Massachusetts	5,573	1956			142,375	T. Roosevelt	1912
Michigan	5,330	1924	4,347	1960	214,584	T. Roosevelt	1912
Minnesota	3,828	1920	3,077	1960	339,192	LaFollette	1924
Mississippi					167,538	States' Rights Demo.	1948
Missouri	2,164	1920			124,371	T. Roosevelt	1912
Montana	247	1924	391	1960	65,876	LaFollette	1924
Nebraska	186	1896			106,701	LaFollette	1924
Nevada					9,769	LaFollette	1924
New Hampshire	228	1896			24,124	National Republican	1828
New Jersey	6,939	1944	11,402	1960	145,674	T. Roosevelt	1912
New Mexico	570	1960			9,543	LaFollette	1924
New York	17,958	1892	14,319	1960	509,559	Wallace	1948
North Carolina					70,144	T. Roosevelt	1912
North Dakota			158	1960	89,922	LaFollette	1924
Ohio	3,025	1924			357,948	LaFollette	1924
Oklahoma	5,234	1924			41,141	LaFollette	1924
Oregon	2,487	1940			68,403	LaFollette	1924
Pennsylvania	7,447	1956	2,678	1960	447,426	T. Roosevelt	1912
Rhode Island	1,423	1900			19,569	Union	1936
South Carolina					102,607	States' Rights Demo.	1948
South Dakota					75,355	LaFollette	1924
Tennessee					73,826	States' Rights Demo.	1948
Texas	442	1912			135,439	Texas Regulars	1944
Utah	510	1912	100	1960	32,662	LaFollette	1924
Vermont					24,365	National Republican	1828
Virginia	1,160	1952			74,701	Constitutional Union	1860
Washington	10,895	1960	705	1960	150,727	LaFollette	1924
West Virginia					79,112	T. Roosevelt	1912
Wisconsin	1,882	1940	1,792	1960	453,678	LaFollette	1924
Wyoming	56	1948			25,174	LaFollette	1924
United States	47,522	1960	40,175	1960	4,831,470	LaFollette	1924

TABLE 113 **High Percentage for Parties in Each State**

1828 to 1960

States	Dem.	Year	Rep.	Year	Whig	Year	Pop.	Year
Alabama	89.84	1828	53.19	1872	49.29	1848	36.60	1892
Alaska	49.06	1960	50.94	1960				
Arizona	69.85	1936	60.99	1956				
Arkansas	85.96	1932	53.73	1868	44.93	1848	8.06	1892
California	66.97	1936	66.24	1920	46.51	1852	9.39	1892
Colorado	84.96	1896	64.72	1928			57.07	1892
Connecticut	55.32	1936	63.73	1956	55.37	1840	.49	1892
Delaware	59.02	1868	65.03	1928	54.99	1840	.12	1904
Florida	84.78	1892	57.20	1956	58.36	1848	13.62	1892
Georgia	100.00	1832	43.77	1872	55.78	1840	19.37	1892
Hawaii	50.03	1960	49.97	1960				
Idaho	78.10	1896	66.02	1920			53.65	1892
Illinois	72.27	1832	67.81	1920	48.83	1840	2.54	1892
Indiana	67.10	1832	59.90	1956	55.97	1836	4.01	1892
Iowa	57.69	1932	70.91	1920	45.61	1848	4.65	1892
Kansas	53.67	1936	78.61	1864			50.20	1892
Kentucky	74.55	1868	59.33	1928	64.20	1840	6.89	1892
Louisiana	92.97	1932	55.69	1872	59.73	1840	2.08	1892
Maine	60.04	1836	72.03	1924	50.13	1840	1.76	1892
Maryland	67.20	1868	60.04	1956	54.64	1856	.37	1892
Massachusetts	60.22	1960	72.22	1864	57.43	1840	.86	1892
Michigan	64.84	1836	75.37	1924	51.67	1840	4.28	1892
Minnesota	61.84	1936	73.95	1904			10.97	1892
Mississippi	100.00	1832	63.47	1872	53.45	1840	19.14	1892
Missouri	100.00	1832	70.17	1864	45.48	1856	7.62	1892
Montana	79.93	1896	61.13	1920			16.55	1892
Nebraska	62.98	1932	70.12	1872			41.52	1892
Nevada	81.21	1896	61.45	1952			66.78	1892
New Hampshire	75.04	1836	68.74	1896	44.63	1840	.33	1892
New Jersey	59.54	1936	67.60	1920	51.75	1840	.86	1904
New Mexico	62.72	1932	59.01	1928				
New York	58.85	1936	64.56	1920	51.18	1840	1.23	1892
North Carolina	84.49	1832	57.48	1872	57.85	1840	15.92	1892
North Dakota	69.59	1932	77.79	1920			49.01	1892
Ohio	58.00	1936	64.89	1928	54.10	1840	1.75	1892
Oklahoma	73.30	1932	63.72	1928			.17	1908
Oregon	64.42	1936	67.06	1904			34.35	1892
Pennsylvania	66.66	1828	67.99	1904	50.42	1848	.87	1892
Rhode Island	63.63	1960	71.94	1872	61.22	1840	.43	1892
South Carolina	98.57	1936	75.95	1872			3.42	1892
South Dakota	63.62	1932	71.09	1904			37.64	1892
Tennessee	95.24	1832	68.33	1868	58.06	1836	8.77	1892
Texas	88.07	1932	55.27	1956	33.41	1856	23.60	1892
Utah	82.70	1896	64.56	1956				
Vermont	44.93	1940	80.10	1896	63.90	1840	.08	1892
Virginia	74.59	1832	56.32	1952	49.20	1848	4.20	1892
Washington	66.38	1936	69.95	1904			21.72	1892
West Virginia	60.56	1936	68.95	1864			2.44	1892
Wisconsin	63.80	1936	70.65	1920	35.10	1848	2.67	1892
Wyoming	60.58	1936	66.71	1904			46.22	1892
United States	60.80	1936	60.31	1920	52.87	1840	8.53	1892

The Indiana Whig vote was cast for Harrison. The Tennessee Whig vote was cast for White.
According to Stanwood, the Democrats had no opposition in Missouri in 1832, but according to the *Tribune Almanac* and the *American Almanac*, the figure shown for the Democrats for that year represents their majority in that state.

The highest percentage for each party is underlined.

1828 to 1960

States	Soc.	Year	Grnb.	Year	Proh.	Year	F. L.	Year
Alabama	2.57	1912	3.05	1880	2.37	1900		
Alaska								
Arizona	13.33	1912			1.99	1916	.02	1920
Arkansas	6.57	1912	3.80	1880	1.20	1916		
California	11.76	1912	2.07	1880	3.47	1912		
Colorado	6.15	1912	2.93	1884	2.39	1888	1.03	1920
Connecticut	5.28	1912	1.23	1884	2.75	1888	.53	1920
Delaware	1.22	1932	.41	1880	1.56	1896	.10	1920
Florida	9.26	1912			6.01	1916		
Georgia	.85	1912	.62	1880	3.44	1896		
Hawaii								
Idaho	11.31	1912			2.04	1908	.00	1920
Illinois	7.09	1912	4.24	1880	3.23	1904	2.37	1920
Indiana	5.64	1912	2.76	1880	3.44	1904	1.31	1920
Iowa	3.44	1912	10.11	1880	2.39	1904	1.15	1920
Kansas	7.33	1912	9.87	1880	2.22	1904		
Kentucky	2.57	1912	4.30	1880	1.89	1892		
Louisiana	6.61	1912	.42	1880	.11	1888		
Maine	2.19	1904	3.11	1880	2.63	1892		
Maryland	2.07	1920	.47	1880	2.76	1892	.38	1920
Massachusetts	3.25	1920	8.05	1884	3.30	1884		
Michigan	4.21	1912	10.29	1884	4.57	1884	1.00	1920
Minnesota	8.23	1912	2.17	1880	5.82	1888	.57	1932
Mississippi	3.19	1912	4.98	1880	1.89	1892		
Missouri	4.07	1912	8.84	1880	1.12	1904	.25	1920
Montana	13.64	1912			1.24	1892	6.82	1920
Nebraska	4.08	1912	4.52	1880	4.65	1888		
Nevada	16.47	1912	.20	1884	1.04	1916		
New Hampshire	2.25	1912	.65	1884	1.86	1884		
New Jersey	3.67	1912	1.34	1884	2.61	1888	.25	1920
New Mexico	5.79	1912			.25	1960	1.05	1920
New York	7.01	1920	1.46	1884	2.86	1892	.64	1920
North Carolina	.79	1932	.47	1880	.98	1888		
North Dakota	8.05	1912			2.49	1892		
Ohio	8.69	1912	.89	1880	3.06	1892		
Oklahoma	16.61	1912			.86	1912	.21	1928
Oregon	9.74	1912	1.71	1876	4.22	1904		
Pennsylvania	6.85	1912	2.36	1880	2.90	1908	.84	1920
Rhode Island	2.63	1912	1.29	1884	3.11	1892		
South Carolina	.33	1912	.33	1880	.35	1944		
South Dakota	4.01	1912			3.52	1908	19.04	1920
Tennessee	1.38	1912	2.45	1880	1.96	1888		
Texas	8.44	1912	11.34	1880	1.83	1904		
Utah	8.03	1912			.22	1900	3.07	1920
Vermont	1.66	1904	1.86	1880	2.95	1884		
Virginia	.80	1932			1.06	1904	.12	1920
Washington	12.43	1912			3.04	1912	19.37	1920
West Virginia	5.70	1912	8.05	1880	1.99	1908		
Wisconsin	12.05	1920	2.99	1880	4.06	1888		
Wyoming	6.53	1912			3.17	1892	3.88	1920
United States	5.99	1912	3.35	1880	2.25	1892	.99	1920

The highest percentage for each election is underlined.

".00" signifies that the party received some votes, but less than .01%.

States	Comm.	Year	S. L.	Year	S. W.	Year	Misc. Parties		Year
Alabama	.25	1936					79.75	S. R. D.	1948
Alaska									
Arizona	.22	1932	.12	1960			29.29	T. R.	1912
Arkansas	.16	1928					37.17	C. U.	1860
California	.42	1940	.54	1896	.00	1948	42.11	T. R.	1912
Colorado	.17	1928	.50	1956	.08	1960	27.09	T. R.	1912
Connecticut	.23	1932	.70	1896	.07	1948	75.68	N. R.	1828
Delaware	.12	1932	.14	1952			50.48	N. R.	1832
Florida	1.46	1928					37.90	C. U.	1860
Georgia	.03	1928					40.31	C. U.	1860
Hawaii									
Idaho	.26	1932					36.52	LaF	1924
Illinois	.46	1932	.44	1904			33.72	T. R.	1912
Indiana	.14	1932	.48	1912			43.40	N. R.	1828
Iowa	.41	1924	.41	1948	.05	1960	32.83	T. R.	1912
Kansas	.04	1928					32.89	T. R.	1912
Kentucky	.03	1928	.21	1912			54.49	N. R.	1832
Louisiana							49.07	S. R. D.	1948
Maine	.13	1940	.29	1892			59.86	N. R.	1828
Maryland	.20	1932	.29	1916			50.96	N. R.	1828
Massachusetts	.31	1932	.63	1900			83.21	N. R.	1828
Michigan	.56	1932	.46	1924	.13	1960	38.95	T. R.	1912
Minnesota	.61	1932	.66	1912	.20	1960	41.26	LaF	1924
Mississippi							87.17	S. R. D.	1948
Missouri	.04	1932	.26	1904			35.27	C. U.	1860
Montana	.82	1932	.32	1904	.14	1960	37.77	LaF	1924
Nebraska			.08	1896			29.14	T. R.	1912
Nevada							36.29	LaF	1924
New Hampshire	.13	1932	.27	1896			53.55	N. R.	1828
New Jersey	.33	1940	1.07	1896	.41	1960	51.98	N. R.	1828
New Mexico	.13	1928	.18	1960			16.90	T. R.	1912
New York	.64	1936	1.34	1892	.20	1960	49.03	N. R.	1828
North Carolina	.00	1936					46.75	C. U.	1860
North Dakota	.39	1928			.06	1960	45.17	LaF	1924
Ohio	.28	1932	.26	1904			48.40	N. R.	1828
Oklahoma			.99	1924			7.79	LaF	1924
Oregon	.46	1932	.64	1920			27.44	T. R.	1912
Pennsylvania	.20	1932	.25	1900	.06	1948	42.31	A. M.	1832
Rhode Island	.21	1932	2.52	1900			77.03	N. R.	1828
South Carolina							71.97	S. R. D.	1948
South Dakota	.13	1932					50.55	T. R.	1912
Tennessee	.07	1936					47.59	C. U.	1860
Texas	.03	1936	.18	1904			24.51	C. U.	1860
Utah	.46	1932	.45	1912	.03	1960	21.51	T. R.	1912
Vermont	.29	1940					74.40	N. R.	1828
Virginia	.06	1928	.19	1952			44.65	C. U.	1860
Washington	.48	1932	1.10	1904	.06	1960	35.76	LaF	1924
West Virginia	.06	1928					29.42	T. R.	1912
Wisconsin	.45	1924	.29	1896	.10	1960	53.96	LaF	1924
Wyoming	.19	1932	.06	1948			31.51	LaF	1924
United States	.26	1932	.26	1896	.06	1960	43.96	N. R.	1828

Extended Socialist Workers percentages: California .003, Washington .011+.

The highest percentage for each party is underlined.
".00" signifies that the party received some votes, but less than .01%.

TABLE 114   High Votes for Winners and Losers of States

States	Winners	Party	Year	Losers	Party	Year
Alabama	324,050	Dem.	1960	237,981	Rep.	1960
Alaska	30,953	Rep.	1960	29,809	Dem.	1960
Arizona	221,241	Rep.	1960	176,781	Dem.	1960
Arkansas	226,300	Dem.	1952	186,287	Rep.	1956
California	3,259,722	Rep.	1960	3,224,099	Dem.	1960
Colorado	402,242	Rep.	1960	330,629	Dem.	1960
Connecticut	711,837	Rep.	1956	565,813	Rep.	1960
Delaware	99,590	Dem.	1960	96,373	Rep.	1960
Florida	795,476	Rep.	1960	748,700	Dem.	1960
Georgia	458,638	Dem.	1960	274,472	Rep.	1960
Hawaii	92,410	Dem.	1960	92,295	Rep.	1960
Idaho	180,707	Rep.	1952	138,853	Dem.	1960
Illinois	2,623,327	Rep.	1956	2,368,988	Rep.	1960
Indiana	1,182,811	Rep.	1956	952,358	Dem.	1960
Iowa	808,906	Rep.	1952	578,800	Dem.	1940
Kansas	616,302	Rep.	1952	397,727	Rep.	1936
Kentucky	602,607	Rep.	1960	521,855	Dem.	1960
Louisiana	407,339	Dem.	1960	306,925	Rep.	1952
Maine	249,238	Rep.	1956	181,159	Dem.	1960
Maryland	565,808	Dem.	1960	489,538	Rep.	1960
Massachusetts	1,487,174	Dem.	1960	1,083,525	Dem.	1952
Michigan	1,713,647	Rep.	1956	1,620,428	Rep.	1960
Minnesota	779,933	Dem.	1960	757,915	Rep.	1960
Mississippi	172,566	Dem.	1952	112,966	Rep.	1952
Missouri	1,111,043	Dem.	1936	962,221	Rep.	1960
Montana	159,690	Dem.	1936	134,891	Dem.	1960
Nebraska	421,603	Rep.	1952	263,677	Dem.	1940
Nevada	56,049	Rep.	1956	52,387	Rep.	1960
New Hampshire	176,519	Rep.	1956	137,772	Dem.	1960
New Jersey	1,606,942	Rep.	1956	1,363,324	Rep.	1960
New Mexico	156,027	Dem.	1960	153,733	Rep.	1960
New York	4,340,340	Rep.	1956	3,446,420	Rep.	1960
North Carolina	713,136	Dem.	1960	655,420	Rep.	1960
North Dakota	191,712	Rep.	1952	124,036	Dem.	1940
Ohio	2,262,610	Rep.	1956	1,944,248	Dem.	1960
Oklahoma	533,039	Rep.	1960	430,939	Dem.	1952
Oregon	420,815	Rep.	1952	367,402	Dem.	1960
Pennsylvania	2,585,252	Rep.	1956	2,439,956	Rep.	1960
Rhode Island	258,032	Dem.	1960	203,293	Dem.	1952
South Carolina	198,129	Dem.	1960	188,558	Rep.	1960
South Dakota	203,857	Rep.	1952	131,362	Dem.	1940
Tennessee	556,577	Rep.	1960	481,453	Dem.	1960
Texas	1,167,932	Dem.	1960	1,121,699	Rep.	1960
Utah	215,631	Rep.	1956	169,248	Dem.	1960
Vermont	110,390	Rep.	1956	69,186	Dem.	1960
Virginia	404,521	Rep.	1960	362,327	Dem.	1960
Washington	629,273	Rep.	1960	599,298	Dem.	1960
West Virginia	502,582	Dem.	1936	419,970	Rep.	1952
Wisconsin	979,744	Rep.	1952	830,805	Dem.	1960
Wyoming	81,047	Rep.	1952	63,331	Dem.	1960
United States	35,589,477	Rep.	1956	34,108,647	Rep.	1960

TABLE 115   High and Low Percentages for Winners and Losers of States

Winners

States	High	Year	Party	Low	Year	Party
Alabama	89.84	1828	Democratic	50.71	1848	Democratic
Alaska	50.94	1960	Republican	50.94	1960	Republican
Arizona	69.85	1936	Democratic	41.26	1924	Republican
Arkansas	85.96	1932	Democratic	50.19	1960	Democratic
California	66.97	1936	Democratic	32.96	1860	Republican
Colorado	84.96	1896	Democratic	42.80	1912	Democratic
Connecticut	82.40	1824	J. Q. Adams	39.16	1912	Democratic
Delaware	65.03	1928	Republican	45.62	1860	Breckinridge
Florida	84.78	1892	Democratic	48.82	1948	Democratic
Georgia	100.00	1832	Democratic	48.81	1860	Breckinridge
Hawaii	50.03	1960	Democratic	50.03	1960	Democratic
Idaho	78.10	1896	Democratic	32.08	1912	Democratic
Illinois	72.27	1832	Democratic	35.34	1912	Democratic
Indiana	67.10	1832	Democratic	43.07	1912	Democratic
Iowa	70.91	1920	Republican	37.60	1912	Democratic
Kansas	78.61	1864	Republican	39.31	1912	Democratic
Kentucky	74.55	1868	Democratic	45.18	1860	Constitutional Union
Louisiana	92.97	1932	Democratic	44.90	1860	Breckinridge
Maine	81.50	1824	J. Q. Adams	39.43	1912	Democratic
Maryland	67.20	1868	Democratic	44.06	1824	J. Q. Adams
Massachusetts	83.21	1828	Nat'l Rep.	35.61	1912	Democratic
Michigan	75.37	1924	Republican	38.95	1912	T. Roosevelt
Minnesota	73.95	1904	Republican	37.66	1912	T. Roosevelt
Mississippi	100.00	1832	Democratic	38.99	1960	Unpledged Democratic
Missouri	100.00	1832	Democratic	35.53	1860	Douglas
Montana	79.93	1896	Democratic	35.00	1912	Democratic
Nebraska	70.12	1872	Republican	43.57	1892	Republican
Nevada	81.21	1896	Democratic	39.70	1912	Democratic
New Hampshire	93.59	1824	J. Q. Adams	39.48	1912	Democratic
New Jersey	67.60	1920	Republican	40.19	1912	Democratic
New Mexico	62.72	1932	Democratic	48.52	1924	Republican
New York	64.56	1920	Republican	41.28	1912	Democratic
North Carolina	84.49	1832	Democratic	47.36	1892	Democratic
North Dakota	77.79	1920	Republican	34.14	1912	Democratic
Ohio	64.89	1928	Republican	38.49	1824	Clay
Oklahoma	73.30	1932	Democratic	46.84	1912	Democratic
Oregon	67.06	1904	Republican	34.34	1912	Democratic
Pennsylvania	76.23	1824	Jackson	36.67	1912	T. Roosevelt
Rhode Island	91.47	1824	J. Q. Adams	39.04	1912	Democratic
South Carolina	98.57	1936	Democratic	45.37	1956	Democratic
South Dakota	71.09	1904	Republican	49.48	1892	Republican
Tennessee	97.45	1824	Jackson	47.59	1860	Constitutional Union
Texas	88.07	1932	Democratic	50.52	1960	Democratic
Utah	82.70	1896	Democratic	37.46	1912	Republican
Vermont	80.10	1896	Republican	37.13	1912	Republican
Virginia	74.59	1832	Democratic	44.65	1860	Constitutional Union
Washington	69.95	1904	Republican	35.22	1912	T. Roosevelt
West Virginia	68.95	1864	Republican	42.09	1912	Democratic
Wisconsin	70.65	1920	Republican	38.30	1848	Democratic
Wyoming	66.71	1904	Republican	36.20	1912	Democratic
United States	60.80	1936	Democratic	39.79	1860	Republican

Extreme highs and lows are underlined. Where there were several losers, the runner-up is used.

High and Low Percentages for Winners and Losers of States (continued)

Losers

States	High	Year	Party	Low	Year	Party
Alabama	49.29	1848	Whig	10.16	1828	National Republican
Alaska	49.06	1960	Democratic	49.06	1960	Democratic
Arizona	44.36	1960	Democratic	26.93	1936	Republican
Arkansas	47.83	1872	Democratic	12.91	1932	Republican
California	49.76	1868	Democratic	24.29	1920	Democratic
Colorado	48.37	1940	Democratic	13.84	1896	Republican
Connecticut	49.31	1836	Whig	17.60	1824	Crawford
Delaware	49.66	1852	Whig	24.03	1860	Constitutional Union
Florida	49.01	1876	Democratic	9.26	1912	Socialist
Georgia	48.79	1844	Whig	3.21	1828	National Republican
Hawaii	49.97	1960	Republican	49.97	1960	Republican
Idaho	48.07	1944	Republican	21.30	1896	Republican
Illinois	49.80	1960	Republican	23.36	1924	Democratic
Indiana	49.03	1940	Democratic	24.75	1912	T. Roosevelt
Iowa	47.62	1940	Democratic	25.46	1920	Democratic
Kansas	48.40	1892	Republican	21.39	1864	Democratic
Kentucky	49.84	1952	Republican	25.45	1868	Republican
Louisiana	48.70	1844	Whig	6.95	1916	Republican
Maine	49.67	1840	Democratic	18.50	1824	Crawford
Maryland	49.99	1832	Democratic	24.91	1912	T. Roosevelt
Massachusetts	49.15	1928	Republican	16.79	1828	Democratic
Michigan	49.52	1940	Democratic	13.13	1924	Democratic
Minnesota	49.16	1960	Republican	18.84	1904	Democratic
Mississippi	49.41	1848	Whig	2.74	1936	Republican
Missouri	49.87	1956	Republican	29.13	1828	National Republican
Montana	48.60	1960	Democratic	19.72	1896	Republican
Nebraska	47.60	1908	Republican	23.44	1904	Democratic
Nevada	48.84	1960	Republican	18.79	1896	Republican
New Hampshire	49.06	1916	Republican	6.41	1824	Crawford
New Jersey	49.48	1836	Democratic	27.40	1924	Democratic
New Mexico	49.41	1960	Republican	35.76	1932	Republican
New York	49.54	1864	Democratic	26.43	1848	Free Soil
North Carolina	49.53	1852	Whig	15.51	1832	National Republican
North Dakota	49.20	1916	Republican	18.19	1920	Democratic
Ohio	49.82	1944	Democratic	23.70	1924	Democratic
Oklahoma	45.41	1952	Democratic	26.70	1932	Republican
Oregon	49.63	1868	Republican	19.43	1904	Democratic
Pennsylvania	49.90	1840	Democratic	11.49	1824	John Quincy Adams
Rhode Island	49.55	1928	Republican	8.53	1824	Crawford
South Carolina	49.74	1876	Democratic	1.43	1936	Republican
South Dakota	49.48	1896	Republican	19.72	1920	Democratic
Tennessee	49.95	1844	Democratic	1.51	1824	Crawford
Texas	48.52	1960	Republican	9.46	1912	T. Roosevelt
Utah	48.30	1900	Democratic	17.27	1896	Republican
Vermont	44.93	1940	Democratic	15.67	1924	Democratic
Virginia	49.50	1872	Democratic	17.00	1912	Republican
Washington	45.44	1956	Democratic	19.36	1904	Democratic
West Virginia	49.03	1888	Republican	29.41	1912	T. Roosevelt
Wisconsin	48.57	1944	Democratic	16.07	1920	Democratic
Wyoming	48.88	1896	Republican	29.08	1904	Democratic
United States	49.55	1960	Republican	27.42	1912	T. Roosevelt

Extreme highs and lows are underlined. Where there were several losers, the runner-up is used.

TABLE 116   High Votes and Percentages for "Third" Parties

(Includes parties other than Democratic, Republican, Whig, and National Republican.)

States	Vote	Parties	Year	Pct.	Parties	Year
Alabama	171,443	S. R. Democratic	1948	79.75	S. R. Democratic	1948
Arizona	17,210	LaFollette	1924	29.29	T. Roosevelt	1912
Arkansas	40,068	S. R. Democratic	1948	37.17	Constitutional Union	1860
California	424,649	LaFollette	1924	42.11	T. Roosevelt	1912
Colorado	72,306	T. Roosevelt	1912	57.07	Populist	1892
Connecticut	42,416	LaFollette	1924	20.51	Breckinridge	1860
Delaware	8,886	T. Roosevelt	1912	24.03	Constitutional Union	1860
Florida	89,755	S. R. Democratic	1948	37.90	Constitutional Union	1860
Georgia	85,055	S. R. Democratic	1948	40.31	Constitutional Union	1860
Idaho	54,160	LaFollette	1924	53.65	Populist	1892
Illinois	432,027	LaFollette	1924	33.72	T. Roosevelt	1912
Indiana	162,007	T. Roosevelt	1912	24.75	T. Roosevelt	1912
Iowa	272,243	LaFollette	1924	32.83	T. Roosevelt	1912
Kansas	163,111	Populist	1892	50.20	Populist	1892
Kentucky	102,766	T. Roosevelt	1912	45.18	Constitutional Union	1860
Louisiana	204,290	S. R. Democratic	1948	49.07	S. R. Democratic	1948
Maine	48,495	T. Roosevelt	1912	37.41	T. Roosevelt	1912
Maryland	57,789	T. Roosevelt	1912	44.91	Constitutional Union	1860
Massachusetts	142,375	T. Roosevelt	1912	29.08	T. Roosevelt	1912
Michigan	214,584	T. Roosevelt	1912	38.95	T. Roosevelt	1912
Minnesota	339,192	LaFollette	1924	41.26	LaFollette	1924
Mississippi	167,538	S. R. Democratic	1948	87.17	S. R. Democratic	1948
Missouri	124,371	T. Roosevelt	1912	35.27	Constitutional Union	1860
Montana	65,876	LaFollette	1924	37.77	LaFollette	1924
Nebraska	106,701	LaFollette	1924	41.52	Populist	1892
Nevada	9,769	LaFollette	1924	66.78	Populist	1892
New Hampshire	17,794	T. Roosevelt	1912	20.23	T. Roosevelt	1912
New Jersey	145,674	T. Roosevelt	1912	33.61	T. Roosevelt	1912
New Mexico	9,543	LaFollette	1924	16.90	T. Roosevelt	1912
New York	509,559	Wallace	1948	26.43	Free Soil	1848
North Carolina	70,144	T. Roosevelt	1912	46.75	Constitutional Union	1860
North Dakota	89,922	LaFollette	1924	49.01	Populist	1892
Ohio	357,948	LaFollette	1924	22.16	T. Roosevelt	1912
Oklahoma	45,527	Socialist	1916	16.61	Socialist	1912
Oregon	68,403	LaFollette	1924	34.35	Populist	1892
Pennsylvania	447,426	T. Roosevelt	1912	36.67	T. Roosevelt	1912
Rhode Island	19,569	Union	1936	21.67	T. Roosevelt	1912
South Carolina	102,607	S. R. Democratic	1948	71.97	S. R. Democratic	1948
South Dakota	75,355	LaFollette	1924	50.55	LaFollette	1912
Tennessee	73,826	S. R. Democratic	1948	47.59	Constitutional Union	1860
Texas	135,439	Texas Regulars	1944	24.51	Constitutional Union	1860
Utah	32,662	LaFollette	1924	21.51	T. Roosevelt	1912
Vermont	22,132	T. Roosevelt	1912	40.79	Anti-Masonic	1832
Virginia	74,701	Constitutional Union	1860	44.65	Constitutional Union	1860
Washington	150,727	LaFollette	1924	35.76	LaFollette	1924
West Virginia	79,112	T. Roosevelt	1912	29.42	T. Roosevelt	1912
Wisconsin	453,678	LaFollette	1924	53.96	LaFollette	1924
Wyoming	25,174	LaFollette	1924	46.22	Populist	1892
United States	4,831,470	LaFollette	1924	27.42	T. Roosevelt	1912

Underlined years indicate that the "third" party carried the state.

The highest percentage for the nation is underlined.

TABLE 117   High Votes for Parties that Were Third within a State

States	Vote	Party	Year	Winner	Runner-Up
Alabama	20,323	Constitution	1956	Democratic	Republican
Arizona	17,210	LaFollette	1924	Republican	Democratic
Arkansas	40,068	S. R. Demo.	1948	Democratic	Republican
California	190,381	Wallace	1948	Democratic	Republican
Colorado	69,945	LaFollette	1924	Republican	Democratic
Connecticut	42,416	LaFollette	1924	Republican	Democratic
Delaware	8,886	T. Roosevelt	1912	Democratic	Republican
Florida	89,755	S. R. Demo.	1948	Democratic	Republican
Georgia	76,691	Republican	1948	Democratic	S. R. Demo
Idaho	25,527	T. Roosevelt	1912	Democratic	Republican
Illinois	432,027	LaFollette	1924	Republican	Democratic
Indiana	151,267	Republican	1912	Democratic	T. Roosevelt
Iowa	162,600	Democratic	1924	Republican	LaFollette
Kansas	98,461	LaFollette	1924	Republican	Democratic
Kentucky	102,766	T. Roosevelt	1912	Democratic	Republican
Louisiana	169,572	States Rights	1960	Democratic	Republican
Maine	26,545	Republican	1912	Democratic	T. Roosevelt
Maryland	54,956	Republican	1912	Democratic	T. Roosevelt
Massachusetts	142,375	T. Roosevelt	1912	Democratic	Republican
Michigan	150,751	Democratic	1912	T. Roosevelt	Republican
Minnesota	74,296	Union	1936	Democratic	Republican
Mississippi	73,561	Republican	1960	Unpledged Demo.	Democratic
Missouri	124,371	T. Roosevelt	1912	Democratic	Republican
Montana	33,805	Democratic	1924	Republican	LaFollette
Nebraska	106,701	LaFollette	1924	Republican	Democratic
Nevada	5,909	Democratic	1924	Republican	LaFollette
New Hampshire	17,794	T. Roosevelt	1912	Democratic	Republican
New Jersey	109,964	LaFollette	1924	Republican	Democratic
New Mexico	9,543	LaFollette	1924	Republican	Democratic
New York	509,559	Wallace	1948	Republican	Democratic
North Carolina	69,652	S. R. Demo.	1948	Democratic	Republican
North Dakota	36,708	Union	1936	Democratic	Republican
Ohio	357,948	LaFollette	1924	Republican	Democratic
Oklahoma	45,527	Socialist	1916	Democratic	Republican
Oregon	67,589	Democratic	1924	Republican	LaFollette
Pennsylvania	307,567	LaFollette	1924	Republican	Democratic
Rhode Island	19,569	Union	1936	Democratic	Republican
South Carolina	75,700	Republican	1956	Democratic	States Rights
South Dakota	34,707	Farmer Labor	1920	Republican	Democratic
Tennessee	73,826	S. R. Demo.	1948	Democratic	Republican
Texas	135,439	Texas Regulars	1944	Democratic	Republican
Utah	32,662	LaFollette	1924	Republican	Democratic
Vermont	15,354	Democratic	1912	Republican	T. Roosevelt
Virginia	43,393	S. R. Demo.	1948	Democratic	Republican
Washington	77,246	Farmer Labor	1920	Republican	Democratic
West Virginia	56,754	Republican	1912	Democratic	T. Roosevelt
Wisconsin	85,041	Socialist	1920	Republican	Democratic
Wyoming	12,868	Democratic	1924	Republican	LaFollette
United States	4,831,470	LaFollette	1924	Republican	Democratic

TABLE 118   High Percentages for Parties That Were Third within a State

States	Pct.	Party	Year	Winner	Runner-Up
Alabama	15.11	Douglas	1860	Breckinridge	Constitutional Union
Arizona	23.27	LaFollette	1924	Republican	Democratic
Arkansas	17.47	T. Roosevelt	1912	Democratic	Republican
California	28.89	Breckinridge	1860	Republican	Douglas
Colorado	21.88	Republican	1912	Democratic	T. Roosevelt
Connecticut	20.51	Breckinridge	1860	Republican	Douglas
Delaware	23.71	Republican	1860	Breckinridge	Constitutional Union
Florida	15.54	S. R. Demo.	1948	Democratic	Republican
Georgia	19.37	Populist	1892	Democratic	Republican
Idaho	24.14	T. Roosevelt	1912	Democratic	Republican
Illinois	22.23	Clay	1824	Jackson	John Quincy Adams
Indiana	23.11	Republican	1912	Democratic	T. Roosevelt
Iowa	24.30	Republican	1912	Democratic	T. Roosevelt
Kansas	20.48	Republican	1912	Democratic	T. Roosevelt
Kentucky	22.65	T. Roosevelt	1912	Democratic	Republican
Louisiana	20.99	States Rights	1960	Democratic	Republican
Maine	20.48	Republican	1912	Democratic	T. Roosevelt
Maryland	23.69	Republican	1912	Democratic	T. Roosevelt
Massachusetts	<u>29.08</u>	T. Roosevelt	1912	Democratic	Republican
Michigan	27.36	Democratic	1912	T. Roosevelt	Republican
Minnesota	19.25	Republican	1912	T. Roosevelt	Democratic
Mississippi	24.67	Republican	1960	Unpledged	Democratic
Missouri	18.92	Breckinridge	1860	Douglas	Constitutional Union
Montana	23.19	Republican	1912	Democratic	T. Roosevelt
Nebraska	22.99	LaFollette	1924	Republican	Democratic
Nevada	21.95	Democratic	1924	Republican	LaFollette
New Hampshire	20.23	T. Roosevelt	1912	Democratic	Republican
New Jersey	24.26	Whig	1856	Democratic	Republican
New Mexico	16.90	T. Roosevelt	1912	Democratic	Republican
New York	25.07	Democratic	1848	Whig	Free Soil
North Carolina	15.92	Populist	1892	Democratic	Republican
North Dakota	26.67	Republican	1912	Democratic	T. Roosevelt
Ohio	24.55	John Quincy Adams	1824	Clay	Jackson
Oklahoma	16.61	Socialist	1912	Democratic	Republican
Oregon	25.89	Douglas	1860	Republican	Breckinridge
Pennsylvania	22.40	Republican	1912	T. Roosevelt	Democratic
Rhode Island	21.67	T. Roosevelt	1912	Democratic	Republican
South Carolina	25.18	Republican	1956	Democratic	States Rights
South Dakota	19.04	Farmer Labor	1920	Republican	Democratic
Tennessee	21.24	T. Roosevelt	1912	Democratic	Republican
Texas	19.28	Republican	1892	Democratic	Populist
Utah	21.51	T. Roosevelt	1912	Republican	Democratic
Vermont	24.50	Democratic	1832	Anti-Masonic	National Republican
Virginia	19.13	Jackson	1824	Crawford	John Quincy Adams
Washington	21.82	Republican	1912	T. Roosevelt	Democratic
West Virginia	21.10	Republican	1912	Democratic	T. Roosevelt
Wisconsin	26.60	Free Soil	1848	Democratic	Whig
Wyoming	21.83	T. Roosevelt	1912	Democratic	Republican
United States	23.15	Republican	1912	Democratic	T. Roosevelt

The highest percentage for the nation is underlined.

TABLE 119   High Percentages for New Parties

States	Pct.	Parties	Year	
Alabama	79.75	States' Rights Democratic	1948	Carried state
Arizona	23.27	LaFollette	1924	
Arkansas	37.17	Constitutional Union	1860	
California	42.11	T. Roosevelt	1912	See footnotes
Colorado	57.07	Populist	1892	Carried state
Connecticut	75.68	National Republican	1828	Carried state
Delaware	53.27	Whig (cast for Harrison)	1836	Carried state
Florida	37.90	Constitutional Union	1860	
Georgia	52.71	Whig (cast for White)	1836	Carried state
Idaho	36.52	LaFollette	1924	
Illinois	45.29	Whig (cast for Harrison)	1836	
Indiana	55.97	Whig (cast for Harrison)	1836	Carried state
Iowa	49.13	Republican	1856	Carried state
Kansas	50.20	Populist	1892	Carried state
Kentucky	52.50	Whig (cast for Harrison)	1836	Carried state
Louisiana	49.07	States' Rights Democratic	1948	Carried state
Maine	61.37	Republican	1856	Carried state
Maryland	53.84	Whig (cast for Harrison)	1836	Carried state
Massachusetts	83.21	National Republican	1828	Carried state
Michigan	56.98	Republican	1856	Carried state
Minnesota	41.26	LaFollette	1924	
Mississippi	87.17	States' Rights Democratic	1948	Carried state
Missouri	40.02	Whig (cast for White)	1836	
Montana	37.77	LaFollette	1924	
Nebraska	41.52	Populist	1892	
Nevada	66.78	Populist	1892	Carried state
New Hampshire	53.59	Republican	1856	Carried state
New Jersey	51.98	National Republican	1828	Carried state
New Mexico	8.46	LaFollette	1924	
New York	49.03	National Republican	1828	See footnotes
North Carolina	46.75	Constitutional Union	1860	
North Dakota	45.17	LaFollette	1924	
Ohio	52.10	Whig (cast for Harrison)	1836	Carried state
Oklahoma	7.79	LaFollette	1924	
Oregon	34.35	Populist	1892	See footnotes
Pennsylvania	48.78	Whig (cast for Harrison)	1836	
Rhode Island	77.03	National Republican	1828	Carried state
South Carolina	71.97	States' Rights Democratic	1948	Carried state
South Dakota	50.55	T. Roosevelt	1912	Carried state
Tennessee	58.06	Whig (cast for White)	1836	Carried state
Texas	24.51	Constitutional Union	1860	
Utah	21.51	T. Roosevelt	1912	
Vermont	78.23	Republican	1856	Carried state
Virginia	44.65	Constitutional Union	1860	Carried state
Washington	35.76	LaFollette	1924	
West Virginia	29.42	T. Roosevelt	1912	
Wisconsin	53.96	LaFollette	1924	Carried state
Wyoming	31.51	LaFollette	1924	
United States	43.96	National Republican	1828	

The highest percentage for the nation is underlined.

The North Carolina Constitutional Union percentage extended was 46.753 in 1860. In 1836, its Whig vote, cast for White, was 46.751%.

If that part of the Democratic Party which supported Breckinridge in 1860 is considered a new party, high percentage records set by that party would include: Florida 59.55 and Texas 75.49.

In 1868, the first campaign in which the Republicans received votes in Arkansas and North Carolina, they carried both states, with 53.73% and 53.37%, respectively. They carried Florida in 1872 with 53.52%; it was their first campaign there.

In 1912, Theodore Roosevelt, Progressive, received 29.29% in Arizona, but, inasmuch as it was that state's first campaign, all parties were new there. Similarly, the Populists received 53.65% in Idaho, 49.01% in North Dakota, and 46.22% in Wyoming, all in 1892; they carried Idaho and received one of three electoral votes in North Dakota. Theodore Roosevelt received 16.90% in New Mexico in 1912, the state's first campaign.

TABLE 120   Highest Total Vote

States	High Vote	Year	States	High Vote	Year
Alabama	569,979	1960	Nebraska	615,878	1940
Alaska	60,762	1960	Nevada	107,267	1960
Arizona	398,491	1960	New Hampshire	295,761	1960
Arkansas	428,509	1960	New Jersey	2,773,111	1960
California	6,506,578	1960	New Mexico	311,107	1960
Colorado	736,246	1960	New York	7,290,824	1960
Connecticut	1,222,868	1960	North Carolina	1,368,556	1960
Delaware	196,683	1960	North Dakota	280,775	1940
Florida	1,544,176	1960	Ohio	4,161,859	1960
Georgia	733,110	1960	Oklahoma	948,984	1952
Hawaii	184,705	1960	Oregon	775,462	1960
Idaho	300,450	1960	Pennsylvania	5,006,101	1960
Illinois	4,757,394	1960	Rhode Island	414,498	1952
Indiana	2,135,360	1960	South Carolina	386,687	1960
Iowa	1,273,810	1960	South Dakota	308,427	1940
Kansas	928,825	1960	Tennessee	1,051,809	1960
Kentucky	1,124,462	1960	Texas	2,311,670	1960
Louisiana	807,891	1960	Utah	374,709	1960
Maine	421,767	1960	Vermont	167,317	1960
Maryland	1,055,346	1960	Virginia	771,449	1960
Massachusetts	2,469,449	1960	Washington	1,241,572	1960
Michigan	3,318,097	1960	West Virginia	873,548	1952
Minnesota	1,541,887	1960	Wisconsin	1,729,082	1960
Mississippi	298,171	1960	Wyoming	140,882	1960
Missouri	1,934,422	1960			
Montana	277,579	1960			
			UNITED STATES	68,836,720	1960

The above figures do not include void, blank, or scattering ballots.

Six states cast their highest total votes in a year other than 1960. Had they cast the same number of votes in 1960 that they did in their record years, the total for the United States would have been increased by 97,632, making a total of 68,934,352.

TABLE 121   Party Gains and Losses

The following analysis shows gains and losses in electoral votes by the various parties from one election to the next, beginning with a comparison of 1828 with 1824.

1828. Jackson gained 79 net: from Crawford 38 (Va. 24, Ga. 9, N. Y. 5), from Clay 37 (Ohio 16, Ky. 14, N. Y. 4, Mo. 3), from Adams 4 (N. Y. 10, La. 2, Ill. 1, Me. 1, N. J. —8, Md. —2). Adams gained 3 from Crawford: Del. 2, Md. 1.

1832. Democrats gained 25 net from National Republicans: N. Y. 16, Me. 8, N. J. 8, N. H. 7, Ky. —14. S. C.'s 11, previously Jackson, for Floyd. Vt.'s 7, previously Adams, for Wirt. Democrats got 27 net on reapportionment and absentees: N. Y. 6, Ohio 5, Ind. 4, Tenn. 4, Ala. 2, Ga. 2, Ill. 2, Penna. 2, Me. 1, Miss. 1, Mo. 1, Md. —2, Va. —1. National Republicans lost 2 net on reapportionment and absentees: Ky. 1, Md. —1, Mass. —1, N. H. —1. Of Md.'s reduction of 3, 2 were absentees.

1836. Whigs gained 67 from Democrats (Ohio 21, Tenn. 15, Ga. 11, Ind. 9, N. J. 8, Md. 3), gained 37 from National Republicans (Ky. 15, Mass. 14, Md. 5, Del. 3), and got Vt.'s 7, previously Wirt, and Md's 2, previously absentee. Democrats gained 12 from National Republicans (Conn. 8, R. I. 4) and got 3 each in Ark. and Mich., new states. Mangum got 11 S. C., previously Floyd.

1840. Whigs gained 121 from Democrats: N. Y. 42, Penna. 30, N. C. 15, Me. 10, Conn. 8, La. 5, Miss. 4, R. I. 4, Mich. 3.

1844. Democrats gained 102 from Whigs (N. Y. 36, Penna, 26, Ga. 10, Ind. 9, Me. 9, La. 5, Miss. 4, Mich. 3) and gained 8 net on reapportionment (Ala. 2, Ill. 4, Ind. 3, La. 1, Mich. 2, Miss. 2, Mo. 3, N. H. —1, S. C. —2, Va. —6). Whigs lost 27 net on reapportionment: Conn. —2, Ga. —1, Ky. —3, Me. —1, Md. —2, Mass. —2, N. J. —1, N. Y. —6, N. C. —4, Ohio 2, Penna. —4, Tenn. —2, Vt. —1.

1848. Whigs gained 55 net from Democrats (N. Y. 36, Penna. 26, Ohio —23, Ga. 10, La. 6) and got 3 Fla., new state. Democrats got 4 each in Iowa, Tex., Wisc., new states.

1852. Democrats gained 118 from Whigs (N. Y. 35, Penna. 26, Ga. 10, N. C. 10, Md. 8, N. J. 7, Conn. 6, La. 6, R. I. 4, Del. 3, Fla. 3), got 4 Calif., new state, and gained 5 net on reapportionment (Ill. 2, Mo. 2, Ark. 1, Ind. 1, Mich. 1, Miss. 1, Penna. 1, Wisc. 1, Va. —2, Me. —1, N. H. —1, S. C. —1). Whigs lost 3 net on reapportionment: Mass. 1, N. Y. —1, N. C. —1, Tenn. —1, Vt. —1.

1856. Republicans gained 96 from Democrats (N. Y. 35, Ohio 23, Me. 8, Conn. 6, Mich. 6, N. H. 5, Wisc. 5, Iowa 4, R. I. 4) and 18 from Whigs (Mass. 13, Vt. 5). Democrats gained 16 net from Whigs: Ky. 12, Tenn. 12, Md. —8.

1860. Republicans gained 59 from Democrats (Penna. 27, Ind. 13, Ill. 11, Calif. 4, N. J. 4) and got 7 in new states (Minn. 4, Oreg. 3). Constitutional Union gained 39 from Democrats: Va. 15, Ky. 12, Tenn. 12. The remaining 76 Democratic votes were divided between Breckinridge and Douglas. The former got 64 Democratic (Ga. 10, N. C. 10, Ala. 9, Fla. 3, S. C. 8, Miss. 7, La. 6, Ark. 4, Tex. 4, Del. 3) and 8 Whig (Md.). Douglas got 9 Mo. and 3 N. J.

1864. Republicans gained 5 net from Democrats (formerly Douglas) (Mo. 9, N. J. —4), gained 7 Md., formerly Breckinridge, and got 10 from new states (W. Va. 5, Kans. 3, Nev. 2—a third Nev. elector died). Democrats gained 11 Ky., formerly Constitutional Union, and 3 Del., formerly Breckinridge. Breckinridge's other votes were all in seceding states: Ga. 10, N. C. 10, Ala. 9, S. C. 8, Miss. 7, La. 6, Ark. 4, Tex. 4, Fla. 3. Other Constitutional Union votes were all in seceding states: Va. 15, Tenn. 12. Republicans gained 10 net on reapportionment: Ill. 5, Iowa 4, Wisc. 3, Mich. 2, Mo. 2, Calif. 1, N. Y. —2, Penna. —1, Ohio —2, Me. —1, Mass. —1. Ky. lost 1, formerly Constitutional Union, and Md. lost 1, formerly Breckinridge. Seceding states gained and lost thus: Ala. —1, Ark. 1, Ga. —1, La. 1, N. C. —1, S. C. —2, Tenn. —2, Tex. 2, Va. —5 (3 to W. Va.). Of these votes, —1 net had been Breckinridge and —7 Constitutional Union.

1868. Democrats gained 43 from Republicans (N. Y. 33, Md. 7, Oreg. 3) and 16 from states returned to Union (Ga. 9, La. 7). Republicans gained 41 from states returned to Union (Tenn. 10, N. C. 9, Ala. 8, S. C. 6, Ark. 5, Fla. 3), got 3 in Nebr., new state, and 1 additional in Nev., which cast but 2 before.

1872. Republicans gained 25 net from Democrats (N. Y. 33, N. J. 7, Del. 3, Oreg. 3, Mo. —11, Tenn. —10) and gained 33 on reapportionment (Ala. 2, Calif. 1, Fla. 1, Ill. 5, Ind. 2, Iowa 3, Kans. 2, Mass. 1, Mich. 3, Minn. 1, N. J. 2, N. Y. 2, N. C. 1, Ohio 1, Penna. 3, S. C. 1, Wisc. 2). Democrats got 10 on reapportionment: Ga. 2, Ky. 1, Md. 1, Mo. 4, Tenn. 2. In the three states returned to Union, Republicans got 8 Miss. and 11 Va., Democrats 8 Tex. Votes of two states rejected, Republicans losing 5 Ark. and 7 La.

1876. Democrats gained 112 from Republicans (N. Y. 35, Ind. 15, Va. 11, Ala. 10, N. C. 10, N. J. 9, Miss. 8, Conn. 6, W. Va. 5, Del. 3) and got 6 Ark., which returned to Union. Republicans got 8 La., which returned to Union, and 3 Colo., new state.

1880. Republicans gained 29 net from Democrats: N. Y. 35, Ind. 15, Conn. 6, La. —8, S. C. —7, Calif. —5, Fla. —4, Nev. —3.

1884. Democrats gained 48 net from Republicans (N. Y. 35, Ind. 15, Conn. 6, Calif. —5, Nev. —3) and gained 16 on reapportionment (Ark. 1, Ga. 1, Ky. 1, Miss. 1, Mo. 1, N. Y. 1, N. C. 1, S. C. 2, Tex. 5, Va. 1, W. Va. 1). Republicans gained 16 net on reapportionment: Calif. 2, Ill. 1, Iowa 2, Kans. 4, Me. —1, Mass. 1, Mich. 2, Minn. 2, Nebr. 2, N. H. —1, Ohio 1, Penna. 1, Vt. —1, Wisc. 1.

1888. Republicans gained 51 from Democrats: N. Y. 36, Ind. 15.

1892. Democrats gained 96 from Republicans (N. Y. 36, Ill. 22, Ind. 15, Wisc. 11, Calif. 7, Mich. 4, Ohio 1) and got 1 from N. D., new state, which also gave Republicans and Populists 1 each. Populists gained 15 from Republicans: Kans. 9, Colo. 3, Nev. 3. Republicans got 14 more from new states: S. D. 4, Wash. 4, Mont. 3, Wyo. 3. On reapportionment, Democrats got 12 (Ala. 1, Ark. 1, Calif. 1, Ga. 1, Ill. 2, Mich. 1, Mo. 1, N. J. 1, Tex. 2, Wisc. 1), Republicans 8 (Mass. 1, Minn. 2, Nebr. 3, Penna. 2), and Populists 3 (Colo. 1, Kans. 1, Oreg. 1). Populists got 3 Ida., new state.

1896. Republicans gained 124 net from Democrats (N. Y. 36, Ill. 24, Ind. 15, Ky. 12, Wisc. 12, N. J. 10, Md. 8, Calif. 7, Conn. 6, W. Va. 6, Mich. 5, Del. 3, Ohio 1, Nebr. —8, S. D. —4, Wash. —4, Mont. —3, Wyo. —3, N. D. 1) and 2 from Populists (N. D. 1, Oreg. 1). Democrats gained 20 from Populists (Kans. 10, Colo. 4, Ida. 3, Nev. 3) and got 3 Utah, new state.

1900. Republicans gained 21 net from Democrats: Kans. 10, Nebr. 8, S. D. 4, Wash. 4, Utah 3, Wyo. 3, Calif. 1, Ky. —12.

1904. Republicans gained 23 net from Democrats (Mo. 17, Colo. 4, Ida. 3, Mont. 3, Nev. 3, Md. —7) and got 21 on reapportionment (Ill. 3, N. Y. 3, Minn. 2, N. J. 2, Penna. 2, Calif. 1, Colo. 1, Conn. 1, Mass. 1, Mo. 1, N. D. 1, Wash. 1, W. Va. 1, Wisc. 1). Democrats got 8 on reapportionment: Tex. 3, and Ark., Fla., La., Miss., and N. C., 1 each.

1908. Democrats gained 15 from Republicans (Nebr. 8, Colo. 5, Nev. 3, Md. —1) and got 7 in Okla., new state.

1912. Democrats gained 238 from Republicans (N. Y. 39, Ohio 23, Ill. 27, Mo. 18, Mass. 16, Ind. 15, Iowa 13, Wisc. 13, N. J. 12, Kans. 10, Conn. 7, W. Va. 7, Me. 6, N. H. 4, N. D. 4, Oreg. 4, R. I. 4, Del. 3, Ida. 3, Mont. 3, Wyo. 3, Calif. 2, Md. 2), got 3 each in Ariz. and N. M., new states, and got 29 on reapportionment (N. Y. 6, Okla. 3, Ill. 2, Mass. 2, N. J. 2, Tex. 2, and 1 each in Ala., Colo., Fla., Ga., Ida., La., Mont., N. D., Ohio, Oreg., R. I., and W. Va.). Republicans got 1 in Utah on reapportionment. Progressives gained 76 from Republicans (Penna. 34, Mich. 14, Minn. 11, Calif. 8, Wash. 5, S. D. 4) and got 12 on reapportionment (Penna. 4, Calif. 3, Wash. 2, Mich. 1, Minn. 1, S. D. 1).

1916. Republicans gained 176 net from Democrats (N. Y. 45, Ill. 29, Mass. 18, Ind. 15, N. J. 14, Iowa 13, Wisc. 13, Conn. 7, W. Va. 7, Me. 6, Oreg. 5, R. I. 5, Utah —4, Del. 3) and got 70 formerly Progressive (Penna. 38, Mich. 15, Minn. 12, S. D. 5). Democrats got 18 formerly Progressive: Calif. 11, Wash. 7.

1920. Republicans gained 150 from Democrats: Ohio 24, Mo. 18, Calif. 13, Tenn. 12, Kans. 10, Okla. 10. Md. 8, Nebr. 8, Wash. 7, Colo. 6, N. D. 5, Ida. 4, Mont. 4, N. H. 4, Utah 4, Ariz. 3, Nev. 3, N. M. 3, Wyo. 3, W. Va. 1.

1924. Democrats gained 9 net from Republicans: Tenn. 12, Okla. 10, Ky. —13. Progressives gained 13 Wisc. from Republicans.

1928. Republicans gained 49 net from Democrats (Tex. 20, N. C. 12, Tenn. 12, Va. 12, Okla. 10, Fla. 6, Mass. —18, R. I. —5) and got 13 Wisc., formerly Progressive.

1932. Democrats gained 366 from Republicans (N. Y. 45, Ill. 29, Ohio 24, Tex. 20, Mich. 15, Mo. 15, Ind. 14, N. J. 14, Calif. 13, N. C. 12, Wisc. 12, Iowa 11, Ky. 11, Minn. 11, Tenn. 11, Va. 11, Okla. 10, Kans. 9, Md. 8, W. Va. 8, Nebr. 7, Wash. 7, Colo. 6, Fla. 6, Oreg. 5, Ida. 4, Mont. 4, N. D. 4, S. D. 4, Utah 4, Ariz. 3, Nev. 3, N. M. 3, Wyo. 3) and gained 19 net on reapportionment (Calif. 9, Mich. 4, N. J. 2, N. Y. 2, Ohio 2, Tex. 3, Fla. 1, N. C. 1, Okla. 1, Wash. 1, Ga. —2, Ala. —1, Mass. —1, Miss. —1, R. I. —1, S. C. —1). Republicans lost 19 net on reapportionment: Conn. 1, Mo. —3, Iowa —2, Ky. —2, Penna. —2, and Ind., Me., Minn., Nebr., N. D., S. D., Kans., Tenn., Vt., Va., and Wisc., —1 each.

1936. Democrats gained 51 from Republicans: Penna. 36, Conn. 8, N. H. 4, Del. 3.

1940. Republicans gained 74 from Democrats: Mich. 19, Ind. 14, Iowa 11, Kans. 9, Nebr. 7, Colo. 6, N. D. 4, S. D. 4.

1944. Republicans gained 21 net from Democrats (Ohio 25, Wisc. 12, Wyo. 3, Mich. —19) and lost 4 on reapportionment (1 each in Ind., Iowa, Kans., and Nebr.). Democrats gained 4 net on reapportionment: Calif. 3, Ariz., Fla., N. M., N. C., Oreg., and Tenn., 1 each; Ill., Mass., Ohio, Okla., and Penna., —1 each.

1948. Republicans gained 90 net from Democrats (N. Y. 47, Penna. 35, Mich. 19, N. J. 16, Conn. 8, Md. 8, Oreg. 6, N. H. 4, Del. 3, Ohio —25, Wisc. —12, Iowa —10, Colo. —6, Wyo. —3). States' Rights Democrats gained 39 from Democrats (Ala. 11, La. 10, Miss. 9, S. C. 8, Tenn. 1).

1952. Republicans gained 249 from Democrats (Ill. 28, Calif. 25, Ohio 25, Tex. 23, Mass. 16, Mo. 15, Wisc. 12, Minn. 11, Tenn. 11, Va. 11, Iowa 10, Okla. 10, Fla. 8, Wash. 8, Colo. 6, Ariz. 4, Ida. 4, Mont. 4, N. M. 4, R. I. 4, Utah 4, Nev. 3, Wyo. 3); got 1 Tenn., formerly States' Rights Democratic; and gained 3 net on reapportionment (Calif. 7, Fla. 2, Md., Mich., Tex., Va., and Wash., 1 each, Penna. —3, Mo., N. Y., and Okla., —2 each. Ill. and Tenn., —1 each). Democrats gained 38 from States' Rights Democrats (Ala. 11, La. 10, Miss. 9, S. C. 8) and lost 3 on reapportionment (Ark., Ky., and Miss., 1 each).

1956. Republicans gained 15 net from Democrats (Ky. 10, La. 10, W. Va. 8, Mo. —13). Democrats lost 1 additional in Ala. to Walter B. Jones.

1960: Democrats gained 240 from Republicans (Conn. 8, Del. 3, Ill. 27, La. 10, Md. 9, Mass. 16, Mich. 20, Minn. 11, Nev. 3, N. J. 16, N. M. 4, N. Y. 45, Penna. 32, R. I. 4, Tex. 24, W. Va. 8), got 3 in Hawaii, new state, and lost 13 to Byrd (Ala. 5, Miss. 8). Republicans got 3 in Alaska, new state, and lost 1 in Okla. to Byrd. Byrd gained 1 in Ala. from Jones.

TABLE 122   Closest Democratic-Republican Races in Each State

States	Democratic	Republican	Dem. %	Rep. %	Year	Electoral D.	Electoral R.
Alabama	127,797	120,725	51.33	48.49	1928	12	
Alaska	29,809	30,953	49.06	50.94	1960		3
Arizona	26,235	30,516	35.47	41.26	1924		3
Arkansas	37,927	41,373	47.83	52.17	1872		6
California	80,443	80,348	48.98	48.92	1880	5	1
Colorado	126,644	123,700	47.99	46.88	1908	5	
Connecticut	74,922	74,586	48.66	48.44	1888	6	
Delaware	67,813	69,588	48.76	50.04	1948		3
Florida	22,923	23,849	49.01	50.99	1876		4
Georgia	76,356	62,550	53.43	43.77	1872	8	
Hawaii	92,410	92,295	50.03	49.97	1960	3	
Idaho	33,921	32,810	32.08	31.02	1912	4	
Illinois	2,377,846	2,368,988	49.98	49.80	1960	27	
Indiana	261,013	263,361	48.61	49.05	1888		15
Iowa	522,380	494,018	50.31	47.58	1948	10	
Kansas	172,915	159,345	51.50	47.45	1896	10	
Kentucky	217,890	218,171	48.86	48.92	1896	1	12
Louisiana	70,566	75,135	48.43	51.57	1876		8
Maine	156,478	163,951	48.77	51.10	1940		5
Maryland	109,446	109,497	48.81	48.83	1904	7	1
Massachusetts	792,758	775,566	50.24	49.15	1928	18	
Michigan	150,751	152,244	27.36	27.63	1912		
Minnesota	179,152	179,544	46.25	46.35	1916		12
Mississippi	108,362	73,561	36.34	24.67	1960	8*	
Missouri	346,574	347,203	48.41	48.50	1908		18
Montana	134,891	141,841	48.60	51.10	1960		4
Nebraska	131,099	126,997	49.14	47.60	1908	8	
Nevada	11,212	10,775	45.71	43.93	1908	3	
New Hampshire	43,779	43,723	49.12	49.06	1916	4	
New Jersey	1,385,415	1,363,324	49.96	49.16	1960	16	
New Mexico	156,027	153,733	50.15	49.41	1960	4	
New York	563,154	562,005	48.25	48.15	1884	36	
North Carolina	590,530	575,062	50.66	49.34	1956	14	
North Dakota	55,206	53,471	50.80	49.20	1916	5	
Ohio	404,115	405,187	47.53	47.66	1892	1	22
Oklahoma	123,907	110,550	48.23	43.03	1908	7	
Oregon	11,125	10,961	50.37	49.63	1868	3	
Pennsylvania	2,556,282	2,439,956	51.06	48.74	1960	32	
Rhode Island	118,973	117,522	50.16	49.55	1928	5	
South Carolina	90,906	91,870	49.74	50.26	1876		7
South Dakota	41,225	41,042	49.70	49.48	1896	4	
Tennessee	443,710	446,147	49.71	49.98	1952		11
Texas	1,167,932	1,121,699	50.52	48.52	1960	24	
Utah	45,006	47,139	48.30	50.59	1900		3
Vermont	64,269	78,371	44.93	54.79	1940		3
Virginia	151,979	150,449	49.98	49.47	1888	12	
Washington	599,298	629,273	48.27	50.68	1960		9
West Virginia	78,677	78,171	49.35	49.03	1888	6	
Wisconsin	177,335	170,846	47.77	46.02	1892	12	
Wyoming	10,375	10,072	50.35	48.88	1896	3	

* Byrd received the electoral votes which had been cast for an unpledged slate.

In 1872, the Georgia electoral vote was divided between Benjamin Gratz Brown, who received six votes, and Charles Jones Jenkins, who received two. Congress rejected the three which had been cast for Greeley, who had died after the popular election and before the counting of the electoral vote. Roosevelt, Progressive, received Michigan's fifteen electoral votes in 1912. Byrd, Democrat, received Mississippi's eight electoral votes in 1960; they had been cast for an unpledged slate.

The closest Democratic-Republican race nationally was that of 1880, when Garfield defeated Hancock, 4,454,433 to 4,444,976. The percentages were 48.32 and 48.21. The closest race in the Electoral College was that of 1876, when Hayes defeated Tilden, 185 to 184.

Contests which were closer than those shown above for the same states, but in which at least one of the parties involved was neither Democratic nor Republican, have been as follows:

TABLE 122 (continued)

States	Winner	Loser	W - %	L - %	Year	Parties		Electoral	
Alabama	31,363	30,482	50.71	49.29	1848	Dem.	Whig	Dem.	9
Delaware	6,319	6,294	49.85	49.66	1852	Dem.	Whig	Dem.	3
Georgia	44,177	42,106	51.20	48.79	1844	Dem.	Whig	Dem.	10
Kansas	163,111	157,241	50.20	48.40	1892	Pop.	Rep.	Pop.	10
Louisiana	13,782	13,083	51.30	48.70	1844	Dem.	Whig	Dem.	6
Maine	46,612	46,190	50.13	49.67	1840	Whig	Dem.	Whig	10
Maryland	19,160	19,156	50.01	49.99	1832	N. R.	Dem.	See below	
Mississippi	26,537	25,922	50.59	49.41	1848	Dem.	Whig	Dem.	6
North Carolina	39,744	39,058	50.40	49.53	1852	Dem.	Whig	Dem.	10
North Dakota	17,700	17,519	49.01	48.50	1892	Pop.	Rep.	See below	
Pennsylvania	144,023	143,784	49.98	49.90	1840	Whig	Dem.	Whig	30
Tennessee	60,033	59,904	50.05	49.95	1844	Whig	Dem.	Whig	13
Vermont	13,106	11,152	40.79	34.71	1832	A. M.	N. R.	A. M.	7
Virginia	74,701	74,379	44.65	44.46	1860	C. U.	Dem.	C. U.	15

In 1832, the Maryland electoral vote was cast by districts, Clay getting five and Jackson three. In 1892, the North Dakota vote was split, Weaver, Harrison, and Cleveland each getting one elector. In 1960, Byrd received the Mississippi electoral votes which had been cast for an unpledged Democratic slate.

The closest three-way race occurred in California in 1860. The vote and percentages were: Lincoln 39,173 - 32.96%, Douglas 38,516 - 32.41%, Breckinridge 34,334 - 28.89%.

TABLE 123   Low Percentages for Democratic and Republican Candidates

States	Dem.	Year	Rep.	Year
Alabama	46.81	1872	3.95	1892
Alaska	49.06	1960	50.94	1960
Arizona	35.47	1924	12.74	1912
Arkansas	46.27	1868	12.91	1932
California	8.23	1924	.58	1912
Colorado	21.98	1924	13.84	1896
Connecticut	21.50	1860	35.88	1912
Delaware	34.60	1928	2.11	1856
Florida	40.12	1928	8.25	1912
Georgia	44.22	1840	4.28	1912
Hawaii	50.03	1960	49.97	1960
Idaho	.01	1892	21.30	1896
Illinois	23.36	1924	22.13	1912
Indiana	38.69	1924	23.11	1912
Iowa	16.65	1924	24.30	1912
Kansas	21.39	1864	20.48	1912
Kentucky	35.80	1840	.26	1856
Louisiana	32.75	1948	4.83	1912
Maine	21.83	1924	20.48	1912
Maryland	39.96	1956	.32	1856
Massachusetts	16.79	1828	31.89	1912
Michigan	13.13	1924	27.63	1912
Minnesota	6.80	1924	19.25	1912
Mississippi	10.09	1948	2.47	1912
Missouri	29.83	1864	10.29	1860
Montana	19.38	1924	19.72	1896
Nebraska	12.46	1892	21.73	1912
Nevada	6.56	1892	15.89	1912
New Hampshire	25.91	1896	37.43	1912
New Jersey	27.40	1924	20.54	1912
New Mexico	40.85	1928	35.76	1932
New York	25.07	1848	28.68	1912
North Carolina	42.14	1840	11.94	1912
North Dakota	6.96	1924	26.58	1936
Ohio	23.70	1924	26.81	1912
Oklahoma	35.44	1928	26.70	1932
Oregon	18.15	1892	25.30	1912
Pennsylvania	19.07	1924	22.40	1912
Rhode Island	22.97	1828	35.57	1912
South Carolina	23.85	1872	1.06	1912
South Dakota	12.88	1892	34.40	1932
Tennessee	31.67	1868	23.84	1912
Texas	43.98	1956	8.86	1912
Utah	29.94	1924	17.27	1896
Vermont	15.67	1924	37.13	1912
Virginia	38.36	1956	.19	1856
Washington	10.16	1924	21.82	1912
West Virginia	31.05	1864	21.10	1912
Wisconsin	8.10	1924	30.26	1936
Wyoming	16.11	1924	34.42	1912
UNITED STATES	28.82	1924	23.16	1912

The Connecticut Democratic percentage is Douglas'; Breckinridge received 20.51%.
Extreme lows are underlined. Cases where candidates received no votes are disregarded.

States	No.	Democratic	No.	Republican
Alabama	4	1928-40	3	1936-44, 1952-60
Arizona	4	1928-40, 1948-60	6	1940-60
Arkansas	7	1872-96	3	1880-8, 1900-8, 1936-44
California	6	1876-96	6	1940-60
Colorado	3	1928-36	4	1916-28
Connecticut	5	1876-92, 1928-44	5	1940-56
Delaware	6	1900-20	6	1888-1908
Florida	4	1876-88, 1908-20, 1928-40	7	1936-60
Georgia	6	1924-44	7	1936-60
Idaho	4	1928-40	3	1900-8
Illinois	7	1876-1900	6	1876-96
Indiana	7	1832-56, 1876-1900	8	1860-88
Iowa	4	1884-96	12	1860-1904
Kansas	6	1868-88	6	1868-88
Kentucky	2	1852-6, 1864-8, 1884-8, 1896-1900, 1916-20, 1928-32	8	1860-88
Louisiana	7	1916-40	6	1936-56
Maine	3	1908-16	4	1916-28
Maryland	7	1868-92	6	1936-56
Massachusetts	8	1912-40	4	1916-28
Michigan	8	1840-68	6	1868-88
Minnesota	7	1864-88	7	1864-88
Mississippi	7	1836-60	2	1896-1900, 1916-20, 1940-4
Missouri	8	1868-96	7	1864-88
Montana	3	1928-36	2	1900-4, 1916-20, 1948-52
Nebraska	5	1872-88	5	1872-88
Nevada	4	1928-40, 1948-60	5	1940-56
New Hampshire	4	1928-40	4	1916-28
New Jersey	6	1916-36	13	1860-1908
New Mexico	4	1948-60	4	1948-60
New York	6	1916-36	8	1860-88
North Carolina	4	1908-20	4	1876-88
North Dakota	2	1928-32, 1956-60	4	1896-1908
Ohio	17	1832-96	8	1860-88
Oklahoma	3	1916-24	2	1916-20, 1936-40
Oregon	4	1876-88	9	1864-96
Pennsylvania	6	1836-56	8	1860-88
Rhode Island	8	1912-40	7	1872-96
South Carolina	3	1928-36	4	1940-52
South Dakota	3	1908-16	3	1896-1904
Tennessee	4	1928-40	7	1936-60
Texas	6	1876-96	4	1916-28
Utah	4	1928-40	5	1940-56
Vermont	4	1928-40	4	1916-28
Virginia	5	1928-44	7	1936-60
Washington	5	1928-44	6	1940-60
West Virginia	18	1868-1936	11	1868-1908
Wisconsin	7	1852-76	4	1876-88
Wyoming	3	1928-36	4	1896-1908, 1916-28
United States	9	1864-96	8	1860-88

Cases where parties received no votes are disregarded.

TABLE 125   Most Consecutive Campaigns in Which Major Parties
Lost Votes from Previous Campaign

States	No.	Democratic	No.	Republican
Alabama	4	1896-1908	2	1876-80, 1888-92
Arizona	2	1920-4	2	1932-6
Arkansas	2	1900-4, 1920-4	2	1892-6
California	2	1900-4, 1920-4	2	1868-72, 1932-6
Colorado	2	1900-4, 1920-4, 1940-4	2	1892-6,1908-12,1932-6,1944-8
Connecticut	2	1904-8	2	1932-6
Delaware	2	1944-8	2	1932-6
Florida	2	1900-4, 1944-8	1	1880,1888,1900,1912,1924,1932
Georgia	2	1880-4, 1896-1900	2	1884-8, 1900-4
Idaho	3	1944-52	2	1932-6, 1956-60
Illinois	3	1940-8	2	1908-12
Indiana	2	1940-4, 1952-6	2	1908-12, 1944-8
Iowa	2	1900-4, 1940-4	2	1908-12, 1944-8, 1956-60
Kansas	2	1900-4, 1920-4, 1940-4	2	1908-12, 1944-8, 1956-60
Kentucky	3	1832-40	2	1932-6, 1944-8
Louisiana	3	1896-1904	5	1888-1904
Maine	4	1884-96	3	1940-8
Maryland	3	1940-8	2	1900-4
Massachusetts	2	1856-60, 1952-6	2	1944-8
Michigan	2	1900-4, 1920-4	2	1908-12, 1932-6
Minnesota	2	1900-4, 1920-4, 1940-4	2	1908-12, 1932-6, 1944-8
Mississippi	2	1956-60	2	1876-80, 1888-92, 1932-6
Missouri	2	1848-52, 1900-4, 1940-4	2	1944-8
Montana	2	1900-4, 1920-4, 1940-4	2	1908-12, 1932-6, 1956-60
Nebraska	5	1936-52	2	1908-12, 1944-8
Nevada	3	1884-92	2	1880-4, 1892-6, 1932-6
New Hampshire	4	1944-56	4	1900-12
New Jersey	3	1940-8	2	1932-6
New Mexico	2	1940-4	1	1924, 1932, 1944
New York	2	1908-12	2	1944-8
North Carolina	3	1940-8	2	1900-4
North Dakota	5	1936-52	2	1908-12,1932-6,1944-8,1956-60
Ohio	3	1940-8	3	1868-76, 1884-92
Oklahoma	3	1936-44, 1952-60	2	1944-8
Oregon	3	1940-8	2	1932-6
Pennsylvania	3	1896-1904, 1940-8	2	1908-12
Rhode Island	2	1868-72	2	1928-32
South Carolina	3	1884-92, 1940-8	7	1880-1904
South Dakota	3	1936-44	2	1944-8
Tennessee	2	1832-6, 1848-52, 1900-4, 1944-8	2	1900-4
Texas	2	1900-4, 1944-8	2	1888-92, 1900-4
Utah	4	1944-56	2	1908-12, 1932-6
Vermont	5	1880-96	4	1900-12
Virginia	3	1896-1904	2	1900-4
Washington	2	1900-4, 1920-4	2	1932-6
West Virginia	2	1940-4	2	1932-6, 1944-8
Wisconsin	5	1940-56	2	1908-12, 1944-8, 1956-60
Wyoming	2	1900-4, 1920-4, 1940-4	2	1932-6, 1944-8
United States	3	1940-8	2	1944-8

Cases where parties received no votes are disregarded.

States	No.	Democratic	No.	Republican
Alabama	2	1884-8, 1932-6	6	1940-60
Arizona	3	1928-36	5	1940-56
Arkansas	2	1852-6, 1872-6, 1892-6	3	1936-44
California	3	1908-16, 1928-36	4	1940-52
Colorado	3	1928-36	2	1884-8, 1900-4, 1916-20, 1940-4
Connecticut	3	1928-36	5	1940-56
Delaware	3	1908-16	5	1888-1904, 1940-56
Florida	2	1876-80, 1888-92	5	1940-56
Georgia	2	1884-8, 1912-6	7	1936-60
Idaho	3	1928-36	2	1900-4, 1916-20, 1940-4
Illinois	3	1884-92, 1928-36	4	1860-72
Indiana	3	1928-36	4	1916-28
Iowa	2	1928-32, 1956-60	3	1896-1904
Kansas	3	1928-36	3	1936-44
Kentucky	2	1852-6, 1864-8	3	1880-8
Louisiana	5	1888-1904	3	1936-44
Maine	3	1908-16	4	1944-56
Maryland	4	1840-52	6	1936-56
Massachusetts	4	1864-76, 1928-40	2	1904-8, 1916-20, 1940-4, 1952-6
Michigan	3	1928-36	3	1896-1904, 1916-24, 1948-56
Minnesota	3	1928-36	3	1896-1904
Mississippi	3	1888-96	2	1896-1900, 1916-20, 1948-52
Missouri	3	1868-76, 1924-32	3	1896-1904, 1936-44
Montana	3	1928-36	2	1900-4, 1916-20, 1940-4
Nebraska	2	1928-32, 1956-60	3	1896-1904, 1936-44
Nevada	3	1928-36	4	1940-56
New Hampshire	4	1928-40	4	1944-56
New Jersey	3	1908-16, 1928-36	5	1940-56
New Mexico	1	1916, 1932, 1948, 1960	3	1936-44
New York	4	1924-36	2	1916-20, 1952-6
North Carolina	3	1896-1904, 1932-40	2	1916-20, 1952-6
North Dakota	2	1928-32, 1956-60	3	1896-1904
Ohio	4	1864-76	3	1896-1904
Oklahoma	1	1916, 1924, 1932, 1948	3	1936-44, 1952-60
Oregon	3	1908-16, 1928-36	4	1940-52
Pennsylvania	3	1928-36	5	1940-56
Rhode Island	3	1884-92, 1924-32	4	1860-72
South Carolina	4	1876-88	2	1916-20, 1940-4
South Dakota	3	1908-16	3	1896-1904, 1936-44
Tennessee	3	1896-1904	2	1880-4, 1916-20, 1940-4
Texas	2	1904-8	3	1948-56
Utah	3	1928-36	5	1940-56
Vermont	4	1928-40	4	1944-56
Virginia	2	1852-6, 1876-80, 1900-4, 1912-6, 1932-6	4	1940-52
Washington	3	1928-36	4	1940-52
West Virginia	3	1868-76	3	1896-1904
Wisconsin	3	1908-16, 1928-36	3	1896-1904
Wyoming	3	1928-36	2	1900-4, 1916-20, 1940-4
United States	3	1928-36	3	1896-1904

Cases where parties received no votes are disregarded.

TABLE 127   Most Consecutive Campaigns in Which Major Parties

Lost Percentagewise from Previous Campaign

States	No.	Democratic	No.	Republican
Alabama	2	1856-60, 1908-12, 1940-4	2	1876-80, 1888-92, 1932-6
Arizona	5	1940-56	2	1932-6
Arkansas	7	1936-60	3	1872-80, 1888-96
California	4	1940-52	2	1876-80, 1888-92, 1908-12, 1932-6, 1956-60
Colorado	2	1884-8, 1900-4, 1920-4, 1940-4	2	1892-6,1908-12,1932-6,1956-60
Connecticut	5	1940-56	4	1924-36
Delaware	5	1940-56	2	1908-12, 1932-6
Florida	5	1940-56	2	1876-80, 1932-6
Georgia	4	1936-48	3	1884-92
Idaho	4	1940-52	2	1908-12, 1932-6, 1956-60
Illinois	3	1864-72, 1948-56	4	1924-36
Indiana	2	1856-60, 1888-92, 1900-4, 1920-4, 1940-4, 1952-6	2	1908-12, 1932-6
Iowa	5	1888-1904	5	1876-92
Kansas	2	1876-80,1900-4,1920-4,1940-4	8	1868-96
Kentucky	5	1880-96	2	1900-4, 1932-6
Louisiana	4	1936-48	5	1888-1904
Maine	4	1944-56	4	1928-40
Maryland	5	1940-56	2	1900-4
Massachusetts	3	1840-8	4	1924-36
Michigan	2	1868-72, 1880-4, 1900-4, 1920-4, 1948-52	3	1928-36
Minnesota	2	1868-72, 1900-4, 1920-4	3	1884-92
Mississippi	3	1940-8	2	1876-80, 1888-92, 1932-6
Missouri	3	1856-64, 1936-44	4	1868-80
Montana	4	1940-52	2	1908-12, 1932-6, 1956-60
Nebraska	3	1936-44	3	1884-92
Nevada	4	1940-52	2	1876-80, 1892-6, 1908-12, 1932-6, 1956-60
New Hampshire	4	1944-56	5	1924-40
New Jersey	5	1940-56	4	1924-36
New Mexico	3	1920-8, 1936-44	1	1924, 1932, 1948, 1960
New York	3	1880-8, 1948-56	4	1924-36
North Carolina	4	1944-56	3	1932-40
North Dakota	2	1900-4,1920-4,1936-40,1948-52	2	1908-12,1932-6,1944-8,1956-60
Ohio	5	1940-56	3	1868-76, 1884-92
Oklahoma	3	1936-44, 1952-60	2	1912-6
Oregon	4	1940-52	2	1876-80,1908-12,1932-6,1956-60
Pennsylvania	5	1940-56	4	1924-36
Rhode Island	3	1864-72, 1948-56	4	1924-36
South Carolina	3	1940-8	4	1876-88
South Dakota	3	1936-44	2	1956-60
Tennessee	3	1940-8	2	1872-6,1888-92,1900-4,1932-6
Texas	6	1936-56	2	1876-80, 1888-92
Utah	5	1940-56	2	1908-12, 1932-6
Vermont	4	1944-56	4	1928-40
Virginia	5	1940-56	2	1876-80,1900-4,1932-6,1956-60
Washington	4	1940-52	2	1908-12, 1932-6, 1956-60
West Virginia	3	1896-1904	4	1868-80
Wisconsin	3	1896-1904	3	1884-92
Wyoming	2	1900-4, 1920-4, 1940-4	2	1908-12, 1932-6, 1956-60
United States	5	1940-56	3	1884-92

Cases where parties received no votes are disregarded.

The six following tables show comparative votes for some of the candidates who ran three or more times each. Three successful candidates, Andrew Jackson, Martin Van Buren, and Theodore Roosevelt, have been included. Jackson, a Democrat, who ran in 1824, 1828, and 1832, led in both the electoral and popular vote all three times, but was unable to get the necessary majority of the former in his first race; he was defeated in the House. Van Buren was elected in 1836 and defeated in 1840 as a Democrat; he met defeat in 1848 as the Free Soil nominee. Roosevelt won in 1904 as a Republican and lost in 1912 as a Progressive; in 1916 he was an unwilling and unsuccessful Progressive candidate.

Of the three unsuccessful candidates who have been included, two secured electoral votes each time they ran. As a Democrat, Henry Clay ran third in the popular vote in 1824 but fourth in the electoral vote, thus being eliminated from consideration by the House. He was defeated in 1832 as a National Republican and in 1844 as a Whig. William Jennings Bryan, a Democrat, made losing efforts in 1896, 1900, and 1908. Eugene Victor Debs, a Socialist, made futile campaigns in 1900, 1904, 1908, 1912, and 1920.

Similar tables for Stephen Grover Cleveland and Franklin Delano Roosevelt, Democrats, Eric Hass, Socialist Labor, Farrell Dobbs, Socialist Workers, Norman Mattoon Thomas, Socialist, and William Zebulon Foster, Communist, each of whom ran three or more times, have not been included, as each was the nominee of the same party each time and ran in consecutive races. The comparisons may be seen in the appropriate party compilations. Cleveland ran in 1884, 1888, and 1892; Roosevelt in 1932, 1936, 1940, and 1944; Hass in 1952, 1956, and 1960; Dobbs in 1948, 1952, 1956, and 1960; Thomas in 1928, 1932, 1936, 1940, 1944, and 1948; and Foster in 1924, 1928, and 1932.

TABLE 128

Jackson's Votes Compared

Number and Percentage of Votes

States	1824	1828	1832	1824	1828	1832
Alabama	9,443	17,138		69.40	89.84	
Connecticut		4,448	11,212		24.32	34.91
Delaware			4,194			49.52
Georgia		19,362	20,750		96.79	100.00
Illinois	1,901	9,560	14,147	40.37	67.22	72.27
Indiana	7,343	22,237	31,552	46.61	56.60	67.10
Kentucky	6,455	39,394	36,247	27.14	55.60	45.51
Louisiana		4,605	4,049		52.92	61.56
Maine		13,927	33,984		40.14	54.68
Maryland	14,523	24,565	19,156	43.73	49.04	49.99
Massachusetts		6,019	14,497		16.79	23.11
Mississippi	3,234	6,772	5,919	64.08	81.07	100.00
Missouri	987	8,272	5,192	36.57	70.87	100.00
New Hampshire		20,922	25,486		46.45	57.28
New Jersey	10,985	21,951	23,859	51.59	48.02	49.98
New York		140,763	168,562		50.97	52.11
North Carolina	20,415	37,857	24,862	56.65	73.12	84.49
Ohio	18,489	67,597	81,246	36.96	51.60	51.33
Pennsylvania	36,100	101,652	90,983	76.23	66.66	57.69
Rhode Island		821	2,126		22.97	36.57
South Carolina						
Tennessee	20,197	44,293	28,740	97.45	95.19	95.24
Vermont		8,385	7,870		25.60	24.50
Virginia	2,861	26,752	33,609	19.13	68.85	74.59
TOTALS	152,933	647,292	688,242	42.16	56.04	54.50

The electoral vote was cast by the legislatures in Delaware in 1824 and 1828; in Georgia, Louisiana, New York, and Vermont in 1824, and in South Carolina in 1824, 1828, and 1832. The highest percentage for each election is underlined.

The 1824 figures are not a fair comparison with 1828 and 1832. In 1824, there were four strong candidates and six states' electoral votes were cast by the legislatures. In 1828, Jackson had only one opponent and in 1832 he had but two; only two states had their electoral votes cast by the legislatures in 1828 and only one in 1832. There was no opposition to Jackson in Alabama, Georgia, and Mississippi in 1832. According to Stanwood, he had no opposition in Missouri in 1832, but according to the *Tribune Almanac* and the *American Almanac*, the figure for Jackson represents his majority in that state.

TABLE 129

Van Buren's Votes Compared

Number and Percentage of Votes

States	1836	1840	1848	1836	1840	1848
Alabama	20,506	33,991		56.78	54.42	
Arkansas	2,400	6,766		65.97	56.73	
Connecticut	19,291	25,296	5,005	50.69	44.32	8.02
Delaware	4,152	4,884	80	46.73	45.01	.64
Georgia	22,333	31,989		47.29	44.22	
Illinois	18,097	47,625	15,804	54.71	51.01	12.58
Indiana	32,478	51,695	8,100	44.03	44.18	5.30
Iowa			1,126			4.63
Kentucky	33,435	32,616		47.50	35.80	
Louisiana	3,653	7,617		51.92	40.27	
Maine	22,900	46,190	12,124	60.04	49.67	13.85
Maryland	22,168	28,759	130	46.16	46.17	.18
Massachusetts	33,542	52,432	38,263	44.82	41.30	28.35
Michigan	7,534	21,131	10,389	64.84	47.61	15.98
Mississippi	9,979	16,995		50.74	46.55	
Missouri	10,995	29,760		59.98	56.44	
New Hampshire	18,722	32,670	7,560	75.04	55.16	15.09
New Jersey	25,847	31,034	829	49.48	48.14	1.07
New York	166,886	212,743	120,510	54.60	48.19	26.43
North Carolina	26,910	33,782	85	53.25	42.14	.11
Ohio	96,916	124,782	35,354	47.90	45.57	10.76
Pennsylvania	91,475	143,784	11,263	51.22	49.90	3.06
Rhode Island	2,966	3,301	730	52.25	38.29	6.54
South Carolina						
Tennessee	26,129	48,289		41.94	44.43	
Vermont	14,039	18,009	13,837	40.08	35.47	28.88
Virginia	30,845	43,893	9	56.85	50.81	.01
Wisconsin			10,418			26.60
TOTALS	764,198	1,130,033	291,616	50.93	46.84	10.13

In South Carolina, the legislature cast the electoral vote in all three elections. In Massachusetts, the legislature cast the electoral vote in 1848, due to the failure of any candidate to receive a majority of the popular vote.

The highest percentage for each election is underlined.

The 1848 figures are not a fair comparison with 1836 and 1840. Although Van Buren defeated three strong candidates in 1836, no state offered more than one opponent. He had only one strong opponent in 1840, the third man getting but .29% of the vote. He had two strong opponents in 1848, when he ran as a third party nominee. The 1836 and 1840 figures are a fair comparison with each other, as the same states participated each time.

TABLE 130

Theodore Roosevelt's Votes Compared

Number and Percentage of Votes

States	1904	1912	1916	1904	1912	1916
Alabama	22,472	22,680		20.65	19.24	
Arizona		6,949			29.29	
Arkansas	46,860	21,673		40.25	17.47	
California	205,226	283,610		61.90	42.11	
Colorado	134,687	72,306	409	55.27	27.09	.14
Connecticut	111,089	34,129		58.13	17.93	
Delaware	23,712	8,886		54.04	18.25	
Florida	8,314	4,535		21.15	8.74	
Georgia	24,003	22,010	20,653	18.32	18.11	13.01
Idaho	47,783	25,527		65.84	24.14	
Illinois	632,645	386,478		58.77	33.72	
Indiana	368,289	162,007	3,915	53.99	24.75	.54
Iowa	307,907	161,819	1,793	63.37	32.83	.35
Kansas	212,955	120,210		64.81	32.89	
Kentucky	205,277	102,766		47.11	22.65	
Louisiana	5,205	9,323	6,349	9.65	11.74	6.83
Maine	64,438	48,495		67.10	37.41	
Maryland	109,497	57,789		48.83	24.91	
Massachusetts	257,822	142,375		57.92	29.08	
Michigan	364,957	214,584		69.50	38.95	
Minnesota	216,651	125,856	290	73.95	37.66	.07
Mississippi	3,187	3,645	520	5.46	5.65	.60
Missouri	321,446	124,371		49.92	17.80	
Montana	34,932	22,456	302	54.21	28.13	.17
Nebraska	138,558	72,689		61.38	29.14	
Nevada	6,864	5,620		56.66	27.94	
New Hampshire	54,180	17,794		60.14	20.23	
New Jersey	245,164	145,674		56.68	33.61	
New Mexico		8,347			16.90	
New York	859,533	390,021		53.13	24.56	
North Carolina	82,625	70,144		39.70	28.62	
North Dakota	52,595	25,726		74.83	29.71	
Ohio	600,095	229,807		59.73	22.16	
Oklahoma			234			.08
Oregon	60,455	37,600	310	67.06	27.44	.12
Pennsylvania	840,949	447,426		67.99	36.67	
Rhode Island	41,605	16,878		60.60	21.67	
South Carolina	2,554	1,293	259	4.63	2.57	.41
South Dakota	72,083	58,811		71.09	50.55	
Tennessee	105,369	54,041		43.40	21.24	
Texas	51,242	28,853		21.90	9.46	
Utah	62,446	24,174		61.45	21.51	
Vermont	40,459	22,132		77.98	35.22	
Virginia	47,880	21,777		36.67	15.90	
Washington	101,540	113,698		69.95	35.22	
West Virginia	132,628	79,112		55.26	29.42	
Wisconsin	280,164	62,460		63.24	15.62	
Wyoming	20,489	9,232		66.71	21.83	
TOTALS	7,628,831	4,127,788	35,034	56.40	27.42	.19

The highest percentage for each election is underlined.

The above figures are given merely to complete the record; they are not a fair comparison. In 1904 Roosevelt had but one major opponent; while he had the two major party nominees running against him in 1912. In 1916 he received the votes shown above, although he had refused the Progressive nomination. Arizona, New Mexico, and Oklahoma were not in the Union in 1904, but were in 1912 and 1916.

TABLE 131   Clay's Votes Compared

Number and Percentage of Votes

States	1824	1832	1844	1824	1832	1844
Alabama	67		26,084	.49		40.87
Arkansas			5,504			36.57
Connecticut		17,617	32,832		54.85	50.81
Delaware		4,276	6,278		50.48	51.15
Georgia			42,106			48.79
Illinois	1,047	5,429	45,790	22.23	27.73	42.43
Indiana	5,315	15,472	67,867	33.74	32.90	48.42
Kentucky	17,331	43,396	61,255	72.86	54.49	54.09
Louisiana		2,528	13,083		38.44	48.70
Maine		27,327	34,619		43.96	40.52
Maryland	695	19,160	35,984	2.09	50.01	52.41
Massachusetts		33,003	67,418		52.61	51.42
Michigan			24,337			43.67
Mississippi			19,206			43.32
Missouri	1,401		31,251	51.91		43.03
New Hampshire		19,010	17,866		42.72	36.32
New Jersey		23,397	38,318		49.01	50.46
New York		154,896	232,482		47.89	47.85
North Carolina		4,563	43,232		15.51	52.39
Ohio	19,255	76,539	155,057	38.49	48.35	49.66
Pennsylvania	1,609		161,203	3.40		48.57
Rhode Island		2,810	7,322		48.33	59.55
South Carolina						
Tennessee		1,436	60,033		4.76	50.05
Vermont		11,152	26,770		34.71	54.90
Virginia	416	11,451	44,790	2.78	25.41	46.91
TOTALS	47,136	473,462	1,300,687	12.99	37.49	48.13

The electoral vote was cast by the legislatures in Delaware, Georgia, Louisiana, New York, and Vermont in 1824, and in South Carolina in 1824, 1832, and 1844.

The highest percentage for each election is underlined.

The above figures are not a fair comparison as to 1824 and 1832. In 1824, there were four strong candidates and six states' electoral votes were cast by the legislatures. In 1832, Clay had only two opponents and only one state had its electoral vote cast by the legislature. The figures are more nearly a fair comparison for 1832 and 1844, although the entrance into the Union of Arkansas and Michigan increased the number of states participating, and Birney's candidacy was the balance of power between Clay and Polk in three states, including pivotal New York.

TABLE 132

Bryan's Votes Compared

Number and Percentage of Votes

States	1896	1900	1908	1896	1900	1908
Alabama	131,226	96,368	74,374	67.44	60.05	71.65
Arkansas	110,103	81,142	87,015	73.70	63.46	57.20
California	144,618	124,985	127,492	48.44	41.33	32.98
Colorado	161,269	122,733	126,644	84.96	55.44	47.99
Connecticut	56,740	74,014	68,255	32.53	41.09	35.92
Delaware	16,615	18,863	22,071	43.01	44.91	45.96
Florida	32,736	28,007	31,104	70.47	71.06	63.01
Georgia	94,733	81,700	72,413	58.03	66.57	54.53
Idaho	23,192	29,414	36,162	78.10	50.98	37.17
Illinois	465,613	503,061	450,810	42.68	44.44	39.02
Indiana	305,573	309,584	338,262	47.96	46.62	46.91
Iowa	223,741	209,265	200,771	42.90	39.42	40.58
Kansas	173,042	162,601	161,209	51.48	45.96	42.88
Kentucky	217,890	234,899	244,092	48.86	50.24	49.74
Louisiana	77,175	53,671	63,568	76.31	79.04	84.59
Maine	34,587	36,823	35,403	29.19	34.83	33.29
Maryland	104,746	122,238	115,908	41.75	46.23	48.59
Massachusetts	106,206	157,016	155,543	26.41	37.86	34.04
Michigan	237,268	211,685	175,771	43.52	38.89	32.44
Minnesota	139,735	112,901	109,401	40.89	35.69	33.02
Mississippi	63,793	51,706	60,287	90.52	87.48	90.07
Missouri	363,652	351,922	346,574	53.95	51.48	48.41
Montana	42,537	37,145	29,326	79.93	58.32	42.61
Nebraska	115,999	114,013	131,099	51.75	47.22	49.14
Nevada	8,376	6,347	11,212	81.21	62.25	45.71
New Hampshire	21,650	35,489	33,655	25.91	38.43	37.56
New Jersey	133,695	164,879	182,567	36.03	41.10	39.08
New York	551,513	678,462	667,468	38.72	43.83	40.74
North Carolina	174,488	157,752	136,995	52.68	53.90	54.30
North Dakota	20,686	20,531	32,885	43.66	35.52	34.71
Ohio	477,497	474,882	502,721	47.07	45.66	44.82
Oklahoma			123,907			48.23
Oregon	46,739	33,385	38,049	47.98	39.64	34.31
Pennsylvania	433,228	424,232	448,778	36.27	36.16	35.41
Rhode Island	14,459	19,812	24,706	26.39	35.04	34.16
South Carolina	58,801	47,283	62,290	85.29	92.96	93.81
South Dakota	41,225	39,544	40,266	49.70	41.14	35.08
Tennessee	168,878	145,356	135,608	52.15	53.02	52.66
Texas	370,434	267,432	217,302	68.00	63.12	73.97
Utah	64,607	45,006	42,601	82.70	48.30	39.22
Vermont	10,640	12,849	11,496	16.67	22.88	21.83
Virginia	154,985	146,080	82,946	52.54	55.23	60.52
Washington	51,646	44,833	58,691	55.19	41.70	31.80
West Virginia	94,488	98,807	111,418	46.83	44.75	43.16
Wisconsin	165,523	159,279	166,632	37.00	35.99	36.67
Wyoming	10,375	10,164	14,918	50.35	41.24	39.67
TOTALS	6,516,722	6,358,160	6,410,665	46.72	45.50	43.05

The highest percentage for each election is underlined.

If Oklahoma, which participated only in 1908, is omitted, the 1908 totals would be: 6,286,758 votes; 42.96%.

TABLE 133 Debs's Votes Compared

Number of Votes

States	1900	1904	1908	1912	1920
Alabama	928	853	1,399	3,029	2,369
Arizona				3,163	222
Arkansas	27	1,816	5,842	8,153	5,111
California	7,572	29,535	28,659	79,201	64,076
Colorado	714	4,304	7,974	16,418	8,046
Connecticut	1,029	4,543	5,113	10,056	10,350
Delaware	57	146	239	556	988
Florida	601	2,337	3,747	4,806	5,189
Georgia		197	584	1,028	465
Idaho		4,949	6,400	11,960	38
Illinois	9,687	69,225	34,711	81,278	74,747
Indiana	2,374	12,013	13,476	36,931	24,703
Iowa	2,790	14,847	8,287	16,967	16,981
Kansas	1,605	15,869	12,420	26,779	15,511
Kentucky	770	3,602	4,060	11,647	6,409
Louisiana		995	2,538	5,249	
Maine	878	2,103	1,758	2,541	2,214
Maryland	904	2,247	2,323	3,996	8,876
Massachusetts	9,716	13,604	10,781	12,662	32,269
Michigan	2,826	9,042	11,586	23,211	28,947
Minnesota	3,065	11,692	14,527	27,505	56,106
Mississippi		392	978	2,061	1,639
Missouri	6,139	13,009	15,431	28,466	20,242
Montana	708	5,676	5,855	10,885	
Nebraska	823	7,412	3,524	10,185	9,600
Nevada		925	2,103	3,313	1,864
New Hampshire	790	1,090	1,299	1,980	1,234
New Jersey	4,611	9,587	10,253	15,928	27,385
New Mexico				2,859	2
New York	12,869	36,883	38,451	63,381	203,201
North Carolina		125	378	128	446
North Dakota	520	2,117	2,421	6,966	8,282
Ohio	4,847	36,260	33,795	90,144	57,147
Oklahoma			21,752	42,262	25,726
Oregon	1,494	7,619	7,339	13,343	9,801
Pennsylvania	4,831	21,863	33,913	83,614	70,021
Rhode Island		956	1,365	2,049	4,351
South Carolina		22	100	164	28
South Dakota	169	3,138	2,846	4,662	
Tennessee	413	1,354	1,870	3,504	2,268
Texas	1,846	2,791	7,870	25,743	8,121
Utah	720	5,767	4,895	9,023	3,159
Vermont		859		928	
Virginia	145	56	255	820	807
Washington	2,006	10,023	14,177	40,134	8,913
West Virginia	219	1,574	3,679	15,336	5,618
Wisconsin	7,051	28,220	28,170	33,481	85,041
Wyoming		1,077	1,715	2,760	1,288
TOTALS	95,744	402,714	420,858	901,255	919,801

Debs's Votes Compared

Percentage of Votes

States	1900	1904	1908	1912	1920
Alabama	.58	.78	1.35	2.57	.98
Arizona				13.33	.33
Arkansas	.02	1.56	3.84	6.57	2.78
California	2.50	8.91	7.41	11.76	6.79
Colorado	.32	1.77	3.02	6.15	2.75
Connecticut	.57	2.38	2.69	5.28	2.83
Delaware	.14	.33	.50	1.14	1.04
Florida	1.52	5.95	7.59	9.26	3.56
Georgia		.15	.44	.85	.30
Idaho		6.82	6.58	11.31	.03
Illinois	.86	6.43	3.00	7.09	3.57
Indiana	.36	1.76	1.87	5.64	1.96
Iowa	.53	3.06	1.67	3.44	1.90
Kansas	.45	4.83	3.31	7.33	2.72
Kentucky	.16	.83	.83	2.57	.70
Louisiana		1.84	3.38	6.61	
Maine	.83	2.19	1.65	1.96	1.12
Maryland	.34	1.00	.97	1.72	2.07
Massachusetts	2.34	3.06	2.36	2.59	3.25
Michigan	.52	1.72	2.14	4.21	2.76
Minnesota	.97	3.99	4.38	8.23	7.65
Mississippi		.67	1.46	3.19	1.99
Missouri	.90	2.02	2.16	4.07	1.52
Montana	1.11	8.81	8.51	13.64	
Nebraska	.34	3.28	1.32	4.08	2.51
Nevada		7.64	8.57	16.47	6.85
New Hampshire	.86	1.21	1.45	2.25	.78
New Jersey	1.15	2.22	2.19	3.67	3.01
New Mexico				5.79	.00
New York	.83	2.28	2.35	3.99	7.01
North Carolina		.06	.15	.05	.08
North Dakota	.90	3.01	2.56	8.05	4.02
Ohio	.47	3.61	3.01	8.69	2.83
Oklahoma			8.47	16.61	5.29
Oregon	1.77	8.45	6.62	9.74	4.11
Pennsylvania	.41	1.77	2.68	6.85	3.78
Rhode Island		1.39	1.89	2.63	2.59
South Carolina		.04	.15	.33	.04
South Dakota	.18	3.09	2.48	4.01	
Tennessee	.15	.56	.73	1.38	.53
Texas	.44	1.19	2.68	8.44	1.67
Utah	.77	5.67	4.51	8.03	2.17
Vermont		1.66		1.48	
Virginia	.05	.04	.19	.60	.35
Washington	1.87	6.91	7.68	12.43	2.24
West Virginia	.10	.66	1.43	5.70	1.10
Wisconsin	1.59	6.37	6.20	8.37	12.05
Wyoming		3.51	4.56	6.53	2.29
TOTALS	.69	2.98	2.83	5.99	3.43

The highest percentage for each election is underlined.

".00" signifies that the candidate received some votes, but less than .01%.

ELECTION OF 1964

   Candidates were Lyndon Baines Johnson, Democrat; Barry Morris
Goldwater, Republican; Eric Hass, Socialist Labor; Clifton DeBerry,
Socialist Workers; Earle Harold Munn, Prohibition; John Kasper, National
States Rights; and Joseph B. Lightburn, Constitution. The Democratic Party
in Alabama ran unpledged electors.

   Data pertaining to this election are from the official records on file
in the National Archives, with the exception of the following, which are
from Statistics of the Presidential and Congressional Election of November
3, 1964: Arkansas, New Hampshire, and Ohio, all; South Dakota, Goldwater;
and Kansas, Hass and Munn.

   The total vote for all candidates was 70,626,632.

Election of 1964

TABLE 134   Electoral and Popular Vote

States	J	G	Johnson	Goldwater	Unpl'd	Hass	DeB'y	Munn	Kasp.	Light
Alabama		10	-	479,085	210,732	-	-	-	-	-
Alaska	3		44,329	22,930		-	-	-	-	-
Arizona		5	237,753	242,535	-	482	-	-	-	-
Arkansas	6		314,197	243,264	-	-	-	-	2,965	-
California	40		4,171,877	2,879,108	-	489	378	305	-	-
Colorado	6		476,024	296,767	-	302	2,537	1,356	-	-
Connecticut	8		826,269	390,996	-	-	-	-	-	-
Delaware	3		122,704	78,078	-	113	-	425	-	-
Florida	14		948,540	905,941	-	-	-	-	-	-
Georgia		12	522,557	616,600	-	-	-	-	-	-
Hawaii	4		163,249	44,022	-	-	-	-	-	-
Idaho	4		148,920	143,557	-	-	-	-	-	-
Illinois	26		2,796,833	1,905,946	-	-	-	-	-	-
Indiana	13		1,170,848	911,118	-	1,374	-	8,266	-	-
Iowa	9		733,030	449,148	-	182	159	1,902	-	-
Kansas	7		464,028	386,579	-	1,901	-	5,393	-	-
Kentucky	9		669,659	372,977	-	-	-	-	3,469	-
Louisiana		10	387,068	509,225	-	-	-	-	-	-
Maine	4		262,264	118,701	-	-	-	-	-	-
Maryland	10		730,912	385,495	-	-	-	-	-	-
Massachusetts	14		1,786,422	549,727	-	4,755	-	3,735	-	-
Michigan	21		2,136,615	1,060,152	-	1,704	3,817	669	-	-
Minnesota	10		991,117	559,624	-	2,544	1,177	-	-	-
Mississippi		7	52,618	356,528	-	-	-	-	-	-
Missouri	12		1,164,344	653,535	-	-	-	-	-	-
Montana	4		164,246	113,032	-	-	332	499	519	-
Nebraska	5		307,307	276,847	-	-	-	-	-	-
Nevada	3		79,339	56,094	-	-	-	-	-	-
New Hampshire	4		182,065	104,029	-	-	-	-	-	-
New Jersey	17		1,867,671	963,843	-	7,075	8,181	-	-	-
New Mexico	4		194,017	131,838	-	1,217	-	543	-	-
New York	43		4,913,156	2,243,559	-	6,085	3,215	-	-	-
North Carolina	13		800,139	624,844	-	-	-	-	-	-
North Dakota	4		149,784	108,207	-	-	224	174	-	-
Ohio	26		2,498,331	1,470,865	-	-	-	-	-	-
Oklahoma	8		519,834	412,665	-	-	-	-	-	-
Oregon	6		501,017	282,779	-	-	-	-	-	-
Pennsylvania	29		3,130,954	1,673,657	-	5,092	10,456	-	-	-
Rhode Island	4		315,463	74,615	-	-	-	-	-	-
South Carolina		8	215,700	309,048	-	-	-	-	-	-
South Dakota	4		163,010	130,108	-	-	-	-	-	-
Tennessee	11		635,047	508,965	-	-	-	-	-	-
Texas	25		1,663,185	958,566	-	-	-	-	-	5,060
Utah	4		219,628	180,682	-	-	-	-	-	-
Vermont	3		108,127	54,942	-	-	-	-	-	-
Virginia	12		558,038	481,334	-	2,895	-	-	-	-
Washington	9		779,699	470,366	-	7,772	537	-	-	-
West Virginia	7		538,087	253,953	-	-	-	-	-	-
Wisconsin	12		1,050,424	638,495	-	1,204	1,692	-	-	-
Wyoming	3		80,718	61,998	-	-	-	-	-	-
Dist. of Columbia	3		169,796	28,801	-	-	-	-	-	-
TOTALS	486	52	43,126,959	27,175,770	210,732	45,186	32,705	23,267	6,953	5,060

Percentage of Popular Vote

States	J	G	Unpl.	H	DeB	M	K	L
Alabama	-	69.45	<u>30.55</u>	-	-	-	-	-
Alaska	65.91	34.09	-	-	-	-	-	-
Arizona	49.45	50.45	-	.10	-	-	-	-
Arkansas	56.06	43.41	-	-	-	-	<u>.53</u>	-
California	59.16	40.83	-	.01	.01	.00	-	-
Colorado	61.27	38.19	-	.04	<u>.33</u>	.17	-	-
Connecticut	67.88	32.12	-	-	-	-	-	-
Delaware	60.95	38.78	-	.06	-	.21	-	-
Florida	51.15	48.85	-	-	-	-	-	-
Georgia	45.87	54.13	-	-	-	-	-	-
Hawaii	78.76	21.24	-	-	-	-	-	-
Idaho	50.92	49.03	-	-	-	-	-	-
Illinois	59.47	40.53	-	-	-	-	-	-
Indiana	55.98	43.56	-	.07	-	.40	-	-
Iowa	61.89	37.92	-	.02	.01	.16	-	-
Kansas	54.09	45.06	-	.22	-	<u>.63</u>	-	-
Kentucky	64.01	35.65	-	-	-	-	.33	-
Louisiana	43.19	56.81	-	-	-	-	-	-
Maine	68.84	31.16	-	-	-	-	-	-
Maryland	65.47	34.53	-	-	-	-	-	-
Massachusetts	76.19	23.45	-	.20	-	.16	-	-
Michigan	66.71	33.10	-	.05	.12	.02	-	-
Minnesota	63.76	36.00	-	.16	.08	-	-	-
Mississippi	12.86	87.14	-	-	-	-	-	-
Missouri	64.05	<u>35.95</u>	-	-	-	-	-	-
Montana	58.95	40.57	-	-	.12	.18	.19	-
Nebraska	52.61	47.39	-	-	-	-	-	-
Nevada	58.58	41.42	-	-	-	-	-	-
New Hampshire	63.64	36.36	-	-	-	-	-	-
New Jersey	65.61	33.86	-	.25	.29	-	-	-
New Mexico	59.22	40.24	-	.37	-	.17	-	-
New York	68.56	31.31	-	.08	.04	-	-	-
North Carolina	56.15	43.85	-	-	-	-	-	-
North Dakota	57.97	41.88	-	-	.09	.07	-	-
Ohio	62.94	37.06	-	-	-	-	-	-
Oklahoma	55.75	44.25	-	-	-	-	-	-
Oregon	63.92	36.08	-	-	-	-	-	-
Pennsylvania	64.96	34.72	-	.11	.22	-	-	-
Rhode Island	80.87	19.13	-	-	-	-	-	-
South Carolina	41.11	58.89	-	-	-	-	-	-
South Dakota	55.61	44.39	-	-	-	-	-	-
Tennessee	55.51	44.49	-	-	-	-	-	-
Texas	63.32	36.49	-	-	-	-	-	<u>.19</u>
Utah	54.86	45.14	-	-	-	-	-	-
Vermont	66.31	33.69	-	-	-	-	-	-
Virginia	53.54	46.18	-	.28	-	-	-	-
Washington	61.96	37.38	-	<u>.62</u>	.04	-	-	-
West Virginia	67.94	32.06	-	-	-	-	-	-
Wisconsin	62.09	37.74	-	.07	.10	-	-	-
Wyoming	56.56	43.44	-	-	-	-	-	-
Dist. of Columbia	85.50	14.50	-	-	-	-	-	-
TOTALS	61.06	38.48	.30	.06	.05	.03	.01*	.01*

* Extended: .009 and .007. The highest percentage for each candidate is underlined.
".00" signifies that the candidate received some votes, but less than .01%.

SUPPLEMENTARY TABLES
1968-1980

ELECTION OF 1968

Candidates were Richard Milhous Nixon, Republican; Hubert Horatio Humphrey, Democrat; George Corley Wallace, American Independent; Henning A. Blomen, Socialist-Labor; Dick Gregory, Peace and Freedom; Fred Halstead, Socialist-Workers; Eldridge Cleaver, Peace and Freedom; Eugene Joseph McCarthy, New Party; Earle Harold Munn, Prohibition; Ventura Chavez, People's Constitutional; Charlene Mitchell, Communist; Kirby James Hensley, Universal; Richard K. Troxell, Constitution; and Kent M. Soeters, Defense. A group of unpledged electors received votes in Alabama.

Data pertaining to this election are from the official records on file in the National Archives.

The total vote for all candidates was 73,171,050.

The following figures show how a switch of 153,572 votes out of the 63,037,928 cast for Nixon and Humphrey—.24%—would have made the latter president:

States	Humphrey	Nixon	Shift
	191	301	
Illinois	26	-26	67,481
Ohio	26	-26	45,215
New Jersey	17	-17	30,631
Missouri	12	-12	10,245
	272	220	153,572

A switch of 111,664 votes in California, which had 40 electoral votes, would have prevented Nixon's election without giving Humphrey the victory, as a decision by the House of Representatives would have become necessary. Nixon would have led, 261 to 231, with Wallace's 46 representing the balance of power. This switch would have been .18% of the total vote cast for Nixon and Humphrey.

Election of 1968

TABLE 135   Electoral and Popular Vote

States	N	H	W	Nixon	Humphrey	Wallace	Blomen	Gregory	Halstead
Alabama			10	146,923	196,579	691,425	-	-	-
Alaska	3			37,540	35,411	10,024	-	-	-
Arizona	5			266,721	170,514	46,573	75	-	85
Arkansas			6	189,062	184,901	235,627	-	-	-
California	40			3,467,644	3,244,318	487,270	341	3,230	-
Colorado	6			409,345	331,063	60,813	3,016	1,393	235
Connecticut		8		556,721	621,561	76,650	-	-	-
Delaware	3			96,714	89,194	28,459	-	-	-
Florida	14			886,804	676,794	624,207	-	-	-
Georgia			12	366,611	334,439	535,550	-	-	-
Hawaii		4		91,425	141,324	3,469	-	-	-
Idaho	4			165,369	89,273	36,541	-	-	-
Illinois	26			2,174,774	2,039,814	390,958	13,878	-	-
Indiana	13			1,067,885	806,659	243,108	-	36	1,293
Iowa	9			619,106	476,699	66,422	241	-	3,377
Kansas	7			478,674	302,996	88,921	-	-	-
Kentucky	9			462,411	397,541	193,098	-	-	2,843
Louisiana			10	257,535	309,615	530,300	-	-	-
Maine		4		169,254	217,312	6,370	-	-	-
Maryland		10		517,995	538,310	178,734	-	-	-
Massachusetts		14		766,844	1,469,218	87,088	6,180	-	-
Michigan		21		1,370,665	1,593,082	331,968	1,762	-	4,099
Minnesota		10		658,643	857,738	68,931	285	-	808
Mississippi			7	88,516	150,644	415,349	-	-	-
Missouri	12			811,932	791,444	206,126	-	-	-
Montana	4			138,835	114,117	20,015	-	-	457
Nebraska	5			321,163	170,784	44,904	-	-	-
Nevada	3			73,188	60,598	20,432	-	-	-
New Hampshire	4			154,903	130,589	11,173	-	-	104
New Jersey	17			1,325,467	1,264,206	262,187	6,784	8,084	8,667
New Mexico	4			169,692	130,081	25,737	-	-	252
New York		43		3,007,932	3,378,470	358,864	8,432	24,517	11,851
North Carolina	12		1	627,192	464,113	496,188	-	-	128
North Dakota	4			138,669	94,769	14,244	-	-	128
Ohio	26			1,791,014	1,700,586	467,495	120	372	69
Oklahoma	8			449,697	301,658	191,731	-	-	-
Oregon	6			408,433	358,866	49,683	-	-	-
Pennsylvania		29		2,090,017	2,259,403	378,582	4,977	7,821	4,862
Rhode Island		4		122,359	246,518	15,678	-	-	383
South Carolina	8			254,062	197,486	215,430	-	-	-
South Dakota	4			149,841	118,023	13,400	-	-	-
Tennessee	11			472,592	351,233	424,792	-	-	-
Texas		25		1,227,844	1,266,804	584,269	-	-	-
Utah	4			238,728	156,665	26,906	-	-	89
Vermont	3			85,142	70,255	5,104	-	-	294
Virginia	12			590,319	442,387	320,272	4,671	1,680	-
Washington		9		588,510	616,037	96,990	488	-	270
West Virginia		7		307,555	374,091	72,560	-	-	-
Wisconsin	12			809,997	748,804	127,835	1,338	-	1,222
Wyoming	3			70,927	45,173	11,105	-	-	-
Dist. of Columbia		3		31,012	139,566	-	-	-	-
TOTALS	301	191	46	31,770,203	31,267,725	9,899,557	52,588	47,133	41,388

One North Carolina elector voted for Wallace, although Nixon had a popular plurality there.

TABLE 135   Electoral and Popular Vote

States	Cleaver	McCarthy	Munn	Unpledged	Chavez	Mitchell	Hensley	Troxell	Soeters
Alabama	-	-	4,022	10,960	-	-	-	-	-
Alaska	-	-	-	-	-	-	-	-	-
Arizona	217	2,751	-	-	-	-	-	-	-
Arkansas	-	-	-	-	-	-	-	-	-
California	27,707	20,721	59	-	-	260	-	-	17
Colorado	-	-	275	-	-	-	-	-	-
Connecticut	-	-	-	-	-	-	-	-	-
Delaware	-	-	-	-	-	-	-	-	-
Florida	-	-	-	-	-	-	-	-	-
Georgia	-	-	-	-	-	-	-	-	-
Hawaii	-	-	-	-	-	-	-	-	-
Idaho	-	-	-	-	-	-	-	-	-
Illinois	-	-	-	-	-	-	-	-	-
Indiana	-	-	4,616	-	-	-	-	-	-
Iowa	1,332	-	362	-	-	-	142	-	-
Kansas	-	-	2,192	-	-	-	-	-	-
Kentucky	-	-	-	-	-	-	-	-	-
Louisiana	-	-	-	-	-	-	-	-	-
Maine	-	-	-	-	-	-	-	-	-
Maryland	-	-	-	-	-	-	-	-	-
Massachusetts	-	-	2,369	-	-	-	-	-	-
Michigan	4,585	-	60	-	-	-	-	-	-
Minnesota	935	585	-	-	-	415	-	-	-
Mississippi	-	-	-	-	-	-	-	-	-
Missouri	-	-	-	-	-	-	-	-	-
Montana	-	470	510	-	-	-	-	-	-
Nebraska	-	-	-	-	-	-	-	-	-
Nevada	-	-	-	-	-	-	-	-	-
New Hampshire	-	421	-	-	-	-	-	-	-
New Jersey	-	-	-	-	-	-	-	-	-
New Mexico	-	-	-	-	1,519	-	-	-	-
New York	-	-	-	-	-	-	-	-	-
North Carolina	-	-	-	-	-	-	-	-	-
North Dakota	-	-	38	-	-	-	-	34	-
Ohio	-	-	19	-	-	23	-	-	-
Oklahoma	-	-	-	-	-	-	-	-	-
Oregon	-	1,496	-	-	-	-	-	-	-
Pennsylvania	-	-	-	-	-	-	-	-	-
Rhode Island	-	-	-	-	-	-	-	-	-
South Carolina	-	-	-	-	-	-	-	-	-
South Dakota	-	-	-	-	-	-	-	-	-
Tennessee	-	-	-	-	-	-	-	-	-
Texas	-	-	-	-	-	-	-	-	-
Utah	180	-	-	-	-	-	-	-	-
Vermont	-	579	-	-	-	-	-	-	-
Virginia	-	-	599	-	-	-	-	-	-
Washington	1,609	-	-	-	-	377	-	-	-
West Virginia	-	-	-	-	-	-	-	-	-
Wisconsin	-	-	-	-	-	-	-	-	-
Wyoming	-	-	-	-	-	-	-	-	-
Dist. of Columbia	-	-	-	-	-	-	-	-	-
TOTALS	36,565	27,023	15,121	10,960	1,519	1,075	142	34	17

Percentage of Popular Vote

States	Nixon	Humphrey	Wallace	Blo	Gre	Hal	Cle	McC	Mun	Unpl	Cha	Mit	Hen	Tro	Soe
Alabama	13.99	18.72	65.86	-	-	-	-	-	.38	1.04	-	-	-	-	-
Alaska	45.24	42.68	12.08	-	-	-	-	-	-	-	-	-	-	-	-
Arizona	54.78	35.02	9.51	.02	-	.02	.04	.56	-	-	-	-	-	-	-
Arkansas	31.01	30.33	38.65	-	-	-	-	-	-	-	-	-	-	-	-
California	47.82	44.74	6.72	.00	.04	-	.38	.29	.00	-	-	.00	-	-	.00
Colorado	50.78	41.07	7.54	.37	.17	.03	-	-	.03	-	-	-	-	-	-
Connecticut	44.36	49.53	6.11	-	-	-	-	-	-	-	-	-	-	-	-
Delaware	45.12	41.61	13.28	-	-	-	-	-	-	-	-	-	-	-	-
Florida	40.53	30.93	28.53	-	-	-	-	-	-	-	-	-	-	-	-
Georgia	29.65	27.05	43.31	-	-	-	-	-	-	-	-	-	-	-	-
Hawaii	38.70	59.83	1.47	-	-	-	-	-	-	-	-	-	-	-	-
Idaho	56.79	30.66	12.55	-	-	-	-	-	-	-	-	-	-	-	-
Illinois	47.08	44.16	8.46	.30	-	-	-	-	-	-	-	-	-	-	-
Indiana	50.29	37.99	11.45	-	.00	.06	-	-	.22	-	-	-	-	-	-
Iowa	53.02	40.82	5.69	.02	-	.29	.11	-	.03	-	-	-	.01	-	-
Kansas	54.84	34.72	10.19	-	-	-	-	-	.25	-	-	-	-	-	-
Kentucky	43.79	37.65	18.29	-	-	.27	-	-	-	-	-	-	-	-	-
Louisiana	23.47	28.21	48.32	-	-	-	-	-	-	-	-	-	-	-	-
Maine	43.07	55.30	1.62	-	-	-	-	-	-	-	-	-	-	-	-
Maryland	41.94	43.59	14.47	-	-	-	-	-	-	-	-	-	-	-	-
Massachusetts	32.89	63.01	3.73	.27	-	-	-	-	.10	-	-	-	-	-	-
Michigan	41.46	48.18	10.04	.05	-	.12	.14	-	.00	-	-	-	-	-	-
Minnesota	41.46	54.00	4.34	.02	-	.05	.06	.04	-	-	-	.03	-	-	-
Mississippi	13.52	23.02	63.46	-	-	-	-	-	-	-	-	-	-	-	-
Missouri	44.87	43.74	11.39	-	-	-	-	-	-	-	-	-	-	-	-
Montana	50.60	41.59	7.29	-	-	.17	-	.17	.19	-	-	-	-	-	-
Nebraska	59.82	31.81	8.36	-	-	-	-	-	-	-	-	-	-	-	-
Nevada	47.46	39.29	13.25	-	-	-	-	-	-	-	-	-	-	-	-
New Hampshire	52.12	43.94	3.76	-	-	.03	-	.14	-	-	-	-	-	-	-
New Jersey	46.10	43.97	9.12	.24	.28	.30	-	-	-	-	-	-	-	-	-
New Mexico	51.85	39.75	7.86	-	-	.08	-	-	-	-	.46	-	-	-	-
New York	44.30	49.76	5.29	.12	.36	.17	-	-	-	-	-	-	-	-	-
North Carolina	39.51	29.24	31.26	-	-	-	-	-	-	-	-	-	-	-	-
North Dakota	55.94	38.23	5.75	-	-	.05	-	-	.02	-	-	-	-	.01	-
Ohio	45.23	42.95	11.81	.00	.01	.00	-	-	.00	-	-	.00	-	-	-
Oklahoma	47.68	31.99	20.33	-	-	-	-	-	-	-	-	-	-	-	-
Oregon	49.90	43.85	6.07	-	-	-	-	.18	-	-	-	-	-	-	-
Pennsylvania	44.04	47.61	7.98	.10	.16	.10	-	-	-	-	-	-	-	-	-
Rhode Island	31.79	64.04	4.07	-	-	.10	-	-	-	-	-	-	-	-	-
South Carolina	38.09	29.61	32.30	-	-	-	-	-	-	-	-	-	-	-	-
South Dakota	53.27	41.96	4.76	-	-	-	-	-	-	-	-	-	-	-	-
Tennessee	37.85	28.13	34.02	-	-	-	-	-	-	-	-	-	-	-	-
Texas	39.88	41.14	18.98	-	-	-	-	-	-	-	-	-	-	-	-
Utah	56.49	37.07	6.37	-	-	.02	.04	-	-	-	-	-	-	-	-
Vermont	52.76	43.54	3.16	-	-	.18	-	.36	-	-	-	-	-	-	-
Virginia	43.41	32.53	23.55	.34	.12	-	-	-	.04	-	-	-	-	-	-
Washington	45.12	47.23	7.44	.04	-	.02	.12	-	-	-	-	.03	-	-	-
West Virginia	40.78	49.60	9.62	-	-	-	-	-	-	-	-	-	-	-	-
Wisconsin	47.95	44.31	7.57	.08	-	.07	-	-	-	-	-	-	-	-	-
Wyoming	55.76	35.51	8.73	-	-	-	-	-	-	-	-	-	-	-	-
Dist. of Columbia	18.18	81.82	-	-	-	-	-	-	-	-	-	-	-	-	-
TOTALS	43.42	42.73	13.53	.07	.07	.06	.05	.04	.02	.01	.00	.00	.00	.00	.00

The highest percentage for each candidate is underlined.

".00" signifies that the candidate received some votes, but less than .01%.

Extended percentages for Mitchell: Washington .00029%, Minnesota .00026%.

ELECTION OF 1972

Candidates were Richard Milhous Nixon, Republican; George Stanley Mc Govern, Democrat; John George Schmitz, American; Benjamin Spock, People's; Louis Fisher, Socialist Labor; Linda Jenness, Socialist Workers; Gus Hall, Communist; _____ Reed, Socialist Workers; Earle Harold Munn, Prohibition; John Hospers, Libertarian; _____ Mahalik, America First; and _____ Green, Universal.

Data pertaining to this election are from the offical records on file in the National Archives.

The vote for all candidates was 77,665,808.

Election of 1972

Electoral and Popular Vote

States	N	Mc	H	Nixon	McGovern	Schmitz	Spock	Fisher	Jenn's	Hall	Reed	Munn
Alabama	9			728,701	256,923	11,918						8,551
Alaska	3			55,349	32,967	6,903						
Arizona	6			402,812	198,540	21,208						
Arkansas	6			445,751	198,899	3,016						
California	45			4,602,096	3,476,117	232,554	55,167	197	574	373		53
Colorado	7			597,189	329,980	17,268	2,403	4,361	666	432		467
Connecticut	8			810,763	555,498	17,239						
Delaware	3			140,357	92,298	2,638						
Florida	17			1,857,759	718,117							
Georgia	12			881,490	289,529	2,288		3				238
Hawaii	4			168,865	101,409							
Idaho	4			199,384	80,826	28,869	903		397			
Illinois	26			2,788,179	1,913,472	2,471		12,344		4,541		
Indiana	13			1,405,154	708,568		4,544	1,688			5,575	
Iowa	8			706,207	496,206	22,056		195	488	272		
Kansas	7			619,812	270,287	21,808						
Kentucky	9			676,446	371,159	17,627	1,118		685	464		
Louisiana	10			686,852	298,142	52,099			14,398			
Maine	4			256,458	160,584							
Maryland	10			829,305	505,781	18,726						
Massachusetts		14		1,112,078	1,332,540	2,877	101	129	10,600	46		43
Michigan	21			1,961,721	1,459,435	63,321		2,437	1,603	1,210		
Minnesota	10			897,569	802,346	31,407	2,855	4,261	940	662		
Mississippi	7			505,125	126,782	11,598			2,458			
Missouri	12			1,153,852	697,147	13,430						
Montana	4			183,976	120,197							
Nebraska	5			406,298	169,991							
Nevada	3			115,750	66,016							
New Hampshire	4			213,724	116,435	3,386			368			
New Jersey	17			1,845,502	1,102,211	34,378	5,355	4,544	2,233	1,263		
New Mexico	4			235,606	141,084	8,767		474				
New York	41			4,192,777	2,951,079			4,530		5,641	7,797	
North Carolina	13			1,054,889	438,705	25,018						
North Dakota	3			174,109	100,384	5,646			288	87		
Ohio	25			2,441,827	1,558,889	80,067		7,107		6,437		
Oklahoma	8			759,025	247,147	23,728						
Oregon	6			480,679	389,741	44,995						

Electoral and Popular Votes (continued)

States	N	Mc	H	Nixon	McGovern	Schmitz	Spock	Fisher	Jenn's	Hall	Reed	Munn
Pennsylvania	27			2,714,521	1,796,951	70,593			4,639	2,686		
Rhode Island	4			220,383	194,645				729			
South Carolina	8			477,044	186,824	10,075						
South Dakota	4			166,476	139,945				994			
Tennessee	10			813,147	357,293	30,373						
Texas	26			2,298,468	1,154,109	6,039			8,664			
Utah	4			323,643	126,284	28,549						
Vermont	3			117,149	68,174		1,010			296		
Virginia	11		1	988,493	438,887	19,721		9,918				
Washington	9			837,135	568,334	58,906	2,644	1,102	623	566		
West Virginia	6			481,950	276,320							
Wisconsin	11			989,430	810,174	47,525	2,701	998		663	506	
Wyoming	3			100,464	44,358	748						
Dist. of Col.			3	35,226	127,627					252	316	
Totals	520	17	1	47,156,965	29,165,356	1,099,835	78,801	53,814	52,117	25,595	14,194	13,540

Hospers: Calif. 980, Colo. 1,111, Wash. 1,537; total 3,628.

Mahalchik: N. J. 1,743; total 1,743.

Green: Colo. 21, Ind. 199; total 220.

Percentage of Popular Vote

States	Nixon	McGvn	Schmz	Spock	Fishr	Jenns	Hall	Reed	Munn	Hosps	Mahal	Green
Alabama	72.43	25.54	1.18						.85			
Alaska	58.13	34.62	7.25									
Arizona	64.70	31.89	3.41									
Arkansas	68.82	30.71	.47									
California	55.00	41.54	2.78	.66	.00	.01	.00		.00	.01		
Colorado	62.61	34.59	1.81	.25	.46	.07	.05		.05	.12		.00
Connecticut	58.60	40.15	1.25									
Delaware	59.59	39.19	1.12						.10			
Florida	72.12	27.88										
Georgia	75.13	24.68			.00							
Hawaii	62.48	37.52	.20									
Idaho	64.24	26.04	9.30	.29	.26	.13						
Illinois	59.06	40.53	.05				.10					
Indiana	66.11	33.34	1.80	.21	.08	.04	.02	.26				.01
Iowa	57.62	40.49	1.80		.02							
Kansas	67.66	29.50	2.38						.46			
Kentucky	63.37	34.77	1.65	.10		.06	.04					
Louisiana	65.32	28.35	4.95			1.37						
Maine	61.49	38.51										
Maryland	61.26	37.36	1.38									
Massachusetts	45.23	54.20	.12	.00	.01	.43	.00					
Michigan	56.21	41.82	1.81		.07	.05	.03		.00			
Minnesota	51.58	46.11	1.80	.16	.24	.05	.04					
Mississippi	78.20	19.63	1.80			.38						
Missouri	62.34	37.66										
Montana	57.93	37.85	4.23									
Nebraska	70.50	29.50										
Nevada	63.68	36.32										
New Hampshire	64.01	34.87	1.01		.15	.11						
New Jersey	61.57	36.77	1.15	.18		.07	.04				.06	
New Mexico	61.05	36.56	2.27			.12						
New York	58.54	41.21			.06		.08	.11				
North Carolina	69.46	28.89	1.65									
North Dakota	62.07	35.79	2.01			.10	.03					
Ohio	59.64	38.07	1.96		.17		.16					
Oklahoma	73.70	24.00	2.30									
Oregon	52.51	42.58	4.92									

Percentage of Popular Vote (continued)

States	Nixon	McGvn	Schmz	Spock	Fishr	Jenns	Hall	Reed	Munn	Hosps	Mahal	Green
Pennsylvania	59.15	39.15	1.54			.10	.06					
Rhode Island	53.01	46.82				.18						
South Carolina	70.78	27.72	1.49									
South Dakota	54.15	45.52										
Tennessee	67.72	29.75	2.53			.32						
Texas	66.29	33.29	.17									
Utah	67.64	26.39	5.97			.25						
Vermont	62.77	36.53		.54		.16						
Virginia	67.84	30.12	1.35		.68							
Washington	56.92	38.64	4.00	.18	.07	.04	.04			.10		
West Virginia	63.56	36.44										
Wisconsin	53.43	43.75	2.57	.15	.05		.04	.00				
Wyoming	68.99	30.47	.51				.15	.19				
Dist. of Col.	21.56	78.10					.15					
Totals	60.72	37.55	1.42	.10	.07	.07	.03	.02	.02	.00	.00	.00

The highest percentage for each candidate is underlined.

".00" signifies that the candidate received some votes, but less than .01%.

ELECTION OF 1976

Candidates were James Earl Carter, Jr., Democrat; Gerald Rudolph Ford, Republican; Eugene Joseph McCarthy, Independent; Roger Lea MacBride, Libertarian; Lester Garfield Maddox, American Independent; Thomas Jefferson Anderson, American; Peter Camejo, Socialist Workers; Gus Hall, Communist; Margaret Wright, Peace and Freedom; Lyndon H. LaRouche, United States Labor; Benjamin C. Bubar, Prohibition; Jules Levin, Socialist Labor; Frank P. Zeidler, Socialist; _____ Blomen, Socialist Labor; Ronald Wilson Reagan; _____ Miller; Edmund G. Brown, Jr.; and Frank Taylor, United American.

Data pertaining to this election are from the official records on file in the National Archives, with the exception of the following, which are from Statistics of the Presidential and Congressional Election of November 2, 1976: Arkansas, Carter; New Mexico, Carter and Ford; Utah, McCarthy and Hall; and Wyoming, McCarthy, MacBride, Maddox, and Anderson.

The total vote for all candidates was 81,420,410.

The following figures show how a switch of 8,354 votes out of the 79,978,100 cast for Carter and Ford--.0001%--would have made the latter president:

States	Ford	Carter	Shift
	241*	297	
Ohio	25	-25	4,667
Hawaii	4	- 4	3,687
	270	268	8,354

* It is assumed that the elector in Washington who voted for Reagan instead of Ford would not have defected under the circumstances outlined here.

Election of 1976

Electoral and Popular Vote

States	C	F	R	Carter	Ford	McCarthy	MacBride	Maddox	Anderson	Camejo	Hall
Alabama	9			659,170	504,070		1,481	9,198			1,954
Alaska		3		44,055	71,555		6,773				
Arizona		6		295,602	418,642	19,229	7,647	85	564	928	
Arkansas	6			498,604	267,903	639			389		
California		45		3,742,284	3,882,244		56,388	51,098		17,259	12,766
Colorado		7		460,801	584,456	27,047	5,339			1,071	403
Connecticut		8		647,895	719,261			7,101			
Delaware	3			122,596	109,831	2,432			645		
Florida	17			1,636,000	1,469,531	23,643			21,325		
Georgia	12			979,409	483,743	159		18	99		
Hawaii	4			147,375	140,003		3,923				
Idaho		4		126,549	204,151		3,558	5,935			
Illinois		26		2,271,295	2,364,269	55,939	8,057		14,048	3,615	9,250
Indiana		13		1,014,714	1,185,958	20,052			3,040	5,695	
Iowa		8		619,931	632,863	13,185	1,452		4,724	265	554
Kansas		7		430,421	502,752		3,242	2,118			
Kentucky	9			615,717	531,852	6,837	814	2,328	8,308	350	426
Louisiana	10			661,365	587,446	6,588	3,134	10,058		2,240	7,417
Maine		4		232,279	236,320	10,874					
Maryland	10			759,612	672,661						
Massachusetts	14			1,429,475	1,030,276	65,637	135		7,555	8,138	
Michigan		21		1,696,714	1,893,742	47,905	5,407			1,804	
Minnesota	10			1,070,440	819,395	35,490	3,529		13,592	4,149	1,092
Mississippi	7			381,329	366,846	4,074	2,609	4,049	6,678	2,805	
Missouri	12			998,387	927,443	24,029					
Montana		4		149,259	173,703				5,772		
Nebraska		5		233,293	359,219	9,383	1,476	3,378			
Nevada		3		92,479	101,273		1,519	1,497			
New Hampshire		4		147,645	185,935	4,095	936			161	
New Jersey		17		1,444,653	1,509,688	32,717	9,449	7,716		1,184	1,662
New Mexico		4		201,148	211,419		277			615	
New York	41			3,389,558	3,100,791		12,197			6,996	10,270
North Carolina	13			927,365	741,960	2,952	5,607		2,219		
North Dakota		3		136,078	153,470		236	269	3,698	43	85
Ohio	25			2,009,959	2,000,626	58,267	8,952	15,508			
Oklahoma		8		532,442	545,708	14,101				4,833	7,817
Oregon		6		490,407	492,120	40,192			1,035		

Electoral and Popular Vote (continued)

States	C	F	R	Carter	Ford	McCarthy	MacBride	Maddox	Anderson	Camejo	Hall
Pennsylvania	27			2,328,677	2,205,604	50,584		25,344		3,009	1,891
Rhode Island	4			227,636	181,249		715			462	334
South Carolina	8			451,653	348,662			2,029	3,125		
South Dakota			4	147,068	151,505		1,619			168	318
Tennessee	10			825,879	633,969	5,004	1,375	2,303	5,769		547
Texas	26			2,082,319	1,953,294	20,118			11,442	1,723	
Utah		4		182,110	337,908	3,907	2,438	1,162	13,304	268	121
Vermont		3		78,789	100,387	4,001				430	
Virginia		12		813,896	836,554		4,648		16,686	17,802	
Washington	8:1			717,323	777,732	36,986	5,042	8,585	5,046	905	817
West Virginia	6			435,864	314,726						
Wisconsin	11			1,040,232	1,004,987	34,943	3,814	8,552	290	1,691	749
Wyoming		3		62,239	92,717	624	89	30			
Dist. of Col.	3			137,818	27,873		274			545	219
Totals	297	240	1	40,827,808	39,150,292	681,633	174,151	168361	149,353	89,154	58,692

States	Wright	LaRouche	Bubar	Levin	Zeidler	Blomen	Reagan	Miller	Brown	Taylor
Alabama			6,669							
Alaska										
Arizona										22
Arkansas										
California	41,731									
Colorado		565	2,836							
Connecticut		1,789								
Delaware		135	103	86						
Florida										
Georgia										
Hawaii										
Idaho		739								
Illinois		2,018				2,422				
Indiana		1,947								
Iowa		241		169	234					
Kansas			1,403							
Kentucky		510								
Louisiana										
Maine			3,495							
Maryland										
Massachusetts	33	4,922	14	19						
Michigan	3,504	1,366		1,148						
Minnesota	635	543		370	354					
Mississippi										
Missouri										
Montana										
Nebraska										
Nevada							388			
New Hampshire		186		66						
New Jersey	1,044	1,650	554	3,686	469					
New Mexico			53		60					
New York		5,413								
North Carolina		755								
North Dakota		142	63		38					
Ohio		4,364	62	68						
Oklahoma										
Oregon										

States	Wright	LaRouche	Bubar	Levin	Zeidler	Blomen	Reagan	Miller	Brown	Taylor
Pennsylvania		2,744								
Rhode Island				188						
South Carolina										
South Dakota										
Tennessee		512	442					316		
Texas										
Utah										
Vermont		196								
Virginia		7,508								
Washington	1,124	903		713	358					
West Virginia										
Wisconsin	943	738		389	4,298					
Wyoming							307		47	
Dist. of Col.		157								
Totals	49,014	40,043	15694	6,902	5,811	2,422	695	316	47	22

Percentage of Popular Vote

States	Carter	Ford	McCar	MacBr	Madox	Ander	Camej	Hall	Wrigh	LaRou	Bubar	Levin	Zeidl	Blomn
Alabama	55.74	42.63		.13	.78			.17			.56			
Alaska	36.00	58.47		5.53										
Arizona	39.80	56.37	2.59	1.03	.01	.08	.12							
Arkansas	64.96	34.90	.08			.05								
California	47.95	49.75		.72	.65		.22	.16	.53					
Colorado	47.08	52.27			.52									
Delaware	51.99	46.57	1.03			.27				.13	.06	.04	.04	
Florida	51.93	46.64	.75			.68								
Georgia	66.93	33.06	.01		.00	.01								
Hawaii	50.59	48.06		1.35										
Idaho	37.12	59.88		1.04	1.74					.22				.05
Illinois	48.15	50.12	1.19	.17			.08	.20		.04		.00		
Indiana	45.66	53.36				.63	.26			.09				
Iowa	48.48	49.49	1.57	.11		.24	.00	.04		.02				
Kansas	44.94	52.49	1.38	.34	.22	.49					.15	.01	.02	
Kentucky	52.75	45.57	.59	.07	.20	.71	.03	.04		.04				
Louisiana	51.24	45.96	.52	.25	.79		.18	.58						
Maine	48.09	48.93	2.25								.72			
Maryland	53.04	46.96	2.58	.01	.30	.32		.00		.19	.00	.00		
Massachusetts	56.14	40.46					.05			.04		.03		
Michigan	46.47	51.86	1.31	.15		.70	.05		.10	.04		.02		
Minnesota	54.91	42.03	1.82	.18		.70	.21	.06	.03	.03		.02	.02	
Mississippi	49.63	47.74	.53	.34	.53	.87	.37							
Missouri	51.20	47.56	1.23			1.76								
Montana	45.40	52.84										/		
Nebraska	38.45	59.20	1.55	.24	.56									
Nevada	47.00	51.47		.77	.76									
New Hampshire	43.50	54.78	1.21	.28			.05			.05		.00		
New Jersey	47.92	50.08	1.09	.31	.26		.04	.06	.03	.05	.02	.12	.02	
New Mexico	48.64	51.12		.07			.15				.01		.01	
New York	51.95	47.52		.19			.11	.16		.08				
North Carolina	55.27	44.22		.33		.13				.04				
North Dakota	45.81	51.66	.99	.08	.09	1.24	.01	.03		.05			.01	
Ohio	48.90	48.67	1.42	.22	.38		.12	.19		.11	.00	.00		
Oklahoma	48.75	49.96	1.29									.00		
Oregon	47.90	48.07	3.93			.10	.07	.04		.06				
Pennsylvania	50.43	47.76	1.10	.17	.55					.06				
Rhode Island	55.44	44.14		.17		.11	.08					.05		

Percentage of Popular Vote (continued)

States	Cartr	Ford	McCar	MacBr	Madox	Ander	Camej	Hall	Wrigh	LaRou	Bubar	Levin	Zeidl	Blomn
South Carolina	56.07	43.29			.25	.39		.11						
South Dakota	48.91	50.39		.54	.09	.16	.06		.04					
Tennessee	55.95	42.95	.34			.39					.03	.03		
Texas	51.18	48.01	.49			.28	.04							
Utah	33.65	62.43	.72	.45	.21	2.46	.05	.02						
Vermont	42.87	54.62	2.18				.23			.11				
Virginia	47.96	49.29			.27	.98	1.05			.44				
Washington	46.23	50.13	2.38	.32	.55	.33	.06	.05	.07	.06		.05	.02	
West Virginia	58.07	41.93		.18	.41		.08		.04	.04		.02		
Wisconsin	49.51	47.84	1.64			.19		.04	.04	.04		.02	.02	
Wyoming	39.81	59.30	.40	.06	.02									
Dist. of Col.	82.58	16.70		.16			.33	.13		.09				
Totals	50.14	48.08	.84	.21	.21	.18	.11	.07	.06	.05	.02	.01	.01	.00

Reagan: N. H. .11, Wyo. .20; total .00.

Miller: Tenn. .02; total .00.

Brown: Wyo. .03; total .00.

Taylor: Ariz. .00; total .00.

The highest percentage for each candidate is underlined.

".00" signifies that the candidate received some votes, but less than .01%.

ELECTION OF 1980

Candidates were Ronald Wilson Reagan, Republican; James Earl Carter, Jr., Democrat; John B. Anderson, Independent; Edward E. Clark, Libertarian; Barry Commoner, Citizens; Gus Hall, Communist; John Rarick, American Independent; Clifton De Berry, Socialist Workers; Ellen McCormick, Right-to-Life; Margaret Smith, Peace and Freedom; Deidre Griswold, Workers World; Benjamin C. Bubar, National Statesman; David McReynolds, Socialist; Percy Greaves, American; Andrew Pulley, Socialist Workers; Richard Congress, Independent; Kurt Lynen, Middle Class; Bill Gahres, Down With Lawyers; Frank Shelton, American; Martin Wendelken, Independent; and Harley McLain, National Peoples League.

Data pertaining to this election are from the official records on file with the Federal Election Commission.

The total vote for all candidates was 86,478,757.

Election of 1980

Electoral and Popular Vote

States	R	C	Reagan	Carter	Anderson	Clark	Commmer	Hall	Rarick	De B'y	McCorm
Alabama	9		654,192	636,730	16,481	13,318	517	1,629	15,010	1,303	
Alaska	3		86,112	41,842	11,156	18,479					
Arizona	6		529,688	246,843	76,952	18,784				1,100	
Arkansas	6		403,164	398,041	22,468	8,970	2,345	1,244			
California	45		4,524,835	3,083,652	739,833	148,434	61,063		9,856		
Colorado	7		652,264	368,009	130,633	25,744	5,614	487			
Connecticut	8		677,210	541,732	171,807	8,570	6,130				
Delaware	3		111,252	105,754	16,288	1,974					
Florida	17		2,046,951	1,419,475	189,692	30,524					
Georgia		12	654,168	890,733	36,055	15,627					
Hawaii		4	130,112	135,879	32,021	3,269	1,548	458			
Idaho	4		290,699	110,192	27,058	8,425			1,057		
Illinois	26		2,358,094	1,981,413	346,754	38,939	10,692	9,711		1,302	
Indiana	13		1,255,656	844,197	111,639	19,627	4,852	702		610	
Iowa	8		676,026	508,672	115,633	13,123	2,273	298		244	
Kansas	7		566,812	326,150	68,231	14,470		967	789		
Kentucky	9		635,274	617,417	31,127	5,531	1,304	348			4,233
Louisiana	10		792,853	708,453	26,345	8,240	1,584		10,333	783	
Maine	4		238,522	220,974	53,327	5,119	4,394	591			
Maryland		10	680,606	726,161	119,537	14,192					
Massachusetts	14		1,056,223	1,053,802	382,539	22,038				5,143	
Michigan	21		1,915,225	1,661,532	275,223	41,597	11,930	3,262			
Minnesota		10	873,268	954,173	174,997	31,593	8,406	1,117		711	
Mississippi	7		441,089	429,281	12,036	5,465					
Missouri	12		1,074,181	931,182	77,920	14,422					
Montana	4		206,814	118,032	29,281	9,825					
Nebraska	5		419,214	166,424	44,854	9,041				1,515	
Nevada	3		155,017	66,666	17,651	4,358					
New Hampshire	4		221,705	108,864	49,693	2,067	1,325	129		72	
New Jersey	17		1,546,557	1,147,364	234,632	20,652	8,203	2,555			3,927
New Mexico	4		250,779	167,826	29,459	4,365	2,202				
New York	41		2,893,831	2,728,372	467,801	52,648	23,186	7,414		2,068	24,159
North Carolina	13		915,018	875,635	52,800	9,677	2,287			416	
North Dakota	3		193,695	79,189	23,640	3,743	429	93		89	
Ohio	25		2,206,545	1,752,414	254,472	49,033	8,564	4,729			
Oklahoma	8		695,570	402,026	38,284	13,828					
Oregon	6		571,044	456,890	112,389	25,838	13,642				

States	Smith	Griswd	Bubar	McRns	Grevs	Pully	Congs	Lymen	Gahrs	Shltn	Wendn	McLan
Alabama		1,743	1,006									
Alaska												
Arizona												
Arkansas		1,350										
California	18,117											
Colorado		1,180				519						
Connecticut												
Delaware					400							
Florida												
Georgia												
Hawaii												
Idaho												
Illinois		2,257										
Indiana					4,750							
Iowa			150	534	189							
Kansas			821									
Kentucky						393						
Louisiana												
Maine												
Maryland												
Massachusetts										1,555		
Michigan				536								
Minnesota		698										
Mississippi		2,402										
Missouri						2,347						
Montana												
Nebraska												
Nevada												
New Hampshire		76										
New Jersey		1,288		1,973		2,198		3,694	1,718		923	
New Mexico			1,281			325						
New York		1,416										
North Carolina												
North Dakota			54	82		235						
Ohio		3,790					4,029					
Oklahoma												
Oregon												296

Electoral and Popular Vote (continued)

States	R	C	Reagan	Carter	Anderson	Clark	Commoner	Hall	Rarick	De B'y	McCorm
Pennsylvania	27		2,261,872	1,937,540	292,921	33,263	10,430	5,184		20,291	
Rhode Island		4	154,793	198,342	59,819	2,458		218		90	
South Carolina	8		439,277	428,220	13,868	4,807			2,086		
South Dakota	4		198,343	103,855	21,431	3,824					
Tennessee	10		787,761	783,051	35,991	7,116	1,112	503		490	
Texas	26		2,510,705	1,881,147	111,613	37,643					
Utah	4		439,687	124,266	30,284	7,156	1,009	139	522	124	
Vermont	3		94,628	81,952	31,761	1,900	2,316	118		75	
Virginia	12		989,609	752,174	95,418	12,821	14,024			1,986	
Washington	9		865,244	650,193	185,073	29,213	9,403	834		1,137	
West Virginia	6		334,206	367,462	31,691	4,356					
Wisconsin	11		1,088,845	981,584	160,657	29,135	7,767	772	1,519	383	
Wyoming	3		110,700	49,427	12,072	4,514					
Dist. of Col.		3	23,313	130,231	16,131	1,104	1,826	369		173	
Totals	489	49	43,899,248	35,481,435	5,719,437	920,859	230,377	43,871	41,172	40,105	32,319

States	Smith	Griswd	Bubar	McRns	Grevs	Pully	Congs	Lynen	Gahrs	Shltn	Wendn	McLan
Pennsylvania												
Rhode Island		77		170								
South Carolina												
South Dakota						250						
Tennessee		400	521	519								
Texas					965							
Utah												
Vermont				136								
Virginia												
Washington		341		956								
West Virginia												
Wisconsin		414		808								
Wyoming												
D. of C.		52										
Totals	18,117	13,211	7,100	6,720	6,539	6,032	4,029	3,694	1,718	1,555	923	296

Percentage of Popular Vote

States	Reagn	Cartr	Ander	Clark	Comnr	Hall	Rarck	DeBry	McCmk	Smith	Grisw	Bubar	McRds	Grevs	Pully
Alabama	48.75	47.45	1.23	.99	.04	.12	1.12	.10					.13	.07	
Alaska	54.64	26.55	7.08	11.73											
Arizona	60.65	28.26	8.81	2.15				.13							
Arkansas	48.13	47.52	2.68	1.07	.28	.15						.16			
California	52.70	35.92	8.62	1.73	.71	.15				.21					
Colorado	55.07	31.07	11.03	2.17	.47	.11						.10			.04
Connecticut	48.18	38.55	12.22	.61	.44	.04									
Delaware	47.21	44.87	6.91	.84										.17	
Florida	55.52	38.50	5.15	.83											
Georgia	40.97	55.79	2.26	.98											
Hawaii	42.90	44.80	10.56	1.08	.51	.15									
Idaho	66.46	25.19	6.19	1.93											
Illinois	49.65	41.72	7.30	.82	.23	.20	.24	.03			.05				
Indiana	56.01	37.65	4.98	.88	.22	.03		.03				.01		.21	
Iowa	51.33	38.62	8.78	1.00	.17	.02		.02				.04			.01
Kansas	57.85	33.29	6.96	1.48		.10	.08					.08			.03
Kentucky	49.03	47.65	2.40	.43	.10	.03	.08		.33						
Louisiana	51.20	45.75	1.70	.53	.10		.67	.05							
Maine	45.61	42.26	10.20	.98	.84	.11									
Maryland	44.18	47.14	7.76	.92											
Massachusetts	41.92	41.82	15.18	.87				.20							
Michigan	49.00	42.51	7.04	1.06	.31	.08									
Minnesota	42.69	46.65	8.56	1.54	.41	.05		.03			.03	.03			
Mississippi	49.42	48.09	1.35	.61							.27		.03		.26
Missouri	51.17	44.36	3.71	.69				.07							
Montana	56.82	32.43	8.04	2.70											
Nebraska	65.55	26.02	7.01	1.41											
Nevada	63.61	27.36	7.25	1.79											
New Hampshire	57.75	28.36	12.94	.54	.35	.03		.02			.02				.07
New Jersey	51.97	38.56	7.88	.69	.28	.09			.13		.04		.07		.07
New Mexico	54.97	36.78	6.46	.96	.48							.28			
New York	46.67	44.00	7.54	.85	.37	.12		.03	.39		.02				
North Carolina	49.30	47.18	2.85	.52	.12			.02							
North Dakota	64.23	26.26	7.84	1.24	.14	.03		.03				.02	.03	.08	
Ohio	51.51	40.91	5.94	1.14	.20	.11					.09				
Oklahoma	60.50	34.97	3.33	1.20											
Oregon	48.40	38.73	9.53	2.19	1.16										

Percentage of Popular Vote (continued)

States	Reagn	Cartr	Ander	Clark	Comnr	Hall	Rarck	DeBry	McCmk	Smith	Grisw	Bubar	McRds	Grevs	Pully
Pennsylvania	49.59	42.48	6.42	.73		.11			<u>.44</u>						
Rhode Island	37.21	47.68	14.38	.59		.05					.02				
South Carolina	49.45	48.21	1.56	.54			.23								
South Dakota	60.53	31.69	6.54	1.17											.08
Tennessee	48.70	48.41	2.23	.44	.23	.03									
Texas	55.29	41.44	2.46	.83	.07		.09	.03							
Utah	72.78	20.57	5.01	1.18	.17	.02		.02			.02	.03			
Vermont	44.45	38.50	14.92	.89	1.09	.06		.04							
Virginia	53.03	40.31	5.11	.69	.75			.11			.02				
Washington	49.66	37.32	10.62	1.68	.54	.05		.07				.05			
West Virginia	45.30	49.81	4.30	.59											
Wisconsin	47.93	43.21	7.07	1.28	.34	.03	.07	.02		.02				.16	
Wyoming	62.64	27.97	6.83	2.55							.03		.04	.06	
Dist. of Col.	13.46	75.19	9.31	.64	1.05	.21		.10							
Totals	50.76	41.03	6.61	1.06	.27	.05	.05	.05	.04	.02	.02	.01	.01	.00	.00

Congress: Ohio .09; total .00.
Lynen: N. J. <u>.12</u>; total .00.
Gahres: N. J. .06; total .00.
Shelton: Kans. <u>.16</u>; total .00.
Heldenken: N. J. .03; total .00.
McLain: N. D. <u>.10</u>; total .00.

The highest percentage for each candidate is underlined.

".00" signifies that the candidate received some votes, but less than .01%.